IFIP Advances in Information and Communication Technology 466

Editor-in-Chief

Kai Rannenberg, Goethe University Frankfurt, Germany

Editorial Board

Foundation of Computer Science
  Jacques Sakarovitch, Télécom ParisTech, France
Software: Theory and Practice
  Michael Goedicke, University of Duisburg-Essen, Germany
Education
  Arthur Tatnall, Victoria University, Melbourne, Australia
Information Technology Applications
  Erich J. Neuhold, University of Vienna, Austria
Communication Systems
  Aiko Pras, University of Twente, Enschede, The Netherlands
System Modeling and Optimization
  Fredi Tröltzsch, TU Berlin, Germany
Information Systems
  Jan Pries-Heje, Roskilde University, Denmark
ICT and Society
  Diane Whitehouse, The Castlegate Consultancy, Malton, UK
Computer Systems Technology
  Ricardo Reis, Federal University of Rio Grande do Sul, Porto Alegre, Brazil
Security and Privacy Protection in Information Processing Systems
  Yuko Murayama, Iwate Prefectural University, Japan
Artificial Intelligence
  Tharam Dillon, La Trobe University, Melbourne, Australia
Human-Computer Interaction
  Jan Gulliksen, KTH Royal Institute of Technology, Stockholm, Sweden
Entertainment Computing
  Matthias Rauterberg, Eindhoven University of Technology, The Netherlands

IFIP – The International Federation for Information Processing

IFIP was founded in 1960 under the auspices of UNESCO, following the First World Computer Congress held in Paris the previous year. An umbrella organization for societies working in information processing, IFIP's aim is two-fold: to support information processing within its member countries and to encourage technology transfer to developing nations. As its mission statement clearly states,

> *IFIP's mission is to be the leading, truly international, apolitical organization which encourages and assists in the development, exploitation and application of information technology for the benefit of all people.*

IFIP is a non-profitmaking organization, run almost solely by 2500 volunteers. It operates through a number of technical committees, which organize events and publications. IFIP's events range from an international congress to local seminars, but the most important are:

- The IFIP World Computer Congress, held every second year;
- Open conferences;
- Working conferences.

The flagship event is the IFIP World Computer Congress, at which both invited and contributed papers are presented. Contributed papers are rigorously refereed and the rejection rate is high.

As with the Congress, participation in the open conferences is open to all and papers may be invited or submitted. Again, submitted papers are stringently refereed.

The working conferences are structured differently. They are usually run by a working group and attendance is small and by invitation only. Their purpose is to create an atmosphere conducive to innovation and development. Refereeing is also rigorous and papers are subjected to extensive group discussion.

Publications arising from IFIP events vary. The papers presented at the IFIP World Computer Congress and at open conferences are published as conference proceedings, while the results of the working conferences are often published as collections of selected and edited papers.

Any national society whose primary activity is about information processing may apply to become a full member of IFIP, although full membership is restricted to one society per country. Full members are entitled to vote at the annual General Assembly, National societies preferring a less committed involvement may apply for associate or corresponding membership. Associate members enjoy the same benefits as full members, but without voting rights. Corresponding members are not represented in IFIP bodies. Affiliated membership is open to non-national societies, and individual and honorary membership schemes are also offered.

More information about this series at http://www.springer.com/series/6102

Mason Rice · Sujeet Shenoi (Eds.)

Critical Infrastructure Protection IX

9th IFIP 11.10 International Conference, ICCIP 2015
Arlington, VA, USA, March 16–18, 2015
Revised Selected Papers

 Springer

Editors
Mason Rice
Department of Electrical and
  Computer Engineering
Air Force Institute of Technology
Wright-Patterson AFB, Ohio
USA

Sujeet Shenoi
Tandy School of Computer Science
University of Tulsa
Tulsa, Oklahoma
USA

ISSN 1868-4238   ISSN 1868-422X   (electronic)
IFIP Advances in Information and Communication Technology
ISBN 978-3-319-38746-8   ISBN 978-3-319-26567-4   (eBook)
DOI 10.1007/978-3-319-26567-4

Springer Cham Heidelberg New York Dordrecht London
© IFIP International Federation for Information Processing 2015
Softcover re-print of the Hardcover 1st edition 2015

Printed on acid-free paper

Springer International Publishing AG Switzerland is part of Springer Science+Business Media
(www.springer.com)

Contents

PART V   INFRASTRUCTURE MODELING AND SIMULATION

PART VI   RISK AND IMPACT ASSESSMENT

Contributing Authors

Abdullah Alsubaie is a Ph.D. candidate in Electrical and Computer Engineering at the University of British Columbia, Vancouver, Canada; and a Researcher at King Abdulaziz City for Science and Technology, Riyadh, Saudi Arabia. His research interests include power systems operation, smart grids and critical infrastructure protection.

Khaled Alutaibi is a Ph.D. candidate in Electrical and Computer Engineering at the University of British Columbia, Vancouver, Canada; and a Senior Officer at the Civil Defense Headquarters, Riyadh, Saudi Arabia. His research interests include decision support systems, critical infrastructure protection and emergency response.

Christopher Badenhop is a Ph.D. student in Computer Engineering at the Air Force Institute of Technology, Wright-Patterson Air Force Base, Ohio. His research interests include computer network security, embedded systems security and RF communications.

Gregory Brainard is a Technical Manager at Honeywell Defense and Space, Albuquerque, New Mexico. His research interests include microgrid design and construction, and microgrid security.

Mike Burmester is a Professor of Computer Science at Florida State University, Tallahassee, Florida. His research interests include computer and network security, cyber-physical system protection, pervasive and ubiquitous systems, trust management and cryptography.

Jonathan Butts, Chair, IFIP Working Group 11.10 on Critical Infrastructure Protection, is the Founder of QED Secure Solutions, Coppell, Texas. His research interests include critical infrastructure protection and cyber-physical systems security.

Marco Caselli is a Ph.D. student in Computer Security at the University of Twente, Enschede, The Netherlands. His research interests include industrial control systems and building automation, with a focus on critical infrastructures.

Yeop Chang is a Senior Member of the Engineering Staff at the National Security Research Institute, Daejeon, South Korea. His research interests include industrial control systems security and reverse engineering.

Dongqing Chen is a Researcher at the China Information Technology Security Evaluation Center, Beijing, China. Her research interests include critical infrastructure protection, cyber-physical system testbeds and complex systems analysis.

Seungoh Choi is a Member of the Engineering Staff at the National Security Research Institute, Daejeon, South Korea. His research interests include critical infrastructure protection and network security.

Kam-Pui Chow is an Associate Professor of Computer Science at the University of Hong Kong, Hong Kong, China. His research interests include information security, digital forensics, live system forensics and digital surveillance.

Antonio Di Pietro is a Staff Scientist at the Laboratory for the Analysis and Protection of Critical Infrastructures, ENEA, Rome, Italy. His research interests include critical infrastructure modeling, decision support systems and data fusion algorithms.

Scott Fischer is a Principal Systems Engineer at Honeywell Defense and Space, Glendale, Arizona. His research interests include microgrid design and construction, and microgrid security.

Chiara Foglietta is a Researcher at the University of Roma Tre, Rome, Italy. Her research interests include industrial control systems (especially, energy management systems), resilience control algorithms for smart grids and data fusion techniques.

Jonathan Fuller is an M.S. student in Computer Science at the Air Force Institute of Technology, Wright-Patterson Air Force Base, Ohio. His research interests include wireless sensor networks and computer and network security.

Haihui Gao is a Researcher at the China Information Technology Security Evaluation Center, Beijing, China. His research interests include critical infrastructure protection, network testbeds, cyber-physical systems and cloud computing.

Andrea Gasparri is an Assistant Professor of Engineering at the University of Roma Tre, Rome, Italy. His research interests include robotics, sensor networks and networked multiagent systems.

Michael Glover is the Managing Partner of Fox Three, McKinney, Texas. His research interests include SCADA systems security, risk analysis and strategic policies.

Dimitris Gritzalis is a Professor of Information Security and the Director of the Information Security and Critical Infrastructure Protection Laboratory at the Athens University of Economics and Business, Athens, Greece. His research interests include critical infrastructure protection, open source intelligence, advanced persistent threats and digital forensics.

Joseph Hall is an M.S. student in Cyberspace Operations at the Air Force Institute of Technology, Wright-Patterson Air Force Base, Ohio. His research interests include network security and wireless sensor networks.

Gerry Howser is an Assistant Professor of Computer Science at Kalamazoo College, Kalamazoo, Michigan. His research interests include computer and network security, cyber-physical system protection, trust management and applications of modal logic to system security and assurance.

Jonathan Jenkins is a Ph.D. student in Computer Science at Florida State University, Tallahassee, Florida. His research interests include computer security and integrity, cyber-physical systems security and trust management.

Frank Kargl is the Director of the Institute of Distributed Systems at Ulm University, Ulm, Germany; and a Professor of Security and Privacy at the University of Twente, Enschede, The Netherlands. His research interests are in the area of mobile and self-organizing networks, and security and privacy of information technology systems, with a special focus on vehicular ad-hoc networks and industrial control systems.

Himanshu Khurana is the Director of Engineering at Honeywell Building Solutions, Golden Valley, Minnesota. His research interests are in the area of secure building automation and control systems.

Woonyon Kim is a Principal Member of the Engineering Staff at the National Security Research Institute, Daejeon, South Korea. His research interests include critical infrastructure protection and SCADA systems security.

Marieke Klaver is a Program Manager at the Netherlands Organisation for Applied Scientific Research (TNO), The Hague, The Netherlands. Her research interests include critical infrastructure protection and resilience.

Panayiotis Kotzanikolaou is an Assistant Professor of Information and Communications Technology Security at the University of Piraeus, Piraeus, Greece. His research interests include network security and privacy, critical infrastructure protection and applied cryptography.

Joshua Lawrence is a Ph.D. student in Computer Science at Florida State University, Tallahassee, Florida. His research interests include critical infrastructure security, cyber-physical systems security and network security.

Frankie Li is a Research Staff Member at the Center for Information Security and Cryptography, University of Hong Kong, Hong Kong, China. His research interests include malware analysis and digital forensics.

Eric Luiijf is a Principal Consultant at the Netherlands Organisation for Applied Scientific Research (TNO), The Hague, The Netherlands. His research interests include information assurance and critical infrastructure protection.

Jose Marti is a Professor of Electrical and Computer Engineering at the University of British Columbia, Vancouver, Canada. His research interests include complex systems, power systems and critical infrastructure protection.

Apurva Mohan is a Cybersecurity Research Scientist at Honeywell Automation and Control Solutions Labs, Golden Valley, Minnesota. His research interests are in the areas of security and privacy for smart grids, industrial control systems, critical infrastructures, cloud computing, mobile computing and healthcare informatics.

Thomas Morris is an Associate Professor of Electrical and Computer Engineering, and the Director of the Center for Cybersecurity Research and Education at the University of Alabama in Huntsville, Huntsville, Alabama. His research interests include industrial control systems security, intrusion detection, machine learning and vulnerability testing.

Cosimo Palazzo is a Ph.D. student in Computer Science and Automation at the University of Roma Tre, Rome, Italy. His research interests include critical infrastructure modeling and simulation, and robotics.

Stefano Panzieri is an Associate Professor of Engineering and the Head of the Models for Critical Infrastructure Protection Laboratory at the University of Roma Tre, Rome, Italy. His research interests include industrial control systems, robotics and sensor fusion.

Yong Peng is a Research Fellow at the China Information Technology Security Evaluation Center, Beijing, China. His research interests include critical infrastructure protection, SCADA systems and complex systems analysis.

Jonathan Petit is a Research Fellow with the Computer Security Group at University College Cork, Cork, Ireland. His research interests include the security and privacy of cyber-physical systems, network security and intelligent transportation systems.

Benjamin Ramsey is an Assistant Professor of Computer Science at the Air Force Institute of Technology, Wright-Patterson Air Force Base, Ohio. His research interests include wireless network security and critical infrastructure protection.

Owen Redwood is a Ph.D. student in Computer Science at Florida State University, Tallahassee, Florida. His research interests include computer and network security, vulnerability analysis and cyber-physical systems security.

Wang Ren is a Researcher at the China Information Technology Security Evaluation Center, Beijing, China. Her research interests include critical infrastructure protection, network security and complex systems analysis.

Mason Rice is an Assistant Professor of Computer Science at the Air Force Institute of Technology, Wright-Patterson Air Force Base, Ohio. His research interests include network and telecommunications security, cyber-physical systems security and critical infrastructure protection.

Riccardo Santini is a Ph.D. student in Computer Science and Automation at the University of Roma Tre, Rome, Italy. His research interests are in the area of cyber-physical systems from a control point of view with an emphasis on the topological properties of interconnected networks.

Lena Schutzle is an M.S. student in Mechanical Engineering at the Technical University of Munich, Munich, Germany. Her research interests are in the area of additive manufacturing.

Siraj Ahmed Shaikh is a Reader in Cyber Security at Coventry University, Coventry, United Kingdom. His research interests include cyber defense and systems security engineering focused on problems in the automotive and transportation domain.

James Shuttleworth is the Associate Head of the Department of Computing and the Digital Environment at Coventry University, Coventry, United Kingdom. His research interests include image analysis, wireless sensor networks, data visualization, in-network processing and systems integration.

George Stergiopoulos is a Ph.D. candidate in Informatics at the Athens University of Economics and Business, Athens, Greece. His research interests include critical infrastructure protection, applications security and software engineering.

Marianthi Theocharidou is a Scientific/Technical Support Officer at the Institute for the Protection and Security of the Citizen, European Commission Joint Research Center, Ispra, Italy. Her research interests include critical infrastructure protection, dependency modeling and risk assessment.

Zach Thornton received his M.S. degree in Electrical and Computer Engineering from Mississippi State University, Mississippi State, Mississippi. His research interests include virtual SCADA systems and industrial control systems security.

Uday Vaidya is the UT/ORNL Governor's Chair of Advanced Composites Manufacturing at the University of Tennessee at Knoxville, Knoxville, Tennessee. His research interests include advanced composites, applications development, prototyping and the commercialization of composites.

Adrian Venables is a Ph.D. student in Cyber Security at Coventry University, Coventry, United Kingdom. His research interests include cyberpower modeling, in particular, the role of innovation in the projection of influence in cyberspace.

Chong Xiang is a Researcher at the China Information Technology Security Evaluation Center, Beijing, China. His research interests include critical infrastructure protection, complex systems analysis, cyber-physical systems and cloud computing.

Mark Yampolskiy is an Assistant Professor of Computer Science at the University of South Alabama, Mobile, Alabama. His research focuses on the security aspects of additive manufacturing, cyber-physical systems and the Internet of Things.

Alec Yasinsac is a Professor and the Dean of the School of Computing at the University of South Alabama, Mobile, Alabama. His research interests include cyber security, critical infrastructure protection, Internet voting and digital forensics.

Ken Yau is a Research Staff Member at the Center for Information Security and Cryptography, University of Hong Kong, Hong Kong, China. His research interests include information security and digital forensics.

Jeong-Han Yun is a Senior Member of the Engineering Staff at the National Security Research Institute, Daejeon, South Korea. His research interests include industrial control systems security and network anomaly detection.

Emmanuele Zambon is a Postdoctoral Researcher with the Services, Cybersecurity and Safety Group at the University of Twente, Enschede, The Netherlands; and the Founder of SecurityMatters, Eindhoven, The Netherlands. His research interests include industrial control systems security and information technology risk management.

Preface

The information infrastructure – comprising computers, embedded devices, networks and software systems – is vital to operations in every sector: information technology, telecommunications, energy, banking and finance, transportation systems, chemicals, agriculture and food, defense industrial base, public health and health care, national monuments and icons, drinking water and water treatment systems, commercial facilities, dams, emergency services, commercial nuclear reactors, materials and waste, postal and shipping, and government facilities. Global business and industry, governments, indeed society itself, cannot function if major components of the critical information infrastructure are degraded, disabled or destroyed.

This book, *Critical Infrastructure Protection IX*, is the ninth volume in the annual series produced by IFIP Working Group 11.10 on Critical Infrastructure Protection, an active international community of scientists, engineers, practitioners and policy makers dedicated to advancing research, development and implementation efforts related to critical infrastructure protection. The book presents original research results and innovative applications in the area of infrastructure protection. Also, it highlights the importance of weaving science, technology and policy in crafting sophisticated, yet practical, solutions that will help secure information, computer and network assets in the various critical infrastructure sectors.

This volume contains nineteen revised and edited papers from the Ninth Annual IFIP Working Group 11.10 International Conference on Critical Infrastructure Protection, held at SRI International in Arlington, Virginia, USA on March 16–18, 2015. The papers were refereed by members of IFIP Working Group 11.10 and other internationally-recognized experts in critical infrastructure protection. The post-conference manuscripts submitted by the authors were rewritten to accommodate the suggestions provided by the conference attendees. They were subsequently revised by the editors to produce the final chapters published in this volume.

The chapters are organized into six sections: themes and issues, control systems security, cyber-physical systems security, infrastructure security, infrastructure modeling and simulation, and risk and impact assessment. The coverage of topics showcases the richness and vitality of the discipline, and offers promising avenues for future research in critical infrastructure protection.

This book is the result of the combined efforts of several individuals and organizations. In particular, we thank Zach Tudor, Heather Drinan and Nicole Hall Hewett for their tireless work on behalf of IFIP Working Group 11.10. We gratefully acknowledge the Institute for Information Infrastructure Protection (I3P), managed by Dartmouth College, for its sponsorship of IFIP Working Group 11.10. We also thank the Department of Homeland Security, National Security Agency and SRI International for their support of IFIP Working Group 11.10 and its activities. Finally, we wish to note that all opinions, findings, conclusions and recommendations in the chapters of this book are those of the authors and do not necessarily reflect the views of their employers or funding agencies.

MASON RICE AND SUJEET SHENOI

I

THEMES AND ISSUES

Chapter 1

A MODEL FOR CHARACTERIZING CYBERPOWER

Adrian Venables, Siraj Ahmed Shaikh and James Shuttleworth

Abstract   Cyberspace may well be the "great equalizer" where nation states and non-state actors can wield cyberpower and compete on relatively equal terms. Leveraging current views and uses of cyberpower, this chapter redefines cyberspace and introduces a three-dimensional model that expresses how cyberpower can be exercised. The model, which is divided into distinct layers, each with its own unique characteristics, offers a notion of distance through a view of cyberspace that introduces the concepts of near, mid and far space. Cyberpower is examined from the perspective of national security. A range of prominent cyber attacks are qualitatively assessed and compared within the context of the model.

Keywords: Cyberspace, cyberpower, cyber attacks, national security

1.   Introduction

This work builds on research by Rowland et al. [18] that describes the anatomy of a cyber power and highlights the essential elements required to achieve and maintain cyberpower. It redefines cyberspace by drawing together and expanding on existing definitions to create a three-dimensional model through which power can be exercised. After deconstructing the notion of cyberpower into a number of constituent components, a range of well-documented examples of cyber attacks are examined within the context of the new model for cyberspace. This provides a foundation for the measurement of cyberpower.

Although power has been defined in a number of ways, this work restricts the definition to national security and conflict, which seek to achieve advantage for political purposes. Thus, the criminally-motivated activities that flourish in cyberspace for financial benefit are excluded as are the social media activities of celebrities and other individuals who seek self-promotion and influence.

As the cyberspace domain is essentially technical in nature, the proposed characterization of cyberpower encompasses several attributes that together

© IFIP International Federation for Information Processing 2015

M. Rice, S. Shenoi (Eds.): Critical Infrastructure Protection IX, IFIP AICT 466, pp. 3–16, 2015.

DOI: 10.1007/978-3-319-26567-4_1

provide a scale of increasing sophistication and capabilities. The ability of an actor to use cyberspace to develop and launch novel, targeted actions that influence the behavior of other persons or devices is considered to be a demonstration of cyberpower. This requires a superior understanding of the nature of cyberspace and ability to precisely maneuver within it. Similarly, acquiring and retaining cyberpower also require an entity to maintain comprehensive situational awareness of its cyberspace assets and to recognize and contain infiltrations and attacks.

2.   Related Work

According to Nye [15], power is a contested concept that is elusive to define and measure. Nye also describes the three facets of power. The first is to get others to do what they would not normally do. The second is agenda setting and framing issues in a manner that does not require coercion. The third is the exercise of power by determining the wants of other entities.

Nye also distinguishes hard power from soft power. Whereas conventional hard power changes the behavior of another entity through inducements or threats in the form of economic or military measures, soft power comes from attraction, which includes non-material means such as culture, political values and foreign policy. Nye [14] also develops the notion of smart power where the concepts of hard and soft power are mutually reinforcing. Smart power enables the full range of political, economic and military options to be articulated in a single strategy that advances national policy objectives.

As with the notion of power, arriving at a definitive description of cyberspace is a notoriously difficult task; one study reports 28 different definitions of cyberspace [10]. The Development, Concepts and Doctrine Centre (DCDC) of the U.K. Ministry of Defence acknowledges the lack of a formal definition of cyberspace and, thus, draws on the Concise Oxford English Dictionary definition of cyberspace as relating to "information technology, the Internet and virtual reality." The Joint Doctrine Note 3/13 formally defines cyberspace for the U.K. defense forces as "the interdependent network of information technology infrastructures (including the Internet, telecommunications networks, computer systems, as well as embedded processors and controllers), and the data therein within the information environment" [30].

This research views the component elements of cyberspace as a series of layers, with each layer fulfilling a particular role. Initially three layers were considered, the physical layer at the base, a syntactic layer above it and a semantic layer at the top [12]. In this model, the physical layer comprises hardware and cabling, the syntactic layer includes the software and protocols that enable data transfer between the hardware components in the physical layer, and the semantic layer contains the information used by a system to achieve its intended purpose.

Subsequent work developed a four-layer model comprising the infrastructure, physical, syntactic and semantic layers [23]. The infrastructure layer consists of hardware, cabling and satellites; the physical layer incorporates the electro-

Table 1. Three horizontal layers of cyberspace.

Environment	Description
Near Space	Local networks and systems that are considered vital to support the critical national infrastructure and services, and are assumed to be controlled and protected by national or governmental agencies.
Mid Space	Networks and systems that are critical to access global cyberspace, but over which there is no local control or protection. Typically, these assets are geographically distant and are owned by foreign companies or third parties.
Far Space	Networks and systems that form the near space of a competitor or adversary, and must be influenced or controlled as part of a campaign to project power and influence in cyberspace.

magnetic spectrum; and the syntactic and semantic layers retain their original definitions.

In addition to representing cyberspace in terms of layers, cyberspace can be considered geographically in terms of near, mid and far operating space as described in Table 1 and based on the U.K. Ministry of Defence *Cyber Primer* [30]. Control and a comprehensive situational awareness of local near space are vital to protect and defend national and local interests. Power is exerted through the "no man's land" of mid space into far space by traditional power projection mechanisms or cyber attacks; the far space corresponds to the near space of a target country or competitor. An analysis of an adversary's strengths and weaknesses in each of these areas can provide information about the most effective methods that can be utilized to reduce its influence and ability to operate freely in cyberspace.

3. Unified Cyberspace Model

The four-layer model of cyberspace expresses the fact that the ability to control one layer does not imply control of any other layer for the purposes of achieving a specific cyber effect. In fact, all four layers must be considered in a coherent mission planning process.

To fully appreciate the planning required to effectively project power as part of a broader campaign, a unified model has been created that incorporates three new layers and expands the definition of the semantic layer. Figure 1 presents the unified model, which comprises seven layers from bottom to top: (i) services layer; (ii) infrastructure layer; (iii) physical layer; (iv) syntactic layer; (v) semantic layer; (vi) human layer; and (vii) mission layer.

The services layer lies below the infrastructure layer and emphasizes the dependencies between components of the infrastructure layer that enable cyberspace to exist and function. It includes resources such as power, water,

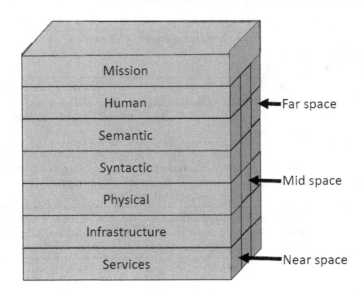

Figure 1. Unified cyberspace model.

materials and even physical security. This layer also includes industrial systems and components that support the infrastructure.

Cyberspace requires human intervention for its creation, maintenance, exploitation and (even) its destruction. Thus, a human layer is included directly above the semantic layer. The semantic layer, which provides information that is useful and understandable to human operators, is necessarily expanded to cover the specific needs of end users. This includes language, culture and user interactions in cyberspace. The importance of this aspect of communicating information is recognized in the field of social network analysis, which investigates the characteristics of relational ties to draw inferences about a network and its entities [22].

The mission layer is the capstone of the unified cyberspace model. It emphasizes the fact that cyberspace serves human needs that are constantly evolving and expanding, and that cyberspace is not a naturally-occurring phenomenon. Every interaction in cyberspace has a specific purpose and consequence, whether intentional or unintentional, innocent or malevolent. By specifying and highlighting the notion of a mission at the top of the model, the roles of all the lower layers can be better understood and contextualized.

Upon combining the seven layers of cyberspace with the concepts of near, mid and far space, cyberspace can be redefined in terms of the three dimensions shown in Figure 1. This can be used to further illustrate that, although cyberpower may be exercised in some elements of cyberspace, it does not guarantee control of all the elements and that a technique that targets a particular aspect may only have a limited overall effect against an adversary. This model also enables attacks to be appreciated in terms of their intended effects and where the greatest risks to an organization exist. It should also be noted that, because the mission element does not vary from mid to far space, it remains a constant throughout.

4. Defining Cyberpower

This section defines the notion of cyberpower and distinguishes between state and non-state actors.

4.1 Cyberpower

Cyberpower may be defined as the ability to alter the behavior of a target subject through the medium of cyberspace in the context of national security and conflict. Such power is exercised by state or non-state actors via cyber campaigns that comprise a singular targeted event (or series of events) using coercive, persuasive or technical means to achieve a specific effect as part of a strategic objective. This ability can be broken down into the following distinct capabilities:

- Active engagement and influence aimed at understanding and opinion forming with a view to directing policy and discourse in the cyber domain using the projection of soft power.

- Targeted and possibly offensive measures designed to deny, degrade, destroy, disrupt or divert service or data to particular devices or components to achieve specific objectives.

- Resilience of the cyber infrastructure through the effective anticipation, absorption, adaptation and recovery from a cyber campaign. A cyber campaign can consist of hard, soft or smart power techniques available to a state or non-state actor and may be realized via a combination of technical and policy mechanisms to strengthen, adapt and defend the infrastructure. This is achieved through reconnaissance and intelligence to maintain a comprehensive situational awareness of assets located in near space.

- Resources and means to achieve attribution of the full spectrum of cyber campaigns in order to counter and, if necessary, take retaliatory action.

- Technical skills and the capacity to underpin the effective and sustained delivery of all of the above.

4.2 State and Non-State Actors

Cyberspace can be regarded as the "great equalizer" in which nation states and non-state actors can compete on relatively equal terms. It can offer entities the same speed, reach, anonymity and protection as well as the ability to develop their own cyber weapons at low cost while profiting economically from on-line commerce [19]. The differences between state and non-state actors are highlighted by comparing their published cyber strategies or previously-demonstrated offensive activities in cyberspace to determine where their priorities lie and where they reside in the unified model of cyberspace.

Several countries have published their national cyber strategies. The United Kingdom and the United States emphasize their increasing dependence on cyberspace and the risks that this brings, noting the dichotomy between the need to tackle security threats while respecting privacy and other fundamental rights. The 2011 United Kingdom Cyber Security Strategy [29] presents a vision to derive economic and social value from cyberspace and emphasizes the economic benefits as well as the need to tackle cyber crime and be resilient to cyber attacks. The human aspect of security is also recognized with the need to develop the knowledge, skills and capabilities required to meet the overall security objectives.

The United States recognized the need for a policy to secure cyberspace as far back as 2003 with the publication of a national strategy [3]. This strategy articulated a framework for protecting the infrastructure that is essential to the economy, security and way of life. The 2011 United States Department of Defense's strategy for operating in cyberspace is predominantly defensive in nature and treats cyberspace as an operational domain [31]. In particular, the strategy covers the protection of Department of Defense networks and systems using the skills of its workforce and through partnerships with other departments and allies. The theme of international cooperation is also the subject of the 2011 U.S. International Strategy for Cyberspace [16]. One of the important goals is to work with the international community to promote an open, interoperable, secure and reliable information and communications infrastructure [16].

The need for international collaboration to secure cyberspace is also recognized by NATO in its National Cyber Security Framework Manual [8]. The manual notes that, although national interests tend to have priority over common interests, international cooperation is needed to achieve cyber security at the global level. The NATO Cooperative Cyber Defense Center of Excellence (CCDOE) has identified international laws that are applicable to cyber warfare in its Tallinn Manual [20]. Released in 2013, the manual specifies 95 rules governing cyber conflicts, addressing issues such as sovereignty, state responsibility, international humanitarian law and the law of neutrality. The European Commission has also recognized the need to achieve an open, safe and secure cyberspace, which it seeks to achieve through its norms and principles of fundamental rights, democracy and the rule of law [4].

Although several nation states have published their official (defensive) cyber policies, they tend to be very reticent about exposing details of their offensive doctrines or capabilities. However, this is not the case with some non-state actors who have amply demonstrated their intent and capabilities to conduct a wide spectrum of cyber attacks [5]. The Anonymous collective is the most prominent western non-state group and it has demonstrated significant cyberpower. The collective, which first came to prominence after its attacks on the

Church of Scientology in 2008, achieved significant publicity with a campaign of action in support of Wikileaks against PayPal and the hacking of the security firm HBGary in 2011 [24]. Anonymous is difficult to quantify because it claims to be a leaderless collective operating under the mantra: "Knowledge is free. We are Anonymous. We are Legion. We do not forgive. We do not forget. Expect us." Its significant social media presence grants it status as a cyber power according to the definition given above, especially when considering the sophistication of its activities (e.g., support of Wikileaks) [21].

The Syrian Electronic Army is a formidable group that has supported the government of Syrian President Bashar al-Assad. Although its relationship with the government is unclear and despite its claims to be independent, some commentators speculate that the Syrian Electronic Army is a state-sponsored entity [17]. State sponsored or not, the group is well organized with its own website, which lists its high profile hacks, including successful attacks on the western media and the U.S. Marine Corps website [28].

In general, nation states publish their cyberspace strategies and emphasize the need for resilience. This concentrates their efforts on the protection of near space for reasons of economic and national security. Non-state actors, however, typically operate in mid space and do not have the burden of protecting their infrastructures in near space. Instead, their activities are limited to exerting cyberpower in the near space of their adversaries according to their political and conflict agendas. This enables non-state actors to maintain resilience through distribution and anonymity, although their capabilities may not be focused and sustained because they primarily rely on volunteers to pursue their agendas. The key difference between nation states and non-state actors is that the former are constrained by domestic and international law, while the latter consider themselves free to use any and all means that are deemed to be effective.

5. Characterizing Cyberpower

This section characterizes cyber attacks, and by extension cyberpower, in terms of six attributes that are used to provide a composite score of the sophistication of a cyber campaign. Also, the section evaluates ten well-publicized cyber attacks from 2007 through 2014 with respect to the six attributes and provides the corresponding composite scores.

5.1 Cyber Attack Attributes

Having defined the concepts of cyberspace and cyberpower in the context of the unified model, it is possible to characterize the effects of cyber attacks and to measure cyber attacks and, by extension, cyberpower. Cyber attacks are measured using a sophistication scale based on the layers in the cyberspace model, which combined with the targeted activities, provides a comparative scaling of the attacks. Sophistication is measured in terms of six characteristics, persistence, propagation, novelty, precision and accuracy, impact and attribution:

- **Persistence:** This is measured in terms of the actions or effort under-taken by the attacker. For example, a denial-of-service attack requiring continued action from an attacker would score less than a virus that does not require human action to propagate. Accordingly, a virus would score less than a self-replicating worm that requires no originator interaction after the initial delivery.

- **Propagation:** This is measured in terms of the effort that is required to deliver the payload. For example, a successful attack on a system that is not connected to the Internet would score higher than a system that is more easily accessed.

- **Novelty:** This is measured in terms of the uniqueness of the technique employed by the attack payload and the amount of effort expended in its development. The use of previously-unknown exploits would receive a high score.

- **Precision and Accuracy:** These are measured in terms of how discreet the attack is in achieving a particular effect. This considers the level of collateral damage to other systems or people and the extent to which the timing of the event can be determined. An attack that focuses on a unique target at a specific time would score more highly than a general widespread attack with no particular timing because it indicates the complexity of the objective or a desire to reduce collateral damage.

- **Impact:** This is measured in terms of the effectiveness of the attack, which depends on its psychological value as well as the actual effect on the target. Impact can also be measured in terms of the temporal effect. The scoring is influenced by the publicity and assessment of cyber security researchers who identify precise attack details that have not been released to the public. The more severe the impact, the higher the score.

- **Attribution:** This is measured in terms of the ability of the target of a cyberpower campaign to accurately identify the originator. The orig-inator may seek total anonymity or may imply that another group or country executed the attack in order to hinder the investigation. The scoring index depends on the mission of the cyber attack; although, in general, the greater the anonymity, the higher the score.

5.2   Cyber Attack Evaluation

Tables 2 and 3 describe ten significant cyber attacks from 2007 through 2014. The attacks are characterized in terms of near, mid and far space, and the layers of the unified cyberspace model in which they were active. Numerous attacks have been publicized, but these ten attacks were selected due to their relevance to the definition of cyberpower as being related to national security

Table 2. Characterization of cyber attacks.

Attack	Attack Details and Degree of Sophistication
DDoS **(2007)** [9]	Coordinated distributed denial-of-service attack on Estonia's infrastructure through near, mid and far space. The attack, although large in scale, used relatively unsophisticated methods and was launched over the Internet. Although it generated considerable publicity, it was relatively short-lived with limited long-term damage. Active Layer: Syntactic. Persistence, Propagation, Novelty, Precision, Attribution: Low; Impact: Medium. *Total Score = 7.*
Aurora **(2009)** [25]	Targeted malware attack against Adobe and Google through near, mid and far space. The attack, thought to be state-sponsored, targeted at least 30 companies and employed a previously unknown Internet Explorer vulnerability that enabled computers to be controlled and data to be exfiltrated [7]. The attack was eventually neutralized by browser and anti-virus updates. Active Layer: Semantic. Propagation, Precision: Low; Persistence, Novelty, Impact, Attribution: Medium. *Total Score = 10.*
Stuxnet **(2010)** [27]	Highly-sophisticated malware thought to be state-sponsored and believed to have targeted an industrial control system in far space that could not be directly accessed via the Internet. The malware used an unprecedented number of previously-unknown Microsoft vulnerabilities and also compromised the human-machine interfaces of the control system. Active Layers: Services, Infrastructure. Persistence, Propagation, Novelty, Precision, Impact, Attribution: High. *Total Score = 18.*
Duqu **(2011)** [1]	Stuxnet-like malware that targeted the Microsoft Windows operating system to steal information located in far space. The malware sought information about industrial control systems and exfiltrated the information through mid space to the originator's near space. Active layer: Syntactic. Propagation, Precision, Impact, Attribution: Medium; Persistence, Novelty: High. *Total Score = 14.*
HBGary **(2011)** [24]	Attack attributed to Anonymous. This relatively-unsophisticated attack against HBGary through mid and far space exploited known vulnerabilities to exfiltrate sensitive data and conduct a denial-of-service attack. Active Layers: Semantic, Human. Propagation, Novelty, Attribution: Low; Persistence: Medium; Precision, Impact: High. *Total Score = 11.*

or conflict. Additionally, the attacks were selected because substantial open source information was available for analysis.

Table 3.   Characterization of cyber attacks (contd.).

Attack	Attack Details and Degree of Sophistication
Flamer **(2012)** [26]	Malware with a complexity similar to Stuxnet and Duqu, albeit unrelated. Thought to be state-sponsored, the malware targeted Eastern Europe and Middle Eastern countries to exfiltrate information from a range of targets in far space through mid space to near space. Active Layer: Syntactic. Precision: Low; Propagation, Impact, Attribution: Medium; Persistence, Novelty: High. *Total Score = 13.*
Shamoon **(2013)** [2]	Highly targeted and widespread attack in far space on the critical infrastructure of Saudi Aramco by means of a self-replicating virus that deleted data and rendered computers unusable. Thought to be state-sponsored. Active Layer: Infrastructure. Propagation: Low; Persistence, Novelty, Precision, Impact, Attribution: High. *Total Score = 16.*
APT1 **(2013)** [13]	Widespread industrial espionage of western commercial enterprises in far space using complex and well-organized procedures with evidence of state-sponsorship in near space. Active Layer: Semantic. Propagation: Low; Persistence, Novelty, Precision, Impact, Attribution: Medium. *Total Score = 11.*
ISIL **(2014)** [6]	Non-state sponsored campaign through social media in mid space targeting domestic and western media using high production quality media to publicize activities, attract and encourage supporters and intimidate adversaries. Active Layers: Semantic, Human. Propagation, Precision, Attribution: Low; Persistence, Novelty: Medium; Impact: High. *Total Score = 10.*
Sony **(2014)** [11]	Possible state-sponsored attack on Sony Corporation that resulted in the exfiltration and publication of sensitive information in far space causing embarrassment and financial loss. Active Layers: Semantic, Human. Persistence, Propagation: Low; Novelty, Attribution: Medium; Precision, Impact: High. *Total Score = 12.*

The grades, low, medium and high, correspond to the numerical scores, 1, 2 and 3, respectively. The numerical scores assigned to the individual characteristics were added to yield the total score. The grades and, thus, the scores were qualitatively assessed based on expert opinion. Note that all the characteristics were given the same weight, although, in some circumstances, certain criteria may necessitate higher relative values.

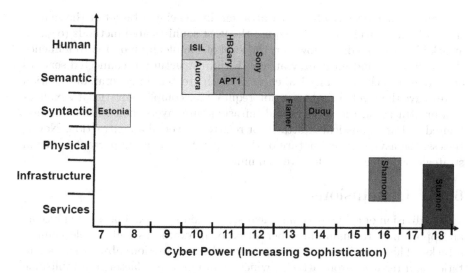

Figure 2. Comparison of cyber attack sophistication and layers of operation.

Figure 2 displays the information provided in Tables 2 and 3 in a graphical format, indicating the relative sophistication of the attacks and the layers of cyberspace in which they were active. The figure shows a general trend that indicates a less complex and less technically-challenging approach is adequate to attack the semantic and human layers. This is because these layers are designed to be readily accessible and, therefore, require less effort to achieve successful interactions. The human targets are not only easier to access, but are also more susceptible to influence and change than programmed technical components, which only have a limited series of responses to the possible inputs.

Creating effects in the layers that are not designed for direct human interaction (e.g., services, infrastructure, physical and syntactic layers) are more complex undertakings. This is because an attack involves creating an effect contrary to that envisioned by the system designers and, consequently, requires a deeper understanding of the system architecture and configuration. In addition, an attack conducted over a network that is designed to cause physical damage to a specific system has to be carefully targeted and calibrated to reduce collateral damage.

If it is determined that a physical effect is desired on a system and that impacting the lower elements of a network would require considerable preparation and planning, an alternative strategy may be more effective. Depending on the circumstances, it may be decided that the most timely, economical and effective way of achieving the desired effect is to attack the target using conventional munitions instead of a cyber attack. However, a decision that weighs the strengths and weaknesses of the different options can only be made after a thorough analysis of the target, which can be aided using the unified model of cyberspace and the measures of attack sophistication discussed above.

From the perspective of a cyber attacker, influencing a target at the semantic and human layers tends to require the least sophisticated methods (e.g., an attack via social media). However, the level of complexity required to influence the lower levels and ultimately attack the infrastructure or connected services or systems to achieve a physical effect is much greater. In general, only nation states have the level of sophistication required for complex covert data exfiltration or attacks on the services and infrastructure layers; non-state actors are limited to less sophisticated attacks or relatively overt data extraction. Nevertheless, the asymmetrical nature of these operations is an important factor in strategic offensive and defensive planning.

6.   Conclusions

The division of cyberspace into near space, mid space and far space presents an opportunity to maintain cyber situational awareness and enable counter attacks. This contributes to resilience via the anticipation, absorption, adaptation and recovery from attacks, which is an important factor in establishing cyberpower. The specification of what constitutes near space enables the articulation of defensive priorities and the identification of far space boundaries that lower the risk of incurring collateral damage. Combining situational awareness with the quantification of the various layers of cyberspace can improve the understanding of cyberspace and how to project cyberpower.

Future research will attempt to further delineate the elements of cyberspace and quantify cyber attacks and the cyberpower of nation states and non-state actors. The goal is to develop a model that can provide numerical indices of cyberspace and cyberpower, and assist with the prediction of attack effectiveness. Such a model would significantly inform defense policy and spending priorities. Clearly, reliable data sources will be required to develop and validate the model. Future research will also evaluate government and industry databases to determine what information is already available and what information remains to be collected.

References

[1] B. Bencsath, G. Pek, L. Buttyan and M. Felegyhazi, Duqu: A Stuxnet-like Malware Found in the Wild, Technical Report, Laboratory of Cryptography and System Security, Department of Telecommunications, Budapest University of Technology and Communications, Budapest, Hungary ((www.crysys.hu/publications/files/bencsathPBF11duqu.pdf), 2011.

[2] C. Bronk, The cyber attack on Saudi Aramco, *Survival: Global Politics and Strategy*, vol. 55(2), pp. 81–96, 2013.

[3] G. Bush, National Strategy to Secure Cyberspace, The White House, Washington, DC, 2003.

[4] European Commission, Cybersecurity Strategy of the European Union: An Open, Safe and Secure Cyberspace, Joint Communication to the European Parliament, the Council, the European Economic and Social Committee and the Committee of the Regions, JOIN(2013) 1 Final, Brussels, Belgium, 2013.

[5] European Union Agency for Network and Information Security (ENISA), National Cyber Security Strategies in the World, Heraklion, Greece, 2014.

[6] F. Irshaid, How ISIS is spreading its message online, *BBC News*, June 19, 2014.

[7] A. Kliarsky, Responding to Zero Day Threats, InfoSec Reading Room, SANS Institute, Bethesda, Maryland (www.sans.org/reading-room/whitepapers/incident/responding-zero-day-threats-33709), 2011.

[8] A. Klimburg (Ed.), National Cyber Security Framework Manual, NATO Cooperative Cyber Defence Centre of Excellence, Tallinn, Estonia (www.ccdcoe.org/publications/books/NationalCyberSecurityFrameworkManual.pdf), 2012.

[9] A. Kozlowski, Comparative analysis of the cyber attacks on Estonia, Georgia and Kyrgyzstan, *European Scientific Journal*, vol. 3, pp. 237–245, 2014.

[10] F. Kramer, Cyberpower and national security: Policy recommendations for a strategic framework, in *Cyberpower and National Security*, F. Kramer, S. Starr and L. Wentz (Eds.), National Defense University Press and Potomac Books, Washington, DC, pp. 3–23, 2009.

[11] T. Lee, The Sony hack: How it happened, who is responsible, and what we've learned, *Vox*, December 17, 2014.

[12] M. Libicki, *Cyberdeterrence and Cyberwar*, RAND, Santa Monica, California, 2009.

[13] Mandiant, APT1: Exposing One of China's Cyber Espionage Units, Mandiant Intelligence Center Report, Alexandria, Virginia (intelreport.mandiant.com), 2013.

[14] J. Nye, *Soft Power: The Means to Success in World Politics*, PublicAffairs, New York, 2004.

[15] J. Nye, *Cyber Power*, Belfer Center for Science and International Affairs, Kennedy School of Government, Harvard University, Cambridge, Massachusetts, 2010.

[16] B. Obama, International Strategy for Cyberspace: Prosperity, Security and Openness in a Networked World, The White House, Washington, DC, 2011.

[17] N. Perlroth, Hunting for Syrian hackers' chain of command, *New York Times*, May 17, 2013.

[18] J. Rowland, M. Rice and S. Shenoi, The anatomy of a cyber power, *International Journal of Critical Infrastructure Protection*, vol. 7(1), pp. 3–11, 2014.

[19] J. Rowland, M. Rice and S. Shenoi, Whither cyberpower? *International Journal of Critical Infrastructure Protection*, vol. 7(2), pp. 124–137, 2014.

[20] M. Schmitt (Ed.), *Tallinn Manual on the International Law Applicable to Cyber Warfare*, Cambridge University Press, Cambridge, United Kingdom, 2013.

[21] M. Schwartz, Who is Anonymous: 10 key facts, *Information Week – Dark Reading*, February 6, 2012.

[22] J. Scott and P. Carrington (Eds.), *The SAGE Handbook of Social Network Analysis*, Sage Publications, London, United Kingdom, 2011.

[23] J. Sheldon, Deciphering cyberpower: Strategic purpose in peace and war, *Strategic Studies Quarterly*, vol. 5(2), pp. 95–112, 2011.

[24] P. Singer and A. Friedman, *Cybersecurity and Cyberwar: What Everyone Needs to Know*, Oxford University Press, New York, 2014.

[25] Sophos, Operation Aurora: What you need to know, Abingdon, United Kingdom (www.sophos.com/en-us/security-news-trends/sec urity-trends/operation-aurora.aspx), 2010.

[26] Symantec, Flamer: Highly Sophisticated and Discreet Threat Targets the Middle East, Mountain View, California (www.symantec .com/connect/blogs/flamer-highly-sophisticated-and-discreet-threat-targets-middle-east), 2012.

[27] Symantec, W32.Stuxnet, Mountain View, California (www.symantec. com/security_response/writeup.jsp?docid=2010-071400-3123-99), 2013.

[28] Syrian Electronic Army, Syrian Electronic Army Homepage (www.sea.sy), 2015.

[29] U.K. Cabinet Office, The U.K. Cyber Security Strategy: Protecting and Promoting the U.K. in a Digital World, London, United Kingdom (www.gov.uk/government/uploads/system/uploads/attachment_ data/file/60961/uk-cyber-security-strategy-final.pdf), 2011.

[30] U.K. Ministry of Defence, Cyber Primer, Development, Concepts and Doctrine Centre, Shrivenham, United Kingdom, 2013.

[31] U.S. Department of Defense, Department of Defense Strategy for Operating in Cyberspace, Washington, DC, 2011.

Chapter 2

CYBER ATTACKS AND POLITICAL EVENTS: THE CASE OF THE OCCUPY CENTRAL CAMPAIGN

Kam-Pui Chow, Ken Yau and Frankie Li

Abstract   Occupy Central was a Hong Kong civil disobedience campaign that began in September 2014 with the goal of forcing Mainland China to allow Hong Kong to implement genuine universal suffrage as demanded by Hong Kong residents. The campaign initially encouraged citizens to block the Central District, Hong Kong's financial center. However, as the campaign evolved, large protests were organized all over Hong Kong.

While vigorous clashes occurred between Occupy Central protesters and police officers on the streets of Hong Kong, cyber attacks were launched quietly by supporters of both sides against each other's assets. The cyber weapons included mobile applications with malware for surveillance, tools for launching distributed denial-of-service (DDoS) attacks and sophisticated phishing emails with advanced persistent threat functionality. This chapter presents information about cyber attacks related to the Occupy Central campaign and classifies the attacks based on their purpose, techniques, targets and propagation. Based on the attack classification and timeline, a framework is provided that helps predict attack patterns and behavior in order to prevent or mitigate attacks launched during similar political events.

Keywords: Political events, cyber attacks, Occupy Central campaign

1.   Introduction

In January 2013, the Occupy Central civil disobedience campaign was proposed by Benny Yiu-Ting Tai, an Associate Professor of Law at the University of Hong Kong. The campaign, which he named "Occupy Central with Love and Peace" (OCLP), encouraged citizens to block roads in Hong Kong's Central District and paralyze its financial infrastructure in order to force the Mainland Chinese and Hong Kong governments to implement universal suffrage for the

© IFIP International Federation for Information Processing 2015
M. Rice, S. Shenoi (Eds.): Critical Infrastructure Protection IX, IFIP AICT 466, pp. 17–27, 2015.
DOI: 10.1007/978-3-319-26567-4_2

Hong Kong Chief Executive election in 2017 and the Legislative Council elections in 2020 according to international standards [18].

On September 22, 2014, the Hong Kong Federation of Students and Scholars began protesting outside the Hong Kong government headquarters against its decision on proposed electoral reforms made by the Standing Committee of the National People's Congress (NPCSC) [17]. This protest triggered the Occupy Central campaign. On September 28, 2014, Benny Tai announced that the civil disobedience campaign would start at 1:45 pm. The *South China Morning Post* reported that the organizers expected about 10,000 supporters to show up at Hong Kong's financial district. However, several tens of thousands of protesters filled the streets, paralyzing not just the Central District, but also parts of Causeway Bay, Admiralty and Mong Kok, through late September and early October 2014.

During the early days of the protests, the Hong Kong Police used tear gas and pepper spray to disperse the swelling crowds, especially when protesters attempted to break police lines to reach Occupy Central's main protest site at Tamar Park. The protesters were equipped with masks, goggles and umbrellas to fend off the tear gas and pepper spray. Therefore, the protest was also referred to as the Umbrella Revolution or the Umbrella Movement.

As the protesters and police clashed on the streets, cyber warfare was initiated on the Internet between protest supporters and the Hong Kong government. A variety of cyber attacks were launched, including injecting spyware into mobile devices for surveillance, executing distributed denial-of-service (DDoS) attacks on various government entities and sending phishing emails with advanced persistent threat (APT) functionality.

The cyber attacks launched by the two sides during the Occupy Central campaign are classified as: (i) silent attacks; and (ii) violent attacks. A silent attack is a low profile attack that mainly targeted protest supporters for purposes of conducting surveillance. A violent attack is a high profile attack that primarily disrupted the opponent's online services. This chapter presents a cyber warfare framework based on the timeline of silent attacks and violent attacks that occurred during the Occupy Central campaign. The framework can be used to predict cyber attack patterns and behavior in order to prevent or mitigate attacks during similar campaigns in the future.

2.   Initial Violent Attacks

In June 2014, the Public Opinion Programme at the University of Hong Kong and the Centre for Social Policy Studies at Hong Kong Polytechnic University were commissioned by the Secretariat of Occupy Central with Love and Peace to organize the Occupy Central with Love and Peace 6.20-29 Civil Referendum [13]. The civil referendum was about the implementation of universal suffrage for the Chief Executive election in 2017 and the Legislative Council elections in 2020 according to international standards [12].

In order to enable citizens to familiarize themselves with the e-voting interface of the 6.22 Civil Referendum, the Public Opinion Programme at the University of Hong Kong launched a mobile application platform for pre-registration and mock voting on June 13, 2014 [13]. Online services for the system were provided by three prominent service providers, Amazon Web Services, CloudFlare and UDomain.

The system worked fine for the first 30 hours. However, after receiving more than 20,000 successful registrations, the three service providers came under large-scale distributed denial-of-service attacks. The attacks paralyzed the voting system, but did not compromise the security of its information. Records reveal that the domain name system (DNS) of Amazon Web Services received more than 10 billion queries in 20 hours, while CloudFlare and UDomain recorded distributed denial-of-service attacks at the rates of 75 Gbps and 10 Gbps, respectively. Reports indicate that the last batch of attacks originated from local Internet service providers.

According to analyses conducted by Internet security experts, the scale and duration of the distributed denial-of-service attacks on one targeted system over two days were unprecedented in Hong Kong (based on attacks known to the public). These large-scale distributed denial-of-service attacks are categorized as violent attacks in the proposed framework.

3.   Silent Attacks on Protest Supporters

Smartphones belonging to Hong Kong democracy protesters were targeted by silent hacking attacks. In early September 2014, Hong Kong residents with Android smartphones received messages saying "Check out this Android app designed by Code4HK for the coordination of OCCUPY CENTRAL!" Code4HK is a group of coders that was attempting to improve government transparency in Hong Kong. However, according to the *South China Morning Post* of October 1, 2014, Code4HK said that it had neither developed nor distributed the Android application.

The silent attacks were discovered by researchers at Lacoon Mobile Security on September 30, 2014, just as the Occupy Central campaign started [11]. According to Lacoon Mobile Security, an advanced tool called mRat was installed on a smartphone after its user clicked on the link via WhatsApp messaging. The tool gave the hackers essentially complete access to an infected smartphone. The hackers could then extract information from the compromised device, including the address book, call logs, email and geographical locations. In addition, the hackers could upload files to a compromised device, call a number and delete specific files [2].

The mRat spyware targeted Android phones as well as iOS devices such as iPhones and iPads. The spyware that targeted iOS devices was given the name Xsser mRat. The attack behavior of Xsser mRat was very similar to mRat, but it only infected jailbroken devices. Since at least 30% of the iPhones in Hong Kong and China were jailbroken as of 2013, the reach of Xsser mRat was significant [11]. Michael Shaulov, CEO of Lacoon Mobile Security, said that mRat was the first attack to target Android and iOS devices simultaneously, and that the iOS version used a "very sophisticated and very polished piece of malware."

The silent attack did not merely target protesters' mobile devices, it also targeted pro-democracy websites. An article posted by Steven Adair from the Volexity security firm on October 9, 2014 claimed that four websites that promoted democracy in Hong Kong had been rigged to deliver malicious software [1, 7]. The websites included the Alliance for True Democracy (www. atd.hk), Democratic Party Hong Kong (www.dphk.org; eng.dphk.org), People Power in Hong Kong (www.peoplepower.hk) and Professional Commons (www.procommons.org.hk).

The Alliance for True Democracy and the Democratic Party Hong Kong websites were injected with a suspected malicious JavaScript linked to the domain java-se.com. This domain was known to be associated with advanced persistent threat activity [1, 7].

The People Power in Hong Kong website contained a malicious iframe, which pointed to a Chinese URL shortened address that redirected visitors to an exploit page hosted by a Hong Kong IP address [1, 7]. The Professional Commons website also contained a suspicious JavaScript, which loaded an iframe that pointed to a South Korean hotel website. Steven Adair from Volexity discovered that the iframe attempted to load an HTML page that did not exist on the South Korean website, which indicated that it was a previously-active attack [1, 7].

In addition to attacks on pro-democracy websites, phishing emails were sent to protesters. Since many of the protesters were students, the phishing emails were a good way to target college and university computer systems and networks. The Chinese University of Hong Kong and the University of Hong Kong sent announcements to their staff and students to ignore phishing emails with the subject Occupy Central written in Chinese. The phishing emails contained a virus-infected file named dblleft Letter To Hong Kong.rar [4, 16].

A cyber attack that targeted Apple iCloud users was discovered on October 2, 2014 [6, 11]. According to the anti-censorship group GreatFire.org, when a user visited Apple's iCloud site in China, the site returned an invalid digital certificate, a sign that the connections had been tampered with using a man-in-the-middle attack. GreatFire.org alleged that the Chinese government was behind the attack, which was used to eavesdrop on communications and steal username and password information from Apple iCloud users. However, a spokeswoman from the Chinese Foreign Ministry emphasized that the country was opposed to any form of hacking.

4.   Violent Attacks on Protest Supporters

Violent attacks were frequently launched on social networking sites to block communications between protest supporters. On September 29, 2014, the *South China Morning Post* [3] reported that access to the Instagram photo-sharing platform appeared to have been blocked in Mainland China on September 28,

2014 after photos of the Hong Kong pro-democracy protests were circulated via Instagram.

On September 29, 2014, the Instagram website could not be accessed by servers in Beijing, Shenzhen, Inner Mongolia, Heilongjiang and Yunnan, according to the Chinese censorship monitoring website, Great Firewall of China (greatfirewallofchina.org). The censors added Instagram to the growing list of foreign services blocked by Mainland China. Facebook, YouTube and Twitter have been blocked for years. Almost all of Google's online services have been blocked since June 2014. The Japanese messaging service Line and South Korea's Kakao Talk have also been blocked. Additionally, DuckDuckGo, a U.S.-based Internet search engine with a focus on user privacy, has been made inaccessible in China.

The shutting down of access to Instagram generated numerous angry comments and turned into one of the highest trending topics in Chinese microblogs on September 29, 2014, according to Weibo's own rankings. Conversations on Weibo with the hashtag Instagram could not be accessed on September 29, 2014. The microblogging service said the conversations were "in the process of being audited."

5. Violent Attacks on the Government

On October 15, 2014, the Anonymous hacker collective officially declared "cyber war" on the Mainland Chinese regime in a video announcement [11]. A few days later, on October 18, 2014, coordinated attacks were launched against Chinese government websites.

According to an October 13, 2014 report in the *South China Morning Post* [8], Anonymous had already released hundreds of phone numbers and email addresses associated with the Ningbo Free Trade Zone in the Zhejiang coastal province and a job-search site run by the Changxing county administration, also in the Zhejiang province. The reason for targeting these websites remains unknown. However, Anonymous did announce that it had successfully penetrated more than 50 Chinese government databases and leaked 50,000 user names and emails.

Anonymous had previously targeted Hong Kong government websites after first issuing a warning on October 2, 2014. In a video message, Anonymous declared cyber war on the Hong Kong government and police force for using tear gas against Occupy Central demonstrators. Attacks by Anonymous on October 3, 2014 rendered some Hong Kong government websites inaccessible or intermittently accessible. Distributed denial-of-service attacks were also launched against Chinese government websites; the sites were overloaded with artificial traffic and taken offline.

According to an October 23, 2014 report in the *South China Morning Post* [15], eleven people were arrested for launching cyber attacks on more than 70 government websites after the hackers' warning about retaliation for the use of tear gas on democracy protesters. The attacks were apparently conducted under the banner of Anonymous, a brand adopted by hackers and activists around the globe.

After the series of the cyber attacks, Kam-Leung So, the Secretary for Commerce and Economic Development of Hong Kong, said that no information was altered or stolen, and that the government's online services were not affected significantly; the attackers merely made the sites intermittently inaccessible by issuing a flood of access requests. He also said that "attacks launched by the hacker group originated partly from Hong Kong, and partly from other regions." Hong Kong police arrested eight men and three women, aged between 13 to 39, on suspicion of accessing computers with criminal or dishonest intent.

6.   Attack Characteristics

Silent attacks mainly target protesters to conduct surveillance. In the case of the Occupy Central protests, the objective of the silent attacks was to steal protesters' personal information and monitor protesters' activities and movements in order to develop a strategy for dealing with the protests.

The first step in conducting a silent attack is to install malicious code on the target device. The target device could be a web server, computer, smartphone or tablet. Smartphones and tablets are the best devices to conduct surveillance because their users (i.e., protesters) carry them wherever they go. These devices also contain valuable information such as photographs, contact lists, email and user locations, making them perfect devices to conduct spying activities [11]. It is important that the attack be performed silently without impacting normal device operations and performance; otherwise, the victims might suspect the presence of spyware and attempt to have it removed. A silent attack must be well planned and organized before it is launched. Indeed, a silent attack always involves a high level of technical skill to ensure that the malicious code is persistent on the target device and performs its activities in a stealthy manner.

Violent attacks mainly target government entities or public organizations to disrupt their online services. The objective typically is to temporarily or indefinitely interrupt or suspend host computer services that are provided over the Internet. Sometimes, violent attacks are launched to disrupt protesters' online social networking activities and online pro-democracy websites, the goal being to disrupt communications and hinder command and control of demonstrations and other protest activities.

Violent attacks are generally implemented as denial-of-service (DoS) or distributed denial-of-service (DDoS) attacks. A violent attack can be implemented with little technical skills because attack tools are easily purchased or downloaded from the Internet. Violent attacks are destructive and difficult to defend against; they can be launched against practically any target, anytime and anywhere. These attacks are often performed by hactivist groups and criminal organizations; however, there are instances where violent attacks have been launched by nation states or their proxies. Unlike their silent counterparts, violent attacks are very high profile and their symptoms are obvious. The U.S.

Computer Emergency Readiness Team (US-CERT) lists the following symptoms of denial-of-service attacks:

- Unusually slow network performance (opening files or accessing web sites).

- Unavailability of a web site.

- Inability to access a web site.

- Dramatic increase in the number of spam email received (this type of attack is called an e-mail bomb).

- Disconnection of wireless or wired Internet connections.

- Long-term denial of access to the web or Internet services.

All the symptoms listed above were observed at the targeted government websites as well as the university websites that supported the online opinion surveys.

7.   Motivation for the Cyber War Framework

According to Kam-Leung So, Secretary of Commerce and Economic Development of Hong Kong, significant damage was not observed as a result of the attacks launched during the Occupy Central campaign. However, cyber attacks can cause massive economic losses when the targeted systems do not have adequate protection. A cyber warfare framework can help predict attack trends and behavior in order to understand the risk and mitigate the damage to systems that may be targeted.

In November 2014, cyber attacks were launched against Sony Pictures Entertainment, whose global operations encompass motion picture production, acquisition and distribution; television production, acquisition and distribution; television networks; digital content creation and distribution; operation of studio facilities; and development of new entertainment products, services and technologies [14]. On December 15, 2014, Sony Pictures Entertainment announced that it had experienced a significant disruption on November 24, 2014. It determined that the cause of the disruption was a cyber attack and passed the case to leading cyber security consultants and law enforcement agencies. On December 1, 2014, Sony Pictures Entertainment was informed that the security of personally identifiable information about its current and former employees, and their dependents who participated in health plans and other benefits, may have been compromised.

According to the Australian news and entertainment website, News.com. au [9], the Guardians of Peace hacker group essentially stole every bit of information and private data in Sony's possession and then deleted the original copies from Sony's computers. The hacker group informed Sony that, if their demands were not met, all the files would be posted online.

The Guardians of Peace began by releasing five Sony movies to the public; four of these movies had not yet been released to theaters. Following this,

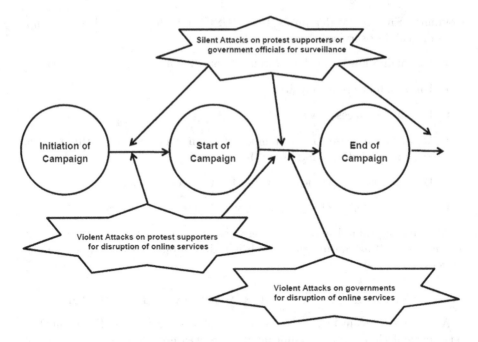

Figure 1.   Cyber warfare framework.

thousands of Sony confidential documents were posted on the Internet. The documents included everything from private email messages between Sony employees to performance data and the salaries of employees, including stars in Sony films – this was considered to be the real damage to Sony.

It is hard to imagine how serious the consequences would be if similar cyber attacks were launched during the Occupy Central campaign. The damage could be mitigated if attack patterns and behavior could be predicted and appropriate actions could be taken before the attacks. Indeed, a cyber warfare framework would be an important and valuable tool for cyber attack prediction and mitigation.

8.   Cyber Warfare Framework

Table 1 provides the timeline and details of the cyber attacks that were launched by both sides during the Occupy Central campaign, Figure 1 presents the cyber warfare framework constructed based on the information in Table 1. According to the cyber warfare framework, a campaign has three stages. The first stage is the initiation of the campaign, the second stage is the start of the campaign and the third and final stage is the end of the campaign. Spyware for the silent attacks would have to be ready before the start of the campaign. After the silent attacks have been launched, the spyware must continue to be active even if the protest ends. This is because the silent attacks seek to gather information about the protesters' plans ahead of time and to monitor

Table 1. Cyber attacks launched during the Occupy Central campaign.

Date	Attack Type	Description	Victim	Purpose	Target Device	Technique	Propagation
06/13/2014	Violent	Mock e-voting system attacked	Protest supporters	Shut down e-voting system	Web server	DDoS attack	N/A N/A
09/29/2014	Violent	Instagram website blocked	Protest supporters	Stop photo sharing	Web server	Website blocking	N/A N/A
10/10/2014	Silent	iCloud user accounts leaked	iCloud users	Steal user information	iCloud server	Man-in-the-middle attack	N/A N/A
10/03/2014	Violent	DDoS attack by Anonymous	Mainland Chinese and Hong Kong governments	Disrupt online services	Web server	DDoS and DoS attacks	N/A N/A
10/09/2014	Silent	Pro-democracy websites attacked	Protest supporters	Surveillance	Web server	Cross-site scripting	Code injection
10/12/2014 10/13/2014	Silent	Phishing attacks on university users	Protest supporters	Unknown	Computer	APT	Email
10/13/2014	Violent	Data leaked by Anonymous	Mainland Chinese and Hong Kong governments	Leak sensitive data	Network	Intrusion	N/A N/A

the protesters' activities after the protest ends [11]. Government officials may well be targets of silent attacks in future campaigns. Also, mobile devices such as smartphones and tablets are most likely to be the targets of silent attacks.

Violent attacks can be launched anytime and anywhere. Tools and services for launching denial-of-service and distributed denial-of-service attacks are easily purchased or downloaded from the Internet. Violent attacks targeting protesters would ideally be launched between the initiation of the campaign and the end of the campaign because they are intended to disrupt communications and information sharing and, thereby, impact planning, coordination and command and control activities. Violent attacks targeting government entities would typically be launched between the start of the campaign and the end of the campaign to influence the government to accept the protesters' demands.

Civil disobedience campaigns are often supported by hacktivist groups such as Anonymous. For example, in 2012, hacktivist groups were involved in a protest against amendments to Japanese copyright laws (#opJapan), dissent against Chinese censorship (#opChina) and anti-government efforts in Russia (#opRussia), Israel (#opIsrael) and North Korea (#opNorthKorea) [10].

Violent attacks almost always involve denial-of-service and distributed denial-of-service attacks. These attacks are destructive and hard to avoid. The attacks mainly target government websites and services, and also expose sensitive government data to the public. It is expected that the Mainland Chinese and Hong Kong governments would be targeted by violent attacks if a campaign similar to Occupy Central were to occur again.

9.   Conclusions

The classification of cyber attacks launched by both sides during the Occupy Central protests in Hong Kong in 2014 provide useful insights into attack timelines, patterns and behavior. The resulting cyber warfare framework involving silent and violent attacks can be used to predict the patterns and behavior of cyber attacks launched in similar campaigns. Additionally, the framework could serve as a valuable tool for risk assessment and mitigation.

Future research will focus on enhancing the framework by incorporating the results of digital forensic investigations. Additionally, cyber attack campaigns launched during recent protests and conflicts in other countries will be analyzed and the results used to refine and augment the cyber warfare framework.

References

[1] S. Adair, Democracy in Hong Kong Under Attack, Volexity, Reston, Virginia (www.volexity.com/blog/?p=33), 2014.

[2] O. Bobrov, Chinese Government Targets Hong Kong Protesters with Android mRAT Spyware, Check Point Software Technologies, San Carlos, California, September 30, 2014.

[3] P. Boehler, Instagram appears blocked in China as photos of "occupied" Hong Kong circulate, *South China Morning Post*, September 29, 2014.

[4] Chinese University of Hong Kong, Phishing Emails Report, Hong Kong, China, 2014.

[5] J. Griffiths, TIMELINE: How Occupy Central's democracy push turned into an Umbrella Revolution, *South China Morning Post*, October 9, 2014.

[6] M. Kan, China attacks push Apple to warn users of iCloud threats, *Computerworld*, October 21, 2014.

[7] J. Kirk, Hong Kong pro-democracy activist websites compromised, *Computerworld*, October 13, 2014.

[8] C. Luo, Anonymous group of hackers release data from Chinese government sites, *South China Morning Post*, October 12, 2014.

[9] News.com.au, FBI confirms North Korea behind Sony hacks: The explainer, December 19, 2014.

[10] P. Paganini, Hacktivism: Means and Motivations ... What Else? InfoSec Institute, Elmwood Park, Illinois (`resources.infosecinstitute.com/hacktivism-means-and-motivations-what-else`), 2014.

[11] J. Philipp, A cyberwar quietly rages over Hong Kong, *Epoch Times*, October 24, 2014.

[12] Public Opinion Programme, 6.20-29 Civil Referendum, University of Hong Kong, Hong Kong, China (`popvote.hk/english/project/vote_622`), 2014.

[13] Public Opinion Programme, Mock voting system of "6.22 Civil Referendum" under severe attack, University of Hong Kong, Hong Kong, China (`hkupop.hku.hk/english/release/release1149.html`), 2014.

[14] Sony Pictures Entertainment, Culver City, California (`www.sonypictures.com`), 2014.

[15] E. Tsang, Eleven arrested over cyber attacks on 70 government websites, *South China Morning Post*, October 22, 2014.

[16] University of Hong Kong, Spam Email Reports, Hong Kong, China (`www.its.hku.hk/spam-report?page=2`), 2014.

[17] Wikipedia, 2014 Hong Kong protests (`en.wikipedia.org/wiki/2014_Hong_Kong_protests#September_2014`), 2014.

[18] Wikipedia, Occupy Central with Love and Peace (`en.wikipedia.org/wiki/Occupy_Central_with_Love_and_Peace`), 2015.

Chapter 3

ON THE SHARING OF CYBER
SECURITY INFORMATION

Eric Luiijf and Marieke Klaver

Abstract   The sharing of cyber security information between organizations, both
public and private, and across sectors and borders is required to increase situational awareness, reduce vulnerabilities, manage risk and
enhance cyber resilience. However, the notion of information sharing
often is a broad and multi-faceted concept. This chapter describes an
analytic framework for sharing cyber security information. A decomposition of the information sharing needs with regard to information
exchange elements is mapped to a grid whose vertical dimension spans
the strategic/policy, tactical and operational/technical levels and whose
horizontal dimension spans the incident response cycle. The framework
facilitates organizational and legal discussions about the types of cyber security information that can be shared with other entities along
with the terms and conditions of information sharing. Moreover, the
framework helps identify important aspects that are missing in existing
information exchange standards.

Keywords: Information sharing, cyber security, resilience, incident management

1.   Introduction

Modern society and citizenry rely on the continuous and undisturbed functioning of critical infrastructure assets that provide vital goods and services [4].
The failure of a critical infrastructure can seriously impact the health and well-
being of citizens, the economy and the environment, and the functioning of governments. Examples of critical infrastructures are power grids, transportation
systems, drinking water treatment and distribution systems, financial services
and government administration. These infrastructures increasingly depend on
information and communications – or so-called "cyber" – technologies. Cyber security and resilience are, therefore, critical topics for modern society [2].
The timely sharing of cyber security information between organizations – in a
critical sector, across sectors, nationally or internationally – is widely recog-

© IFIP International Federation for Information Processing 2015
M. Rice, S. Shenoi (Eds.): Critical Infrastructure Protection IX, IFIP AICT 466, pp. 29–46, 2015.
DOI: 10.1007/978-3-319-26567-4_3

nized as an effective means to address the cyber security challenges faced by organizations, especially those that are part of a critical infrastructure. For example, the sharing of information across organizations at the boardroom level is stimulated by the World Economic Forum [19, 20]. Another example is the European Network Information Security (NIS) Platform, which promotes collaboration and information exchange between stakeholders from the private and public sectors [6].

The notion of "sharing" cyber security information is often misunderstood. As a result, it may create internal organizational and legal barriers to sharing information with other organizations. To address the problem, this chapter presents an analytic framework for information sharing. A decomposition of the information sharing needs with regard to information exchange elements is mapped to a grid whose vertical dimension spans the strategic/policy, tactical and operational/technical levels and whose horizontal dimension spans the incident response cycle [7]. The mapped elements facilitate discussions about the types of information that can be shared with other organizations and the conditions under which they can be shared. The time criticality of the elements, if it exists, is a factor that may influence sharing decisions. This chapter explains how existing standards for information exchange as well as standards under development are mapped to the elements. It also shows that a number of information sharing elements are not supported or even mentioned by standards or standardization efforts.

2.   Definitions

A critical infrastructure (CI) consists of assets and parts thereof that are essential to the maintenance of critical societal functions, including the supply chain, health, safety, security, economy or social well-being of people [4]. Similar national definitions and sets of national critical infrastructure sectors can be found in [3].

Cyber resilience is the ability of systems and organizations to withstand cyber events. It is measured in terms of the mean time to failure and the mean time to recovery [20].

Cyber security constitutes the safeguards and actions that can protect the cyber domain, both in the civilian and military realms, from threats that are associated with or that may harm the interdependent network and information infrastructures in the cyber domain [5].

3.   Previous Work

The increased focus on cyber security has demonstrated that information sharing is a very important good practice for improving cyber security across collaborating organizations. Although information sharing has proved its value in practice, little work has been done on the theoretical and practical aspects. This section discusses some of the earlier studies that provide the foundation of the research described in this chapter.

MITRE has developed a set of technical/operational-level standards for uniquely classifying and identifying threats, vulnerabilities and assets, and for exchanging intrusion detection data (e.g., [13, 14]) in order to speed up the prevent-detect-respond cycle. However, the wider incident management cycle and the tactical and strategic levels are not (yet) fully covered by these efforts.

From 2008 through 2012, a NATO Research and Technology Organization (RTO) Research Task Group focused on developing a common operating picture of coalition network defense [1]. To ease the effort, the task group emphasized the need to identify possible information exchange elements. Information exchange classes and elements within the types, specifically aimed at the defense of coalition networks, were outlined during a brainstorming session. The final report of the task group is yet to be published; only a draft final report exists that contains an initial set of ten information exchange classes and thirty-nine elements.

Research by the authors of this chapter has extended the initial set of information exchange classes and elements to the exchange of cyber security information between military entities and/or non-military coalition partners, as well as to information exchange in civilian settings. One information exchange class (actor information) and twelve new elements were added to the original set. Some of the new elements were identified after mapping the set of elements to the analysis framework, which is outlined in its final form in Section 4. This chapter uses the expanded incident management cycle as one axis of the grid to map the information exchange elements. The cycle, which is described in the National Cyber Security Framework Manual (NCSFM) [7], comprises several phases: proaction, prevention, preparation, incident response, recovery and aftercare/legal follow up.

4. Analytic Framework for Information Sharing

This section describes the analytic framework for information sharing.

4.1 Information Exchange Classes and Elements

Detailed descriptions of the cyber security information exchange classes and elements are provided in the Appendix. The information exchange classes range from technical data on incidents (Class I) and detection data (Class D) to background and context information (Class B) and good practices (Class G). Each class comprises a set of information sharing elements. Note that the classes and elements differ by the type of stakeholders that they aim to reach, ranging from cyber security operations specialists to policy makers. The stakeholder aims form the basis of the vertical dimension of the analysis framework.

4.2 Framework Levels

Based on the NCSFM governance model [7], the sharing of cyber security information takes place at three levels: (i) combined strategic and policy making

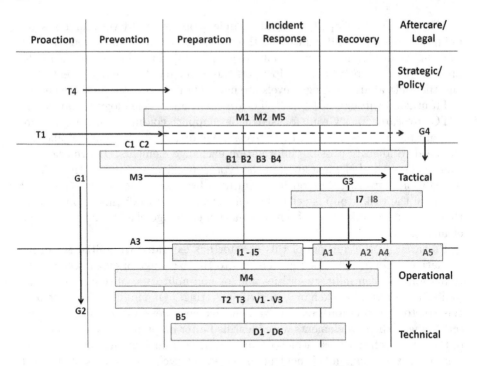

Figure 1. Analytic framework (grid from [7]).

levels; (ii) tactical steering level; and (iii) operational/technical levels. The level at which cyber security information is shared largely depends on the job positions and responsibilities in an organization. Information sharing usually takes place horizontally within the same decision making level when the information exchange is cross-organizational or cross-sectoral. Horizontal information exchange may involve the sharing of data at the original level of detail, although, in general, some form of anonymization or aggregation is employed. Shared information can also propel vertically, but then the information is usually (and preferably [8]) exchanged internal to an organization. Vertical information exchange generally involves a form of analysis in which more detailed data is aggregated and/or assessed in support of decision making at the higher levels.

4.3   Incident Management Cycle

Information sharing is a cross-mandate that spans various public and private mandates as outlined in the NCSFM [7]. Based on the incident management cycle outlined in the NCSFM, it is clear that an information sharing activity may span one or more phases of the cycle. The cycle comprises several phases: proaction, prevention, preparation, incident response, recovery and aftercare/legal follow up. For example, an organization may decide to concentrate on sharing information about proaction and prevention activities given the mandates of

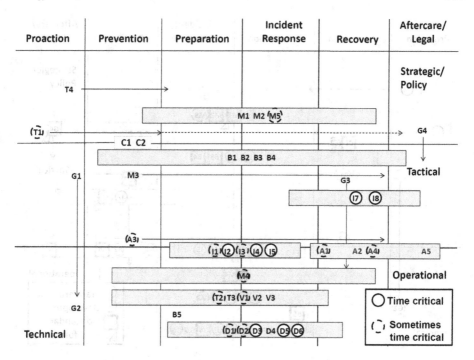

Figure 2. Time criticality of the information exchange elements.

the participants. Other sharing communities (e.g., CERT) focus on sharing incident response and recovery information. Finally, law enforcement may concentrate on collecting shared intelligence to disrupt and prevent incidents from occurring, or on deriving incident-specific evidence and situational information for criminal investigations and eventual prosecution.

4.4 Mapping the Elements to the Grid

The combination of the incident management cycle described in Section 4.3 and the three decision making and activity levels described in Section 4.2 results in a grid that constitutes the background of Figure 1. The 41 information sharing elements of nine information exchange classes are mapped to the grid. Note that the R* and S* military information exchange classes and the I6* elements are not described in this chapter.

Each information sharing element has different properties in terms of dynamics, time frame, amount of information, complexity of information, factual or weak indication, etc. Figure 2 shows the outcome of the analysis of the time criticality of the information sharing elements. Note that the most time critical information concerns the detection/incident response part of the incident management cycle. The sharing of detection data is most valuable when shared

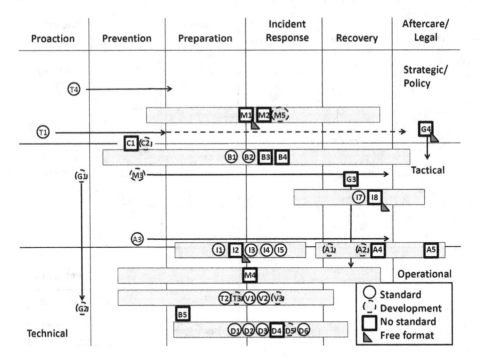

Figure 3.   Standards and standardization efforts mapped to exchange elements.

promptly, preferably as enriched actionable data, in order for other organizations to be able to act on the information [8].

5.   Standards and Standardization Efforts

Certain information elements can be exchanged during face-to-face meetings or via voice communications. The decision partly depends on the time criticality of the information that is to be shared [8]. Other information sharing elements can or must be exchanged via electronic means (e.g., because of time criticality or the amount of information to be shared). Simple information can be exchanged in free format (e.g., via unstructured emails). The exchange of more complex information requires structured exchange mechanisms, in other words, using standardized methods. As part of this research, mappings were performed for each element to existing standards (if any) as well as to *de facto* standards and to other efforts that may partially satisfy the needs of an identified information exchange element. Table 1 in the Appendix provides details of the mappings. Figure 3 shows the mappings to the analysis framework grid.

The analysis shows that:

- Most information exchange standards target the detection and incident response phases, and the technical/operational levels. This agrees with the statement on time criticality, which also shows that the sharing of detection and incident response data is most valuable when shared promptly. Prompt information sharing requires a uniform and efficient approach as well as clear definitions of the data to be exchanged as reflected by the development of standards.

- Some standards target the sharing of strategic threat information.

- For a large number of information sharing elements, no standards or active standardization efforts exist.

- Not many information exchange elements bridge the strategic/policy and tactical levels or the tactical and operational/technical levels.

- Currently, there is a lack of interoperability of standards that would allow the forwarding of information to other stakeholders in a subsequent phase of the incident management cycle. For instance, there is a gap in moving and reusing (technical) detection information to law enforcement.

6.   Conclusions

Information sharing of cyber security information is a complex organizational topic as outlined by the good practice document on sharing cyber security information [8]. This chapter has discussed the decomposition of the information sharing domain into a set of information sharing classes and elements using a grid based on the incident management cycle and decision making levels. The mapping shows where information exchange elements fit, the level of decision making they support and the phases of the incident management cycle in which they are involved

The grid of mapped elements facilitates discussions in organizations about the types of information that can be shared with other organizations and the conditions under which the information may be shared. Some information elements can be shared easily while other elements require a base level of trust and a secure means of transfer, processing and storage. For example, the sharp distinction between information exchange elements of strategic importance to organizations and technical intrusion detection data may eliminate internal organizational barriers to information sharing with other public and private organizations.

An organization may decide that the risk of an information security breach is too high to allow the electronic exchange of the information. The information exchange elements help split (i.e., conduct a "triage" of) cyber security information into classes and elements that can be shared without restrictions, that can never be shared, and that can be shared on a case-by-case basis. The grid can also be used to identify the time criticality of elements. The understanding of time criticality of information exchange elements may encourage organizations to fine-tune the triage process before an incident occurs, thereby enhancing organizational preparation for cyber resilience and incident response.

The grid also reveals the lack of standards or standardization efforts for some cyber security information exchange elements. The identified gaps may be used to develop a roadmap for developing future interoperable standards, especially related to Class A (actors) and Class M (metrics). Moreover, some standardization efforts have overlooked certain needs – these come to the fore in the mappings shown in Figures 1–3 and Table 1. In some cases, only minor changes are required to create a *de facto* standard that provides the required functionality (e.g., merely extending the standard with additional information exchange fields).

Acknowledgement

This research is partly based on the collaborative work of the NATO RTO Research Task Group on Coalition Network Defense Common Operating Picture and on funding from the Dutch Ministry of Security and Justice for research in cross-sector information sharing.

References

[1] L. Beaudoin, M. Gregoire, P. Lagadec, J. Lefebvre, E. Luiijf and J. Tolle, Coalition network defense common operational picture, presented at the *Symposium on Information Assurance and Cyber Defense*, 2010.

[2] R. Bruce, S. Dynes, H. Brechbuhl, B. Brown, E. Goetz, P. Verhoest, E. Luiijf and S. Helmus, International Policy Framework for Protecting Critical Information Infrastructure: A Discussion Paper Outlining Key Policy Issues, TNO Report 33680, TNO, Delft, The Netherlands; and Center for Digital Strategies, Tuck School of Business, Dartmouth College, Hanover, New Hampshire, 2005.

[3] CIPedia, CIPedia Main Page (www.cipedia.eu), 2014.

[4] Council of the European Union, European Council Directive 2008/114/EC of 8 December 2008 on the Identification and Designation of European Critical Infrastructures and the Assessment of the Need to Improve Their Protection, Brussels, Belgium, 2008.

[5] European Commission, Joint Communication to the European Parliament, the Council, the European Economic and Social Committee and the Committee of the Regions – Cybersecurity Strategy of the European Union: An Open, Safe and Secure Cyberspace, JOIN(2013) 1 Final, Brussels, Belgium, 2013.

[6] W. Grudzien and W. Semple, WG2 Outcome Draft, European Union Agency for Network and Information Security, Heraklion, Greece (resilience.enisa.europa.eu/nis-platform/shared-documents/wg2 -documents/wg2-outcome-draft/view), 2013.

[7] E. Luiijf and J. Healey, Organizational structures and considerations, in *National Cyber Security Framework Manual*, A. Klimburg (Ed.), NATO Cooperative Cyber Defence Centre of Excellence, Tallinn, Estonia, pp. 108–145, 2012.

[8] E. Luiijf and A. Kernkamp, Sharing Cyber Security Information: Good Practices Stemming from the Dutch Public-Private-Partnership Approach, TNO, The Hague, The Netherlands, 2015.

[9] E. Luiijf, M. Klaver, R. Wolthuis and S. van Hooft, Cross-Sector Information Sharing (in Dutch), TNO Report 2014 R10945, TNO, The Hague, The Netherlands, 2014.

[10] Mandiant, OpenIOC: An Open Framework for Sharing Threat Intelligence, Alexandria, Virginia (www.openioc.org), 2014.

[11] Ministry of Security and Justice, Cyber Security Assessment Netherlands 2014, The Hague, The Netherlands, 2014.

[12] Multi-State Information Sharing and Analysis Center, Cyber Alert Level Indicator, Center for Internet Security, East Greenbush, New York (msisac.cisecurity.org/alert-level), 2014.

[13] National Institute of Standards and Technology, Common Platform Enumeration (CPE) Dictionary, National Vulnerability Database, Gaithersburg, Maryland (nvd.nist.gov/cpe.cfm), 2014.

[14] National Institute of Standards and Technology, National Vulnerability Database, Gaithersburg, Maryland (nvd.nist.gov), 2014.

[15] P. Pawlinski, P. Jaroszewski, P. Kijewski, L. Siewierski, P. Jacewicz, P. Zielony and R. Zuber, Actionable Information for Security Incident Response, European Union Agency for Network and Information Security, Heraklion, Greece, 2014.

[16] P. Pawlinski, P. Jaroszewski, J. Urbanowicz, P. Jacewicz, P. Zielony, P. Kijewski and K. Gorzelak, Standards and Tools for Exchange and Processing of Actionable Information, European Union Agency for Network and Information Security, Heraklion, Greece, 2014.

[17] SANS Internet Storm Center, InfoCon, SANS Institute, Bethesda, Maryland (isc.sans.edu/infocon.html), 2014.

[18] VERIS, VERIS Community Database (veriscommunity.net/vcdb.html), 2014.

[19] World Economic Forum, Risk and Responsibility in a Hyperconnected World: Pathways to Global Cyber Resilience, Cologny/Geneva, Switzerland, 2012.

[20] World Economic Forum, Risk and Responsibility in a Hyperconnected World (WEF Principles), Cologny/Geneva, Switzerland, 2014.

Appendix: Information Sharing Classes and Elements

This appendix contains detailed information about the information sharing classes and elements. It characterizes the classes and elements. Note that the class name abbreviation is derived from the information exchange type. An element with an asterisk is a military cyber security information exchange element that is not described in this chapter. Table 1 outlines the standards and standardization efforts related to specific information exchange elements. In particular, it shows the existing standards (if any) as well as *de facto* standards and other efforts that may partially satisfy the needs of an information exchange element.

Class M: Sharing Cyber Situational Awareness Metrics

Instead of exchanging large amounts of detailed cyber anomaly information to improve collaborative situational awareness, a number of metrics or (aggregation) indicators may be shared to provide a high-level collaborative situational overview.

- **M1 – Cyber alert level:** A single value defines the overall alert level of another organization, denoting whether a significant threat is currently active or whether the other organization is under attack. Examples are the Multi-State Information Sharing and Analysis Center [12] and the SANS Internet Storm Center [17].

- **M2 – Incident summary metrics and statistics:** The number of open incidents that another organization is currently handling and the number of incidents that occurred in the past, including quarterly or yearly aggregates.

- **M3 – Vulnerability assessment metrics:** The number of open vulnerabilities that another organization has identified in total and per type of system (or network) presented in the context of the total number of scanned systems in order to obtain comparable metrics (e.g., average number of open vulnerabilities per host).

- **M4 – Cyber security sensor alert metrics:** The number of intrusion detection system alerts that another organization has received in the form of trend indicators or a top-ten list of intrusion alerts. An absolute number is of less value because it depends on the numbers, types and configurations of sensors and the types of monitored networks.

- **M5 – Risk and impact metrics:** Indicators of the (potential) impact to the mission or business continuity of an organization such as the percentage of automated teller machines affected at a financial institution.

Class I: Sharing Incident Information

Active sharing of cyber incident information enables one collaborating organization to inform the other collaborating organizations about incident observations, detection methodologies and mitigation techniques so that the other organizations may better detect and respond to similar incidents in their infrastructures.

- **I1 – Sharing information about own incident(s):** An organization shares incident information that it has been attacked and that its cyber operational capabilities may be impacted.

- **I2 – Warning a partner organization that it is targeted:** An organization that monitors network traffic may encounter signs of a cyber attack targeting a partner organization. Sharing such information benefits the potentially affected organization and increases collaborative situational awareness.

- **I3 – Warning a partner organization that it is a cyber attack source:** Warning an organization that it is a source of cyber attacks on other organizations may quickly initiate mitigation actions that are beneficial to all the collaborating organizations.

- **I4 – Sharing cyber actions:** Sharing information about on-going incident response actions and other cyber actions that may impact collaborative business services (missions). Situational reports include on-going actions, mitigation planning, assets affected, estimated time of completion, etc. Hot phase information is highly sensitive and should not be released to the public.

- **I5 – Querying another organization for similar incidents:** An organization queries other organizations for incidents similar to the incident of interest. Useful (sensitive) information may be shared in order to improve the speed and the quality of the (collaborative) incident response.

- **I6* – Tasking order to manage a cyber incident or to take a mitigation action.**

- **I7 – Requesting help to manage a cyber incident:** Another organization with unique capabilities (e.g., knowledge and resources) may be asked to help with the incident response.

- **I8 – Requesting the management of a cyber incident:** Another organization may be asked to manage the cyber incident response.

Class T: Sharing Threat Information
A threat is the potential for compromise, loss or theft of information or supporting cyber services and resources. A threat may be defined by its source, motivation or result; it may be deliberate or accidental, violent or surreptitious, external or internal. Sharing threat information is crucial to achieve and maintain the right cyber defensive posture in collaborating organizations.

- **T1 – Sharing intelligence about threat agents, vectors and consequences:** Sharing intelligence about adversarial cyber threats (source, intent, capability, tactics, techniques, procedures, recent activity, etc.) in order to maximize collaborative cyber defenses (e.g., [10]).

- **T2 – Sharing information on malware analysis:** Malware analysis requires advanced technical capabilities as well as resources that may be available at other organizations. The shared information could include captured malware, signatures, indicators of compromise, analysis techniques, tools and analysis results.

- **T3 – Sharing information on exploit analysis:** Information that allows better detection of a specific threat, effective protection against exploits and information about exploit code availability and its efficiency against various system and network configurations.

- **T4 – Sharing strategic threat information:** This could involve regular strategic level threat analysis and trend prediction [11] or a current situational picture [18].

Class V: Sharing General Vulnerability Information

Vulnerability information is critical to assess an organization's defense posture and to guide the mitigation measures needed to protect against the hostile exploitation of a vulnerability. Inadequate knowledge about a vulnerability exposes networks and systems to hostile exploitation.

- **V1 – Sharing non-public (closed) information about a specific vulnerability:** This involves sharing information within a trusted community.

- **V2 – Sharing public information about a specific vulnerability:** This is accomplished by direct access (e.g., NVD [14]) or by the selective relaying of information by a Computer Emergency Response Team (CERT) or Information Sharing and Analysis Center (ISAC).

- **V3 – Sharing alert and advisory information:** This involves sharing alerts, general advice and background information on a specific vulnerability.

Class D: Sharing Detection and Mitigation Information

Collaborative organizations can mitigate adversary tactics, techniques and procedures by sharing malware and intrusion signatures, patch information, defensive strategies, attack correlation patterns and domain blacklists.

- **D1 – Sharing intrusion signatures:** Sharing intrusion signatures with other collaborating organizations enables all the organizations to enhance their detection capabilities with minimal additional investments. Feedback on the efficiency of signatures could lead to signature refinement.

- **D2 – Sharing patch information:** This involves sharing test procedures, patch efficiency, deployment experiences and information about side effects.

- **D3 – Sharing vulnerability assessment signatures:** Vulnerability scanners allow users to add their custom signatures. Sharing these signatures with other organizations enhances the collaborative resources and may reduce the impact on collaborative services.

- **D4 – Sharing blacklists and whitelists:** Blacklists are lists of suspicious or malicious IP addresses, website URLs and email addresses that can be used to block traffic and detect cyber attacks. Sharing provides collaborating organizations with access to more extensive and up-to-date blacklists. Whitelists provide the reverse filtering capabilities of blacklists.

- **D5 – Sharing malware/exploit file signatures:** Collaborating organizations may share signature patterns of malware or other suspicious files, including file names, patterns, locations, sizes and identifying byte sequences.

- **D6 – Sharing indicator patterns:** An indicator pattern is used to verify that a system or network has been affected by a cyber attack. If the attack cannot be verified, deeper analysis may be required to determine whether a compromise took place.

Class R*: Sharing Dynamic Risk Assessment and Operational Dependencies

Within a military coalition environment, coalition partners may critically rely on shared cyber assets for the successful completion of a mission. Sharing operation dependencies and information about the utilization of certain assets are, therefore, important. Three elements have been identified: (i) R1 – Sharing assets and operational dependencies; (ii) R2 – Sharing dynamic risk assessment information; and (iii) R3 – Sharing information about cyber events that increase coalition risk.

Class S*: Sharing Information about Coalition-Shared Assets

If coalition partners share (security) health information of shared assets, other coalition partners can make better use of shared assets and react to changes in the health of an asset. Six elements have been identified: (i) S1 – Identifying shared cyber assets; (ii) S2 – Sharing the security status of shared cyber assets; (iii) S3 – Sharing the changes in the criticality of shared cyber assets; (iv) S4 – Sharing the security status of coalition cyber assets; (v) S5 – Sharing security events concerning coalition cyber assets; and (vi) S6 – Sharing risk assessments of coalition mission objectives and cyber assets.

Class C: Sharing Compliance Policies and Status

If an organization knows the compliance requirements and the status of other organizations with which it collaborates to provide an end-to-end service, the cyber defensive posture can be tuned.

- **C1 – Sharing compliance policies:** Strong compliance may correlate with a lower risk of incidents; detection and reaction to certain threats may be faster. Collaboration with a weaker organization requires more security controls at the interface. Sharing compliance information may help organizations fine-tune their security efforts.

- **C2 – Sharing compliance status:** Even if an organization has a strong compliance policy, all its assets may not comply with the security policy. Knowledge of the actual compliance status enables collaborating organizations to tune their security measures. One example is whether or not an organization can be reached 24/7 in order to report a security incident.

Class B: Sharing Background and Reference Information

This category concerns background information that is not directly cyber security information (e.g., contact details and reference information).

- **B1 – Sharing contact information:** This information may include the contact details of the CERT team and the chief information security officer.

- **B2 – Sharing software and hardware product identifiers and characteristics:** This information may include Common Platform Enumeration (CPE) Dictionary data [13].

- **B3 – Sharing network topology information:** Understanding the network structure of another organization may increase the joint cyber situational awareness. Understanding the types of threats and vulnerabilities and the attack paths existing in other organization also improves the joint cyber situational awareness.

- **B4* – Sharing physical locations of sites and mobile platforms:** This helps understand the geolocation-dependent risk of an organization.

- **B5 – Sharing time zone information:** This helps interpret logging and other information pertaining to synchronized attacks against multiple organizations.

Class G: Sharing Good Practices
Similar to sharing threat and incident information, the sharing of product, architecture and configuration information between collaborating organizations can help reduce costs and improve the joint security posture.

- **G1 – Sharing good practice information:** This includes good practice guides, white papers and security architectures.

- **G2 – Sharing security settings:** This includes system configuration information such as the steps required to harden a system.

- **G3 – Sharing recovery procedures and good practices:** This may increase the resilience of cyber services.

- **G4 – Sharing lessons identified:** Sharing information about what was good and what went wrong may help other organizations avoid pitfalls during incident response. This information also increases the level of trust in partner organizations.

Class A: Sharing Actor Information
Multiple organizations, including law enforcement, may need to exchange information about cyber criminal or cyber espionage activities and the actors to be apprehended and potentially prosecuted.

- **A1 – Sharing attribution information:** This includes detailed technical, analytical and sensitive intelligence about attack attribution.

- **A2 – Sharing actor information:** This includes information about the suspected actors.

- **A3 – Sharing lawful interception information:** This involves (electronic) requests to tap certain information flows and to deliver the collected information to law enforcement.

- **A4 – Requesting legal assistance or cooperation:** This involves an (international) request for legal assistance/cooperation to arrest actors, collect and safeguard evidence, and handle notice-and-takedown requests.

- **A5 – Sharing evidence and prosecution information:** This involves sharing information in criminal investigations and for possible prosecution.

Table 1: Information exchange classes and elements.

Class	Standards (see [16])	De facto standards and other efforts
Class M: Sharing Cyber Situational Awareness		
M1: Cyber alert level		MS-ISAC cyber alert level; InfoCon
M2: Incident summary metrics and statistics		Incident statistics [11]; VERIS [18]

Continued on next page

Table 1. Information exchange classes and elements (continued).

Class	Standards (see [16])	De facto standards and other efforts
M3: Vulnerability assessment metrics		CWSS; CVSS/CCSS
M4: Cyber security sensor alert metrics		No efforts identified
M5: Risk and impact metrics		CWRAF (and CWSS); EBIOS method; Risk management language
Class I: Sharing Incident Information		
I1: Sharing information about own incident(s)	IODEF over RID	IDMEF; VERIS (Commercial)
I2: Warning a partner organization that it is targeted		IODEF (Partial)
I3: Warning a partner organization that it is a cyber attack source	ARF	IODEF (Purpose is mitigation)
I4: Sharing cyber actions	IODEF over RID (Report)	
I5: Querying another organization about similar incidents	IODEF over RID (Query)	VERIS (Commercial)
I6: Tasking order (Military*)		*Military
I7: Requesting help to manage a cyber incident	IODEF over RID (Trace request, Investigation request)	
I8: Requesting the management of a cyber incident		No efforts identified
Class T: Sharing Threat Information		
T1: Sharing intelligence about threat agents, vectors and consequences	STIX over TAXII [16]	OpenIOC; CybOX; CAPEC; NASL
T2: Sharing information on malware analysis	MAEC	OpenIOC; CybOX
T3: Sharing information on exploit analysis		OpenIOC

Continued on next page

Table 1. Information exchange classes and elements (continued).

Class	Standards (see [16])	De facto standards and other efforts
T4: Sharing strategic threat information	SCAP/CAPEC	STIX over TAXII
Class V: Sharing General Vulnerability Information		
V1: Sharing non-public information about a vulnerability	OVAL, CVRF on top of CVE, CWE, ITU-T X.1206; IODEF-SCI/ RFC7203	CWSS; CVSS; CWRAF; DAF Relates to ISO/IEC 29147:2014 and ISO/IEC 30111:2013
V2: Sharing public information about a vulnerability	CVRF, NVD on top of CVE, CWE, ITU-T X.1206	CWSS; CVSS; CWRAF Relates to ISO/IEC 29147:2014 and ISO/IEC 30111:2013
V3: Sharing alert and advisory information		CAP; CVRF; CAIF (Simple factsheets)
Class D: Sharing Detection and Mitigation Information		
D1: Sharing intrusion signatures	OpenIOC	OVAL; XCCDF
D2: Sharing patch information	OVAL; ITU-T X.1206	ISA-TR 62443-2-3 (Draft)
D3: Sharing vulnerability assessment signatures	OVAL; XCCDF	NASL
D4: Sharing blacklists and whitelists		Blacklists and whitelists (ASCII)
D5: Sharing malware/exploit file signatures		OpenIOC
D6: Sharing indicator patterns	CybOX; MEAC	OpenIOC; NASL
Class B: Sharing Background and Reference Information		
B1: Sharing contact information	SCAP	AI

Continued on next page

Table 1. Information exchange classes and elements (continued).

Class	Standards (see [16])	De facto standards and other efforts
B2: Sharing hardware and software product identifiers and characteristics	SCAP/CPE	AI; CPE; CCE; SACM (Draft)
B3: Sharing network topology information		AI; CCE; SACM (Draft)
B4*: Sharing physical locations of sites and mobile platforms		*Military (Possible civilian use)
B5: Sharing time zone information		No efforts identified
Class C: Sharing Compliance Policies and Status		
C1: Sharing compliance policies		No efforts identified
C2: Sharing compliance status		PLARR (ASR/ARF); XCCDF; XDAS
Class G: Sharing Good Practices		
G1: Sharing good practice information		CVRF (Mitigation)
G2: Sharing security settings		OVAL; XCCDF; PLARR (ASR/ARF); CCE
G3: Sharing recovery procedures and good practices		No efforts identified
G4: Sharing lessons identified		No efforts identified
Class A: Sharing Actor Information		
A1: Sharing attribution information		STIX over TAXII; CDESF (Terminated)
A2: Sharing actor information		STIX over TAXII
A3: Sharing lawful interception information	RFC 3924; TIIT (Transport of intercepted traffic)	ETSI lawful intercept standards

Continued on next page

Table 1. Information exchange classes and elements (continued).

Class	Standards (see [16])	De facto standards and other efforts
A4: Requesting legal assistance or cooperation		No efforts identified
A5: Sharing evidence and prosecution information		STIX over TAXII (Incomplete)
Class S*: Sharing Information about Shared Cyber Assets		
S1*: Identifying shared cyber assets		*Military
S2*: Sharing the security status of shared cyber assets		*Military
S3*: Sharing changes in the criticality of shared cyber assets		*Military
S4*: Sharing the security status of coalition cyber assets		*Military
S5*: Sharing security events concerning coalition cyber assets		*Military
S6*: Sharing risk assessments of coalition mission objectives and cyber assets		*Military
Class R*: Sharing Dynamic Risk Assessment and Operational Dependencies		
R1*: Sharing assets and operational dependencies		*Military
R2*: Sharing dynamic risk assessment information		*Military
R3*: Sharing information about cyber events that increase coalition risk		*Military

II

CONTROL SYSTEMS SECURITY

Chapter 4

MODELING MESSAGE SEQUENCES FOR INTRUSION DETECTION IN INDUSTRIAL CONTROL SYSTEMS

Marco Caselli, Emmanuele Zambon, Jonathan Petit and Frank Kargl

Abstract   Compared with standard information technology systems, industrial control systems show more consistent and regular communications patterns. This characteristic contributes to the stability of controlled processes in critical infrastructures such as power plants, electric grids and water treatment facilities. However, Stuxnet has demonstrated that skilled attackers can strike critical infrastructures by leveraging knowledge about these processes. Sequence attacks subvert infrastructure operations by sending misplaced industrial control system messages. This chapter discusses four main sequence attack scenarios against industrial control systems. Real Modbus, Manufacturing Message Specification and IEC 60870-5-104 traffic samples were used to test sequencing and modeling techniques for describing industrial control system communications. The models were then evaluated to verify the feasibility of identifying sequence attacks. The results create the foundation for developing "sequence-aware" intrusion detection systems.

Keywords: Industrial control systems, sequence attacks, intrusion detection

1.   Introduction

Critical infrastructure assets such as power plants, electric grids and water treatment facilities have used control systems for many decades; however, until the turn of the century, they were primarily standalone systems. The Internet and network convergence have brought about many changes to critical infrastructure assets, the most important being their transformation from standalone systems to highly interconnected systems. This transformation has introduced advantages and disadvantages. On one hand, it facilitates the remote monitoring and management of industrial processes. On the other hand, traditional information technology attacks can be launched from afar, includ-

© IFIP International Federation for Information Processing 2015
M. Rice, S. Shenoi (Eds.): Critical Infrastructure Protection IX, IFIP AICT 466, pp. 49–71, 2015.
DOI: 10.1007/978-3-319-26567-4_4

ing over the Internet, to compromise industrial control systems and the critical infrastructure assets they manage.

This is the case of denial-of-service and distributed denial-of-service attacks. These attacks can target a specific device in an industrial control network and flood it with a massive number of packets until it is no longer able to operate normally. This can reduce or eliminate operator situational awareness and eventually impact the coordination and control of infrastructure assets, potentially affecting the larger infrastructure and connected infrastructures, leading to serious consequences to industry, government and society.

Another example involves semantic attacks. Unlike standard cyber attacks, semantic attacks exploit knowledge of specific control systems and physical processes to maximize damage. Stuxnet [4, 16] is probably the most well-known attack of this type. Meanwhile, numerous reports from the U.S. ICS-CERT have described exploits on industrial devices, such as programmable logic controllers and SCADA servers, that are triggered by carefully-crafted messages (see, e.g., [9]). Sequence attacks are a type of semantic attack. Instead of using modified message headers or payloads, these attacks employ misplaced messages in industrial control system communications to cause targeted devices to malfunction or even strike directly at physical processes.

Detecting sequence attacks relies on two assumptions: (i) industrial control system communications can be monitored; and (ii) industrial control system communications are generally regular over time. Traditional industrial technology networks rarely have regular network traffic due to their high variability (e.g., web users downloading different kinds of content from the Internet or interacting among themselves). However, even if an industrial control network maintains the same topology (i.e., a device always communicates with the same devices) [6], no checks are performed – nor is evidence is maintained – that the same sequences of messages are present in the inter-device communications.

Another problem is that traditional network intrusion detection systems generally search for unusual messages and rarely focus on message sequences, causing sequence attacks to go unnoticed. Specification-based intrusion detection systems can deal with sequence attacks based on the misuse of communications protocols. However, they require a precise and comprehensive documentation of system operation (e.g., the TCP/IP protocol suite [22]).

This chapter describes several sequence attack scenarios against industrial control systems. Real Modbus, Manufacturing Message Specification (MMS) and IEC 60870-5-104 traffic samples are used to evaluate the feasibility of sequence analysis and detection. Indeed, the goal is to identify all the traffic data needed to model and analyze the behavior of industrial control protocols over time. Furthermore, the feasibility of "sequence-aware" detection is investigated by identifying model-related information that can be leveraged to detect malicious activities. The implementation of sequence-aware intrusion detection is left as future work because the objective of this research has been to identify plausible sequence detection methodologies that can be used to differentiate attack traffic from normal traffic in industrial control systems.

2.   Background

Industrial control systems include supervisory control and data acquisition (SCADA) systems, distributed control systems (DCSs) and generic control systems such as skid-mounted programmable logic controllers (PLCs) [23]. Industrial control networks usually interconnect a field network and a process network. The field network hosts devices that are directly connected to the physical process. The process network hosts the servers that supervise the control of the physical process. Field devices include sensors, actuators, remote terminal units and programmable logic controllers. Process networks include SCADA servers, human-machine interfaces (HMIs) and engineering workstations.

Industrial control systems use special communications protocols on top of TCP/IP, open protocols like Modbus, MMS and IEC 60870-5-104 and proprietary protocols such as Siemens S7. This research focuses on Modbus, MMS and IEC 60870-5-104 because, in addition to being widely used, these protocols demonstrate different communications patterns and behaviors (e.g., synchronous vs. asynchronous communications, and pushing vs. polling paradigms).

- **Modbus:** This application layer protocol uses a polling client/server scheme [19, 24]. SCADA servers (i.e., masters) always act as clients and initiate communications by sending requests to programming logic controllers (i.e., slaves) and wait for responses. Common Modbus commands can, for example, instruct a server to read or write values in its memory-mapped registers.

- **Manufacturing Message Specification (MMS):** This protocol implements the seven layers of the ISO/OSI stack, even when it operates on top of TCP/IP [12, 13]. MMS is a client/server protocol with synchronous or asynchronous communications patterns. The protocol defines read and write control operations for a set of standard objects, a set of messages to be exchanged and a set of encoding rules that map the messages.

- **IEC 60870-5-104 (IEC104):** This application layer protocol operates on top of TCP/IP [10, 11]. The protocol mostly uses asynchronous balanced or unbalanced data transfer modes. In the balanced mode, a master or slave can initiate communications while the unbalanced mode only allows a master to initiate communications, In the remainder of this chapter, the IEC 60870-5-104 protocol is referred to as IEC104.

3.   Sequence Attacks

This section presents four sequence attacks that are classified according to the targeted industrial control system component (i.e., device or physical process) and the type of compromise (i.e., manipulation of the timing or order of messages).

With regard to the first dimension (i.e., attack targets), this section distinguishes between attacks targeting the implementations of protocol stacks in devices and attacks targeting the industrial processes controlled by the devices. Specifically, the first, and more traditional, class of attacks exploit vulnerabilities in protocol stack implementations. The second class of attacks, which are specific to industrial control systems, attempt to divert or take control of industrial processes by leveraging the lack of integrity and authentication mechanisms. To take control of a process, an attacker may either reprogram the logic executed by a programmable logic controller [18] (e.g., as in the case of Stuxnet), or directly control the process from the network using the same control messages used by legitimate operators. This research focuses on the second type of attacks that are less explored in the literature.

With regard to the second dimension, this research distinguishes between attacks that send messages or commands in incorrect (malicious) order and attacks that send messages or commands with incorrect (malicious) timing. The first type of attacks violate the state machines that underlie application protocols or send sequences of messages or commands that move processes to unsafe states. The second type of attacks leverage the limitations of embedded devices in processing input data or exploit weaknesses of process equipment (e.g., motors or valves) by changing their operational states in ways not foreseen by their manufacturers.

Based on these two dimensions, four attack scenarios are described and a simple, yet realistic, example is provided for each of the four scenarios:

- **Message-Order-Based Device Compromise:** The majority of application level protocols used to manage programmable logic controllers provide for loading and storing logic programs from engineering workstations with network connectivity to programmable logic controllers. The load and store functionalities are typically achieved by sending sequences of messages. The sequence of messages for uploading a logic program to a programmable logic controller typically involves: (i) locking the programmable logic controller; (ii) stopping the running program(s); (iii) deleting the existing program(s); (iv) transferring the program code to the programmable logic controller; (v) creating new program(s) with the new program code; (vi) starting the new program(s); and (vi) unlocking the programmable logic controller. Each step is achieved by sending one of more messages to the programmable logic controller. Experiments in an industrial control laboratory environment have revealed that it is possible to attack some programmable logic controllers merely by sending some of these messages in an inconsistent order. For example, sending a (valid) start program message when the program is still running causes an error that is not properly handled by the programmable logic controller firmware, which causes the programmable logic controller to crash.

- **Message-Order-Based Process Compromise:** Carcano et al. [20] describe an example attack scenario for a process system comprising a pipe with high pressure steam. The pressure is regulated by two valves (V1 and V2). An attacker with the appropriate access sends a write message to the programmable logic controller to completely close valve V2 and another write message to completely open valve V1. This maximizes the flow of steam into the pipe and maximizes the pressure in the pipe because the incoming steam cannot exit the pipe. Both these commands are perfectly legal when considered individually, but they bring the system to a critical state because they are sent in the wrong sequence.

- **Message-Timing-Based Device Compromise:** Many embedded devices used in industrial control systems have limited computing capabilities and have weak protocol stack implementations (because they incorrectly assume that all devices use the protocols correctly). As a result, it is fairly easy to mount attacks that exhaust the resources of these embedded devices by simply flooding the network with (valid) protocol messages (e.g., TCP SYN messages). However, laboratory experiments conducted as part of this research have revealed that the same effects can be achieved using application-level messages. This is particularly true for programmable logic controllers that use UDP-based application protocols. Flooding these devices with application-level messages that require expensive operations (e.g., diagnostic functions) quickly exhausts programmable logic controller resources, compromising their ability to complete their scan-loops in real time and eventually leading to complete resets of the devices.

- **Message-Timing-Based Process Compromise:** A report by the U.S. President's Commission on Critical Infrastructure Protection [21] describes an example attack scenario involving a water distribution facility. In this scenario, major control valves on the water pipeline are rapidly opened and closed to cause water hammer, resulting in a number of simultaneous water main breaks. Such an attack could be carried out by rapidly sending a sequence of write messages that direct programmable logic controllers to open and close the valves.

4.   Sequences and Sequence Events

Detecting sequence attacks requires the ability to extract a sequence of messages from network traffic and identify information that is needed to construct intrusion detection systems. This section investigates the process of transforming a set of network frames into ordered lists of network events that represent device communications.

The easiest way to define an event in the context of network communications is to consider all the traffic frames one by one. However, all traffic frames are not equally important and not all frames need to be included in a sequence. Moreover, all the attacks presented in Section 3 involve a single connection between a sender and a receiver (i.e., one TCP stream). Therefore, it is necessary to group traffic frames into communications channels. The following definitions are used in the ensuing discussion:

Definition 1: *A sequence $\{m_{t_n}\}$ with $n \in [0, \infty[$ is a time-ordered list of application-level messages $(t_n < t_{n+1})$ exchanged over a network channel established between two devices that use a specific communications protocol.*

Because the Modbus, MMS and IEC104 protocols have different communications types (e.g., synchronous vs. asynchronous) and communications patterns (e.g., pushing vs. polling), Definition 1 is redefined for each protocol. Note that the term m is substituted by the sequence event e that details the properties and attributes of each protocol.

Definition 2: *A sequence of Modbus events is a time-ordered list of events $\{e_{t_n}\}$ where e is a three-tuple $<ID, Code, Data>$ derived from two messages $(m^{Req}_{t_n}, m^{Res}_{t>t_n})$.*

Note that ID denotes the transaction identifier, $Code$ indicates the type of operation performed and $Data$ represents the information carried by Modbus requests m^{Req} and responses m^{Res}.

Definition 3: *A sequence of MMS events is a time-ordered list of events $\{e_{t_n}\}$ where e is a four-tuple $<ID, PDU, Service, Data>$ derived from two messages $(m^{Req}_{t_n}, m^{Res}_{t>t_n})$ in the case of synchronous communications, and from m_{t_n} in the case of asynchronous communications.*

Note that ID denotes the invoke identifier, PDU indicates the type of communications (e.g., initiate, request, response, error, etc.), $Service$ describes the operation requested or performed (e.g., read, write, etc.) and $Data$ represents the information carried by MMS requests and responses.

Definition 4: *A sequence of IEC104 events is a time-ordered list of events $\{e_{t_n}\}$ where e is a three-tuple $<Format, Service, Data>$ derived from two messages $(m^{Req}_{t_n}, m^{Res}_{t>t_n})$ in the case of synchronous communications, and from m_{t_n} in the case of asynchronous communications.*

Note that $Format$ denotes the format of the messages, $Service$ defines the performed service and $Data$ represents the information carried by IEC104 messages.

5.   Modeling Message Sequences

Section 4 described how to transform network traffic traces into time-ordered lists of events. The next step involves the modeling of message sequences to perform communications analysis and identify sequence attacks. A discrete-time Markov chain (DTMC) is used to model communications patterns and protocol behaviors. The modeling is done for two reasons:

- First, a flexible definition of event is needed that does not necessarily consider all the attributes used to build the sequence (e.g., ID, $Code$, $Data$). For example, two Modbus events that only differ in their transaction identifier (ID) are considered to be the same event because a

---

Algorithm 1 : DTMC modeling of sequences.

1: **for all** $e_{t_n} \in$ sequence **do**
2:      State$_{DTMC} \leftarrow$ extractAttributes(e_{t_n});
3:      **if** State$_{DTMC} \in$ DTMC **then**
4:          update(State$_{DTMC}$);
5:      **else**
6:          add(State$_{DTMC}$, DTMC);
7:      **end if**
8:      **if** Transition$_{previousState,State_{DTMC}} \in$ DTMC **then**
9:          update(Transition$_{previousState,State_{DTMC}}$);
10:     **else**
11:         add(Transition$_{previousState,State_{DTMC}}$, DTMC);
12:     **end if**
13:     previousState $\leftarrow$ State$_{DTMC}$;
14: **end for**

---

transaction identifier does not determine the meaning of a message or the significance of an event itself. DTMC states are used as sets of sequence events that share the same semantic meaning.

- Second, it is necessary to identify temporal consequent events. DTMC transitions are used to: (i) indicate the strength of the relationship between an event and its successor (e.g., how many times a state follows another); and (ii) understand if the relationship changes over time (e.g., the time interval between two states remains constant over time). A transition between two states A and B indicates an "episode of consequentiality" between two events belonging to A and B, respectively.

Modeling industrial control system communications with DTMCs has some advantages over using other modeling techniques such as n-grams or deterministic finite automata. Analysis using n-grams requires communications to be split into subsequences of messages of length n. Therefore, a model of industrial control system communications would be defined by the statistical distribution of the n-grams included in the entire sequence of messages. The resulting analysis would fail to identify subsequences of messages larger than n that remain the same during the entire communications. Modeling communications using a deterministic finite automaton would allow sequences of any length to be identified, but it would not be suitable for stochastic events (e.g., message delays). Without considering the probabilities of event occurrence, it would be impossible to evaluate the importance of transition functions and, consequently, to assess the correct behavior of industrial control system communications.

The construction of a DTMC is independent of the modeled protocol and is completely automated. From an implementation point of view, the algorithm used to build a DTMC reads a sequence of events one by one and populates the model. For every event in the sequence, the algorithm either assigns it to a state or creates a new state if the event does not match the attributes of a state already in the model. Moreover, in each step, the algorithm adds or updates a transition function that links the previously-visited state to the current state. Algorithm 1 formalizes the DTMC modeling process.

Every state S is defined by a five-tuple $<Data, Type, \#Events, FTS, LTS>$ where $Data$ denotes the information carried by events stored in S, $Type$ indicates the type of events included in S (e.g., requests and responses, asynchronous requests), $\#Events$ denotes the number of events included in S, FTS (first time seen) is the timestamp of the first event in S and LTS (last time seen) is the timestamp of the last event in S.

Every transition T from a source state A to a destination state B is defined by a six-tuple $<TP, \#Jumps, FJ, LJ, ATE, \sigma ATE>$ where TP (transition probability) is the ratio of the number of jumps from A to B to the total number of jumps from A to any other state in the DTMC, $\#Jumps$ represents the number of jumps from A to B, FJ (first jump) is the timestamp of the first jump in T, LJ (last jump) is the timestamp of the last jump in T, ATE (average time elapsed) is the average time between two consequent events of A and B, and σATE is the standard deviation over all the intervals between the two consequent events of A and B.

To illustrate how the DTMC modeling process works, consider the following sequence of events:

1. **MMS Initiate Request/Response Event**: Invoke ID = –, PDU = Initiate, Service = –, Data = mmsInitRequestDetails, Timestamp = 15 Jun 2014 17:14:12.79

2. **MMS Confirmed Request/Response Event**: Invoke ID = 1, PDU = Confirmed Request/Response, Service = write (5), Data = octet-string (9) 00, Timestamp = 15 Jun 2014 17:14:12.973

3. **MMS Confirmed Request/Response Event**: Invoke ID = 2, PDU = Confirmed Request/Response, Service = write (5), Data = octet-string (9) 00, Timestamp = 15 Jun 2014 17:14:13.059

4. **MMS Confirmed Request/Response Event**: Invoke ID = 3, PDU = Confirmed Request/Response, Service = write (5), Data = octet-string (9) 00, Timestamp = 15 Jun 2014 17:14:13.311

Figure 1 shows the DTMC obtained by applying the modeling algorithm. The first event of the sequence creates a DTMC state of type Initiate Request/Response representing MMS initialization messages (state A). The second event of the sequence creates another state in the model of type Confirmed Request/Response that represents MMS messages used to write an octet-string at 00 (state B). At this point, the model also has a transition between the two states that describes the sequential nature of the two events of the sequence (Transition 1). The third event of the sequence has the same attributes as the second event and, thus, increases the attribute $\#Events$ of state B. However, a new transition connects state B in a self-loop to show the new relationship observed in the sequence. Finally, the fourth event of the sequence is still part of

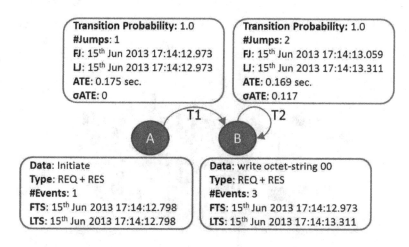

Transition Probability: 1.0
#Jumps: 1
FJ: 15th Jun 2013 17:14:12.973
LJ: 15th Jun 2013 17:14:12.973
ATE: 0.175 sec.
σATE: 0

Transition Probability: 1.0
#Jumps: 2
FJ: 15th Jun 2013 17:14:13.059
LJ: 15th Jun 2013 17:14:13.311
ATE: 0.169 sec.
σATE: 0.117

T1   T2
A   B

Data: Initiate
Type: REQ + RES
#Events: 1
FTS: 15th Jun 2013 17:14:12.798
LTS: 15th Jun 2013 17:14:12.798

Data: write octet-string 00
Type: REQ + RES
#Events: 3
FTS: 15th Jun 2013 17:14:12.973
LTS: 15th Jun 2013 17:14:13.311

Figure 1. DTMC modeling algorithm example.

state B because it has the same attributes as the second event of the sequence. Since the model already has a transition that links state B in a self-loop, the algorithm only increases the *#Jumps* attribute of this transition.

6.   Experiments and Analysis

This section analyzes the DTMCs generated from real Modbus, MMS and IEC104 traffic. The network traces were captured at three utilities. The Modbus traffic was obtained from the control network of a water treatment plant. The MMS traffic was obtained from a gas storage and pipeline infrastructure; log files of the SCADA servers at this facility were also obtained. The IEC104 traffic was obtained from a gas distribution system and refers to secondary substations for distribution.

The timeframes of the data range from one day (MMS) to five days (Modbus and IEC104). It is worth noting that, during the traffic captures, no constraints were imposed on operations. All three infrastructures were running normally and operators were free to perform their tasks. The three samples represent the most realistic use cases in which a security system could be deployed, tested and tuned.

Figure 2 shows the topologies of the three networks tested. Sequencing and modeling operations were implemented on top of Tshark parsing services, which eliminated problems related to TCP stream reconstruction (e.g., retransmission and segment reordering). The Tshark output for a specific TCP stream was forwarded to a custom tool that selected the information needed to transform a message in a sequence event, and concatenated events to create sequences. At the same time, the modeling algorithm constructed the DTMC representing the sequence.

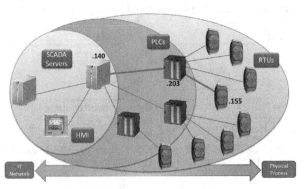

(a) Modbus network topology.

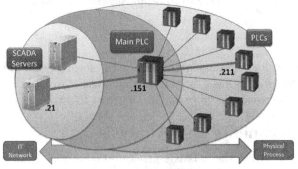

(b) MMS network topology.

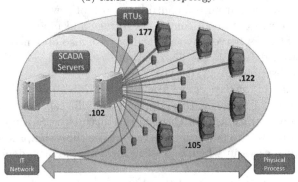

(c) IEC104 network topology.

Figure 2.   Network topologies.

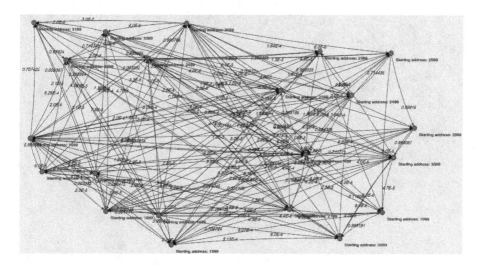

Figure 3. Modbus communications between SCADA server 140 and PLC 203.

6.1   Modbus

In the Modbus experiment, 47 GB of traffic and more than 260M frames were captured. Every communication between a programming logic controller and remote terminal unit involved one Read Holding Register message sent in a loop. For this reason, the analysis focused on the connections between the SCADA server and the programming logic controllers. These TCP streams contained about 43M frames and each related sequence contained about 10M events. The generated models consisted of 21 to 22 states and a variable number of transitions (between 172 and 291). As mentioned above, Read Holding Register was the only message used, each message had a different set of addresses.

Figure 3 shows the Modbus communications between SCADA server 140 and programmable logic controller 203. Note that the models do not present the sequences of states with periodic behavior. However, the analysis of the DTMCs revealed the following outcomes:

- Given the total number of possible transitions within a DTMC (calculated by summing the possible edges $\#States \times (\#States - 1)$ and self-loops $\#States$), the observed transitions cover 40% to 60% of the domain. This means that, on average, half of the transitions did not occur even after five days of analysis.

- Not all the transitions have the same probability. Figure 4 shows a link with a transition probability higher than 0.7. Every involved transition has more than 150K jumps. The results indicate that hidden sequentiality exists even if it is disturbed by random delays. Only one-third of the states have two transitions with probability higher than 0.25 (more than

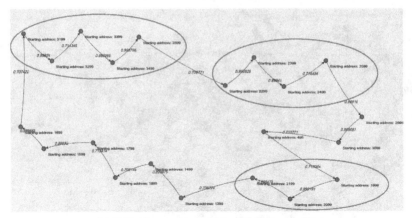

(a) DTMC transitions with probability > 0.7.

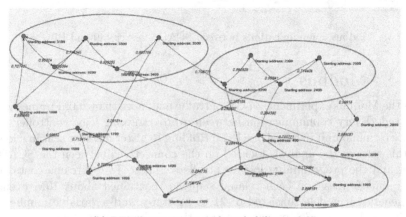

(b) DTMC transitions with probability > 0.25.

Figure 4. Modbus communications between SCADA server 140 and PLC 203.

130K jumps) and the 30 transitions shown in Figure 5 cover 99.8% of the jumps.

- No self-loops exist. None of the states in the model has a transition that goes back to itself. This means that no Read Holding Register operation was performed twice in a row.

- The transition distribution in the models is not uniform. Some states have higher numbers of transitions than others.

Moreover, it was possible to identify clusters of states (see Figure 4) with two properties: (i) each cluster has several edges that connect to states belonging to other clusters; and (ii) each cluster has a few edges that connect internal states to each other and, among these edges, there is a path that connects all the states of the cluster and that contains almost all the jumps performed in the cluster ($\sim$99.9998%).

These clusters denote the presence of several threads in the SCADA server operating system process (one per cluster) that multiplex requests in the same TCP stream. The task of each thread is to ask for a specific interval of registers. This hypothesis explains the difficulty in finding clear sequences (each thread can be randomly scheduled by the CPU) and the absence of some transitions (threads are always created in a loop and operations within the same thread are likely to be sequential).

6.2   MMS

In the MMS experiment, 4 GB of traffic and more than 18.3M frames were captured. TCP streams that connected the main programmable logic controller (i.e., the device that coordinated all the field devices) to the other programmable logic controllers involved on average 2M frames. The generated sequences consisted of about 600K events with models containing two to seven states. The DTMCs had variable numbers of transitions that covered 35% to 75% of all the possible edges in the graphs. Models with the highest percentages of transitions consisted of TCP streams with only Read Request messages that were used to read two variables in the field programmable logic controllers. These models had three transitions (one self-loop and two transitions connecting the two states in each model). Models with higher numbers of states were suitable for sequence modeling in most of the cases.

Figure 5(a) shows the communications model for the main programmable logic controller and a field programmable logic controller. The model has seven states and seventeen transitions. As in the Modbus experiments, there is a path that involves eight of the seventeen transitions; this path covers 99.99% of the jumps. Unlike the Modbus models, the MMS models show instances of strict consequentiality (e.g., between the two read operations at the bottom of Figure 5(a)). Although it is not known if altering the order of these two messages causes problems to the control process, it appears that their sequentiality is enforced by the system and, for this reason, it is likely to remain the same unless the control process changes.

The TCP streams that link the two SCADA servers to the main programmable logic controller include almost the same number of frames (1.9M) and sequence events (570K). This data is comparable with the MMS TCP streams discussed above. However, the related models change completely. The two new models include about 280 states and 1,280 transitions (see Figure 6). This is due to two reasons:

- The number of different operations performed among the SCADA servers and the main programmable logic controller is higher than the number of operations performed among the programmable logic controllers.

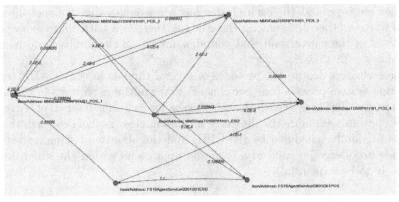

(a) Complete DTMC.

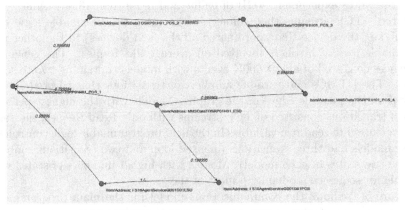

(b) DTMC transitions with probability > 0.19.

Figure 5.   MMS communications between the main PLC 151 and PLC 211.

- The states in the new models mostly represent Read Unconstrained Address operations and the implementation of unconstrained addresses is proprietary. This causes every state to be identified by a byte string and, as a consequence, only events that share the exact same information are grouped together.

The correct parsing of Read Unconstrained Address operations would reduce the number of states. However, it is worth noting that:

- The percentage of performed transitions corresponds to 0.02% of all possible transitions. In the case of Modbus, the definition of a set of allowed sequences would be much more restrictive.

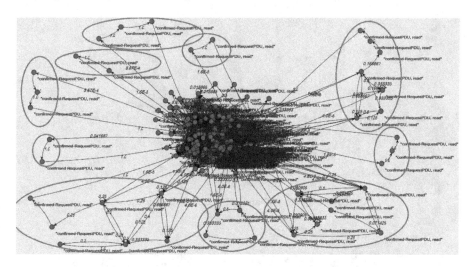

Figure 6. MMS communications between SCADA server 21 and PLC 151.

- About 45% of the states have "univocal relationships" between two other states (a state Y has a univocal relationship between states X and Z if transitions from X to Y are always followed by transitions from Y to Z; moreover, these states are often chained together). Such structures highlight subsets of MMS messages with strong consequentiality (i.e., subsets of messages that always follow each other).

- The model yields several clusters of states (see Figure 6). More precisely, there is a densely-connected core with some smaller groups of states at the edges. Most of the little clusters are linked to the core by a few transitions that often involve only one jump.

  These clusters are the measurable effects of human intervention. This hypothesis is supported by the analysis of the process log file. First, human operations timestamps were matched against the starting times of the transitions. About 50% of the entries labeled as human operations were recorded in the same time frames as when the transitions occurred. Second, the time frames with no human operations were examined; almost the same time gaps were observed for the transitions. Finally, it was observed that the two time frames with the highest numbers of transitions of this kind corresponded to the only two operations recorded as "suppress" in the log file. According to plant operators, these operations correspond to the manual termination of system alarms with a consequent reset of several system control parameters to the "normal" state.

The analyses of Modbus and MMS traffic samples emphasize the differences between programmable logic controller to programmable logic controller (or remote terminal unit to remote terminal unit) and server to programmable

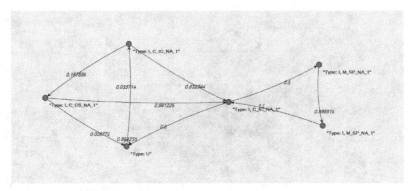

(a) SCADA server 102 and RTU 122 communications.

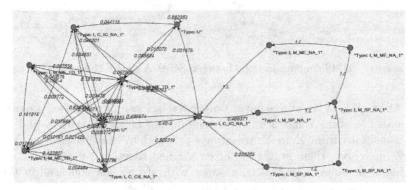

(b) SCADA server 102 and RTU 177 communications.

Figure 7.   IEC104 communications.

logic controller (or server to remote terminal unit) communications. The models demonstrate that the former type of communications exhibits fewer states and transitions while the later usually has a greater variety of messages.

6.3   IEC104

In the IEC104 experiment, 51 GB of traffic and more than 203 M frames were captured. TCP streams linking the SCADA server and the remote terminal units were analyzed. These connections contained 70K to 96K frames and 13K to 24K sequence events. As in the MMS experiments, the number of sequence events did not depend on the number of frames.

Most of the models had a number of transitions that covered 20% to 33% of all possible transitions. Figures 7(a) and 7(b) illustrate this case with TCP streams of about 24K events. Figure 7(a) shows a model with six states and

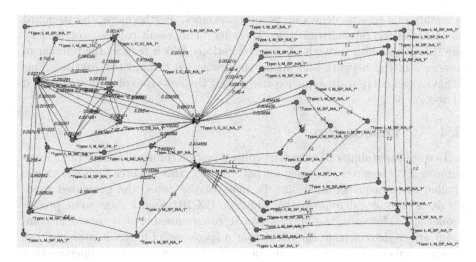

Figure 8. IEC104 communications between SCADA server 102 and RTU 105.

ten transitions while Figure 7(b) shows a model with fourteen states and 43 transitions. Both the models have two sets of states with different densities of transitions. The group of states on the left involves different types of commands and is responsible for the majority of transitions that do not show sequentiality. The other group of states on the right involves "single point information" commands and shows some clear paths. As discussed in the case of MMS, this portion of the model allows some assumptions to be made regarding state sequences (e.g., consequentiality of single point information messages).

The model in Figure 8 corresponds to another server to remote terminal unit TCP stream with fewer events (13K), but with a greater number of states (49) and transitions (92). The percentage of transitions out of the total number of possibilities is lower than in the previous cases (around 0.04%). The model shows also several precise paths. The IEC104 results lead to the following outcomes:

- All the examples demonstrate specific parts of the model with no sequentiality. Messages that create these clusters are almost the same in the three cases (e.g., TESTFR functions, Measured Value – Normalized Value commands).

- The remaining part of the model includes several definite sequences. The analysis reveals that, despite the presence of different paths, the involved states all relate to a precise sequence of addresses to be read. Every state collects single point information commands with a different number of object addresses. The set of object addresses at the end of every path is always the same as well as the order in which they are used.

Finally, it is finally worth noting that the analysis of the IEC104 traffic reveals a lower number of events compared with Modbus and MMS traffic. This is mainly due to long delays for several messages. Furthermore, the standard deviation of the related transitions is higher. This result can be explained by the IEC104 pushing pattern of communications, which reduces the number of messages in the network and makes the transition timings less precise. This behavior can complicate sequence analysis for the two types of misuse discussed in Section 3.

6.4   Discussion

Despite the stability of industrial control system communications (e.g., long-running TCP sessions and constant patterns) [6], this research highlights some challenges to sequence analysis. In most of the cases, the generated models do not present definite paths (only the IEC104 results show some precise sequences). Moreover, the MMS server to programmable logic controller communications demonstrate the effect that a larger set of different messages has on the numbers of states and transitions. Nevertheless, certain properties that should be considered when developing sequence-aware intrusion detection systems were identified.

All the models produce numbers of edges that are much lower than the maximum permitted by the graphs. This result suggests that messages cannot be combined to create every possible sequence, but that only specific sequences are permitted. This is a necessary condition for sequence-aware intrusion detection. Furthermore, the analysis shows that only a small fraction of the transitions are used most frequently. This information emerges from the models by filtering out transitions with few jumps. The remaining transitions often form precise paths through the states and, thus, strengthen the hypothesis of substantial sequentiality in the communications. The sequentiality can be weakened by random delays, but this does not compromise the operations of a sequence-aware intrusion detection system.

From this analysis, it is possible to envision two different, yet interoperable, sequence detection mechanisms. The first mechanism enforces sequentiality constraints defined by the referenced models (e.g., by observing the univocal relationships defined for MMS). The second focuses on the probability distributions of the constraints (e.g., requiring the relative probabilities of the transitions between a state and its neighbors to remain the same).

The first mechanism could be used to detect the "order-based" attacks described in Section 3, because these attacks involve observing a sequence that should not be found (i.e., a sequence that is not present in the model constructed using normal (attack-free) traffic). The second mechanism could be used to detect "timing-based" attacks. Indeed, these attacks involve sequences allowed by the model that occur much more frequently compared with the normal. In this case, the DTMC would allow the transitions until the probability of choosing a path exceeds the one computed based on normal traffic.

Finally, some observations must be made regarding the relationships between transitions that involve low numbers of jumps and human operations. MMS traffic samples together with the process log file permit the extraction of temporal matches. Certain correlations were observed and the analysis supports the assumption that links human interactions to such transitions and, specifically, to some of the clusters shown in Figure 6. This supports the profiling of operator actions and differentiating them from malicious activities. Additional experimentation and analysis would be valuable for sequence-aware intrusion detection because they would decrease the number of false positives by helping filter out sequences that are known to be operator actions.

7. Related Work

Protocol sequence analysis and modeling are activities that are usually related to communications-model-based verification and validation. Aarts et al. [1] have presented an example of this approach. They implemented a regular inference technique based on Mealy machines and tested it on the SIP and TCP protocols. Then, a predicate abstraction framework was used to infer finite state models of network components from observations of external behavior.

Chandola et al. [2] have presented three formulations of the sequence anomaly detection problem: (i) identifying anomalous sequences with respect to a set of known normal sequences; (ii) identifying anomalous subsequences within long sequences; and (iii) identifying subsequences whose frequencies of occurrence are anomalous. They identified suitable approaches for each formulation and detailed their advantages and disadvantages.

A search of the literature reveals that few examples of sequence-aware network intrusion detection systems exist. Sekar et al. [22] have proposed a specification-based modeling approach based on extended finite state automata. They demonstrated the feasibility of analysis based on well-defined network protocols such as UDP and TCP. However, they did not test their approach on application layer protocols and did not investigate the possibility of automatically learning communications patterns in cases where comprehensive specifications are not available.

Krueger et al. [14] went beyond the approach of Sekar et al., using n-grams and Markov chains to model protocols such as SIP, DNS and FTP. They demonstrated the effectiveness of the detection mechanisms on text protocols, but they did not test them against binary protocols. Industrial control systems mainly use binary protocols and studies such as [7] highlight the problems of using n-gram analysis in industrial control environments.

Some researchers have attempted to address this issue [5, 26]. Goldenberg and Wool [5] used a deterministic finite state automaton to create a model from real Modbus traffic. Their system identifies communications channels for each pair of devices that communicate with each other (e.g., human-machine interface and programmable logic controller, and programmable logic controller and programmable logic controller). After the channel is set, the system records the permitted transitions of the deterministic finite state automaton by examining the sequence of Modbus messages within the channel. During the detection phase, every unexpected transition is flagged as an anomaly. Anomalies are of three types: retransmission (occurrence of a deterministic finite state automaton symbol that is the same as the previous symbol), miss (occurrence of a known symbol in an unexpected position) and unknown (appearance of an unknown symbol). Goldenberg and Wool rely on the assumption that Modbus traffic is highly periodic. However, the tests conducted in this research have demonstrated that Modbus traffic is periodic only if random delays are filtered from the model. The approach of Goldenberg and Wool, if applied to the Modbus traffic samples used in this work, would have been inadequate to model communications and would have created an unmanageable number of automaton states and a large number of false positives.

Yoon et al. [26] have also focused on Modbus, but they modeled communications using dynamic Bayesian networks and probabilistic suffix trees. Each communications channel is reduced to a sequence of elements by parsing Modbus messages and pairing requests and responses. The given sequence is fed to the probabilistic suffix tree model and becomes the dataset that is used to detect anomalous communications. In the detection phase, the system evaluates every new sequence of messages by considering the likelihood of generating the sequence using the probabilistic suffix tree model. The system triggers an alert if the result is below a threshold. Yoon et al. tested their intrusion detection system on traffic generated by a testbed as well as on a synthetic data trace. However, they relied on the predictability of industrial control system traffic. Yoon et al. also implemented a mechanism to deal with false positives caused by single missing messages. This mechanism evaluates the probability that an anomalous sequence is missing a message (e.g., due to network delays). The mechanism considers a sequence to be normal traffic if the action of restoring the message allows the sequence to be accepted by the probabilistic suffix tree model, and the detection process proceeds to the next sequence. However, although the mechanism handles most of the false positives, Yoon et al. did not consider the impact on false negatives (e.g., caused by attacks that opportunistically filter specific network messages).

Finally, it is worth mentioning that there are several examples of sequence-aware, host-based intrusion detection systems. Most of these systems profile program activities and system calls (see, e.g., [8, 17, 25]) while other systems focus on user activities (see, e.g., [15]).

8.   Conclusions

This chapter has presented a methodology for modeling and analyzing industrial control system communications. The methodology models sequences of messages as discrete time Markov chains (DTMCs). This is accomplished by extracting information from network frames. An algorithm is then used to model specific features of the communications. Finally, DTMCs are used to understand the communications patterns and the consequentiality among messages. Two sequence detection mechanisms have been proposed based on the information provided by the DTMCs. The first is a deterministic approach that enforces specific sequentiality constraints. The second is a probabilistic approach that exploits transition probability distributions.

Future research will focus on developing a sequence-aware intrusion detection system. Research will also analyze other industrial control system protocols such as DNP3 and Profinet to expand the variety of communications patterns that can be handled, with the ultimate goal of developing high-performance intrusion detection systems for industrial control environments.

Acknowledgements

This research was partially supported by the European Commission via Project FP7-SEC-285477-CRISALIS of the 7th Framework Programme [3]. This research was also supported by a CTVR Grant (SFI 10/CE/I 1853) from Science Foundation Ireland.

References

[1] F. Aarts, B. Jonsson and J. Uijen, Generating models of infinite-state communications protocols using regular inference with abstraction, *Proceedings of the Twenty-Second IFIP WG 6.1 International Conference on Testing Software and Systems*, pp. 188–204, 2010.

[2] V. Chandola, A. Banerjee and V. Kumar, Anomaly detection for discrete sequences: A survey, *IEEE Transactions on Knowledge and Data Engineering*, vol. 24(5), pp. 823–839, 2012.

[3] CRISALIS Project, CRISALIS – Securing Critical Infrastructures, Siemens, Munich, Germany (www.crisalis-project.eu), 2012.

[4] N. Falliere, L. O'Murchu and E. Chien, W32.Stuxnet Dossier, version 1.4, Symantec, Mountain View, California, 2011.

[5] N. Goldenberg and A. Wool, Accurate modeling of Modbus/TCP for intrusion detection in SCADA systems, *International Journal of Critical Infrastructure Protection*, vol. 6(2), pp. 63–75, 2013.

[6] D. Hadziosmanovic, D. Bolzoni, S. Etalle and P. Hartel, Challenges and opportunities in securing industrial control systems, *Proceedings of the Workshop on Complexity in Engineering*, 2012.

[7] D. Hadziosmanovic, L. Simionato, D. Bolzoni, E. Zambon and S. Etalle, N-gram against the machine: On the feasibility of n-gram network analysis for binary protocols, *Proceedings of the Fifteenth International Symposium on Research in Attacks, Intrusions and Defenses*, pp. 354–373, 2012.

[8] S. Hofmeyr, S. Forrest and A. Somayaji, Intrusion detection using sequences of system calls, *Journal of Computer Security*, vol. 6(3), pp. 151–180, 1998.

[9] Industrial Control Systems Cyber Emergency Response Team, Advisory (ICSA-14-073-01), Siemens SIMATIC S7-1500 CPU Firmware Vulnerabilities, Department of Homeland Security, Washington, DC (ics-cert.us-cert.gov/advisories/ICSA-14-073-01), March 17, 2014.

[10] International Electrotechnical Commission, IEC 60870-5-101, Telecontrol Equipment and Systems – Part 5-101: Transmission Protocols – Companion Standard for Basic Telecontrol Tasks, Geneva, Switzerland, 2003.

[11] International Electrotechnical Commission, IEC 60870-5-104, Transmission Protocols, Network Access for IEC 60870-5-101 Using Standard Transport Profiles, Geneva, Switzerland, 2006.

[12] International Organization for Standardization, ISO 9506-1: Industrial Automation Systems – Manufacturing Message Specification, Part 1: Service Definition, Geneva, Switzerland, 2003.

[13] International Organization for Standardization, ISO 9506-2: Industrial Automation Systems – Manufacturing Message Specification, Part 2: Protocol Specification, Geneva, Switzerland, 2003.

[14] T. Krueger, H. Gascon, N. Kramer and K. Rieck, Learning stateful models for network honeypots, *Proceedings of the Fifth ACM Workshop on Security and Artificial Intelligence*, pp. 37–48, 2012.

[15] T. Lane and C. Brodley, Sequence matching and learning in anomaly detection for computer security, *Proceedings of the AAAI-97 Workshop on AI Approaches to Fraud Detection and Risk Management*, pp. 43–49, 1997.

[16] R. Langner, To Kill a Centrifuge: A Technical Analysis of What Stuxnet's Creators Tried to Achieve, The Langner Group, Arlington, Virginia, 2013.

[17] G. Mao, J. Zhang and X. Wu, Intrusion detection based on the short sequence model, *Proceedings of the Seventh World Congress on Intelligent Control and Automation*, pp. 1449–1454, 2008.

[18] S. McLaughlin and P. McDaniel, SABOT: Specification-based payload generation for programmable logic controllers, *Proceedings of the ACM Conference on Computer and Communications Security*, pp. 439–449, 2012.

[19] Modbus Organization, Modbus Application Protocol Specification (v1.1a), Hopkinton, Massachusetts (www.modbus.org/specs.php), 2004.

[20] I. Nai Fovino, A. Carcano, T. De Lacheze Murel, A. Trombetta and M. Masera, Modbus/DNP3 state-based intrusion detection system, *Proceedings of the Twenty-Fourth IEEE International Conference on Advanced Information Networking and Applications*, pp. 729–736, 2010.

[21] President's Commission on Critical Infrastructure Protection, Critical Foundations: Protecting America's Infrastructures, The Report of the President's Commission on Critical Infrastructure Protection, The White House, Washington, DC, 1997.

[22] R. Sekar, A. Gupta, J. Frullo, T. Shanbhag, A. Tiwari, H. Yang and S. Zhou, Specification-based anomaly detection: A new approach for detecting network intrusions, *Proceedings of the Ninth ACM Conference on Computer and Communications Security*, pp. 265–274, 2002.

[23] K. Stouffer, J. Falco and K. Scarfone, Guide to Industrial Control Systems (ICS) Security, NIST Special Publication 800-82, National Institute of Standards and Technology, Gaithersburg, Maryland, 2011.

[24] A. Swales, Open Modbus/TCP Specification, Release 1.0, Schneider Electric, Rueil-Malmaison, France, 1999.

[25] C. Warrender, S. Forrest and B. Pearlmutter, Detecting intrusions using system calls: Alternative data models, *Proceedings of the IEEE Symposium on Security and Privacy*, pp. 133–145, 1999.

[26] M. Yoon and G. Ciocarlie, Communication pattern monitoring: Improving the utility of anomaly detection for industrial control systems, presented at the *NDSS Workshop on Security of Emerging Networking Technologies*, 2014.

Chapter 5

INDUSTRIAL CONTROL SYSTEM FINGERPRINTING AND ANOMALY DETECTION

Yong Peng, Chong Xiang, Haihui Gao, Dongqing Chen and Wang Ren

Abstract   Industrial control systems are cyber-physical systems that supervise and control physical processes in critical infrastructures such as electric grids, water and wastewater treatment plants, oil and natural gas pipelines, transportation systems and chemical plants and refineries. Leveraging the stable and persistent control flow communications patterns in industrial control systems, this chapter proposes an innovative control system fingerprinting methodology that analyzes industrial control protocols to capture normal behavior characteristics. The methodology can be used to identify specific physical processes and control system components in industrial facilities and detect abnormal behavior. An experimental testbed that incorporates real systems for the cyber domain and simulated systems for the physical domain is used to validate the methodology. The experimental results demonstrate that the fingerprinting methodology holds promise for detecting anomalies in industrial control systems and cyber-physical systems used in the critical infrastructure.

Keywords: Industrial control systems, fingerprinting, anomaly detection

1.   Introduction

Industrial control systems (ICSs), which include supervisory control and data acquisition (SCADA) systems, distributed control systems (DCSs) and programmable logic controllers (PLCs), supervise and control physical processes in critical infrastructure assets such as electric grids, water and wastewater treatment plants, oil and natural gas pipelines, transportation systems and chemical plants and refineries [15, 18]. With the increasing use of commercial-off-the-shelf (COTS) information technology products, TCP/IP-based industrial control protocols and connectivity with other networks, industrial control

© IFIP International Federation for Information Processing 2015
M. Rice, S. Shenoi (Eds.): Critical Infrastructure Protection IX, IFIP AICT 466, pp. 73–85, 2015.
DOI: 10.1007/978-3-319-26567-4_5

systems have become attractive targets for cyber attacks. Malware such as Stuxnet [9], Duqu [3] and Flame [17] have demonstrated the enhanced cyber threats to critical infrastructure assets.

In the information technology field, fingerprinting techniques usually exploit information in TCP/IP protocol headers to automatically identify devices and software; these techniques are used in attacks as well as for protection purposes. Caselli et al. [5] have noted that industrial control system characteristics make device fingerprinting more challenging compared with conventional information technology networks due to device heterogeneity, proprietary protocols, device computational power and long-standing TCP sessions. On the other hand, from the system perspective, industrial control systems – unlike conventional information technology networks – tend to have stable and persistent control flow communications patterns, including characteristics such as long lifecycles, static topologies, periodic behavior and a limited number of applications and protocols [1, 16]. At the same time, every industrial control system is a unique cyber-physical system that is customized to its controlled physical process, control software and hardware.

For these reasons, a methodology is required to discriminate against specific industrial control systems. The fundamental questions are: Can the concept of a fingerprint from the information technology networking field that is used at the component level be translated to the industrial control system field where it is used at the system level? Furthermore, can the system-level fingerprint that represents an industrial control system that is operating normally be used to detect anomalous behavior in the control system?

This chapter attempts to answer these questions. Inspired by device fingerprinting as used in information technology networks, it is argued that industrial control protocol based behavior analysis can derive system-level characteristics of industrial control systems that may be used to discriminate between industrial control systems used in the critical infrastructure. Unlike pure simulation approaches described in the literature, an experimental testbed that incorporates real systems for the cyber domain and simulated systems for the physical domain is employed for validation; such an experimental setup is well suited to analyzing the characteristics of industrial control systems. The experimental results demonstrate that the proposed industrial control system fingerprinting methodology can discriminate between normal system behavior and abnormal behavior.

2.   Related Work

Unlike conventional information technology systems that are versatile and variable at the system level, industrial control systems are production systems that are somehow more fixed and regular for long periods of time at the system level. This is one of the characteristics that can be leveraged to extract control system fingerprints. A number of researchers (see, e.g., [6, 15, 18]) have noted that industrial control systems (and cyber-physical systems) have long lifecycles, hierarchical and structural architectures, relatively static topologies and less variability than information technology systems. Barbosa et al. [1] and Pleijsier et al. [16] have demonstrated that control traffic has characteristics such as periodicity, time-series nature, and static and stable topologies (with stable connections).

With regard to fingerprinting information technology systems, Caselli et al. [5] observe that the most widely adopted fingerprinting technique uses a 67-bit signature from TCP/IP protocol headers to identify an operating system on a machine in a standard network. Caselli and colleagues also describe the challenges involved in fingerprinting industrial control devices. Crotti et al. [8] have proposed the concept of a protocol fingerprint and have demonstrated its utility in discriminating between different network protocols. Their protocol fingerprint is based on three simple properties of IP packets: (i) size; (ii) inter-arrival time; and (iii) arrival order. This research has been inspired by their work, but there is a substantial difference. Crotti and colleagues use IP packet features to derive two statistical vectors that correspond to the protocol fingerprint. On the other hand, this research uses industrial control protocol packet features to derive sets of interactive patterns that represent normal industrial control system behavior and use them to identify anomalous behavior.

Garitano et al. [10] have proposed a method for generating realistic industrial control network traffic. This research is inspired by their observation that industrial control systems can be uniquely discriminated by their communications patterns that embody protocol behavior features. However, the research described in this chapter has different goals and employs a different methodology.

Intrusion and anomaly detection in industrial control systems is an emerging area of research. Cheung et al. [7], Goldenberg et al. [11] and Morris et al. [14] have developed intrusion detection systems for industrial control networks that use the Modbus protocol. Barbosa et al. [2] have used flow whitelists to describe legitimate traffic based on the properties of network packets. However, the research described in this chapter differs from these and other efforts in that it focuses on system-level characteristics. In fact, a search of the literature reveals a lack of research on system-level fingerprinting of industrial control systems and its use in discriminating between normal and abnormal system behavior.

3. Background

A reference model provides a common framework and terminology for describing and understanding industrial control systems. The ANSI/ISA-99 [13] and IEC 62443 [12] standards provide a five-level reference model: (i) level 4 is the enterprise system; (ii) level 3 is for operations management; (iii) level 2 is for supervisory control; (iv) level 1 is for local or basic control; and (v) level 0 is the process. Industrial control systems involve levels 3 through 0. As shown in Figure 1, the reference model used in this chapter is simplified as the process network, control network and physical process.

The cyber domain of an industrial control system includes the process network and the control network; the physical domain is the controlled physical

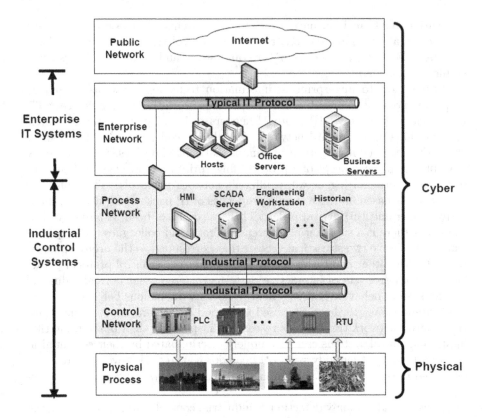

Figure 1. Typical industrial control system architecture.

process (Figure 1). The process network usually hosts human-machine interfaces (HMIs), SCADA servers, engineering workstations and historians. The human-machine interfaces are used by human operators to supervise and control the physical process.

The control network hosts devices such as programmable logic controllers (PLCs) and remote terminal units (RTUs) that, on one side, interact with the physical domain (i.e., the controlled physical process such as a chemical plant) and, on the other side, provide control interfaces to the process network and eventually to human operators. Process network components communicate with control network components using industrial control protocols such as Modbus and DNP3.

4.   Experimental Setup

The availability of experimental environments and real-world data pose major barriers to industrial control system security research. Some researchers have used industrial control system traffic traces captured from real installations. However, such traffic contains a lot of noise and is too complex for

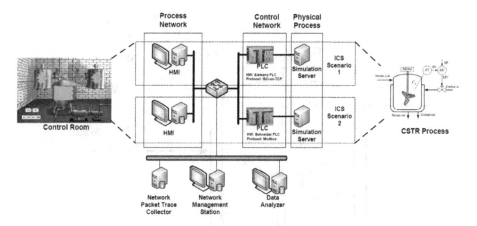

Figure 2. Experimental testbed.

the preliminary research described in this chapter. Other researchers use pure simulations to acquire traffic data, but this data is often inaccurate and the results may be of limited utility. This research focuses on industrial control system traffic in the cyber domain, more specifically, network traffic between a human-machine interface and programmable logic controller. The experimental testbed used in the research engages real hardware and software for the cyber domain and a simulation of the physical domain. This approach yields real control traffic that provides the ground truth of the normal behavior of the industrial control system without any interference or noise. Figure 2 shows the experimental testbed that offers the possibility of acquiring realistic and effective results.

The testbed adheres to the reference architecture presented in Figure 1. It is a part of the larger Cyber-Physical-System-Based Critical Infrastructure Integrated Experimental Platform (C^2I^2EP). The testbed incorporates: (i) an industrial control system that controls a continuous stirred tank reactor (CSTR); and (ii) an experiment analysis system. The process network contains an Intouch human-machine interface. The control network incorporates a Siemens programmable logic controller that communicates with the human-machine interface via the ISO-over-TCP protocol. The physical process is a continuous stirred tank reactor that is simulated in Matlab. The experiment analysis system is used to capture network traffic, perform operations management and analyze data.

Figure 3 shows the continuous stirred tank reactor model used in the research. The model corresponds to a two-state jacketed continuous stirred tank reactor with an exothermic irreversible first-order reaction: A → B. The process is modeled by two nonlinear ordinary differential equations obtained from the material and energy balances under the assumptions of constant volume, perfect mixing and constant physical properties.

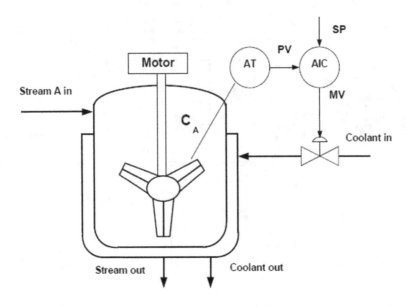

Figure 3. Continuous stirred tank reactor model.

5.   Fingerprinting Methodology

The core of an industrial control system is its physical domain, which comprises the controlled physical process. The cyber domain of the industrial control system is used to interactively and/or automatically control the physical process. From the viewpoint of control system designers, every unique industrial control system is a combination of control logic and parameter values [10]. The designers need to specify the control logic and download it to programmable logic controllers and design human-machine interfaces so that human operators can interact with the control system and, thus, the physical system. Specifically, the human-machine interfaces and programmable logic controllers interact via sensor variable values and control variable values using an industrial control protocol. Therefore, by analyzing the interactive behavior characteristics of an industrial control protocol, it is possible to obtain a fingerprint that represents the designers' understanding of the mission requirements of the controlled physical process and the characteristics of the industrial control system components, as long as there are no changes to the physical process and the industrial control system components.

In the context of this research, an industrial control system fingerprint is a set of transaction patterns between a human-machine interface and programmable logic controller. A transaction pattern is, itself, a set of interactive industrial protocol packets that are characterized by properties such as packet arrival order, packet size, direction (from the human-machine interface to the programmable logic controller or from the programmable logic controller to the human-machine interface) and inter-arrival time.

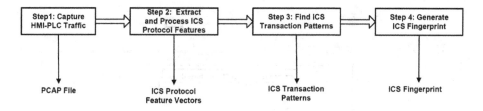

Figure 4. Fingerprinting methodology.

Figure 4 presents the methodology for acquiring an industrial control system fingerprint.

No.	Time	Source	Destination	Protocol	Length	Info
1	0.000000	192.168.0.66	192.168.0.5	T.125	90	detachuserRequest
2	0.001280	192.168.0.5	192.168.0.66	TCP	60	iso-tsap > 49352 [ACK] Seq=1 Ack=37 win=2048 Len=0
3	0.019027	192.168.0.5	192.168.0.66	T.125	76	detachuserRequest
4	0.216685	192.168.0.66	192.168.0.5	TCP	60	49352 > iso-tsap [ACK] Seq=37 Ack=23 win=62938 Len=0
5	0.310048	192.168.0.66	192.168.0.5	T.125	90	detachuserRequest
6	0.311000	192.168.0.5	192.168.0.66	TCP	60	iso-tsap > 49352 [ACK] Seq=23 Ack=73 win=2048 Len=0
374888	21328.213487	192.168.0.66	192.168.0.5	T.125	76	detachuserRequest
374889	21328.422935	192.168.0.66	192.168.0.5	TCP	60	49352 > iso-tsap [ACK] Seq=5425541 Ack=7840531 win=63372 Len=0
374890	21328.510301	192.168.0.66	192.168.0.5	T.125	90	detachuserRequest
374891	21328.511306	192.168.0.5	192.168.0.66	TCP	60	iso-tsap > 49352 [ACK] Seq=7840531 Ack=5425577 win=2048 Len=0
374892	21328.526905	192.168.0.5	192.168.0.66	T.125	76	detachuserRequest
374893	21328.726974	192.168.0.66	192.168.0.5	TCP	60	49352 > iso-tsap [ACK] Seq=5425577 Ack=7840553 win=63350 Len=0

Figure 5. PCAP file of network traffic.

The fingerprinting methodology incorporates four steps:

- **Step 1:** The first step is to capture traffic traces between the human-machine interface and programmable logic controller. Network traffic capture software such as Wireshark can be used to passively capture the traffic. Figure 5 shows the captured PCAP file for the experimental testbed.

- **Step 2:** The second step is to extract and process the industrial control protocol features. A custom data analyzer or tool such as Scapy [4] may be used to extract packet properties such as packet arrival order, packet size, direction and inter-arrival time. Next, the data is filtered and processed to obtain a set of industrial control protocol packet feature vectors P_i:

$$P_i = (s_i, \Delta t_i, d_i) \tag{1}$$

where i is the sequence number of a packet exchanged between the human-machine interface and programmable logic controller, s_i is the size of the packet, Δt_i is the packet inter-arrival time between packet$_{i-1}$ and packet$_i$, and d_i is the direction of the packet flow (d_i has a value of +1 for HMI→PLC and −1 for PLC→HMI). Note that Δt_i is a discretized value that is obtained using a discretization algorithm.

In the experiment, the continuous stirred tank reactor simulation was run for six hours and the network traffic between the human-machine

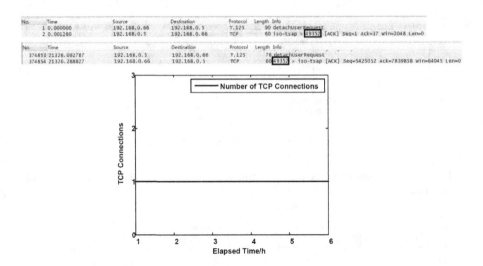

Figure 6.   Long-standing TCP connection between the HMI and PLC.

interface and the programmable logic controller was collected. The following interactive industrial control protocol packet characteristics were discerned from the collected data:

1. The industrial control protocol has a long-standing TCP connection that spans several hours (Figure 6). This observation matches that of Caselli et al. [5] and shows that TCP characteristics are not well suited to industrial control system fingerprinting.

2. Each protocol packet has a limited size s_i and a limited number of vectors (s_i, d_i). In the experiment, six types of vectors (s_i, d_i) were distinguished from among the millions of packets that were captured: (i) (60, +1); (ii) (90, +1); (iii) (133, +1); (iv) (60, –1); (v) (76, –1); and (vi) (227, –1). An analysis of the timescales revealed that almost fixed numbers of (s_i, d_i) vectors were observed each hour (Table 1).

3. The packet inter-arrival times can help discriminate between interactive sessions or transaction patterns between the human-machine interface and programmable logic controller. Figure 7 shows that Δt_i has three orders of magnitude: 100 ms, 10 ms and 1 ms.

■ **Step 3:** The third step is to find the transaction patterns. The observations in Step 2 imply that certain transaction patterns exist between the human-machine interface and programmable logic controller. Each transaction pattern M_j is a set of bi-directional packet feature vectors:

$$M_j = \{P_1, P_2, \ldots, P_m\} \tag{2}$$

where m is the number of feature vectors.

Table 1. Numbers of vectors (s_i, d_i) at different timescales.

Arrrival Order	Packet Size	Direction	Packet Vector	Inter-Arrival Time (ms)
1	90	+1	90	0
2	60	−1	−60	1
3	76	−1	−76	20
4	60	+1	60	200
5	133	+1	133	100
6	60	−1	−60	1
7	227	−1	−227	30
8	133	+1	−133	1
9	60	−1	−60	1
10	90	+1	90	10

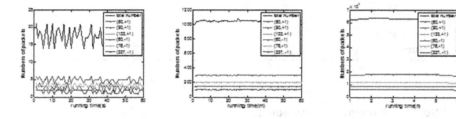

Figure 7. Orders of magnitude of interactive packet inter-arrival times.

Algorithm 1 specifies the procedure for obtaining the industrial control system transaction patterns.

Analysis of the data from the continuous stirred tank reactor simulation revealed exactly eight types of transaction patterns. Figure 8 shows the transaction patterns.

■ **Step 4:** The fourth and final step is to obtain the industrial control system fingerprint. The fingerprint Φ^S is given by:

$$\Phi^S = (M_1, M_2, \ldots, M_n) \tag{3}$$

where n is the number of transaction patterns.

In the case of the continuous stirred tank reactor, it is adequate to use the set of transaction patterns as the industrial control system fingerprint. The processing of transaction patterns to obtain a more compact and more accurate fingerprint is a topic for future research.

Algorithm 1: Obtaining industrial control system transaction patterns.

Input: $P_i = (s_i, \Delta t_i, d_i)$, i = 1, 2, ... I
Output: $\Phi^S = \{M_1, M_2, \ldots M_n\}$
% After the analysis, each interaction is observed to end with a packet
% of length 60 without any data
function Patterns($P_i = (s_i, \Delta t_i, d_i)$)
   i = 1
   $\Phi^S = \phi$
   while(i < I)
     k = i
     while($s_k \neq 60$)
       k = k + 1
     end while
       if $\{(s_i, d_i), \ldots, (s_k, d_k)\} \in \Phi^S$
         then $M_j = \{(s_i, d_i), \ldots, (s_k, d_k)\}$
         $\Phi^S = \Phi^S \cup M_j$
       end if
     i = k + 1
   end while
   return Φ^S

No.	Patterns			Amounts
1	-227	60	-	5021
2	-76	60	-	47703
3	90	-60	-	45269
4	133	-60	-	7475
5	-76	90	-60	9464
6	-76	133	-60	13910
7	-227	90	-60	16366
8	-227	133	-60	14909

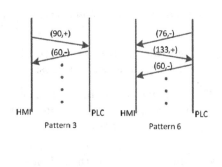

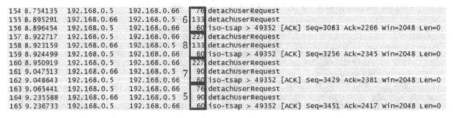

Figure 8.   Continuous stirred tank reactor transaction patterns.

No.	Time	Source	Destination	Length	Info
1	0.000000	140.90.36.1	140.90.37.1	60	56219 > iso-tsap [SYN] Seq=0 Win=0 Len=0 MSS=1460
2	0.001262	140.90.37.1	140.90.36.1	60	iso-tsap > 56219 [SYN, ACK] Seq=0 Ack=1 Win=1024 Len=0 MSS=1460
3	0.001764	140.90.36.1	140.90.37.1	60	56219 > iso-tsap [ACK] Seq=1 Ack=1 Win=1024 Len=0
4	0.244687	140.90.36.1	140.90.37.1	82	CR TPDU src-ref: 0x4431 dst-ref: 0x0000[Malformed Packet]
5	0.246343	140.90.37.1	140.90.36.1	60	iso-tsap > 56219 [ACK] Seq=1 Ack=29 Win=1024 Len=0
6	0.247109	140.90.37.1	140.90.36.1	82	CC TPDU src-ref: 0x4431 dst-ref: 0x4431[Malformed Packet]
7	0.247854	140.90.36.1	140.90.37.1	60	56219 > iso-tsap [ACK] Seq=29 Ack=29 Win=1024 Len=0

Figure 9. PCAP file for the ISO-on-TCP protocol.

6. Fingerprint-Based Anomaly Detection

The industrial control system fingerprint that is derived from normal system behavior can be used to detect anomalous behavior. To detect an anomaly, it is necessary to repeat Steps 1 through 3 for the industrial control system of interest and obtain the set of transaction patterns for the new traffic. Each transaction pattern corresponding to the new traffic is then compared with the corresponding transaction pattern in the fingerprint; a transaction pattern mismatch indicates anomalous behavior.

Two examples are presented to demonstrate the utility of the fingerprint-based anomaly detection methodology. Note that the two examples involve attack traffic with legitimate protocol messages sent from legitimate sources. These correspond to highly stealthy and dangerous attacks on an industrial control system.

The first example involves ISO-on-TCP traffic from a vendor. Figure 9 shows the PCAP file of the ISO-on-TCP traffic. Although the same protocol is used, the packet characteristics are different from those in the original experiment. In particular, packets of length 82 were not seen under normal operating conditions.

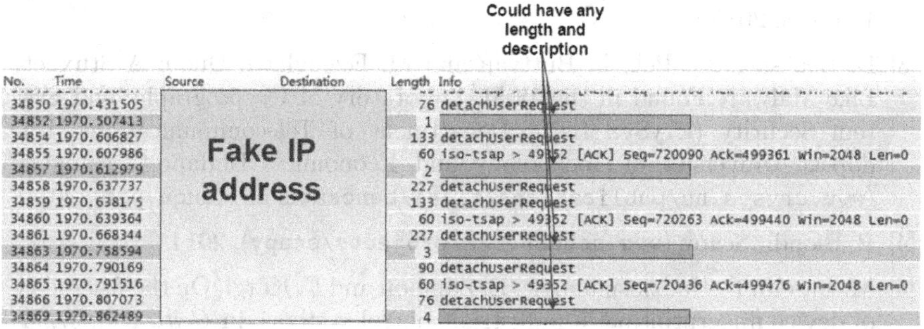

Figure 10. PCAP file for a programmable logic controller scanning attack.

The second example involves a programmable logic controller scanning attack. The assumption is that the attacker is sophisticated enough to use a fake IP address to defeat whitelisting and can adjust the lengths of attack packets. Figure 10 shows the PCAP file corresponding to the attack. Note that any fake length of the second attack packet does not match any combination of the patterns and is, therefore, detected as an anomaly.

7. Conclusions

The industrial control system fingerprinting methodology presented in this chapter leverages the stable and persistent control flow communications patterns in industrial control systems to create fingerprints that correspond to normal behavior of industrial control systems. The fingerprinting methodology is validated using an experimental testbed that incorporates real systems for the cyber domain and simulated systems for the physical domain. The experimental results demonstrate that the fingerprinting methodology holds promise for detecting anomalies in industrial control systems and cyber-physical systems used in the critical infrastructure.

Future research will focus on incorporating real-world industrial control equipment in the Cyber-Physical-System-Based Critical Infrastructure Integrated Experimental Platform (C^2I^2EP) and evaluating complex attack scenarios. Efforts will also be made to acquire and experiment with real traffic from production environments. Additionally, the industrial control system fingerprinting research will attempt to extend the feature set to incorporate lower-level TCP/IP characteristics extracted from real traffic using data mining and statistical analysis techniques.

References

[1] R. Barbosa, R. Sadre and A. Pras, A first look into SCADA network traffic, *Proceedings of the IEEE Network Operations and Management Symposium*, pp. 518–521, 2012.

[2] R. Barbosa, R. Sadre and A. Pras, Flow whitelisting in SCADA networks, *International Journal of Critical Infrastructure Protection*, vol. 6(3-4), pp. 150–158, 2013.

[3] B. Bencsath, G. Pek, L. Buttyan and M. Felegyhazi, Duqu: A Stuxnet-Like Malware Found in the Wild, Laboratory of Cryptography and System Security (CrySyS Lab), Department of Telecommunications, Budapest University of Technology and Economics, Budapest, Hungary (www.crysys.hu/publications/files/bencsathPBF11duqu.pdf), 2011.

[4] P. Biondi, Scapy (www.secdev.org/projects/scapy), 2014.

[5] M. Caselli, D. Hadziosmanovic, E. Zambon and F. Kargl, On the feasibility of device fingerprinting in industrial control systems, in *Critical Information Infrastructures Security*, E. Luiijf and P. Hartel (Eds.), pp. 155–166, 2013.

[6] M. Cheminod, L. Durante and A. Valenzano, Review of security issues in industrial networks, *IEEE Transactions on Industrial Informatics*, vol. 9(1), pp. 277–293, 2013.

[7] S. Cheung, B. Dutertre, M. Fong, U. Lindqvist, K. Skinner and A. Valdes, Using model-based intrusion detection for SCADA networks, *Proceedings of the SCADA Security Scientific Symposium*, 2007.

[8] M. Crotti, M. Dusi, F. Gringoli and L. Salgarelli, Traffic classification through simple statistical fingerprinting, *ACM SIGCOMM Computer Communication Review*, vol. 37(1), pp. 5–16, 2007.

[9] N. Falliere, L. O'Murchu and E. Chien, W32.Stuxnet Dossier, Version 1.4, Symantec, Mountain View, California, 2011.

[10] I. Garitano, C. Siaterlis, B. Genge, R. Uribeetxeberria and U. Zurutuza, A method to construct network traffic models for process control systems, *Proceedings of the Seventeenth IEEE International Conference on Emerging Technologies and Factory Automation*, 2012.

[11] N. Goldenberg and A. Wool, Accurate modeling of Modbus/TCP for intrusion detection in SCADA systems, *International Journal of Critical Infrastructure Protection*, vol. 6(2), pp. 63–75, 2013.

[12] International Electrotechnical Commission, IEC TS 62443-1-1:2009, Industrial Communication Networks – Network and System Security – Part 1-1: Terminology, Concepts and Models, Geneva, Switzerland, 2009.

[13] International Society of Automation, ANSI/ISA-62443-1-1 (99.01.01)-2007, Security for Industrial Automation and Control Systems: Terminology, Concepts and Models, Research Triangle Park, North Carolina, 2007.

[14] T. Morris, R. Vaughn and Y. Dandass, A retrofit network intrusion detection system for Modbus RTU and ASCII industrial control systems, *Proceedings of the Forty-Fifth Hawaii International Conference on System Science*, pp. 2338–2345, 2012.

[15] Y. Peng, C. Jiang, F. Xie, Z. Dai, Q. Xiong and Y. Gao, Industrial control system cybersecurity research, *Journal of Tsinghua University*, vol. 52(10), pp. 1396–1408, 2012.

[16] E. Pleijsier, Towards anomaly detection in SCADA networks using connection patterns, presented at the *Eighteenth Twente Student Conference on Information Technology*, 2013.

[17] sKyWIper Analysis Team, sKyWIper (a.k.a. Flame a.k.a. Flamer): A Complex Malware for Targeted Attacks, v1.05, Technical Report, Laboratory of Cryptography and System Security (CrySyS Lab), Department of Telecommunications, Budapest University of Technology and Economics, Budapest, Hungary (www.crysys.hu/skywiper/skywiper.pdf), 2012.

[18] K. Stouffer, J. Falco and K. Scarfone, Guide to Industrial Control Systems (ICS) Security, NIST Special Publication 800-82, National Institute of Standards and Technology, Gaithersburg, Maryland, 2011.

Chapter 6

TRAFFIC-LOCALITY-BASED CREATION OF FLOW WHITELISTS FOR SCADA NETWORKS

Seungoh Choi, Yeop Chang, Jeong-Han Yun and Woonyon Kim

Abstract   The security of supervisory control and data acquisition (SCADA) networks has attracted considerable attention since the discovery of Stuxnet in 2010. Meanwhile, SCADA networks have become increasingly interconnected both locally and remotely. It is, therefore, necessary to develop effective network intrusion detection capabilities. Whitelist-based intrusion detection has become an attractive approach for SCADA networks. However, when analyzing network traffic in SCADA systems, general properties such as TCP handshaking and common ports are insufficient to create flow whitelists. To address the problem, this chapter proposes a methodology for locality-based creation of flow whitelists and conducts experiments to evaluate its effectiveness in seven SCADA systems. The experimental results demonstrate that the methodology generates effective whitelists for deployment in SCADA networks.

Keywords: SCADA networks, intrusion detection, whitelists, traffic locality

1.   Introduction

Industrial control systems, especially supervisory control and data acquisition (SCADA) systems, are widely used in the critical infrastructure. SCADA networks were traditionally considered to be safe from cyber threats because they employed proprietary protocols and were generally isolated from information technology (corporate) networks. This situation has changed and, as Stuxnet has demonstrated, a highly protected and carefully isolated control network can be compromised by a simple USB drive. Malware targeting SCADA networks has proliferated in recent years with examples such as Duqu, Flame, Gauss, Mahdi, Shamoon and SkyWiper [8].

According to the U.S. Industrial Control Systems Cyber Emergency Response Team (ICS-CERT) [6], SCADA vulnerabilities and incidents are in-

© IFIP International Federation for Information Processing 2015

M. Rice, S. Shenoi (Eds.): Critical Infrastructure Protection IX, IFIP AICT 466, pp. 87–102, 2015.

DOI: 10.1007/978-3-319-26567-4_6

creasing rapidly. Meanwhile, SCADA networks are becoming interconnected with other networks, including the Internet, to link local and remote sites [7]; this greatly increases the ability of SCADA malware to propagate. Hence, it is necessary to develop effective intrusion detection schemes for SCADA networks used in the critical infrastructure.

Whitelisting has been recommended for intrusion detection in SCADA networks because of their stable structure and predictable traffic [1, 9]. Several researchers have studied whitelisting and have proposed novel approaches [4, 5, 10]. However, a challenge when designing a whitelisting solution is to identify client-server relationships without requiring information from operators or manufacturers. Some whitelisting solutions (e.g., [4]) assume that the relationships are known; other researchers (e.g., [5, 10]) simply ignore the problem. Moreover, comprehensive evaluations of whitelist generation techniques and their experimental results have not been performed.

Barbosa et al. [2] have developed a state-of-the-art intrusion detection technique for SCADA networks using flow whitelisting. They inferred client-server relationships from TCP handshaking information (TCP flags) and well-known ports. However, when traffic from a real-world SCADA network is analyzed, problems still exist. First, three-way handshaking relationships cannot be identified when TCP sessions are maintained throughout a traffic collection period. Second, different ports numbers may be used for well-known services to enhance security. Third, network flows may not provide adequate operational information because SCADA systems frequently use proprietary protocols for communications and port assignments on devices that may not be publicly documented.

This chapter focuses on flow whitelisting based on the determination of client-server relationships in a SCADA network. A flow whitelist, which corresponds to a permissible access list, comprises IP addresses, port numbers and transport protocol information such as client-server relationships. This chapter describes a methodology for constructing flow whitelists for SCADA networks based on traffic locality, including degree centrality and locally frequently-used ports. The experimental results demonstrate that the whitelists are very effective at securing SCADA networks.

2.   Background

This section provides background information. In particular, it discusses two important characteristics of SCADA network traffic flow. These characteristics, degree centrality and locally frequently-used ports, form the basis of the proposed methodology for extracting flow whitelists from SCADA network traffic.

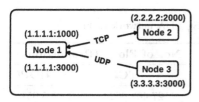

Src.IP	Src.Port	Dst.IP	Dst.Port	Protocol
1.1.1.1	1000	2.2.2.2	2000	TCP
2.2.2.2	2000	1.1.1.1	1000	TCP
3.3.3.3	3000	1.1.1.1	3000	UDP

(a) Directed graph.   (b) Flows as five-tuples.

Figure 1. Flow representation.

2.1 Network Flow and Flow Whitelists

A network flow is a directional edge between two network nodes that is represented by pairs of IP addresses and port numbers. A directional edge identifies the flow protocol and direction of flow.

The directed graph in Figure 1(a) shows network traffic flows: a bidirectional TCP traffic flow between Node 1 and Node 2, and a unidirectional UDP traffic flow from Node 3 to Node 1. A directed graph represents flows using five-tuples (i.e., source IP address, source port number, destination IP address, destination port number, protocol) as shown in Figure 1(b).

A flow whitelist is a set of rules. A rule is also represented as a five-tuple (i.e., source IP address, source port number, destination IP address, destination port number, protocol). However, the source and destination ports are considered to be explicit ports or "ANY."

2.2 Traffic Summary

For the experimental evaluations, SCADA network traffic was captured using mirroring techniques from seven sites in two domains. The collection periods varied from 3 to 29 days. As shown in Table 1, there were distinct distribution differences between the TCP and UDP traffic from each site. A large proportion of traffic did not have many flows for both TCP and UDP communications, such as at Site A. However, Site B had an extremely large proportion of TCP traffic because Site B backed up the other sites using TCP.

All the flows were analyzed to extract a flow whitelist. The analysis revealed two key characteristics, degree centrality and locally frequently-used ports (LFPs), which are discussed below.

2.3 Degree Centrality

Degree centrality is the number of links associated with a node [3]. Two types of degree centrality can be calculated for directional edges: (i) in-degree flow, which is the number of incoming links; and (ii) out-degree flow, which is the number of outgoing links. As shown in Figure 1, the degree centrality of Node 1 comprises an in-degree flow of two (incoming from Node 2 and Node 3) and an out-degree flow of one (outgoing to Node 2).

Table 1.   Summary of captured SCADA network traffic.

Site	Size of Traffic (Proportion)		No. of Flows (Proportion)	
	TCP	UDP	TCP	UDP
A	450 GB	3 GB	27,402,062	25,385,051
	(0.9934)	(0.0066)	(0.5191)	(0.4809)
B	37 GB	0.1 GB	371,908	7
	(0.9973)	(0.0027)	(0.99998)	(0.00002)
C	409 GB	83 GB	4,405,006	4,793,932
	(0.8313)	(0.1687)	(0.4789)	(0.5211)
D	131 GB	76 GB	2,087,740	2,773
	(0.6329)	(0.3671)	(0.9987)	(0.0013)
E	370 GB	55 GB	1,479,011	1,113,938
	(0.8706)	(0.1294)	(0.5704)	(0.4296)
F	2,429 GB	193 GB	47,412,410	26,832,080
	(0.9264)	(0.0736)	(0.6386)	(0.3614)
G	277 GB	3 GB	357,399	24,729
	(0.9893)	(0.0107)	(0.9353)	(0.0647)

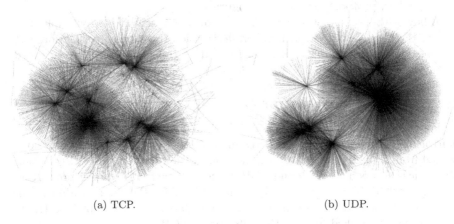

(a) TCP.   (b) UDP.

Figure 2.   Graphs of network flows during a five-hour period at Site C.

Figure 2 presents graphs of TCP and UDP flows seen during a five-hour period at Site C. Note that most of the flows are concentrated at specific nodes.

Based on this observation, it appears that degree centrality could be used to identify client-server relationships. To help identify the nodes, the results were ranked in descending order of degree centrality as shown in Figure 3. Note that, in the figure, the node ID is a unique IP address and port number pair. Most server nodes (IP_{server}, $PORT_{Server}$) had degree centrality values of more than 1,000, which covered approximately half of the flows for both TCP and UDP.

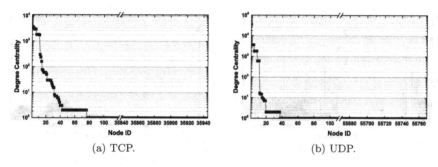

(a) TCP. (b) UDP.

Figure 3. Degree centrality during a five-hour period at Site C.

Upon analyzing the network traffic degree centrality, the fixed port numbers of each IP_{Server} were readily identified. Rules were then extracted from the flows associated with the server nodes. For example, if a server node (IP_{Server}, $PORT_{Server}$) had TCP incoming edges from nodes using the same IP_{Client}, the following rule could be extracted: (IP_{Client}, ANY, IP_{Server}, $PORT_{Server}$, TCP). In the case of TCP, there may be a counter rule, (IP_{Server}, $PORT_{Server}$, IP_{Client}, ANY, TCP), which is similar to the case of UDP.

2.4 Locally Frequently-Used Ports

Although degree centrality helps extract rules that cover a considerable amount of flows, it cannot help extract all the rules for a flow whitelist. Moreover, degree centrality may yield incorrect rules in two situations. One is when one client communicates with many servers and the other is when communications occur via the same port.

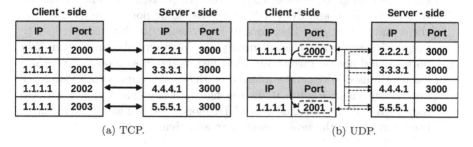

(a) TCP. (b) UDP.

Figure 4. Limitations of degree centrality.

- **One Client to Many Servers:** A device, such as a front end processor (FEP), requires connections to other devices such as programmable logic controllers (PLCs) or remote terminal units (RTUs) with different IP addresses, but the same port number. The application of degree centrality does not yield rules in this case because no nodes have high degree centrality. As shown in Figure 4(a), TCP flows do not converge on a specific

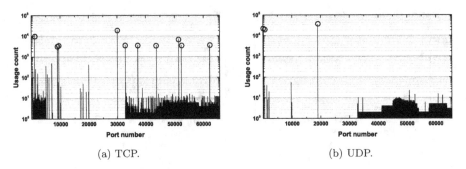

Figure 5.   Port number usage during a five-hour period at Site C.

server IP address and server port pair. One port (3000) on the server side is frequently used, but no rules are generated due to the low degree centrality of every server.

This problem is more acute for UDP flows. As shown in Figure 4(b), one client opens a UDP port (2000) and sends packets to several servers with different IP addresses but the same port number. According to degree centrality, the client node (1.1.1.1, 2000) is a server node. When the client begins the next communications session using another UDP port (2001), another client node (1.1.1.1, 2001) is considered to be a new server node. To solve these problems, it is necessary to consider locally frequently-used server ports in SCADA networks.

■ **Communications via a Fixed Port:** A client can use a fixed port. To communicate with programmable logic controllers, the client and server sides are configured to use fixed ports. In particular, some protocols, such as NetBIOS and SUN RPC, force the same port to be used by the client and the server. Therefore, it is necessary to also discover locally frequently-used ports that primarily use local sites because client-side ports should not be mistakenly identified as server-side ports. A locally frequently-used port can be inferred by the usage count, which varies per port as shown in Figure 5. In the figure, it is evident that there are roughly ten TCP ports and three UDP ports that are locally frequently-used ports when the usage count is greater than 1,000.

3.   Flow Whitelist Creation

This section describes the methodology for creating a flow whitelist based on the observations discussed in the previous section.

3.1   Overview

The flow whitelist creation methodology, which is presented in Figure 6, has three phases: (i) preparation; (ii) generation; and (iii) inspection. The initial

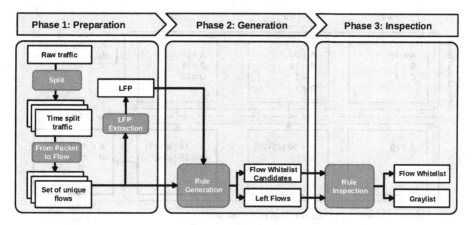

Figure 6. Flow whitelist creation.

preparation phase divides raw traffic into a set of unique flows in each hourly interval without redundant flows. In addition, it lists the locally frequently-used ports based on all flows. The generation phase selectively identifies candidates for the flow whitelist using a generation algorithm. The final inspection phase analyzes the flow whitelist candidates and omits flows that do not match the results of the algorithm executed in the previous phase. Thus, it helps administrators decide whether or not candidates should be placed in the final whitelist.

3.2   Phase 1: Preparation

The preparation phase processes raw traffic to make it appropriate as an input to the second phase. It splits the raw traffic according to a timeline, creates a set of unique flows and lists the locally frequently-used ports.

Raw traffic is first separated by time because flow whitelist generation examines flows within a given period. Next, a set of unique flows is produced; this set includes essential traffic information (i.e., represented as five-tuples) to reduce the processing burden. Finally, the ports that are frequently used with different IP addresses at a local site are listed.

Figure 7 presents the locally frequently-used port extraction process. Two threshold values, θ_{Unit} and θ_{Final}, are employed. The θ_{Unit} threshold is used to filter specific ports that are rarely found in a given set of unique flows. During the filtering, the number of a used port is set to zero as long as the number does not exceed the threshold; otherwise, the value is retained until the end of the process. The θ_{Final} threshold is used in the second phase to obtain the final locally frequently-used port list. In Figure 7, the thresholds used for θ_{Unit} and θ_{Final} are 5 and 25, respectively.

To overcome the lack of knowledge of flows in a SCADA network, the locally frequently-used ports serve as an informative reference to infer server-side ports

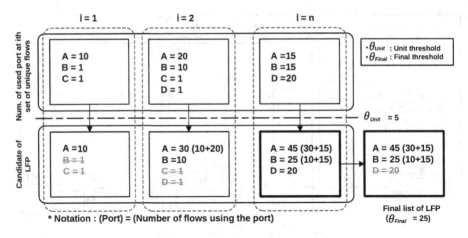

Figure 7. Locally frequently-used port extraction.

without mistakenly identifying the client side as the server side for TCP and UDP traffic. Moreover, based on the observations in Section 2.4, it can be an opportunity to quickly generate a flow whitelist and accurately use the locally frequently-used ports because many uses of server IP addresses are converted in advance to a flow whitelist.

3.3   Phase 2: Generation

The generation phase creates the flow whitelist. The set of unique flows is input to Algorithm 1, which uses two indicators, degree centrality and locally frequently-used ports, as discussed in Section 2.

The algorithm initially checks if a unique flow matches an already-generated rule. When a flow is covered by a rule, the flow is ignored and a new rule is not generated. If a flow is not covered by a rule, then the locally frequently-used port list is examined for a port associated with the source or destination IP address. Three cases exist: the locally frequently-used port list includes: (i) only a source-side port; (ii) only a destination-side port; or (iii) both. As mentioned above, a port is designated as "ANY" if it is not present in the locally frequently-used port list. Thus, the inference of the server side based on the locally frequently-used ports is prioritized when generating the flow whitelist.

Next, the degree centrality with direction is analyzed to handle nodes in which the flow is centralized. Node in-degree and out-degree centrality values are computed by counting the numbers of incoming and outgoing links, respectively. When the in-degree or out-degree centrality of a node exceeds the port threshold (θ_{Port}) defined by an administrator, rule generation is triggered, which depends on the direction of flow at the node. For example, a rule is generated at Lines 14–17 of the algorithm if the node in-degree centrality exceeds the port threshold because many flows head to the destination. In the rule

---

Algorithm 1 : Flow whitelist generation.

Main:

1: **for** each *file* in *files* **do**
2:     MakeUniqueFlows (...)
3:     **for** each *flow* in *flows* **do**
4:         RuleGeneration(protocol, dIP, dPort, sIP, sPort)
5:     **end for**
6: **end for**

RuleGeneration:

1: **if** *IsInRule*() == *True* **then return**
2: **end if**
3: **if** sPort and dPort ∈ LFP **then**
4:     AddRule(sIP, sPort, dIP, dPort)
5: **else**
6:     **if** sPort ∈ LFP **then**
7:         AddRule(sIP, sPort, dIP, ANY)
8:     **else**
9:         **if** dPort ∈ LFP **then**
10:             AddRule(sIP, ANY, dIP, dPort)
11:         **end if**
12:     **end if**
13: **end if**
14: **if** *In–degree of DestinationNode* > θ_{Port} **then**
15:     Find sIPs connected with dNode
16:     AddRules(sIPs, ANY, dIP, dPort)
17: **end if**
18: **if** *Out–degree of SourceNode* > θ_{Port} **then**
19:     Find dIPs connected with sNode
20:     AddRules(sIP, sPort, dIPs, ANY)
21: **end if**
22: **if** *AddRule* == *True* **then**
23:     Remove all flows matched with the rule
24: **end if**

---

generation process, all flows that match a rule generated based on the locally frequently-used ports and degree centrality are eliminated.

3.4   Phase 3: Inspection

The inspection phase confirms if a generated (candidate) rule is whitelisted. Because of the use of the threshold in rule generation, remaining flows may exist. In fact, the inspection phase could generate rules flow by flow. However, not all flows in a SCADA network are legitimate; such flows arise due to link failures or problems with field devices. Therefore, guidelines are provided to serve as a graylist for the remaining flows as well as for the inspection of whitelist candidates. The following are some example guidelines:

Table 2. Preparation phase results.

Site	Volume of Raw Traffic	Volume of Unique Flows	Number of LFPs $(\theta_{Unit} = 25, \theta_{Final} = 100)$
A	453 GB	3.9 GB	49
B	37.1 GB	0.027 GB	11
C	492 GB	0.65 GB	39
D	207 GB	5.8 GB	215
E	425 GB	0.18 GB	6
F	2,622 GB	0.2 GB	77
G	280 GB	0.028 GB	19

- **Unidirectional Rule:** A unidirectional rule represents a one-way flow. It can result from the operational objective of a device or a problem situation. For example, a node may need to send or receive data from other nodes due to an operational objective. However, a packet may not reach its destination because of a problem in a SCADA device or network.

- **Usage Rule Frequency:** It is possible to identify a small rule usage count when a flow is not created often. At times, an unpopular rule may be meaningful if the rule deals with an essential service in a device. Otherwise, it is necessary to inspect the rule to identify if it is normal and can be entered in the whitelist.

- **Dynamic Port:** A port is dynamically assigned by a service such as FTP. In this case, the flow whitelist is not generated because the flows do not satisfy the degree centrality threshold. Therefore, a rule must be created with "ANY" for the source and destination ports if there are many flows between two nodes after inspecting the remaining flows.

4. Experimental Results

This section presents the results obtained during the preparation, generation and inspection phases of the experiments.

4.1 Phase 1: Preparation

Table 2 shows the results after processing raw traffic and running the locally frequently-used port (LFP) extraction procedure. As seen in the table, the volumes of the flows decreased dramatically compared with the raw traffic flow. In addition, several locally frequently-used ports were obtained when θ_{Unit} and θ_{Final} were defined as 25 and 100, respectively.

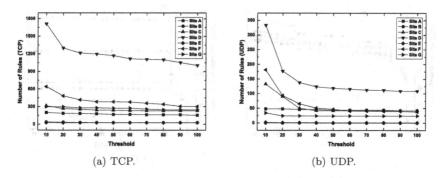

(a) TCP.   (b) UDP.

Figure 8. Numbers of rules for varying degree centrality thresholds.

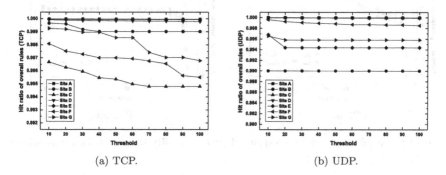

(a) TCP.   (b) UDP.

Figure 9. Hit ratios of overall rules for varying degree centrality thresholds.

4.2   Phase 2: Generation

The experimental results were analyzed in terms of two factors: (i) degree centrality threshold; and (ii) time. Figures 8 and 9 present the numbers of generated rules and the hit ratios of generated rules for varying degree centrality thresholds for the seven sites. When the generated rule number was represented as in Figure 8, it was discovered that the number of rules decreased as the threshold increased. Although the extent of the decrease differed between sites, the numbers of rules for both TCP and UDP sharply decreased when the threshold rose from 10 to 20. Notably, all the hit ratios of the rules were close to one, as shown in Figure 9. The minimum hit ratios were 0.995 and 0.990 for TCP and UDP, respectively. However, unlike the UDP rules, the TCP rules were sensitive to an increasing threshold. The remaining hit ratios could possibly have been in the graylist, which must be inspected by an administrator. In summary, all the results decreased and nearly stabilized at particular values, regardless of the transport protocols and sites; only the amounts of the decreases differed.

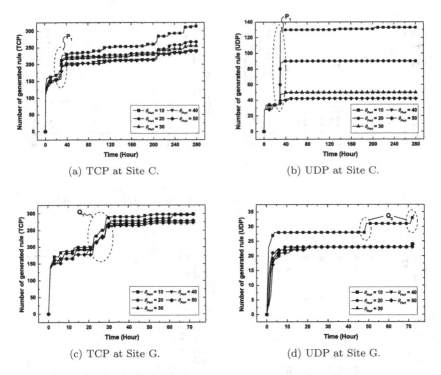

Figure 10. Numbers of rules for varying degree centrality thresholds in a time series.

This enabled a reasonable threshold to be chosen so that a flow whitelist could be created for optimal performance with respect to protocol-specific or site-specific operations. For example, the appropriate threshold for TCP at Site C was 70 whereas it was 30 for UDP. In the case of TCP, the number of rules decreased to between 10 to 50 for the threshold, and the hit ratio noticeably decreased to 70 for the threshold. Thus, 70 was deemed to be the suitable threshold for TCP at Site C. Otherwise, the number of rules for UDP rapidly decreased until a threshold value of 30 was reached; however, the hit ratio did not change significantly over the range of thresholds. Consequently, it was determined that a threshold of 30 would be most appropriate for UDP at Site C.

Figure 10 shows the rule counts for varying thresholds for TCP and UDP at several sites. In particular, Figures 10(a) and 10(b) show that the number of generated rules for every threshold steadily increased, except for the marking period of P_1 at Site C because new services began during the period. On the other hand, during the marking period of Q_1 and Q_2 in Figures 10(c) and 10(d), the reason for a significant increase was different from that for P_1. Specifically, the degree centrality during the period finally exceeded its threshold, causing a rule to be created. In fact, the percentage of flows for UDP (0.06%) was much lower than that for TCP at Site G. Thus, the number of flows for UDP was continuously maintained when the threshold was greater than or equal to 20.

4.3   Phase 3: Inspection

Similar results were observed during the inspection phase regardless of the sites. An interesting result was obtained for Site C, which was much more indicative in terms of what can be discovered via inspection. Figure 11 lists the usage of the rules, including the number of rules used during each hourly interval and the total hours for each rule over 281 hours at Site C. The total number of generated rules was 447. For convenience, each rule was arranged in descending order according to the rule usage frequency. A dot denotes at least one flow that matches the rule at the given time, the top polygonal graph represents the number of rules used in the time interval and the right polygonal graph represents the number of hours during which the rule was used.

- **Flow Whitelist:** As shown in the upper graph of Figure 11, 203 rules (Rule ID 1 to Rule ID 203) were used during all the time intervals; the subsequent 140 rules (Rule ID 204 to Rule ID 343) were frequently used in 89% of the entire timeline. More than 84% of the rules were always active after 30 hours. This was explained in Section 4.2 as being due to new services that began during the period. Therefore, most generated rules were recommended for inclusion in the flow whitelist.

- **Graylist:** All the generated rules may not be included in a flow whitelist. In the experiments, some generated rules were rarely or ever used within one hour. In addition, there were one-way TCP rules between some IP addresses. These rules were determined to be graylist rules. The graylist could be processed without any assistance from a vendor: it was easy to identify unusual rules; moreover, the number of rules was adequate for inspection. Administrators are encouraged to use graylists to investigate SCADA networks and devices.

- **Left Flows:** Analysis revealed 1,062 left flows for TCP and 20 flows for UDP. In the case of TCP, 790 flows (approximately 53%) were identified; they were inferred as a dynamic port and twelve unidirectional TCP flows. Thus, 260 TCP flows and 20 UDP flows remained.

4.4   Discussion

Rules in a flow whitelist have interesting characteristics, correlations and periodicities. As shown at the bottom of Figure 11, a deactivation of Rule Group A and an activation of Rule Group B occurred at hour 209. The rules in the two groups were compared to ascertain the reason for the rule transition. The conclusion was that the transition was due to the service port assigned at the time. Although the two rule groups were both valid, the simultaneous appearance of Rule Groups A and B may have been abnormal. If the

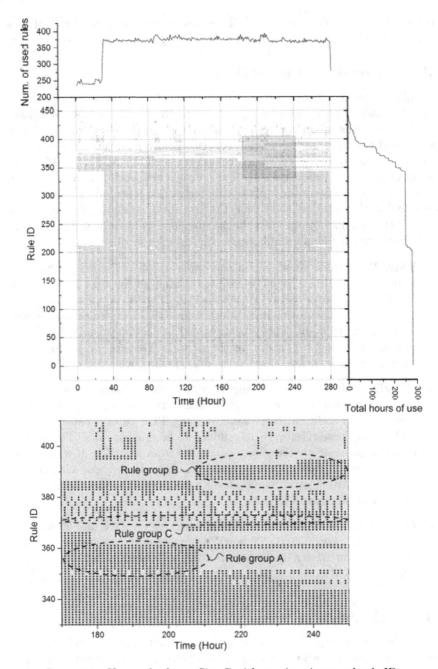

Figure 11. Usage of rules at Site C with varying times and rule IDs.

switchover from Rule Group A to B was sufficiently informative, an intrusion detection system that employs the flow whitelist could be programmed to alert an administrator.

In addition, periodicity was discovered in the flow whitelist. The rules in Rule Group C matched the flows for two hours. If these rules were to relate to an important regular activity (e.g., data backup), the disappearance of matched flows could be reported to an administrator, even if the issues were not security-related.

5. Conclusions

SCADA networks are often interconnected with other networks, including corporate networks and the Internet, greatly increasing the risk of intrusions by malicious entities. Whitelist-based intrusion detection is an attractive network security solution, but flow whitelist extraction from SCADA network traffic is a challenging task. The proposed methodology for creating flow whitelists using degree centrality and locally frequently-used ports addresses the challenges. Experimental results involving seven SCADA systems demonstrate that the methodology generates effective whitelists for deployment in SCADA networks. Indeed, the whitelists can be deployed in a variety of network devices, including switches, firewalls and intrusion detection systems. The approach also supports rule updating because a flow whitelist can indicate the services that have been added or removed by repeatedly updating itself; this enables administrators to easily handle the tasks of flow whitelist extraction and updating. Future research will focus on the deep inspection of SCADA network traffic to address non-disclosure characteristics.

References

[1] R. Barbosa, R. Sadre and A. Pras, A first look into SCADA network traffic, *Proceedings of the IEEE Network Operations and Management Symposium*, pp. 518–521, 2012.

[2] R. Barbosa, R. Sadre and A. Pras, Flow whitelisting in SCADA networks, *International Journal of Critical Infrastructure Protection*, vol. 6(3-4), pp. 150–158, 2013.

[3] L. Freeman, Centrality in social networks: Conceptual clarification, *Social Networks*, vol. 1(3), pp. 215–239, 1978-1979.

[4] Y. Jang, I. Shin, B. Min, J. Seo and M. Yoon, Whitelisting for critical IT-based infrastructure, *IEICE Transactions on Communications*, vol. 96(4), pp. 1070–1074, 2013.

[5] D. Kang, B. Kim, J. Na and K. Jhang, Whitelist generation technique for industrial firewalls in SCADA networks, in *Frontier and Innovation in Future Computing and Communications*, J. Park, A. Zomaya, H. Jeong and M. Obaidat (Eds.), Springer, Dordrecht, The Netherlands, pp. 525–534, 2014.

[6] National Cybersecurity and Communications Integration Center, ICS-CERT Year in Review: Industrial Control Systems Cyber Emergency Response Team, Department of Homeland Security, Washington, DC, 2013.

[7] National Cybersecurity and Communications Integration Center, ICS-CERT Monitor, Department of Homeland Security, Washington, DC, January – April 2014.

[8] A. Sood and R. Enbody, *Targeted Cyber Attacks: Multi-Staged Attacks Driven by Exploits and Malware*, Syngress, Waltham, Massachusetts, 2014.

[9] K. Stouffer, J. Falco and K. Scarfone, Guide to Industrial Control Systems (ICS) Security, NIST Special Publication 800-82, National Institute of Standards and Technology, Gaithersburg, Maryland, 2011.

[10] J. Yun, S. Jeon, K. Kim and W. Kim, Burst-based anomaly detection on the DNP3 protocol, *International Journal of Control and Automation*, vol. 6(2), pp. 313–324, 2013.

Chapter 7

A SYMBOLIC HONEYNET FRAMEWORK FOR SCADA SYSTEM THREAT INTELLIGENCE

Owen Redwood, Joshua Lawrence and Mike Burmester

Abstract   Current SCADA honeypot technologies present attackers with static or pseudo-random data, and are unlikely to entice attackers to use high value or zero-day attacks. This chapter presents a symbolic cyber-physical honeynet framework that addresses the problem, enhances the screening and coalescence of attack events for analysis, provides attack introspection down to the physics level of a SCADA system and enables forensic replays of attacks. The work extends honeynet methodologies with integrated physics simulation and anomaly detection utilizing a symbolic data flow model of system physics. Attacks that trigger anomalies in the physics of a system are captured and organized via a coalescing algorithm for efficient analysis. Experimental results are presented to demonstrate the effectiveness of the approach.

Keywords: SCADA systems, honeypots, threat intelligence, visualization

1. Introduction

Cyber-physical systems are computational systems that monitor and control physical systems; they encompass control systems, sensor-based systems, autonomous systems, robotic systems and more. Cyber-physical systems that control critical infrastructures span across many industries and, depending on their application, may be called supervisory control and data acquisition (SCADA) systems, process control systems, industrial control systems or distributed control systems. These control systems are usually composed of sensors, actuators, communications devices and control processing units such as networked remote telemetry/terminal units (RTUs), programmable logic controllers (PLCs) and intelligent electronic devices (IEDs). While most older control systems were designed to be air gapped, studies show that many current systems are directly or indirectly connected to the Internet [1].

© IFIP International Federation for Information Processing 2015
M. Rice, S. Shenoi (Eds.): Critical Infrastructure Protection IX, IFIP AICT 466, pp. 103–118, 2015.
DOI: 10.1007/978-3-319-26567-4_7

Historically, proprietary SCADA protocols and the complexity of SCADA systems provided some degree of security (albeit through obscurity). However, as SCADA protocols have become increasingly standardized and open, researchers have found increasing numbers of vulnerabilities [20]. Meanwhile, tools such as the Sentient Hyper-Optimized Data Access Network (SHODAN) (www.shodanhq.com), Every Routable IP Project (ERIPP) (eripp.com) and Industrial Risk Assessment Map (IRAM) (www.scadacs.org/iram.html) make Internet-facing SCADA systems easy to track and, sometimes, trivial to exploit. In fact, using these and other tools, researchers have estimated that between 2,000 to 8,000 new SCADA devices are connected directly to the Internet each day [2].

Unfortunately, the anatomy of cyber attacks and the range of potential physical impacts against SCADA systems are poorly understood [7]. Moreover, few solutions are available that simultaneously address both issues.

Honeypots are a promising approach for detecting, analyzing, deflecting and possibly counteracting the unauthorized use of information systems. This is achieved by replicating the behavior of the targeted systems and devices. The degree to which system behavior is replicated by a honeypot leads it to be characterized as a low-interaction or high-interaction device. Honeypots generally have no production value and interactions with these devices are likely to constitute reconnaissance or attack activity; this renders them effective for deployment in networks for the purpose of intrusion detection. Two or more honeypots that are networked together can simulate a network and can be configured such that all activity is monitored and recorded. Interested readers are referred to [6] for a detailed discussion of honeypots.

This chapter describes the Symbolic Cyber-Physical Honeynet (SCyPH) framework, which provides SCADA administrators with a solution that bridges the understanding of cyber attack anatomy and potential physical impacts. The design addresses the three main challenges of honeypot operation: maintenance, attack analysis and attack screening and coalescence [6]. For operators, the end result is greater situational awareness, deep attack introspection and threat intelligence about various types of SCADA system attacks. However, the ultimate goal is to push honeypot development into a new direction and provide a common ground for research in security vulnerabilities and attack impact for critical infrastructures. Only the ROS honeypot [14] presents the ability to detect deeper problems in SCADA systems, enabling the discovery of the objectives and techniques of sophisticated attackers. Modeling the underlying cyber-physical system helps capture a wide range of post-exploitation activities by attackers. Performing anomaly detection on the cyber-physical system model helps filter common automated activities by worms and botnets and focus the analysis on sophisticated attacks. Sophisticated attackers are enticed and kept engaged by using interactive human-machine interfaces that react to attacker changes in a realistic manner.

2. Related Work

Despite significant advances in general honeynet technology, few honeypots are available for cyber-physical systems in general and SCADA systems in particular. In 2004, CISCO's Critical Infrastructure Assurance Group launched the first SCADA honeynet project [16], which extended Honeyd to simulate services for a popular programmable logic controller. While the CISCO project is no longer active, its contributions to fingerprinting banners and honeypot services are still very useful. Two other open-source honeynet projects are currently active: one is the SCADA Honeynet Project launched by Digital Bond [4] in 2010 and the other is Conpot launched by the Honeynet Project [3] in 2013.

The SCADA Honeynet from Digital Bond [4] utilizes two virtual machines, a target virtual machine that simulates a Modicon Quantum programmable logic controller and the Honeywall virtual machine that monitors traffic and activity on the target. The Honeywall virtual machine can be placed in front of an actual programmable logic controller or other control device. Honeywall captures attacks on the target, creates reports, generates alerts and provides other management functions. The provided target simulates a limited-interaction HTTP HMI service, Modbus TCP, FTP, SNMP, VxWorks Debugger and Telnet.

The Conpot honeynet [3] provides virtual programmable logic controller slaves controlled by a master server that simulates a Siemens S7-200 CPU with a CP 443-1 communications processor to handle a large set of industrial control system protocols. By default, Conpot provides low-interaction and supports Modbus TCP and SNMP, but it can be configured to support the BACnet protocol and the Intelligent Platform Management Interface (IPMI). The default virtual slaves in Conpot can publish captured data to the `hpfeeds` system in order to share honeypot data.

Researchers at Harvard and Los Alamos National Laboratory have developed the RobotOS (ROS) honeypot [14], the first true cyber-physical honeypot that utilizes real robotic hardware as the target. The ROS honeypot provides a high-interaction, vulnerable human-machine interface that connects with robotic hardware running ROS. Other closed-source honeypot projects are almost certainly active. For example, in 2013, Trend Micro [21] released data from its three closed-source projects dealing with a water pressure station honeypot, a production programmable logic controller honeypot and a factory temperature control programmable logic controller.

3. SCyPH Framework

This section describes the Symbolic Cyber-Physical Honeynet (SCyPH) framework, including its principal design features and layers.

3.1   Overview

The SCyPH framework can capture exploitation and post-exploitation activities against SCADA human-machine interfaces and programmable logic controllers, respectively, as well as model the resulting physics impacts. The novel honeypot feature is the symbolic simulation of a cyber-physical system to implement anomaly detection and the screening and coalescence of real attacks that succeed in altering the physics of the system. The simulation of the physics of the cyber-physical system allows for the presentation of a high-interaction human-machine interface and emulated programmable logic controllers that interact with the human-machine interface, which ultimately allow attackers to influence the system physics (voltage, current, pressure, etc.). The SCyPH framework incorporates the following design features:

- **Modular Components:** All the components, namely, the anomaly detection engine, interactive human-machine interface and sampling services, are modular. This facilitates crowdsourcing as in the ROS honeynet [14].

- **Human-Machine Interface and Physical Model Coupling:** Human-machine interface interactions are coupled with the simulated physical model. This enables adversarial interactions with the human-machine interface and the sampling services to be logged, simulated and organized depending on how they influence the simulated physical model.

- **Partitioned Layers:** All the layers are strictly partitioned. This provides a clear divide of component responsibilities and facilitates community development of the framework.

3.2   Honeynet Layer

The purpose of the honeynet layer (HL) is to abstract common honeynet technologies that are independent of cyber-physical systems so that the framework can isolate activity in a cyber-physical-centric manner. The composition of the honeynet is flexible – many existing honeynet technologies can coexist with the SCyPH framework inside the honeynet layer. The primary target is the human-machine interface, which ultimately has to be integrated to communicate with the devices in the interaction layer (described below).

Figure 1 presents a general architecture of the SCyPH framework. The framework utilizes anomaly detection on the simulated physics to perform attack screening. Other attack screening and detection mechanisms can be integrated into the framework.

As shown in Figure 1, attacker activity originates from the Internet-exposed human-machine interface (or honeynet), which provides a web-based interface on port 80 (or 8080). For instance, by default, the human-machine interface could present standard web application attack vectors for an adversary to exploit. These include injection attacks (i.e., SQL, operating system commands,

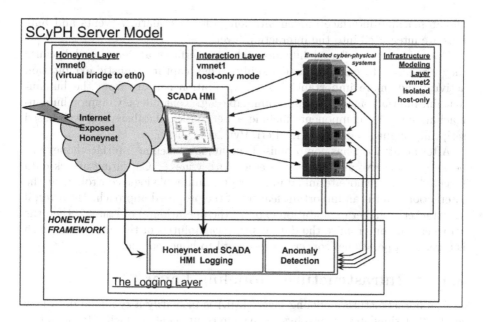

Figure 1. SCyPH architecture.

LDAP and Xpath), broken authentication, session management attacks, cross-site scripting attacks and others, depending on the attack surface of the human-machine interface [15]. Furthermore, services provided by the operating system potentially expose additional attack vectors.

The key requirement for other tools is that data collection and coalescence should be compatible with the logging layer; as described below, the hpfeeds protocol is used for logging. Furthermore, according to the honeypot tool survey presented in [6], it is beneficial to use server-side honeypot tools that have equal or better than good ratings for accuracy of emulation, good ratings for reliability; fair for support, and useful or essential ratings for utility. Specifically Dionea, Glastopf, Kippo and Conpot are recommended for their usefulness, support, reliability and support of hpfeeds. Readers should consult [6] for the ethical and legal issues involved in setting up SCADA or cyber-physical system honeypots.

3.3 Interaction Layer

The interaction layer (IL) facilitates the integration of the human-machine interface and the emulated cyber-physical system. This helps present a believable and highly-interactive human-machine interface for monitoring exploitation and post-exploitation activities. The features and inputs of the human-machine interface directly influence the firing rules of the actors of the process(es) in the interaction layer. The approach is agnostic to the specific human-machine interface implementation. Interface alarms, events and buttons are integrated into the interaction layer.

Open-source, web-based human-machine interfaces are employed because they are easier to configure and modify. They capture realistic exploitation activity and, more importantly, post exploitation activity from the human-machine interface against the programmable logic controllers. Common human-machine interface components include a web server, database and web-based scripting language engine (PHP, Perl, Python or Java).

After an attacker has compromised the human-machine interface honeypot, he/she can observe and directly interact with vmnet1. Capturing attack data targeted at the remote terminal units or programmable logic controllers at the interaction layer is an important feature of the proposed approach. However, if an attacker's further exploitation exposes the operation(s) of vmnet2, then the attacker can compromise the data capture capabilities of the honeynet, which is a general operational concern with regard to honeypots [6].

3.4   Infrastructure Modeling Layer

The infrastructure modeling layer (IML) is primarily a symbolic data flow model that simulates cyber-physical system components to facilitate the interaction of programmable logic controllers with their human-machine interfaces. The programmable logic controllers each need to be integrated with the infrastructure modeling layer simulation.

Similar to a Kahn process network [8, 10], the data flow model in the infrastructure modeling layer defines a process as a set of signals, actors, firing rules and (optionally) one or more sampling service(s) to provide interaction with the human-machine interface.

- A signal φ is an output channel from one actor to the input of another actor. A signal φ comprises a sequence of tokens $x_m, x_{m-1}, \ldots, x_n$.

- An actor α maps input tokens to output tokens. Actors process incoming tokens from input signals in a first-in first-out (FIFO) manner.

- A set of one or more firing rules dictates when an actor α can fire. The token(s) that result from the most recent firing provide the state of the actor. When actor α fires, it consumes input tokens and produces output tokens.

Most tokens are numerical (e.g., voltage, current, pressure); however, exceptions require that tokens be symbolic to support the application of the approach to general cyber-physical systems (e.g., chemical and/or biological mixing).

Formally, an actor α is defined as $\{\varphi_{in}, F, \varphi_{out}, S\}$ where F is a set of firing rules and S is a set of sampling services. An actor for which φ_{in} is null can be seen as a source of tokens if φ_{out} is not null. Likewise, an actor for which φ_{out} is null, but φ_{in} is not null, can be seen as a sink. A set of concurrent actors $\{\alpha_0, \alpha_1, \ldots, \alpha_n\}$ compose a process, which can be extrapolated to mimic a variety of cyber-physical systems.

Theoretically, this approach allows the parallel simulation of continuous, discrete, multirate discrete or even totally ordered discrete time processes through the flexibility provided by the firing rules [8], without having to account for the timing costs of many measurements, conversions, industrial Ethernet latency and signals processing that would be necessary in a formally-modeled Kahn process network. However, this prevents the capture of attacks that target industrial Ethernet latency or signal processing. For ease of implementation, the proposed model does not attempt to meet the execution requirements of a formal Kahn process network [5, 8]. Thus, the model is, at best, a weak Kahn process network.

The operation of actors and their firing rules over signal channels simulate a process over vmnet2. The sampling service S supports the interactions of a remote terminal unit or programmable logic controller with a human-machine interface across vmnet1 (Figure 1). The sampling service is instantiated by the interaction layer and handles the protocol(s) and interval(s) when a human-machine interface samples and/or interacts with the actor. For example, the Modbus, DNP3, MMS and BACnet protocols can be emulated to provide believable interactions with a human-machine interface.

The interaction layer provides the required names, numbers and information (i.e., system names, module identifiers, firmware identifiers, serial numbers, etc.) at initialization time. Optionally, specifications and variables utilized for anomaly detection may be provided by the logging layer at initialization time as well.

Each sampling service is defined as a control protocol between the human-machine interface and programmable logic controllers (or between programmable logic controllers) in the interaction layer. Protocol emulation can have significant engineering and reverse engineering costs because it is necessary to extract the protocol from actual programmable logic controller firmware/kernel images or software and emulate it in a compatible virtualization environment. This facilitates the monitoring of real post-exploitation activity against programmable logic controllers. However, sensors, merging units and other devices have to be simulated in order to integrate an emulated programmable logic controller with the infrastructure modeling layer simulation.

This research uses Conpot as a proxy to capture interactions and traffic with emulated programmable logic controllers. Conpot can be configured to integrate real SCADA hardware; however, the functionality of the hardware would still have to be integrated with the infrastructure modeling layer simulation.

3.5   Logging Layer

The logging layer utilizes anomaly detection in the infrastructure modeling layer physics simulation to filter uninteresting attacks. Data is collected using common honeynet solutions.

Data Collection. Honeynet deployment, administration and capture of network traffic are technical problems that have been addressed [6]. However, the main candidates considered for this task are again tools that use hpfeeds, although this is a choice left to the implementation. The collection of non-network-traffic data (i.e., files and/or processes created or manipulated by attackers) are usually specific to an individual honeypot; however, robust solutions for coalescing this data from a network of honeypots are not yet available.

Anomaly Detection.   Given the state machine in the infrastructure modeling layer and a method for sampling the state of an actor, it is possible to execute a variety of anomaly detection algorithms. The following anomaly detection schemes are currently supported:

- Median absolute deviation

- Grubb's score

- First hour average

- Standard deviation from average

- Standard deviation from moving average

- Mean subtraction cumulation

- Least squares

- Histogram bins

- Kolmogorov-Smirnov test

Data Coalescing.   Anomaly detection is performed on the physics in the infrastructure modeling layer solely for attack screening and detection. Attacks that do not cause anomalies are screened as uninteresting attacks. Attacks that have relevant information from each layer are coalesced into an analysis report (Figure 2). Note that the detection of a physics anomaly serves as a temporal point to coalesce attack data within a time or event window.

The coalescing algorithm is as follows:

- If a new anomaly is detected within a time window δ, then the additional data collected to this point is grouped with the anomaly.

- Else, if there are one or more active connections from the Internet to the honeypot over the eth0 gateway, then all the data is highlighted as being related to the anomaly.

- Else, if no active Internet connections exist at the time of the anomaly, then a search is conducted for the connections spawned by files created by attackers (these could be due to an automated worm or delayed payload).

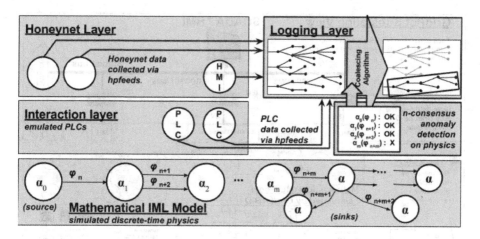

Figure 2. Anomaly detection in the infrastructure modeling layer.

4. GridPot

An electric grid was selected to demonstrate the SCyPH framework due to its mission-critical nature, widespread adoption of insecure automation protocols [9, 13, 17, 19] and the potentially severe consequences of attacks. Cyber attack effects and malware can persist in an electric grid long after the initial attack, exacerbating the fact that the "replacement of large transformers essential to the reliable operation of the grid may require twenty months or longer" [18].

The electric industry is moving to the IEC 61850 standard for automating the control of remote substations in the power grid. IEC 61850 incorporates numerous protocols for substation automation that run over a substation LAN or even a regional WAN. Also, IEC 61850 has communications protocols designed for intelligent electronic devices to communicate with other intelligent electronic devices as well as human-machine interfaces.

This section illustrates the applicability of the SCyPH framework using a sample implementation that simulates the IEC 61850 communications protocols as described in Figure 3. The section discusses the experiment design, infrastructure modeling, IEC 61850 protocol emulation, anomaly detection and logging mechanisms. However, details about the honeynet layer and human-machine interface used in the experiments are not provided for reasons of sensitivity.

4.1 IEC 61850

Most utility communications standards, such as IEC 61850, have largely restricted access to source code or documentation and usually assume domain-specific knowledge, making the subject largely inaccessible to outsiders (including security researchers and software developers). Intelligent electronic

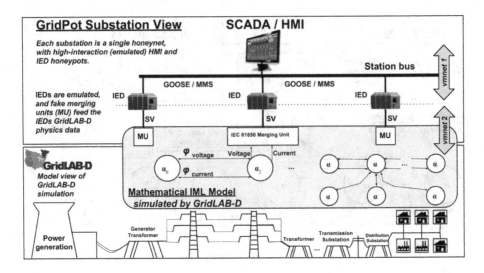

Figure 3. GridPot implementation.

devices are important components in electric power grids; they are embedded microprocessor-based controllers that send and receive data and control commands to/from external sources. These devices are similar to desktop computers (and may even run Linux-based operating systems), but they often contain special digital logic chips for performing domain-specific tasks such as voltage measurement and power regulation. Example intelligent electronic devices are circuit breaker controllers, smart meters, voltage regulators and relay devices [11].

Many intelligent electronic devices are legacy components that were not developed under the IEC 61850 standard; thus, they are often used in conjunction with an "IEC 61850 wrapper" device [11]. Regardless, intelligent electronic devices directly or indirectly interface with a substation (or simply station) bus (as shown in Figure 3) and are controlled by a human-machine interface. The human-machine interface may be remotely accessed by an operator via a secure gateway or a virtual private network. Electric grids comprise numerous distributed substations and the role of IEC 61850 is to implement substation automation. Interested readers are referred to [11] for details about the IEC 61850 standard and to [17] for a discussion of IEC-61850-specific attacks.

4.2 Experiment Design

The experiment simulated the power flow of an electric grid using GridLAB-D from Pacific Northwest National Laboratory, which comprises multiple substations and emulates the IEC 61850 digital communications protocol by extending Conpot as shown in Figure 3. The voltages and currents at major components across the electric grid are simulated in the infrastructure modeling layer. A number of substation honeynets were constructed, each tied in with the overall infrastructure modeling layer for the entire electric grid. Each substation honeynet comprised emulated intelligent electronic devices that interacted with each other and the human-machine interface over a substation bus.

The goal of the experiment was to capture cyber attack activities against the emulated IEC 61850 protocols and understand how they affect the underlying simulated physical model. The honeynets presented to attackers represented transmission and distributional substations; however, every actor in the grid was simulated all the way upstream to the power generators.

4.3 Infrastructure Modeling

The voltage and current of the power flow between each actor was modeled. The Newton-Raphson power flow solver algorithm was used to solve the power flow during each iteration of the simulation. Figure 3 shows the GridPot implementation, including the architectures of the interaction and infrastructure modeling layers. As shown the figure, the channels are bidirectional according to the physics of the electric grid. A change in the voltage of a middle node can cause an influx in the electric grid and send voltage drops and currents in all directions before stabilizing. Thus, for each actor, a bidirectional voltage channel $\varphi_{voltage}$ and a bidirectional current channel $\varphi_{current}$ were modeled.

Generally, the firing rules for each actor regulate the voltage and current of the power flow and the opening and closing of switches and relays, and also adjust the power flow to react to system feedback from other actors. The firing rule specifications differ from actor to actor.

To support interactions between the infrastructure modeling layer actors and the human-machine interface, the MMS, GOOSE and Modbus protocols in IEC 61850 were implemented as sampling services. The emulation of these protocols requires the engineering and reverse engineering of intelligent electronic device binaries so that the real software logic handles the protocol implementations. MMS was used to provide real-time measurements from the intelligent electronic devices to the human-machine interface. GOOSE communications were emulated for time synchronization, intelligent electronic device configuration and status changes. The emulated GOOSE communications directly influenced the firing rules of the individual actors. This facilitated the simulation and analysis of denial, disruption, destruction and degradation of service attacks against the electric grid by sophisticated adversaries. A sample intelligent electronic device switch based on `rapid61850` may be downloaded from `gridpot.org`. The experimental system will implement additional IEC 61850 protocols in the future.

4.4 Logging and Anomaly Detection

The SCyPH framework employs a library of anomaly detection algorithms supported by the ETSY Skyline Project (`github.com/etsy/skyline`). The algorithms do not require manual fine tuning or static assignment of thresholds.

Each data point in a data series is assessed by all the selected anomaly detectors; if any anomaly is detected, a consensus vote of the detectors determines whether or not an anomaly is indicated. The consensus is configurable and can range from requiring just one detector to requiring all the detectors to agree that a data point is, in fact, anomalous. The convenient simulation data export features of GridLAB-D reduce the training time of the anomaly detectors. Indeed, the SCyPH framework is launched by feeding in months' or years' worth of baseline data into the anomaly detection engine, which takes only seconds to minutes to be processed. However, the training lead time ultimately depends on the grid architecture and configuration of GridLAB-D.

Experiments revealed that the minimum window of baseline data for reliable anomaly detection is in the order of hours, not months or years. Furthermore, incorporating additional factors in the simulation (e.g., weather) are also facilitated by GridLAB-D. However, weather, loads and other simulation factors can affect the false-positive and false-negative alarm rates.

Upon detecting an anomaly, the coalescing algorithm processes the recent data (within the $t - \delta$ time period) from the honeynet, interaction and infrastructure modeling layers. It then attempts to determine the point of origin in the network traffic and/or honeypot files to provide a rough event chain that shows how the cyber-physical anomaly was triggered.

Typically honeypots utilize intrusion detection systems to detect attacks. Attacks that trigger anomalies in the GridLAB-D simulation, but do not raise any intrusion flags, are potentially zero-day attacks that can be highlighted for prioritized analysis.

4.5 Experimental Results

A switching attack [12] against the GOOSE/MMS protocols was executed to demonstrate the analysis capabilities of GridPot. An electric grid based on the IEEE 13-node test feeder model was represented in GridLAB-D. Malware was written to exploit the GOOSE/MMS vulnerabilities presented in [19]; the malware caused the status of an intelligent electronic device switch in a substation to be flipped. Figure 4 demonstrates the attack. Note that the malware is not shared on `gridpot.org` as it can potentially impact any IEC-61850-based intelligent electronic device switch [17].

Details about the human-machine interface software used in the experiment are not presented so that the honeypot is not made trivially fingerprintable by attackers. However, a vulnerability in the default configuration of the human-machine interface was exploited to gain code execution rights. The human-machine interface vendor has been notified about this vulnerability. In any case, the second stage of the experimental attack downloaded the GOOSE/MMS malware and executed it.

The malware was designed to send GOOSE/MMS messages over the appropriate interface to the control network in order to affect the target switch. Figure 5 illustrates the real-time physics impact displayed by the system analytics during the attack. Cyber and control events are represented as vertical lines;

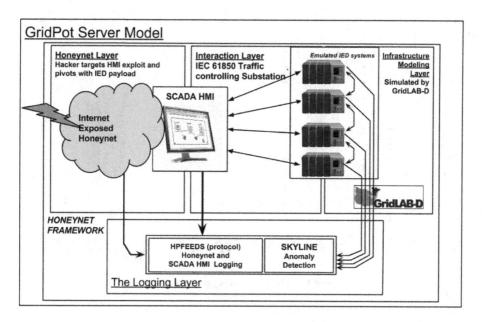

Figure 4. GridPot architecture and experimental attack.

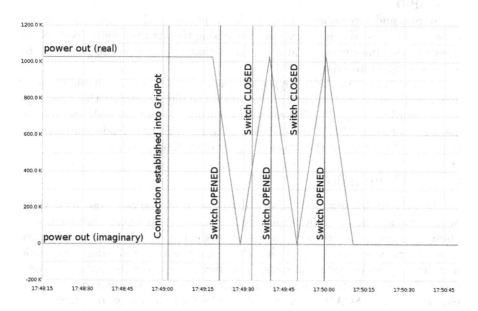

Figure 5. Attack analysis presented by GridPot.

the original image has only been modified by adding text labels for explanatory purposes. The power input and power output parameters were captured for anomaly detection at the switch; however, the physics analysis can be triv-

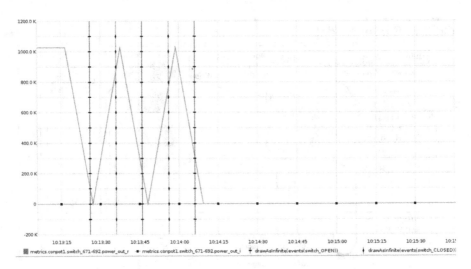

Figure 6. Dynamic analysis capability.

ially extended to any of the numerical parameters of the objects supported by GridLAB-D.

Samples and screenshots of the packet captures of the attack are also not presented because this is equivalent to releasing the malware source code itself. However, this information and other important information are presented to users to support analysis.

New files added to the honeypot are presented to users to enable them to dynamically analyze the malware to confirm the physics impact that was orig- inally recorded. Figure 6 illustrates this feature. Note that malware may be dangerous or impossible to test on real hardware. Interested readers are referred to [12] for details about the physics impact of switching attacks.

5.   Conclusions

The SCyPH framework is designed to entice attackers to use high value or zero-day attacks, thereby helping collect novel threat intelligence for cyber- physical systems. In particular, the framework extends honeynet methodologies with integrated physics simulation and anomaly detection utilizing a symbolic data flow model of system physics. This facilitates the screening and coales- cence of attack events for analysis, provides attack introspection down to the physics level of a SCADA system and enables forensic replays of attacks. Ex- perimental results demonstrate the effectiveness of the approach.

Future research will augment GridPot to be deployable by MHN and to sup- port forensic replays of honeypot events. Additional intelligent electronic de- vices and human-machine interfaces will also be emulated to extend the SCyPH framework. Finally, efforts will be undertaken to extend the framework with a sandbox to support malware testing and analysis.

Acknowledgement

This research was partially supported by NSF Grant Nos. DUE 1241525, CNS 1347113 and DGE 1538850.

References

[1] R. Bodenheim, J. Butts, S. Dunlap and B. Mullins, Evaluation of the ability of the Shodan search engine to identify Internet-facing industrial control devices, *International Journal of Critical Infrastructure Protection*, vol. 7(2), pp. 114–123, 2014.

[2] E. Byres, Project SHINE: 1,000,000 Internet-Connected SCADA and ICS Systems and Counting, Tofino Security, Lantzville, Canada, 2013.

[3] Conpot Development Team, Conpot: ICS/SCADA Honeypot (`conpot. org`), 2013.

[4] Digital Bond, SCADA Honeynet, Sunrise, Florida (`www.digitalbond. com/tools/scada-honeynet`), 2015.

[5] M. Geilen and T. Basten, Requirements on the execution of Kahn process networks, *Proceedings of the Twelfth European Conference on Programming*, pp. 319–334, 2003.

[6] K. Gorzelak, T. Grudziecki, P. Jacewicz, P. Jaroszewski, L. Juszczyk and P. Kijewski, Proactive Detection of Network Security Incidents, European Union Agency for Network and Information Security, Heraklion, Greece, 2011.

[7] N. Hadjsaid, C. Tranchita, B. Rozel, M. Viziteu and R. Caire, Modeling cyber and physical interdependencies – Application in ICT and power grids, *Proceedings of the IEEE Power Engineering Society Power Systems Conference and Exposition*, 2009.

[8] G. Kahn, The semantics of a simple language for parallel programming, *Proceedings of the IFIP Congress*, pp. 471–475, 1974.

[9] E. Knapp and J. Langill, *Industrial Network Security: Securing Critical Infrastructure Networks for Smart Grid, SCADA and Other Industrial Control Systems*, Syngress, Waltham, Massachusetts, 2015.

[10] E. Lee and T. Parks, Dataflow process networks, *Proceedings of the IEEE*, vol. 83(5), pp. 773–801, 1995.

[11] Y. Liang and R. Campbell, Understanding and Simulating the IEC 61850 Standard, Technical Report UIUCDCS-R-2008-2967, Department of Computer Science, University of Illinois at Urbana-Champaign, Urbana, Illinois, 2008.

[12] S. Liu, S. Mashayekh, D. Kundur, T. Zourntos and K. Butler-Purry, A framework for modeling cyber-physical switching attacks in the smart grid, *IEEE Transactions on Emerging Topics in Computing*, vol. 1(2), pp. 273–285, 2014.

[13] P. Maynard, K. McLaughlin and B. Haberler, Towards understanding man-in-the-middle attacks on IEC 60870-5-104 SCADA networks, *Proceedings of the Second International Symposium on ICS and SCADA Cyber Security Research*, pp. 30–42, 2014.

[14] J. McClean, C. Stull, C. Farrar and D. Mascarenas, A preliminary cyber-physical security assessment of the Robot Operating System (ROS), *Proceedings of the SPIE, Unmanned Systems Technology XV*, vol. 8741, 2013.

[15] Open Web Application Security Project (OWASP), OWASP Top 10 – 2013: The Ten Most Critical Web Application Security Risks (www.owasp.org/index.php/Top_10_2013-Top_10), 2013.

[16] V. Pothamsetty and M. Franz, SCADA HoneyNet Project: Building Honeypots for Industrial Networks, Critical Infrastructure Assurance Group, Cisco Systems, San Jose, California (scadahoneynet.sourceforge.net), 2005.

[17] M. Rashid, S. Yussof, Y. Yusoff and R. Ismail, A review of security attacks on IEC 61850 substation automation system networks, *Proceedings of the International Conference on Information Technology and Multimedia*, pp. 5–10, 2014.

[18] Staff of E. Markey and H. Waxman, Electric Grid Vulnerability: Industry Responses Reveal Security Gaps, U.S. House of Representatives, Washington, DC, 2013.

[19] A. Timorin, SCADA deep inside, presented at the *Balkan Computer Congress*, 2014.

[20] S. Wade, SCADA Honeynets: The Attractiveness of Honeypots as Critical Infrastructure Security Tools for the Detection and Analysis of Advanced Threats, M.S. Thesis, Department of Electrical and Computer Engineering, Iowa State University, Ames, Iowa, 2011.

[21] K. Wilhoit, Who's Really Attacking Your ICS Equipment? Research Paper, Trend Micro, Irving, Texas, 2013.

Chapter 8

ENHANCING A VIRTUAL SCADA LABORATORY USING SIMULINK

Zach Thornton and Thomas Morris

Abstract   This chapter describes a virtual supervisory control and data acquisition (SCADA) security laboratory and the improvements made using Simulink. The laboratory was initially constructed using virtual devices written in Python that simulate industrial processes, emulate control system ladder logic functionality and utilize control system communications protocols. However, given the limitations of Python programs with regard to modeling industrial processes, an improved model was constructed using the Simulink modeling environment. Custom and commercially-available human-machine interfaces used in real-world SCADA environments were deployed in the new laboratory. In addition, various attacks were developed and implemented against the virtual SCADA system. The behavior of the improved laboratory and its earlier version are compared against the physical system after which both were modeled.

Keywords: SCADA laboratory, virtualization, Simulink

1.   Introduction

Industrial control systems, including supervisory control and data acquisition (SCADA) systems, are essential components of critical infrastructure assets such as electric power grids, oil and gas pipelines, chemical processing facilities, water treatment and supply systems, and transportation systems. Cyber threats – and actual attacks – targeting SCADA systems are well documented, making it imperative to design and implement sophisticated defensive techniques and countermeasures [10].

Fundamental risks in SCADA systems can be identified by researching attack patterns, attack vectors and attack impact. Traditionally, these research efforts have engaged testbeds that incorporate scaled physical models and the accompanying hardware, software and information and communications technologies to realize complete cyber-physical systems. However, these testbeds

© IFIP International Federation for Information Processing 2015
M. Rice, S. Shenoi (Eds.): Critical Infrastructure Protection IX, IFIP AICT 466, pp. 119–133, 2015.
DOI: 10.1007/978-3-319-26567-4_8

present two limitations to researchers. First, only researchers with hands-on access to a testbed can engage in SCADA intrusion studies. Second, a testbed is typically expensive, difficult to expand and difficult to maintain.

A virtual SCADA laboratory was developed to help address these limitations. The laboratory was designed to be portable, distributable and expandable. It closely models and communicates with commercial SCADA products, and executes in a virtual computing environment. However, the physical process model, initially a curve-fit of a laboratory process, did not adequately capture the real-world process. This chapter describes the original laboratory as well as recent improvements that employ Simulink to model physical processes.

This research has two main contributions. The first is the detailed workings of a virtual laboratory that is designed for SCADA security research. The second contribution is the integration of Simulink in the testbed to model physical processes with high fidelity.

2.　　Related Work

Most modern industrial processes in sectors such as electricity, oil and gas, water, transportation and chemicals are controlled by SCADA systems. These systems incorporate numerous components that can be broken down into four major categories. At the lowest level are sensors and actuators. Sensors include meters, gauges, calipers and transmitters; they are transducers that convert physical phenomena into electrical signals. Actuators, such as pumps/compressors, valves and motors, receive control signals and manipulate physical processes; thus, they are controllers themselves. The second level comprises distributed controllers, which include programmable logic controllers (PLCs), programmable automation controllers (PACs) and intelligent electronic devices (IEDs). Special-purpose computer systems interface with sensors, implement custom control logic and control actuators based on the control logic and system state. Distributed controllers also include network communications interfaces that connect to upstream systems, including the higher supervisory control layer and human-machine interfaces. The third level is the supervisory control layer, which stores process data, implements system-level control schemes and manages the distributed controllers. At the highest level reside the human-machine interfaces that enable human operators to monitor and control physical processes.

Morris et al. [9] describe a typical small-scale research environment that uses commercial-available equipment to model industrial processes and control systems. The laboratory testbed comprises seven systems: a gas pipeline, storage tank, water tower, industrial blower, assembly line conveyor, steel rolling process and chemical mixing system. Two of the physical systems, the gas pipeline and storage tank, were used as the basis for the virtual systems described in this chapter. Figure 1 shows images of the physical systems and human-machine interface screens in the laboratory.

The Idaho National Laboratory (INL) National SCADA Testbed is a research facility that is designed to evaluate control systems representative of

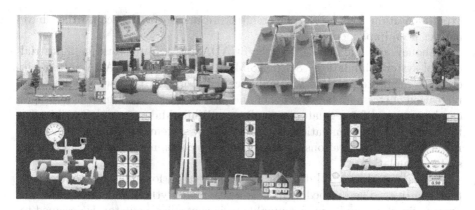

Figure 1. Laboratory systems and human-machine interfaces.

those used in the critical energy infrastructure [6]. Idaho National Laboratory's 890-square-mile Critical Infrastructure Test Range is designed to accurately model physical systems. The test range incorporates industrial-scale sensors, actuators, automation systems, human-machine interfaces and more.

Sandia National Laboratory's National Supervisory Control and Data Acquisition Testbed is sponsored by the Department of Energy's Office of Electricity Delivery and Energy Reliability. Like the Idaho National Laboratory facilities, the Sandia testbed is designed to research the effects of cyber attacks. The testbed incorporates a real power generation system and power loads to analyze the impacts of cyber attacks on power grid components. Current activities include applying autonomous agents in SCADA systems, creating novel cryptographic security mechanisms and conducting system assessments and red-teaming [12].

Hahn et al. [4] describe an experimental testbed that models two electric substations connected to a control center. The testbed incorporates commercial human-machine interfaces, a soft remote terminal unit and physical overprotection relays and autotransformers [4].

While the four laboratory testbeds described above have numerous research applications, they are not easily portable, distributable or expandable. This significantly limits the number of individuals or groups that could use these testbeds for education, training and research activities.

Genge et al. [3] have proposed a framework based on Emulab and Simulink to recreate cyber components and physical processes when conducting security analyses of industrial control networks. The underlying architecture strikes a balance between experiments that consist entirely of physical components as in [2] and experiments that are based entirely on simulated components. Genge and colleagues also list several functionalities required to conduct cyber-physical experiments. The list includes supporting a wide range of physical processes, real malware and SCADA software, high fidelity cyber/physical layers and typical industrial control network components. However, the SCADA experimentation framework and architecture are notional because they have not yet been implemented.

Mahoney and Gandhi [7] describe SCADASim, a framework for industrial control system simulation. SCADASiM simulates legacy SCADA systems in order to facilitate regulatory compliance monitoring. It allows for the rapid recreation of messages between cyber and physical systems so that the messages can be analyzed for regulatory compliance. While Mahoney and Gandhi refer to a control system simulation of a water supply system, their paper focuses on monitoring communications for compliance purposes, not on industrial control system simulation.

Reeves and Morris [11] describe a virtual testbed for industrial control system security. The testbed, which is written in Python and incorporates a process simulator and a programmable logic controller emulator, is designed to be interoperable with commercial industrial control equipment. The testbed implements realistic communications protocols and closely approximates programmable logic controller programming functionality and the physical behavior of the systems described in [9]. The testbed of Reeves and Morris served as the foundation of the work described in this chapter.

Simulators for programmable logic controllers and physical processes are available from Rockwell Automation, Mathworks Simulink, MHJ Software, Modellica and other vendors. These simulators have good modeling capabilities in their respective fields. However, they are not designed for SCADA system modeling and would require custom tools, such as those described in this chapter, to create a comprehensive industrial control system testbed.

This chapter describes a laboratory testbed that combines the benefits of a physical system and simulators. It closely models the behavior of real systems and is easily expandable; although it is designed for SCADA system modeling, it can incorporate other simulators. The laboratory testbed also facilitates the integration of open-source tools and commercial software, simplifying future enhancements.

3.   SCADA Laboratory Overview

The virtual laboratory described in this chapter incorporates three of the four components described in the previous section: (i) a gas pipeline simulation with sensors and actuators; (ii) a programmable logic controller simulation; and (iii) a human-machine interface. Also included are attack generation and attack detection systems. Each laboratory component is run on a separate virtual machine (VM). This makes maintenance of the systems much easier – when errors occur, the system can easily be restored to its previous working state. It also means that a virtual network can be utilized across the virtual machines. Thus, all traffic between the virtual machines is real network traffic that can be logged, disrupted and modified as in a physical system.

3.1   Process Simulation

Physical process simulation is the fundamental component of the laboratory. In a real-world environment, the process is typically a physical/chemical/mechanical system that has to be measured and controlled. The process is usually described in terms of high-order differential equations.

In the case of the gas pipeline simulation, the components modeled included a gas compressor and a solenoid release valve. Four scenarios were considered for pressure changes to the system:

1. If the gas compressor is operating and the valve is closed, then the pressure will rise indefinitely.

2. If the gas compressor is not operating and the valve is open, then the pressure will fall until it reaches zero.

3. If the gas compressor is operating and the valve is open, then the pressure will rise to an equilibrium pressure.

4. If the gas compressor is not operating and the valve is closed, then the pressure will remain constant.

The simulations employ a curve-fitted model described by Morris et al. [9]. The first two scenarios are modeled using the quadratic equations:

$$p = 2.0052t^2 \tag{1}$$

$$p = 0.098t^2 - 4.439t + 49.83 \tag{2}$$

where t is the time and p is the pressure.

The third scenario is modeled using a piecewise model such that the pressure converges to an equilibrium value of about 7.8 psi. This value was discovered empirically for the system described in [2]. The following equation describes the response as the pressure rises to 7.8 psi:

$$p = -0.0210857t^2 + 0.77319t + 0.151637 \tag{3}$$

The following equation describes the response after the pressure exceeds 7.8 psi:

$$p = 7.3 + \mathbf{rand}(-0.02, 0.01) \tag{4}$$

where **rand** is a Python function that generates a uniform random number between the values −0.02 and 0.01.

In the fourth scenario, the pressure is constant.

These equations are implemented in a Python script and are executed as a separate process that runs continuously. The process receives updated commands for the actuators from the virtual controller and sends updates about the current state to the controller.

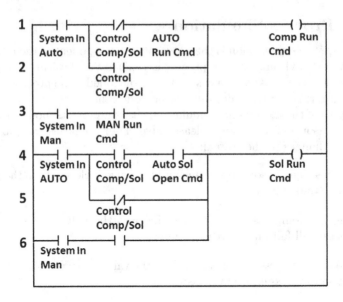

Figure 2. Ladder logic program.

3.2   Programmable Logic Controller Simulation

A central part of the laboratory is the simulation of programmable logic controller hardware and software. In a real-world system, a typical programmable logic controller is programmed to perform four steps in an infinite loop: read inputs, analyze current state, calculate responses and write outputs. This process is captured by the controller simulation. The responses are written to a set of output registers, which are converted to analog signals and sent to actuators.

Almost all programmable logic controllers are programmed using ladder logic. The programming paradigm is so named because each individual program resembles a ladder with one or more rungs. Figure 2 shows a ladder logic program used in the SCADA laboratory [9].

The virtual programmable logic controller devices (VDEVs) in the laboratory simulate the ladder logic programs in [2]. The virtual programmable logic controller devices emulate the gas pipeline process as closely as possible within the confines of Python programming. Each data read, calculation and output setting takes place sequentially, corresponding to each successive ladder logic rung (top to bottom). Figure 3 shows the emulation of the ladder logic program in Figure 2.

The virtual programmable logic controller devices communicate with the process simulator by emulating the analog and digital communications received from the sensors and actuators. The responses are calculated and sent back to the process simulator. The JavaScript Object Notation (JSON) is used to interface with the process simulator. This was chosen for reasons of simplicity and debugging purposes [11].

```
## Ladder Logic: Set compressor and
## solenoid open or closed
Points['CompRunCmd'].set(False)
if points['SystemInAUTO'].get():
  if (points['AUTOCompRunCmd']get() and
      not points['ControlComp/Sol'].get()):
    points['CompRunCmd'].set(True)
  elif points['ControlComp/Sol']get():
    points['CompRunCmd'].set(True)
if (points['SystemInMAN'].get() and
    points['ManCompRunCmd'].get()):
  points['CompRunCmd'].set(True)

points['SolOpenCmd'].set(False)
if points['SystemInAUTO'].get():
  if (points['AUTOSolOpenCmd'].get() and
  points['ControlComp/Sol'].get():
    points['SolOpenCmd'].set(True)
  elif not points['ControlComp/Sol'].get():
    points['SolOpenCmd'].set(True)
if (points['SystemInMAN'].get() and
points['MANSolOpenCmd'].get()):
  points['SolOpenCmd'].set(True)
```

Figure 3. Ladder logic emulation.

The virtual programmable logic controller devices communicate with other virtual devices via Modbus/TCP by using the modbus-tk Python library. This enables the virtual programmable logic controller devices to communicate with external devices such as physical programmable logic controllers and human-machine interfaces using a standard SCADA communications protocol. It also enables researchers and students to route, view, capture and analyze traffic as in a real SCADA system. The Modbus/TCP traffic in the simulation is indistinguishable from Modbus traffic in real SCADA devices. This was demonstrated by using the Snort intrusion detection system to capture all the Modbus traffic between a virtual programmable logic controller device and an external SCADA device such as a human-machine interface. Because Snort has pre-configured rules for detecting various communications protocols, including Modbus/TCP, an instance of Snort was executed and configured to capture all Modbus/TCP traffic.

Figure 4 shows an entry in the Snort system log. The first line shows that an event was logged according to the Modbus/TCP response detected rule. The time, date, IP addresses and TCP information pertaining to the Modbus/TCP transaction are also provided. The figure shows that Snort sees the traffic from the virtual programmable logic controller device to the human-machine interface as typical Modbus/TCP traffic.

```
Snort IDS: Modbus TCP - Response Detected [**]
[Classification: Not Suspicious Traffic] [Priority: 1]
06/09-11:08:30.265212 00:0C:29:1E:3B:A6 -> 00:0C:29:90:D1:3F
type:0x800 len 0x4C
10.128.0.1:502 -> 10.128.0.4:50983 TCP TTL:64 TOS:0x0 ID:20393
IpLen:20 DgmLen:62 DF
***AP*** Seq: 0x5C15A47A Win: 0xE3 TcpLen: 32
TCP Options (3) => NOP NOP TS: 36095 435179
```

Figure 4. Snort log entry.

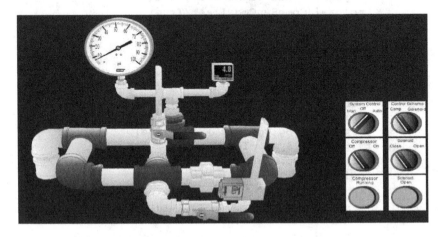

Figure 5. GE iFix human-machine interface.

3.3   Human-Machine Interface

Human-machine interfaces constitute the third main type of component in the laboratory. A human-machine interface is needed by a human operator of an industrial control system to visualize the changing process and interface with the control system. Two human-machine interfaces are incorporated in the laboratory. The first is a GE iFix human-machine interface, which is identical to the gas pipeline interface described in [9]. Figure 5 shows an image of the gas pipeline human-machine interface screen.

The GE iFix human-machine interface is a widely-used SCADA product. However, because the software is proprietary and not easily distributable, a second human-machine interface was developed using the Python TkInter library. Figure 6 shows an image of the Python TkInter human-machine interface screen.

The laboratory configuration enables commercial and custom human-machine interfaces to be ported to the laboratory and tested for vulnerabilities. This enables research on human-machine interface vulnerabilities as in [8] to be conducted without the need to access a physical SCADA laboratory.

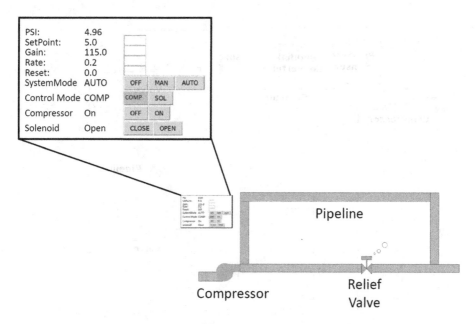

Figure 6. Python `TkInter` human-machine interface.

4.   SCADA Laboratory Enhancements

A real-world process system such as a gas pipeline is typically a complex physical/chemical/mechanical system that has to be measured and controlled. The interrelationships of pressure, temperature, velocity and density of the fluid in the pipeline are approximated by a set of high-order differential equations While these equations are often approximated for computation and simulation, it is clear that the simple quadratic equations presented above are inadequate to study the complex behavior of a pipeline during a cyber attack. Although the differential equations could be programmed using Python and the complex interactions of the fluid with mechanical devices such as compressors and valves could be simulated, native Python is not designed to support such complex mathematics. Also, having to hand code the equations for each new simulation is an unnecessary step, especially if the equations are already available.

Simulink was chosen as the process modeling tool to enhance the existing laboratory due to its popularity as an engineering design and research tool. The SimHydraulics package provided by Simulink offers libraries for modeling and simulating hydraulic systems, including components such as compressors, pumps, valves, actuators and pipelines. Not only does SimHydraulics include pre-configured models of these components, but it also supports the use of custom components via the Simscape language [2].

Initially, a system very similar to the one described in [9] was constructed in Simulink. A simple system comprising a compressor, valve, pipeline and fluid was incorporated. (In the physical system, the fluid is air and its source

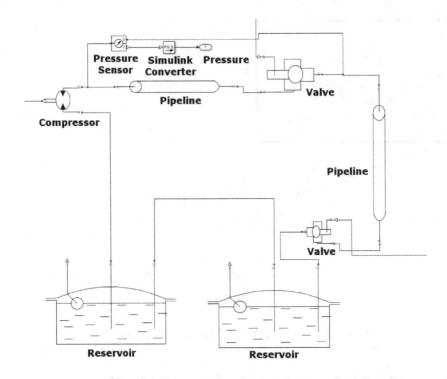

Figure 7.   Initial Simulink design.

is a compressor; however, because Simulink requires a source and an open air supply is not an option, a reservoir of non-descript fluid was chosen as the fluid source.) A valve was also positioned between the valve controlled by the virtual programmable logic controller device and the return reservoir; this valve simulates the load and changes position at least once a second.

Figure 7 shows the initial design of the pipeline system in Simulink. Not pictured in the figure are the conversions from physical signals to Simulink signals, the angular velocity source for the motor and other Simulink components. Each component was modeled in terms of its properties.

Table 1.   Hydraulic motor properties.

Motor Displacement	$5\,\text{in}^3/\text{rev}$
Volumetric Efficiency	0.92
Total Efficiency	0.8
Nominal Pressure	$100\,\text{psi}$
Nominal Angular Velocity	$188\,\text{rpm}$
Nominal Kinematic Viscosity	$18\,\text{cSt}$

As an example, Table 1 lists the properties of the hydraulic motor. The motor displacement in the table indicates the volume of fluid displaced per revolution. The volumetric efficiency is the percentage of fluid that flows out of the compressor. The total efficiency is the volumetric efficiency taking into account the mechanical efficiency of the compressor. The nominal pressure, nominal angular velocity and nominal kinematic viscosity are the expected operating conditions of the compressor.

Because the states of the compressor and valve are controlled by virtual programmable logic controller devices, the Simulink model must communicate with the virtual programmable logic controller devices. Simulink also contains libraries for communicating via UDP packets.

Rate limiters and zero-order holds ensure that the UDP transmission rate and the data transmission rate in the actual pipeline are compatible. The ASCII value conversions transform the commands received from the virtual programmable logic controller devices to binary values for opening/closing the valve and turning the compressor on/off. Each of the three values (compressor, valve and pressure) from the simulation is sent to a different UDP port and each command from a virtual programmable logic controller device is received on a different UDP port. As discussed earlier, the virtual programmable logic controller devices communicate with the process simulator by sending JSON attribute-value pairs. To address the difficulty involved in processing text in Simulink, an interface was written in Python to operate between the virtual programmable logic controller devices and the Simulink model. The interface receives JSON attribute-value pairs, strips the plaintext attribute portion and sends each command from a virtual programmable logic controller device to the appropriate UDP port. It also receives each individual value sent from Simulink, formats the values to be sent as an attribute-value paired UDP packet and sends the packet to a virtual programmable logic controller device.

5.   Experimental Results

This section demonstrates the fidelity of the simulation by comparing the Python and Simulink simulations against the physical model. Normal behavior as well as startup and attack behaviors are compared and contrasted.

5.1   Normal Operation

Figures 8, 9 and 10 show the physical, Python and Simulink systems operating under normal conditions. The setpoints for all three systems are 15 psi, the time range is close to four minutes and the pressure scale is 0–25 psi. The dashed line represents the 15 psi setpoint.

As can be seen, the pressure changes in the Simulink simulation resemble those in the physical system much more closely than the Python simulation. While the Python simulation can be modified to resemble the physical model more closely, this would require the modification of the system equations described above. In the Simulink model, a change to the compressor speed, compressor efficiency, valve size or other physical property can alter the pressure response of the system.

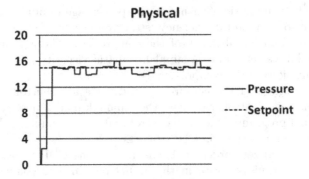

Figure 8.   Physical system (normal operation).

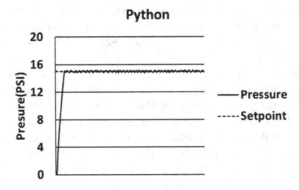

Figure 9.   Python system (normal operation).

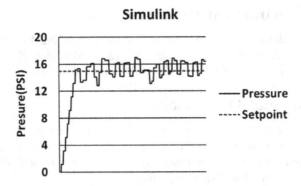

Figure 10.   Simulink system (normal operation).

5.2   Startup Operation

Figure 11 shows the system behavior at startup. As seen in the figure, the stair-step increase and the initial overshoot of the physical model are more closely replicated by the Simulink model than by the Python model.

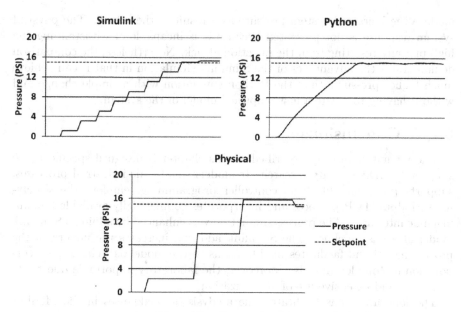

Figure 11. System startup.

5.3 Attack Operation

Command injection attacks can be used by malicious entities to adjust the settings in a SCADA system. One way to implement such an attack is to impersonate a SCADA client, send a command to the server and modify settings such as the setpoint, control (PID) parameters and valve state. An example altered control setpoint attack was implemented. In this attack, the attacker purported to be a Modbus device with a unique Modbus device number, acted as a client and sent a command to the server to alter the system setpoint. Upon receiving the command, the server proceeded to alter the setpoint and adjust the process actuators to achieve the new setpoint.

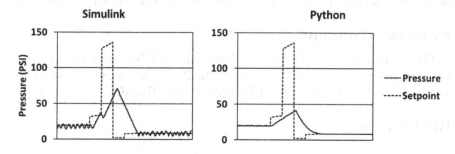

Figure 12. Python and Simulink simulations under attack.

Figure 12 shows the Python and Simulink simulations under the altered control setpoint attack. The graph has been rescaled to 0–150 psi to accommodate the increased system pressure as a result of the attack. The physical system response is not presented because it is incapable of withstanding the high pressure resulting from the injection attack. Nevertheless, the comparison demonstrates the advantages of the Simulink simulation in that it can achieve much higher pressures than the Python simulation with a simple change and without having to create a new empirical model of the system.

6.   Conclusions

The virtual laboratory described in this chapter is designed specifically to support SCADA security research. It models small-scale industrial processes, supports programmable logic controller programming, employs the widely-used Modbus/TCP protocol and incorporates commercially-available human-machine interfaces. The process simulation was enhanced by adding a Simulink model of a gas pipeline. The Simulink addition increases the fidelity of the process model and facilitates modifications to the model as well as the incorporation of complex models. Moreover, the laboratory is portable due to its small size and extensive use of virtualization.

The laboratory has facilitated the analysis of weaknesses in the Modbus protocol as well as the identification and exploration of a number of attacks. It is capable of producing normal and malicious Modbus traffic for intrusion detection, anomaly detection and machine learning research.

Future research will focus on implementing a network of programmable logic controllers and a larger gas pipeline system with multiple gas compressor stations. This new configuration will support the investigation of the effects of cyber attacks on a large distributed infrastructure. Other activities will focus on creating datasets of normal and malicious SCADA network traffic to support the development of sophisticated intrusion and anomaly detection techniques. Another enhancement will involve the communications between the Simulink simulation and virtual programmable logic controller devices that currently employ JSON attribute-value pairs in UDP packets. This method is not used by industrial sensors. Therefore, efforts will be undertaken to replace the current method with an industrial sensor protocol such as WirelessHART or ZigbeePro.

Acknowledgement

This research was supported by the NSF Secure and Trustworthy Cyberspace Program under Grant No. 1315726 and by the Pacific Northwest National Laboratory under U.S. Department of Energy Contract DE-AC05-76RL01830.

References

[1] J. Beaver, R. Borges-Hink and M. Buckner, An evaluation of machine learning methods to detect malicious SCADA communications, *Proceedings of the Twelfth International Conference on Machine Learning and Applications*, vol. 2, pp. 54–59, 2013.

[2] J. Dabney and T. Harman, *Mastering Simulink*, Prentice Hall, Upper Saddle River, New Jersey 2003.

[3] B. Genge, C. Siaterlis, I. Nai Fovino and M. Masera, A cyber-physical experimentation environment for the security analysis of networked industrial control systems, *Computers and Electrical Engineering*, vol. 38(5), pp. 1146–1161, 2012.

[4] A. Hahn, B. Kregal, M. Govindarasu, J. Fitzpatrick, R. Adnan, S. Sridhar and M. Higdon, Development of the PowerCyber SCADA security testbed, *Proceedings of the Sixth Annual Workshop on Cyber Security and Information Intelligence Research*, article no. 21, 2010.

[5] J. Hutchinson, Vertebrate flight, University of California Museum of Paleontology, Berkeley, California (`www.ucmp.berkeley.edu/vertebrates/flight/physics.html`), 1996.

[6] Idaho National Laboratory, Common Cyber Security Vulnerabilities Observed in Control System Assessments by the INL NSTB Program, INL/EXT-08-13979, Idaho Falls, Idaho, 2008.

[7] W. Mahoney and R. Gandhi, An integrated framework for control system simulation and regulatory compliance monitoring, *International Journal of Critical Infrastructure Protection*, vol. 4(1), pp. 41–53, 2011.

[8] R. McGrew, Vulnerability Analysis Case Studies of Control System Human-Machine Interfaces, Ph.D. Dissertation, Department of Computer Science and Engineering, Mississippi State University, Mississippi State, Mississippi, 2012.

[9] T. Morris, R. Vaughn and Y. Dandass, A testbed for SCADA control system cybersecurity research and pedagogy, *Proceedings of the Seventh Annual Workshop on Cyber Security and Information Intelligence Research*, article no. 27, 2011.

[10] B. Obama, Executive Order 13636: Improving Critical Infrastructure Cybersecurity, The White House, Washington, DC, 2013.

[11] B. Reaves and T. Morris, An open virtual testbed for industrial control system security research, *International Journal of Information Security*, vol. 11(4), pp. 215–229, 2012.

[12] M. Schwartz, J. Mulder, J. Trent and W. Atkins, Control System Devices: Architectures and Supply Channels Overview, Sandia Report SAND2010-5183, Sandia National Laboratory, Albuquerque, New Mexico, 2010.

Chapter 9

HOW INDUSTRIAL CONTROL SYSTEM SECURITY TRAINING IS FALLING SHORT

Jonathan Butts and Michael Glover

Abstract   Industrial control systems monitor and manage critical infrastructure assets. Every sector relies extensively on the proper operation of control systems and a major disruption could have devastating consequences to the economy and society. Protecting industrial control systems requires large numbers of well-trained security personnel to detect and respond to increasingly sophisticated cyber attacks. This chapter evaluates current government and industry training courses in the area of industrial control systems security. The results indicate that training is typically geared towards the basic or intermediate knowledge levels and that adequate advanced training programs are not readily available. A primary deficiency is the lack of robust training facilities that incorporate real critical infrastructure assets. Additionally, the curricula do not sufficiently incorporate the physical components and processes associated with industrial control systems. Indeed, there is a great need for training facilities that incorporate real-world industrial control systems and processes to provide trainees with a strong understanding of the effects that cyber-initiated actions have on physical processes. While major investments are required to create advanced curricula and training facilities, they will contribute significantly to the important task of protecting the critical infrastructure.

Keywords: Industrial control systems, training, facilities, curricula

1.   Introduction

Industrial control systems (ICSs) monitor and manage critical infrastructures such as the electric power grid, water treatment systems, oil and gas pipelines, and chemical and nuclear plants. In recent years, industrial control systems have increasingly become interconnected with enterprise networks and the Internet to take advantage of cost savings and operational benefits. This

© IFIP International Federation for Information Processing 2015 (outside the US)
M. Rice, S. Shenoi (Eds.): Critical Infrastructure Protection IX, IFIP AICT 466, pp. 135–149, 2015.
DOI: 10.1007/978-3-319-26567-4_9

trend, however, has introduced myriad attack entry points associated with the networking environment. As a result, formerly isolated critical infrastructure assets are now susceptible to a wide range of threats that previously did not exist. Exacerbating the concern is that approximately 85% of the U.S. critical infrastructure is privately owned and operated [7].

Unfortunately, the majority of infrastructure owners and operators – especially private entities and municipalities – do not understand the risks and have minimal capabilities to respond to sophisticated cyber attacks that target industrial control systems. Training programs are primarily focused on information and communications security rather than industrial control system security.

This chapter evaluates government and industry training programs that specifically focus on industrial control system security professionals. The results indicate that deficiencies exist with respect to training facilities and curricula. Additionally, the training programs do not incorporate coordinated efforts for responding to targeted attacks against critical infrastructure sectors. To overcome the deficiencies, regional facilities are recommended that would support industrial control system security training that utilizes real-world systems. Due to the significant costs and coordination that will be involved, active federal government sponsorship and participation will be required. However, these investments are needed to ensure that adequate numbers of trained personnel are available to prevent and respond to cyber attacks that target industrial control systems and, by extension, the critical infrastructure.

2.   Background

Coordinated cyber attacks target two primary categories of computing systems: (i) traditional information and communications technology (ICT) systems; and (ii) cyber-physical systems [9]. Note that, although the fundamental principles for exploiting the two categories of computing systems may overlap, the effects of cyber-initiated actions on these two types of systems are quite different. Information and communications technology includes systems and applications associated with computer and network hardware, software and communications media [6]. The technology encompasses computers, enterprise software, middleware and data storage that enable users to access, manipulate, store and transmit information. The exploitation of information and communications systems can result in the loss of sensitive or proprietary information, degraded communications, loss or unavailability of data processing and computing systems, and data manipulation. Cyber-physical systems comprise embedded devices and are system-of-systems that are typically associated with the critical infrastructure. Cyber-physical systems, such as industrial control systems, are designed for the "seamless integration of computational algorithms and physical components" [2]. Attacks on these systems can achieve direct kinetic effects that could result in equipment damage and the loss of human life.

Due to the extensive private ownership of the critical infrastructure, the government must largely rely on civilian personnel to protect these national assets. It is imperative that these personnel are adequately trained to protect against, respond to and recover from cyber-initiated attacks on critical infrastructure systems.

Due to the increased threats to the critical infrastructure, myriad courses have been developed to help train control system security professionals in government and industry. In this discussion, only training courses that are publicly available to security professionals are considered.

Government training on industrial control system security is primarily offered by the Department of Homeland Security (DHS) and the Department of Energy (DoE) National Laboratories [4, 8]. The courses incorporate lectures and hands-on training focused on how attacks are launched, why they work and how to develop mitigation strategies. The topics include reviews of industrial control system security, comparative analysis of information and communications system and industrial control system architectures, security vulnerabilities and mitigation strategies. The DHS ICS-CERT advanced training course uses a representative industrial control system to demonstrate how exploits can affect process systems and the utility of mitigation solutions. The training culminates in a red team/blue team exercise that divides students into teams of attackers and teams of defenders. Students are expected to have a strong understanding of industrial control networks and information and communications networks in order to register for the course. The hands-on course is offered only at specific locations in the United States and students must to travel to one of the sites to take the course.

Industry training is primarily offered in the form of one-week courses conducted by vendors. Although a number of vendors offer industrial control system security training, the curricular outlines and training environments are quite similar. The topics covered include industrial control system fundamentals, assessing and managing risk, auditing and assessing systems, defense strategies and implementing security controls. The majority of training courses offer hands-on laboratory assignments that incorporate components such as programmable logic controllers (PLCs) that may be networked in a simulated operational environment. Instructors typically travel to various locations to conduct the training courses, although on-site training tailored to individual organizations is also available. Some vendors offer training at facilities that incorporate simulation testbeds and table-top experimental set-ups that are representative of real industrial control systems. Trainees have a wide range of backgrounds and typically no prerequisites are required to attend the courses.

3.   Gap Analysis

A gap analysis was performed to examine industrial control system security training requirements and existing capabilities. The following shortfalls were identified:

■ **Training Facilities:** The primary shortfall is the lack of appropriate training facilities. A training facility must incorporate real-world systems that adequately prepare students to deal with the situations encountered in industrial environments. Current training facilities either engage simulations or systems that are scaled-down models of physical processes. A real-world, high-fidelity training facility is often overlooked or is considered to be impractical due to the extensive costs associated with incorporating full-scale systems and physical processes. As a result, the courses only provide an abstract understanding of the systems and the associated attacks and defensive strategies. It is imperative that training programs offer hands-on experience and immersion in actual industrial control environments. Without the incorporation of actual physical processes and full-scale systems in training programs, it is impossible for trainees to acquire the skills needed to operate industrial processes in the face of attacks and failures that emanate from the cyber domain.

■ **Training Curricula:** The primary gap in training curricula is the lack of emphasis on physical processes. Current training programs focus primarily on defending and exploiting traditional information and communications systems; they do not adequately incorporate the physical components and processes that are encountered in industrial environments. As a result, the courses do not provide a strong understanding of the implications of cyber-physical correlations and the effects that cyber actions have on physical controls and instrumentation. Although the curricula may offer foundational training, they are not tailored to provide the advanced skills required to detect and mitigate attacks on critical infrastructure assets.

3.1   Training Facility Evaluation

A robust training facility is the key to developing industrial control system security specialists. The training facility must incorporate real-world process systems and control systems and provide hands-on experience. Testbeds and simulation environments may be used to supplement real-world learning experiences, but it is important to be cognizant of the fact that they do not adequately reflect real-world system implementations.

One of the primary challenges when creating a training facility is the integration of a full-scale industrial control system. Real-world industrial control systems comprise equipment from a number of vendors and use diverse protocols, configurations and instrumentation. As a result, the costs associated with designing and implementing a realistic training facility are significant. However, training on real-world industrial control systems exposes personnel to the configuration and deployment intricacies encountered in industrial environments. Additionally, the use of real-world systems emphasizes the importance of physical-safety-override systems and how they affect functionality.

Table 1. Industrial control system (ICS) training environments.

	Government	Industry
Individual ICS Subcomponents	A	A
Interconnected ICS Subcomponents	P	P
Real-World Cyber-Physical Interactions	P	P
Full-Scale Functional ICSs	–	–
Incorporation of Safety Systems	–	–
Ability to Assess Multiple Access Points	–	P
Ability to Manipulate Physical Processes	P	P
Ability to Measure Effects	P	P
Remote Control Center	P	–
Modular Training Environment	–	–
Multiple Vendor Exposure	–	P
Multiple Communications Media	–	P
Interactive Training Capability	P	P

Requirements. A training facility that incorporates real-world industrial control systems is needed to ensure that trainees acquire an in-depth understanding of industrial control systems and the effects that cyber-initiated actions have on physical processes. Simulated environments and small-scale testbeds simply do not provide the required functionality, processes or physical components.

Analysis of Existing Capabilities. Several leading government and industry training facilities were evaluated to assess their ability to support industrial control system training objectives. Table 1 summarizes the findings. Note that "A" indicates that training facilities adequately cover the requirement while "P" indicates that the requirement is partially covered.

Current training facilities lack real-world systems and the ability to manipulate physical processes and measure effects. To meet industrial control system training requirements, personnel must be exposed to hands-on training that incorporates real physical systems. Current training facilities primarily use individual components, simulated environments or small-scale testbeds – the vast majority of facilities use only individual subcomponents. Some of the more advanced training facilities incorporate simulations for traffic generation and provide notional targets for practicing exploitation and defense. A few training facilities offer small-scale testbeds that model real-world systems and provide opportunities to manipulate physical devices and observe minor effects. It is important to note, however, that the testbeds provide only a fraction of real-world functionality and do not adequately replicate the processes, interactions and sophistication associated with fully operational systems. Even at the most basic level, trainees must be exposed to functioning systems to observe the physical processes and control systems in operation and to gain insight into their complex behavior. Unfortunately, it is often the case that trainees never get to see, let alone experiment with, operational industrial control systems.

The majority of training courses use control system subcomponents and virtualized applications for training. For example, trainees are often assigned programmable logic controllers for the duration of a course, but the controllers typically have limited or no interconnections to other control system components. Additionally, the training may not incorporate a remote control center, which is a core component of industrial control systems and one that is frequently targeted by attackers. In many instances, the training facility fails to incorporate key components such as human-machine interfaces, historians and input/output servers. A training facility should incorporate a variety of common access points to expose trainees to methods for gaining unauthorized access to industrial control systems. For example, a primary training requirement should be the ability to identify industrial control system subcomponents from within a corporate network, understand how to pivot and then gain access to the control network.

Communications infrastructures provide different attack vectors and can also alter the operating characteristics of industrial control systems. A training facility should incorporate the range of communications infrastructures that are likely to be encountered in operational environments. The training facility should provide modularity to create the different configurations that meet training objectives, advance student skills and replicate the myriad environments encountered in real-world infrastructures. Most training courses use simulations or testbeds that focus on single, isolated instances of systems. It is important that training courses provide professional with opportunities to work on multiple types of systems used in the various infrastructure sectors.

Well-trained industrial control system professionals should be knowledgeable about how cyber actions can manipulate physical processes and how altering physical processes can affect the cyber components. For example, several cyber options may be available to achieve a desired effect such as shutting down power to a targeted area – these include the available access, types of field devices, operating systems and applications, available exploits and system configurations. It is also critical that a specialist understands and can identify the various risks to individual system components as well as the system as a whole.

3.2   Training Curricula Evaluation

Industrial control system training curricula must prepare professionals for the range of threats that are likely to be encountered when operating critical infrastructure assets. The research results indicate that that training programs are generally inadequate – they primarily focus on exploiting and defending conventional information and communications systems and do not sufficiently incorporate physical components and process systems. A well-designed training program must emphasize the physical aspects and effects associated with industrial control systems.

A professional with strong expertise in process systems and cyber capabilities has the ability to identify the range of threats, comprehend their implications, articulate the strengths and weaknesses of mitigation options and perform the appropriate actions. Indeed, understanding the many ways in which a cyber attack can alter a physical process provides the insight needed to develop and apply strategies to protect against system manipulation. If a physical process has been altered, an experienced operator should be able to discern if the physical effect was cyber-initiated, identify attack vectors, determine the risks to other components and systems, modify configurations and parameters to minimize operational impact and eliminate the threat.

Requirements. Industrial control system security training must provide comprehensive knowledge of the cyber components and physical processes. It is woefully inadequate to understand just the cyber components or physical processes when defending against targeted attacks. In industrial environments, cyber professionals and control engineers have historically been segregated, with each group focusing on its specific area of expertise [3]. The separation of duties and responsibilities has resulted in a lack of understanding of the holistic functionality of industrial control systems. The incorporation of sophisticated automation technologies in industrial environments means that definitive lines cannot be drawn between the engineering aspects of the physical processes and the cyber aspects. This is similar to the case of an automobile technician who, due to advancements in technology, must have knowledge of and the ability to work on the mechanical and electrical systems of modern automobiles.

Industrial control system security specialists must have the ability to analyze a system, understand its functionality, comprehend the risks, evaluate potential secondary effects and articulate mitigation strategies. The core knowledge areas for training curricula that would meet these requirements are: (i) industrial control system principles; (ii) cyber manipulation; and (iii) response coordination. The knowledge areas corresponding to the three core areas are:

- **Industrial Control System Principles:**

    - System functionality

    - Control theory

    - System architecture and operating requirements

    - Instrumentation devices

    - Field device components

    - Control and data acquisition

    - System applications

    - Communications and interconnections

    - Real-world configuration and deployment

- **Cyber Manipulation:**

  - Industrial control systems versus information and communications systems
  - Access vectors
  - Asset enumeration and identification
  - Field device, application and operating system analysis
  - Communications and protocol analysis
  - Vulnerability analysis
  - Availability, integrity and confidentiality
  - Exploitation
  - Pivoting
  - Implanting malware
  - Manipulating physical processes
  - Network protection
  - Forensics
  - Hardening strategies

- **Response Coordination:**

  - Prioritizing system components
  - Identifying attacks
  - Determining system impact
  - Minimizing impact
  - Eradicating malware
  - Recovering from attacks
  - Determining the root cause
  - Implementing safeguards to prevent recurrence
  - Analyzing attacks to obtain intelligence and insights
  - Evaluating defense strategies

The knowledge areas were derived from the skill-set required to defend against targeted attacks on industrial control systems. A specialist should understand: system operating principles; components and functionality; underlying physical processes; cyber-physical correlations; means for gaining access to cyber-physical systems; implications of cyber actions on physical processes; how cyber capabilities are leveraged to achieve physical effects; how to evaluate second-order and cascading effects; limitations of cyber capabilities; and how cyber-kinetic actions are incorporated into requirements, planning and operations.

Table 2. Industrial control system (ICS) training curricula.

	Government	Industry
ICS Fundamentals	B	B
Control Theory	–	B
ICS System Architecture	B	B
Physical Controls	–	–
Instrumentation	–	B
Field Device Operations and Programming	B	I
Control and Data Acquisition	B	B
ICS System Applications	B	I
Communications Media and Protocols	B	I
Implications of Safety Systems	–	B
System Effect Analysis	B	B
ICS vs. ICT Exploitation	A	A
Asset Enumeration and Identification	B	I
Access Vectors	B	B
Field Device and Application Analysis	B	I
Operating System Analysis	I	A
Vulnerability Analysis	B	I
Exploitation	I	I
Pivoting	B	B
Implanting Malware	–	B
Physical Process Manipulation	B	B
Forensics	B	B
Hardening Strategies	I	I
Asset Prioritization	–	–
Time Factors	–	–
Second-Order Effects	–	–
Malware Eradication	–	B
Minimizing Operational Impact	–	–
Response and Recovery Actions	B	B

Analysis of Existing Capabilities. Several government and industry training programs for industrial control system security were evaluated. The training curricula were mapped to the core knowledge areas to identify shortfalls. Table 2 summarizes the findings. Note that "B" indicates that training is available that covers the requirements at a basic level with no practical applications; "I" indicates that training is available that covers the requirements at an intermediate level with practical applications; and "A" indicates that training is available that covers the requirements at an advanced level with in-depth practical applications.

The findings revealed little variance in the training courses with regard to industrial control system fundamentals and cyber manipulation. The primary gaps for all the training courses include the lack of emphasis and material relating to physical systems, instrumentation, safety systems and system effect analysis. From the knowledge and skills perspective, the course material ranged primarily from the beginner level to the intermediate level.

A common theme identified during the curriculum analysis was the traditional information and communications system penetration testing (assessment) mentality. Traditional information and communications system assessments involve a network focus, freedom to maneuver to discover vulnerabilities, a known environment (e.g., Windows operating system) and common vulnerabilities discovered via network assessment tools. Although industrial control systems comprise traditional information and communications systems, understanding how targeted physical effects are achieved requires an evaluation of the overall system-of-systems architecture beyond just the cyber aspects. Current training programs examine individual subcomponents in isolation and do not adequately consider the holistic system. It is imperative that programs cover the interactions between subcomponents and how manipulating parameters in one subsystem or device can cascade throughout a system.

Current training programs rarely go beyond the basic programming and functionality of industrial control system subcomponents. Also, communications protocols are analyzed at a functional level and only a few protocols are incorporated in the training regimens. As a result, there is a major gap related to the implications of the cyber-physical correlations and the effects that cyber actions have on physical controls and instrumentation. Indeed, most training programs are geared towards information and communications technology professionals and primarily expose them to control system functionality and security threats. Although the curricula do help develop awareness and provide basic knowledge, they are not tailored to impart advanced knowledge and skills. As a result, the training programs mainly prepare individuals to protect against attacks directed at information and communications systems instead of preparing them to address sophisticated, targeted attacks on control systems and the infrastructures they operate.

4. Recommendations

The recommendations are focused on delivering training programs that meet the requirements associated with securing critical infrastructure assets across the various sectors. As an initial step, investments must be made to develop realistic training facilities. Curricula should also be developed, ideally through government sponsorship and public-private cooperation, that would provide the best possible training.

4.1 Training Facilities

The primary obstacle to providing adequate training is a sufficient number of facilities that incorporate real-world control systems and processes. These facilities would support the delivery of intense hands-on courses that would enable trainees to observe and learn from the effects of real attacks on industrial control systems. To truly understand the security implications and response strategies, real-world environments are required that comprise multiple interconnected systems (e.g., oil and gas, electric power, water/wastewater and building automation systems).

To overcome the deficiencies, it is recommended to construct several regional facilities that would support industrial control system security training on real-world systems. The primary challenges are the significant costs and coordination that will be required to deploy and operate these facilities. To address these challenges, active federal government sponsorship and participation is required (it would be exceedingly difficult for private entities to independently fund and operate large-scale facilities). Indeed, the Departments of Homeland Security, Energy and Defense, the Government Accounting Office and other government organizations have a vested interest in industrial control system security. The federal government can leverage critical infrastructure assets at legacy sites (e.g., closed military bases) to develop real-world training environments. The various regional training facilities could focus on different combinations of critical infrastructures.

4.2 Training Curricula

Intense training courses that incorporate actual physical systems are required. The proposed training curriculum should cover three core areas: (i) industrial control system principles; (ii) cyber manipulation; (iii) and response coordination. The industrial control system principles and cyber manipulation areas are divided into specific training blocks aligned to the required knowledge and skill sets. The response coordination core area focuses on the practical application of knowledge gained from the industrial control system principles and cyber manipulation core areas. Table 3 lists the recommended course topics.

Industrial Control System Principles. The industrial control system principles core area focuses on physical system attributes and cyber-physical relationships. System functionality includes operating principles, the common vernacular and implementation details in the various sectors. Control theory provides the fundamental knowledge of processes, control systems, systems dynamics and systems engineering required to understand system function and design specifications. System architecture and operating requirements detail the types of configurations and parameters that support system functionality. Note that system functionality is dependent on the underlying physical process. For example, a liquid pipeline has strict timing requirements because liquid is incompressible and an increase in pressure due to a blockage could result in a pipeline rupture, whereas a gas pipeline has less restrictive timing requirements because gas is compressible [1]. Deep knowledge about such system properties is critical to understanding and mitigating the effects of attacks.

Instrumentation devices measure physical system properties such as temperature, pressure, flow and level. It is important to understand how the current and voltage input/output signals to/from field devices impact sensors and actuators that instantiate the physical changes in the process system. Under-

Table 3.   Industrial control system (ICS) course topics.

CORE I: Industrial Control System Principles
Block I: Fundamentals
Block II: Physical Systems and Instrumentation
Block III: Field Devices
Block IV: Industrial Control System Software
Block V: Communications
Block VI: Advanced Control
CORE II: Cyber Manipulation
Block I: Familiarization
Block II: System Profile
Block III: Vulnerability Analysis and Exploitation
Block IV: Defending Against Attacks
CORE III: Response Coordination
Block I: Coordination of Internal and External Responses
Block II: Prioritization of System Components
Block III: Determination of System Impact
Block IV: Minimization of System Impact
Block V: Determination of the Root Cause
Block VI: Eradication of the Cause
Block VII: Implementation of Recovery Strategies

standing the programming languages and field device system architecture (i.e., hardware, firmware and software) provides the ability to manipulate system control via device exploitation. Control and data acquisition covers system interaction and how data is processed and used throughout the system. Applications includes programs for managing system functionality, providing process visualization and enabling operator interfaces. Knowledge of communications protocols, network design and topology are critical to determining access capabilities and how network traffic is routed.

Cyber Manipulation.   The cyber manipulation core area emphasizes the ability to defend against exploitations of cyber vulnerabilities that affect a physical process. It is important to understand the differences between traditional information and communications systems and industrial control systems. Fundamentally, the methods for identifying vulnerabilities in hardware, software or system configurations do not change; however, the exploitation of a vulnerability and the resulting impact are highly dependent on the targeted system. For example, scanning a traditional IP network can identify and provide details of the workstations in the network. On the other hand, performing a similar scan on an industrial control network can cause field devices to malfunction and potentially render them inoperable [5]. It is important to know how to obtain system configuration data and parameters, as well as to understand the capabilities and limitations of available tools.

Understanding access vectors provides insights into leveraging communications systems and other access points to gain entry to industrial control systems. Asset enumeration and identification helps discern the components that comprise a system, including their technical details and network interconnections. This information is used to analyze field devices, applications, operating systems, communications and protocols and determine system configuration and software/firmware information. A vulnerability analysis reveals weaknesses in system configuration, design and implementation for exploitation and implanting malware. Confidentiality, integrity and availability considerations help determine how attacks can manipulate physical processes. Pivoting involves leveraging access gained to one system to compromise other systems. In the case of industrial control systems, pivoting enables attackers to access appropriate subcomponents to achieve their desired effects. Defensive capabilities ensure appropriate configurations and that safeguards are implemented to prevent compromise or minimize damage to the physical process should an attack occur. Forensic capabilities help determine how an attack occurred, the extent of damage and preventive measures to prevent future compromises, as well as obtain intelligence about the attack.

Response Coordination. Knowledge of response coordination is best obtained through mission-oriented training that immerses trainees in environments that mirror real-world operations and scenarios. The response coordination core area involves the application of industrial control system and cyber manipulation knowledge to tailored missions that emphasize the consideration of combined effects, determination of second-order effects and communications with internal and external agencies.

Defending systems against attacks and recovering from attacks require the prioritization of assets to ensure that the physical processes continue to operate as intended. Safeguards should be in place prior to attacks and routine assessments should be performed to identify weaknesses. After an attack is identified, the system impact should be analyzed to prevent or minimize further damage. Recovering from an attack requires the ability to determine the root cause, eradicate malware if it is present and prevent the recurrence of the attack. Digital forensic capabilities are required to understand the details of an attack and its impact as well as gain intelligence about the attack and attacker.

The recommended training curriculum is tailored specifically to meet industrial control system requirements. Each training module should combine classroom lectures with significant hands-on laboratory projects. The training should begin with modules that cover industrial control system principles and provide exposure to actual systems and subcomponents. The next set of modules should cover control engineering principles and control theory, system design, instrumentation and the programming and configuration of field devices, applications and interfaces. Following this, the training should cover the intricacies associated with cyber attacks on industrial control systems and how targeted effects are achieved through cyber-initiated actions that manipulate physical processes. The training should also cover the prioritization of assets, defense strategies and recovery. The training should culminate in mission-oriented activities that apply the knowledge gained in real-world scenarios tailored to industrial control operations.

5. Conclusions

Advanced training is required to ensure that cyber security and industrial control professionals can respond appropriately to sophisticated cyber attacks on industrial control systems and the critical infrastructure assets they monitor and operate. The evaluation of existing government and industry training courses has revealed shortfalls with regard to training facilities and training curricula. Current industrial control system security training relies on individual components, simulated environments or small-scale testbeds. Although these may be effective for beginner and intermediate levels of training, they are inadequate for advanced training, which must provide strong hands-on experience with real industrial control systems and physical processes. Unfortunately, current training facilities have few, if any, real-world systems and do not provide the ability to manipulate physical processes and measure attack impact.

To overcome the deficiencies, regional facilities are recommended that would support industrial control system security training that utilizes real-world systems. The training curricula should cover industrial control system principles, cyber manipulation and response coordination in learning environments that blend classroom lectures with hands-on projects involving real control systems and physical processes. Due to the significant costs and coordination that will be involved, active federal government sponsorship and participation are recommended. These investments are needed to ensure that adequate numbers of trained personnel are available to prevent and respond to cyber attacks that target industrial control systems and, by extension, the critical infrastructure.

Note that the views expressed in this chapter are those of the authors and do not reflect the official policy or position of the U.S. Department of Defense or U.S. Government.

Acknowledgement

This research was partially supported by the Office of the Under Secretary of Defense for Personnel and Readiness.

References

[1] J. Couper, W. Penney and J. Fair, *Chemical Process Equipment: Selection and Design*, Butterworth-Heinemann, Waltham, Massachusetts, 2012.

[2] National Science Foundation, Cyber-Physical Systems, Program Solicitation, NSF 14-542, Arlington, Virginia (www.nsf.gov/pubs/2014/nsf14542/nsf14542.htm), 2014.

[3] L. Neitzel and B. Huba, Top ten differences between ICS and IT cyber-security, *InTech*, International Society of Automation, Research Triangle Park, North Carolina, May/June 2014.

[4] Sandia National Laboratories, SCADA Training Courses, Albuquerque, New Mexico (`energy.sandia.gov/energy/ssrei/gridmod/cyber-security-for-electric-infrastructure/scada-systems/education-and-training/training-courses`), 2014.

[5] K. Stouffer, J. Falco and K. Scarfone, Guide to Industrial Control Systems (ICS) Security, Special Publication 800-82, National Institute of Standards and Technology, Gaithersburg, Maryland, 2011.

[6] U.S. Department of Defense, Protection of Mission Critical Functions to Achieve Trusted Systems and Networks, Instruction No. 5200.44, Washington, DC, 2012.

[7] U.S. Department of Homeland Security, Critical Infrastructure Sector Partnerships, Washington, DC (`www.dhs.gov/critical-infrastructure-sector-partnerships`), 2015.

[8] U.S. Department of Homeland Security, Training Available Through ICS-CERT, Washington, DC (`ics-cert.us-cert.gov/Training-Available-Through-ICS-CERT`), 2015.

[9] B. Zhu, A. Joseph and S. Sastry, A taxonomy of cyber attacks on SCADA systems, *Proceedings of the International Conference on the Internet of Things and the Fourth International Conference on Cyber, Physical and Social Computing*, pp. 380–388, 2011.

III

CYBER-PHYSICAL SYSTEMS SECURITY

Chapter 10

RUNTIME INTEGRITY FOR CYBER-PHYSICAL INFRASTRUCTURES

Jonathan Jenkins and Mike Burmester

Abstract   Cyber-physical systems integrate cyber capabilities (e.g., communications and computing) with physical devices (e.g., sensors, actuators and control processing units). Many of these systems support safety-critical applications such as electric power grids, water distribution systems and transportation systems. Failures of these systems can cause irreparable damage to equipment and injury or death to humans. While most of the efforts to protect the systems have focused on reliability, there are urgent concerns regarding malicious attacks. Trusted computing is a security paradigm that enables platforms to enforce the integrity of execution targets (code and data). However, protection under this paradigm is restricted to static threats.

This chapter proposes a dynamic framework that addresses runtime integrity threats that target software programs in cyber-physical systems. It is well known that the attack surface of a multi-functional program (Swiss-army knife) can be much larger than the sum of the surfaces of its single-function components (e.g., the composition of programs that are secure in isolation is not necessarily secure). The proposed framework addresses this issue using calibration techniques that constrain the functionality of programs to the strict specifications of the cyber-physical application, thus steering execution flow away from the attack surface. Integrity is assured by verifying the calibration, while the burden of validation rests with system designers. The effectiveness of the approach is demonstrated by presenting a prototype for call integrity.

Keywords: Cyber-physical systems, integrity threats, runtime

1.   Introduction

Attacks on the executable code of cyber-physical systems exploit cyber vulnerabilities or physical component vulnerabilities. Attacks of the first kind focus on badly-designed software (e.g., leading to a buffer overflow) or com-

© IFIP International Federation for Information Processing 2015
M. Rice, S. Shenoi (Eds.): Critical Infrastructure Protection IX, IFIP AICT 466, pp. 153–167, 2015.
DOI: 10.1007/978-3-319-26567-4_10

promised code (e.g., malware). Attacks of the second kind exploit outputs from faulty or compromised sensors. This chapter focuses on badly-designed software because attacks on compromised code or compromised sensors can be thwarted via well-understood techniques such as static integrity engines in trusted computing architectures [30] and risk management architectures.

Attacks that exploit software vulnerabilities have been studied extensively and several protection techniques have been proposed (see, e.g., [3, 8, 11, 14, 15, 19, 20, 22, 23, 25, 26]). However, these techniques target specific system vulnerabilities, meaning that they do not transfer to other types of attacks. This chapter proposes a trust framework that addresses the dynamic (real-time) integrity of executable code using calibration techniques. The framework is intended to extend the capabilities of trusted computing architectures to support static as well as dynamic integrity verification.

2.   Related Work

Several techniques exist for the dynamic protection of the integrity of software execution as opposed to the protection of data residing in system memory. Although these techniques do not offer complete dynamic integrity protection of software at runtime, they address important aspects of dynamic integrity and are a major contributor to trusted software execution. Nevertheless, the application of these techniques to secure cyber-physical systems requires adjustments in order to meet the stringent requirements imposed by the systems.

Taint tracking is a technique for tracking untrusted data (e.g., network sources) as they propagate during execution [9, 24]. Copying, arithmetic functions and control flow logic enable the spread of "taint" among data and to subsequent executions. The tracking proceeds by marking sources of suspect data in memory and causes a non-trivial slowdown factor ranging from 5.5 to 30. Taint tracking has been successfully implemented to detect attacks such as buffer overflows, format string attacks and control data overwrites [9].

Control flow integrity is a technique for constraining the control flow of software to its control flow graph, which is a representation of the control flow edges that program code can traverse. A control flow graph is produced by static analysis or by the application of analysis programs. The technique is readily implemented using software instrumentation via rewriting to insert checks of control flow jumps against the control flow graph [2].

The performance cost of full control flow integrity enforcement as implemented in software has been shown to vary from negligible to approximately 45% with some variance based on the application [2, 32]. One limitation is that attacks that obey the control flow graph (e.g., format string attacks) are not addressed. Furthermore, the high performance penalty of software-based, fine-grained (full) control flow integrity protection has resulted in weaker, coarse-grained versions (e.g., reducing the frequency or types of checks) that are subject to attack [17, 32].

Trusted computing is an architecture that supports the measurement and preservation of system integrity, as well as secure network connectivity [28, 29].

Trusted computing is distinct from other integrity protection methodologies due to its provision of an implementation-independent set of abstract engines for creating, maintaining and using robust static integrity information about software in platforms. Trusted computing defines a trust structure in which the trust in a computing platform is created by checking the static integrity of each boot stage program before execution.

Trusted computing provides static integrity protection, but it does not address the dynamic integrity of executing software. However, it can be an important factor when considering dynamic integrity protection for a cyber-physical infrastructure because employing static measurements of integrity such as digests may help. Beyond the integrity of the literal memory state of program code, techniques are required for protecting software execution.

3.   Dynamic Integrity

If the designers of future critical infrastructure systems were to adopt the security practices of conventional systems, they might, for example, design an electric power grid whose data processing devices undergo regular security scans, software updates and enforce access control policies that protect resources. Such an approach cannot protect the system from every security violation. Implementing reactive security policies that address new exploits requires the deployment of resources that analyze and defeat the exploits. The financial investment required for endless attack-specific protection of critical infrastructure assets as adversaries discover new exploits would be substantial and ultimately futile. What is needed is a general protection framework of policies and mechanisms that identify and mitigate violations that appear fundamentally as deviations from correct operation.

A promising solution is to shift the burden of providing integrity for executable code from the security analyst to the software designer. The runtime integrity of code must be guaranteed via techniques that constrain code execution to the envelope of proper operations as intended by the designers. Such an approach is necessary because adding patches or fixes to badly-designed code will not prevent adversaries from bypassing the protection mechanisms by leveraging inherent code vulnerabilities. Another advantage is that the protection framework is not dependent on specific protection mechanisms (e.g., against ROP [25]) that a determined adversary can easily bypass. Note that the integrity of the code content by itself does not guarantee the security of execution – it only guarantees that the state of the code matches that intended by the designers. Thus, measures beyond the verification of code content are necessary to protect software execution and create trusted critical infrastructure devices.

The objective of this research is to extend the integrity protection of a trusted platform module to capture dynamic integrity. In the proposed approach, the software designers are ultimately responsible for code integrity provided that the code is executed within the strict confines of calibrations as specified by the designers. Cyber-physical system security has three traditional requirements:

- **Availability:** Cyber and physical components obey timing and response requirements.

- **Integrity:** Cyber and physical components have static and dynamic integrity. Dynamic integrity protection mechanisms address runtime attacks.

- **Confidentiality:** Observations of data streams/events do not cross user-user, device-device or user-device boundaries unless the observing system node holds the appropriate security level. For real-time confidentiality, forward device secrecy is required [18].

The availability of state information in real-time is crucial in critical infrastructure environments. This is because the failure of system components or other faults can lead to cascading failures and large-scale system shutdown. To prevent this from occurring, it is necessary to enforce "need-to-get-now" policies [6] because quality of service or best effort policies may be inadequate.

This work uses the Byzantine threat model [21] in which the adversary can act arbitrarily and is not restricted by any constraints other than being computationally bounded (modeled by a probabilistic polynomial-time Turing machine). The focus is mainly on dynamic integrity threats.

4.   Trusted Infrastructures

Critical infrastructure systems require appropriate references, measurement and enforcement in order to guarantee their integrity. Software integrity is defined by static references for the literal conditions of memory content and by conditions for safe execution by virtue of safe memory interactions. Software designers and creators are best positioned to provide such references because they express the system functionality as well as the non-functional conditions for safe memory interactions. Thus, in order to protect critical infrastructure assets, it is essential that software designers specify the appropriate reference constraints.

In the case of cyber-physical systems, the addition of physical components means that protection methods must consider a new type of interaction between software, memory and physical components, and must also represent the integrity of the physical components. The integrity of the interface between cyber and physical objects is also a critical part of any protection scheme, and it may introduce security violations when it fails to preserve information as it is transmitted between cyber and physical devices.

A physical data source conceptually provides an event stream. No explicit program logic is presented by physical nodes to their communicating counterparts. Therefore, the integrity of the physical data source can be directly evaluated only by a physical reference value or a physical condition for its safe operation (e.g., voltage level range). Secure interactions between cyber and physical components require the integrity of cyber component execution, the adherence of physical components to references as verified by inspection and the integrity of the cyber-physical interface components. The interactions between the cyber and physical components of a cyber-physical system must be monitored for conditions and failure modes appropriate to the potentially serious threats arising from system failure via the cyber-physical interface.

5.   Dynamic Software Integrity

For runtime security, the operation of software components of cyber-physical systems must exhibit integrity, apart from the (static) intactness of the program code and data on devices that can be protected with architectures such as trusted computing [30]. This task is approached by applying constraints to operate at two stages of deployment in two fundamentally different ways.

First, a form of integrity protection is achieved by reducing the space of vulnerabilities exposed to attack at runtime. Functional constraints on the software designed for critical infrastructure assets is one way to reduce the extent of protection needed before software is executed (e.g., no non-essential functionality is included). Second, it is necessary to constrain software execution by enforcing dynamic integrity conditions at runtime. These conditions are derived from the analysis of programs, but also require input from program creators for application-dependent conditions. Program creators express the intent of algorithms in code and are, therefore, best able to characterize the envelope within which executions should remain. However, as will be shown later, the evaluation of execution with respect to such conditions must be carried out by an external engine to ensure the integrity of the measurement process itself as a general property of systematic infrastructure protection.

The proposed efforts for constraining software execution to benefit integrity can be summarized as follows:

- Software program creators must supply dynamic integrity conditions with respect to:

  - The degree of trust conferred on data sources and the degree to which they are permitted to propagate when used by programs (taint).

  - The control flow of the program (e.g., with respect to a control flow graph).

  - The procedure calls of the program.

- Software program creators must provide attestation for the calibration constraints.

- A dynamic integrity monitoring engine with system memory access must be deployed to measure the dynamic integrity of executing programs with respect to conditions. The engine can be implemented in hardware to significant advantage in a cyber-physical system.

- Appropriate responses to integrity violations must be set.

6.   Constraining Software by Calibration

This section describes the design and dynamic constraints, specifically, taint tracking, control flow integrity and call integrity protection.

6.1   Design Constraints

The conventional software production process must undergo adjustments in order to comply with the stringent requirements imposed by cyber-physical systems, especially with regard to design practices and functional constraints. Non-essential functionalities may interfere with the performance of critical, required functionalities. When a software program implements additional, non-essential functionalities, some degree of resource sharing and interaction (e.g., memory) across functionalities will occur. Thus, program functionalities are subject to conflict in terms of time and resource use, potentially impacting performance and availability.

In addition to resource conflicts, non-essential program functionalities become a threat vector for compound security vulnerabilities that are constructed from conditions created by instructions for the separate functionalities. For example, consider a program that implements a search function and a maintenance function that accesses working memory. The exploitation of flaws during the execution of maintenance instructions may expose a memory address used by the search function to launch an attack; this violates the operational integrity of the entire program. Note that a program may not remain secure if arbitrarily composed with other programs or with instances of itself (universal composability) [7].

Cyber-physical system software, with its stringent demands on availability and failure consequences, must be functionally constrained to avoid introducing resource conflicts and threat vectors. The failure to implement such measures for critical infrastructure assets is unacceptable.

6.2   Dynamic Constraints

To protect the operation of cyber-physical system software, measures are necessary to preserve the dynamic integrity of software execution with regard to memory use and other properties. The enormity of this task is made more manageable by the availability of protection mechanisms for some aspects of dynamic integrity. To address this issue, a hardware dynamic integrity monitor extension is proposed to potentially achieve complete dynamic integrity. Indeed, the combination of taint tracking, control flow integrity and call integrity protection enables the comprehensive dynamic integrity monitoring of cyber-physical system software.

Taint Tracking. Recent research has demonstrated the effectiveness of taint tracking systems [9, 24]. Critical infrastructure systems justify the implementation of taint tracking using specialized hardware as detailed in [10, 12, 27], allowing for a significant reduction in performance impact.

Suh et al. [27] add tracking logic to processors (including tag tracking hardware components). Their technique involves dynamic information flow tracking, which analyzes information flows between memory areas due to program execution. They evaluate two security policies by simulating a set of information flows; the more robust policy tracks flows based on the use of tainted values in computations. The measured performance overhead for both policies is low – less than 1% for the lighter policy and at most 6% for the more robust policy.

Hardware-based tracking is also a necessary part of a dynamic integrity monitor for a cyber-physical system. This is the result of isolation from monitored executions and their resources, a requirement for a systematic cyber-physical system dynamic integrity protection mechanism that cannot itself be attacked.

Control Flow Integrity. Software-based techniques can effectively protect the control flow integrity of software, albeit with a potentially significant performance impact that hampers the adoption of pure fine-grained protection [2, 32]. Weaker versions of control flow integrity protection are inadequate to combat threats to cyber-physical infrastructures [13]. Clearly, the imposition of additional protection delays on cyber-physical systems is also unacceptable due to stringent availability demands, not to mention integrity requirements.

For the unique, critical usage scenarios of cyber-physical devices, hardware-based control flow integrity protection is justified and necessary for the isolation, functional constraints and robustness conferred on the protection functionality as well as the reduced performance burden. Nevertheless, in terms of complexity and difficulty, the hardware-based implementation of full control flow integrity protection is feasible and straightforward. Budiu et al. [4] report that simulations of coarse-grained control flow integrity introduce an average runtime overhead of 3.75% and a maximum of overhead of 7.12%. Further improvements in performance are possible via scheduling.

Call Integrity Protection. The integrity of procedure calls within programs is a relatively unrecognized, but critical, aspect of the dynamic integrity of executing software. It is possible to monitor runtime call integrity to detect sequences of integrity violations and the potentially damaging security attacks they may comprise.

Computer memory is the space in which software integrity is demonstrated by the soundness of literal memory as well as the compliance of program execution with developer intent. Thus, call integrity is measured by examining the memory associated with procedure calls, typically the stack.

Implementing call integrity protection in cyber-physical system software involves three processes: (i) instrumentation; (ii) instruction analysis or introspection; and (iii) specification creation and enforcement. Since the integrity of procedure calls and the integrity of software execution, in general, are not exposed to direct measurement as an inherent property of programs, the substrate of call integrity must be made to expose itself for measurement. This exposure is readily achieved via software instrumentation, which involves inserting instructions into a target program to enable logic or analysis distinct from that of the target application. Such exposure is a fundamental requirement due to the lack of access by external evaluators to the syntactic memory-to-object information that is available in source code. Essentially, instrumentation for call integrity protection inserts source code or binary instructions for the purpose of measurement, exposure of integrity and detection of events.

The use of instrumentation for the call integrity measurement engine as proposed here requires the runtime analysis of instructions in order to access integrity-relevant data exposed by the instrumentation. Instruction analysis (introspection) is the inspection of target program instructions (i.e., opcodes and operands) by an analysis program. This analysis needs a runtime access interface to the signaling data exposed by the instrumentation process. At the level of instruction introspection, aggregate analysis and detection of integrity relevant events can be performed across instructions (e.g., analyzing integrity properties of arguments to a runtime call).

Finally, dynamic call integrity constraint conditions must be specified and enforced. The specification of call integrity conditions requires input from the program creators for some requirements, but in reality, many broadly applicable conditions can be constructed from application-independent relations that apply to categories of calls.

With dynamic call integrity exposed via software instrumentation and constraints on procedure call memory interactions available, dynamic call integrity evaluation and enforcement must be carried out. Clearly, if call integrity is measured and exposed in memory via instrumentation, evaluations can be performed as an additional instrumentation step. The ideal evaluation engine is robust, resource-independent and external to the program being analyzed to mitigate attacks on the protection functionality.

The particular combination of the techniques mentioned above demonstrates two critical facts concerning software integrity protection and cyber-physical infrastructure protection. First, the inclusion of taint, control flow and call integrity produces a comprehensive coverage of software execution integrity via the revelation of key memory interactions that implement execution and exhibit integrity. Second, the combination demonstrates one crucial property of workable systematic software integrity protection for cyber-physical infrastructures – protection is general via the application to integrity itself instead of particular attack profiles or effects. Approaches that apply a patchwork of techniques directed at particular attacks achieve no better protection than conventional security software and do not respect the intolerance of cyber-physical infrastructures to regular violations or conventional remediation strategies. In general, a protection strategy analyzes the integrity of critical systems as it transitions instead of reactively developing protections for each new attack. Reactive, attack-focused integrity strategies impose a cost and maintenance burden that are incompatible with large, heavily interconnected cyber-physical infrastructures.

7.   Dynamic Call Integrity via Calibration

In order to protect cyber-physical system software execution in a general manner, the hardware-based taint and control flow constraints proposed in this work must be combined with call integrity constraint enforcement, thus extending the static protection offered by trusted computing to dynamic execution protection. Dynamic call integrity information must be measured, transmitted to a location accessible to a measurement entity and evaluated before enforcing the appropriate policy.

7.1   Experimental Setup

A prototype was implemented on Linux with C source code using executable and linkable format binaries and the x86 instruction set. Source code instrumentation was implemented using a script that inserts protection-related instructions near procedure calls. The DynamoRIO runtime instruction manipulation library [16] was used to instrument binaries. The prototype was run on a laptop with an Intel Core i5-2520m 2.5 GHz dual-core processor with 3 MB cache.

7.2   Evaluation and Calibration

The goal and scope of the evaluation was to demonstrate the principles and techniques proposed: that the runtime integrity of a call can be measured and that integrity violations can be detected by combining several forms of instrumentation with introspection without requiring the original protected program to be modified by developers. The evaluation code can easily be adapted to other environments that use a working memory stack and registers by making adjustments to system parameters.

Source instrumentation was performed automatically using a script that processes C source code calls. A preamble of instrumentation instructions (e.g., source code and assembly code) was added to all procedure calls residing within a range of code specified by special start and end tags. Figure 1 shows the preamble of function foo(a,b,c,d,e) (i.e., the instructions above the function).

The preamble includes a set of k split calls where k is the number of analyzed arguments contained in the source code call. Each split call accepts only its individual argument and induces a compiler to produce executable instructions that manipulate the stack layout to cause the argument to be isolated at the end of the stack for integrity measurement.

Each split call has a set of instrumentation instructions inserted before and after the call. In particular, each call is marked with a special variable allocation to present a marker to the instruction introspection layer that indicates the

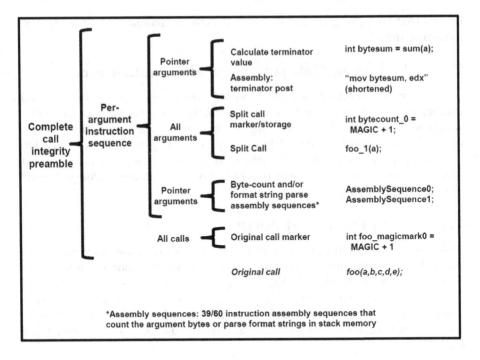

Figure 1.   C code procedure call instrumentation with preamble.

presence of a split call instead of an existing call instruction (`int bytecount_0=` `MAGIC+1` in Figure 1). An instrumented function call (`int bytesum=sum(a)`) is inserted to compute a terminating condition value for the enumeration of parameter bytes in memory. In this case, a call to an instrumented function is incorporated to calculate the sum of the bytes as integers. Finally, inline assembly instructions are inserted to copy the terminator value to a register for the byte-enumerating measurements (abbreviated as `mov bytesum, edx`).

Assembly instructions (`AssemblySequence0`; `AssemblySequence1`) are inserted immediately following each split call. The instructions implement two types of primitive integrity measurements on calls that are the basis for more complex call integrity measurements. They assume that the parameter bytes can be located at a predictable location at the end of the stack in working memory before the assembly byte measurement sequence is reached in the program source code during execution.

7.3   Parameter Length

One critical primitive component of call integrity is the relationships between the lengths of parameters in working memory (especially pointer types) that may be known only during execution. Source instrumentation was applied to insert instructions to measure the parameter lengths in runtime memory using the byte-enumerating assembly sequence detailed earlier, based on the

Integrity performance measurements		Argument run-time length measurement	Argument count + format string count extraction (2 specifier, 2 arguments)	Argument count + run-time format string count extraction (2 specifier, 2 arguments)
Source instrumentation	Average relative slowdown	4.1812, 0.19/byte	0.9984,0.3328042027 per argument	1.05866696, 0.3528889878 per argument
	Absolute additional time (ms)	0.00015558, 0.00000707/byte	negligible	negligible

Figure 2. C source code call integrity measurement performance.

termination sum condition prestored in a register. Counting loop termination is based on the encountered byte sum exceeding the prestored sum. Typically, the number of additional source instructions inserted by this method for length counting is $5 + 48\,k$, where k is the number of arguments whose length is to be measured in memory.

Figure 2 shows that the average relative slowdown for length measurement is 4.1812 or 0.19 per byte measured. The memory space requirement per argument for runtime argument length measurement includes space for two integers to store a bytesum and the count result, and the use of the general purpose x86 registers.

7.4   Call Parameter Parity

Another critical aspect of procedure calls that holds valuable integrity information is the parity of call parameters. The number of parameters required by format string parameters in conversion procedure calls (such as format functions `scanf` and `printf` in C) is an important integrity information primitive that measures dangerous mismatches between the requirements of call parameters. In the case of C format functions, an entire major category of attacks is based on this disparity.

Measurements of the interactions between format string and regular parameters are implemented using the assembly sequence byte-enumerating technique as with parameter length. If the format string is visible in the source code, it is parsed to determine the number of format specifiers. The number of non-format string arguments is extracted via source code analysis during the instrumentation pass. The two values are compared during execution by inserting instructions for simple numeric relational comparison, a mismatch being indicative of a call integrity violation and a potentially dangerous call.

If the format string is known only at runtime, then the methods for isolation and bounding of parameters used for argument length measurement are reapplied to allow the format string to be analyzed in working memory. Inline assembly instructions were inserted to parse the format string in memory during execution to determine the number of format specifiers, each of which is identified by a "%" byte in C format strings. The combination of format string parsing and argument count measurement resulted in the small performance impact shown in Figure 2. The average relative slowdown for measurement was timed at 0.9984 or approximately 0.33 per argument.

Exposure of Integrity Primitives to Evaluation. In the experiments, the exposure of integrity information to an external evaluator was carried out by adding source code instructions that perform initialization assignments with marking identifier values. Such assignments induce a compiler to emit instructions that expose to memory-accessing integrity evaluating entities the location of integrity information (e.g., stack memory offset) or meta-information about instrumented target program code that facilitates protection (e.g., a signal to the evaluation layer about the availability of an integrity measurement during execution). These capabilities allow the general exposure of measurements to a memory-accessing evaluation engine. In the prototype, DynamoRIO [16] intercepts integrity information exposed in memory via source instrumentation using its instruction introspection ability.

Evaluation of Call Integrity. The final process required to demonstrate call integrity is the evaluation of integrity information with respect to a set of integrity conditions. Appropriate enforcement of policy can be carried out based on the result of the evaluation. The conditions demonstrated in the research were:

- The relationships between the lengths of parameters in memory must comply with given relations (e.g., source does not exceed destination). A useful universal example length condition is "no length may exceed another."

- The number of format string specifiers must match the number of non-format string parameters.

Although the number of instantiations of runtime procedure calls is large, conditions for protecting categories of procedure calls can be created based on the primitives (length and parity) demonstrated with the help of developer-assistive tools.

The evaluator engine was demonstrated with DynamoRIO [16] via the analysis of the measurement results held within the instructions inserted by source instrumentation. The instruction introspection feature of DynamoRIO was applied to locate the exposed measurements during runtime, demonstrating the ability to intercept integrity information necessary for enforcing policy (i.e., simply exit upon a violation). Since DynamoRIO is unable to access working stack memory (only instructions), the evaluation was simulated (first, in the source code for demonstration purposes) via the ability to insert new executable instructions to evaluate arbitrary relational expressions on the intercepted numerical integrity measurements (as opposed to analyzing the measurements in memory as an ideal hardware evaluator would).

During the experiments, DynamoRIO was able to illustrate the characteristics and levels of component access necessary to analyze and evaluate integrity information exposed by other techniques (e.g., tool-assisted source code instrumentation). Also, it was able to demonstrate the validity of the relocatability of integrity information, a fundamental requirement of general dynamic integrity protection architectures as proposed in this work.

8. Conclusions

The principal contribution of this research is a dynamic framework that addresses runtime integrity threats to software programs in cyber-physical systems. The framework constrains the design and execution of software so that its functionality adheres to the strict requirements of cyber-physical applications. Constraints are imposed on both software design and execution and are implemented via calibration. The framework is intended to extend the protection offered by trusted computing architectures to address dynamic threats during software execution.

Acknowledgement

This research was partially supported by the National Science Foundation under Grant Nos. DUE 1241525, CNS 1347113 and DGE 1538850.

References

[1] M. Abadi, M. Budiu, U. Erlingsson and J. Ligatti, Control-flow integrity, *Proceedings of the Twelfth ACM Conference on Computer and Communications Security*, pp. 340–353, 2005.

[2] M. Abadi, M. Budiu, U. Erlingsson and J. Ligatti, Control-flow integrity principles, implementations and applications, *ACM Transactions on Information and System Security*, vol. 13(1), article no. 4, 2009.

[3] J. Bridges, T. Sartorius and S. Millendorf, Methods and Systems for Checking Run-Time Integrity of Secure Code Cross-Reference to Related Applications, United States Patent 8,639,943, 2014.

[4] M. Budiu, U. Erlingsson and M. Abadi, Architectural support for software-based protection, *Proceedings of the First Workshop on Architectural and System Support for Improving Software Dependability*, pp. 42–51, 2006.

[5] M. Burmester and B. de Medeiros, On the security of route discovery in MANETs, *IEEE Transactions on Mobile Computing*, vol. 8(9), pp. 1180–1188, 2009.

[6] M. Burmester, E. Magkos and V. Chrissikopoulos, T-ABAC: An attribute-based access control model for real-time availability in highly dynamic systems, *Proceedings of the IEEE Symposium on Computers and Communications*, pp. 143–148, 2013.

[7] R. Canetti, Universally composable security: A new paradigm for cryptographic protocols, *Proceedings of the Forty-Second IEEE Symposium on Foundations of Computer Science*, pp. 136–145, 2001.

[8] M. Castro, M. Costa and T. Harris, Securing software by enforcing dataflow integrity, *Proceedings of the Seventh Symposium on Operating Systems Design and Implementation*, pp. 147–160, 2006.

[9] W. Cheng, Q. Zhao, B. Yu and S. Hiroshige, TaintTrace: Efficient flow tracing with dynamic binary rewriting, *Proceedings of the Eleventh IEEE Symposium on Computers and Communications*, pp. 749–754, 2006.

[10] J. Chow, B. Pfaff, T. Garfinkel, K. Christopher and M. Rosenblum, Understanding data lifetime via whole system simulation, *Proceedings of the Thirteenth USENIX Security Symposium*, 2004.

[11] C. Cowan, C. Pu, D. Maier, H. Hinton, J. Walpole, P. Bakke, S. Beattie, A. Grier, P. Wagle and Q. Zhang, StackGuard: Automatic adaptive detection and prevention of buffer-overflow attacks, *Proceedings of the Seventh USENIX Security Symposium*, 1998.

[12] J. Crandall and F. Chong, Minos: Control data attack prevention orthogonal to memory model, *Proceedings of the Thirty-Seventh International Symposium on Microarchitecture*, pp. 221–232, 2004.

[13] L. Davi, A. Sadeghi, D. Lehmann and F. Monrose, Stitching the gadgets: On the ineffectiveness of coarse-grained control-flow integrity protection, *Proceedings of the Twenty-Third USENIX Security Symposium*, pp. 401–416, 2014.

[14] L. Davi, A. Sadeghi and M. Winandy, Dynamic integrity measurement and attestation: Towards defense against return-oriented programming attacks, *Proceedings of the ACM Workshop on Scalable Trusted Computing*, pp. 49–54, 2009.

[15] L. Davi, A. Sadeghi and M. Winandy, ROPdefender: A detection tool to defend against return-oriented programming attacks, *Proceedings of the Sixth ACM Symposium on Information, Computer and Communications Security*, pp. 40–51, 2011.

[16] DynamoRIO, Dynamic Instrumentation Tool Platform (dynamorio.org), 2009.

[17] E. Goktas, E. Athanasopoulos, H. Bos and G. Portokalidis, Out of control: Overcoming control-flow integrity, *Proceedings of the IEEE Symposium on Security and Privacy*, pp. 575–589, 2014.

[18] C. Gunther, An identity-based key-exchange protocol, in *Advances in Cryptology – EUROCRYPT '89*, J. Quisquater and J. Vandewalle (Eds.), Springer, Heidelberg, Germany, pp. 29–37, 1990.

[19] J. Hiser, A. Nguyen-Tuong, M. Co, M. Hall and J. Davidson, ILR: Where did my gadgets go? *Proceedings of the IEEE Symposium on Security and Privacy*, pp. 571–585, 2012.

[20] V. Kiriansky, D. Bruening and S. Amarasinghe, Secure execution via program shepherding, *Proceedings of the Eleventh USENIX Security Symposium*, pp. 191–206, 2002.

[21] L. Lamport, R. Shostak and M. Pease, The Byzantine generals problem, *ACM Transactions on Programming Languages and Systems*, vol. 4(3), pp. 382–401, 1982.

[22] Y. Li, J. McCune, J. Newsome, A. Perrig, B. Baker and W. Drewry, Minibox: A two-way sandbox for x86 native code, *Proceedings of the Annual USENIX Technical Conference*, pp. 409–420, 2014.

[23] D. Malan, CS50 sandbox: Secure execution of untrusted code, *Proceedings of the Forty-Fourth ACM Technical Symposium on Computer Science Education*, pp. 141–146, 2013.

[24] J. Newsome and D. Song, Dynamic taint analysis for automatic detection, analysis and signature generation of exploits on commodity software, *Proceedings of the Network and Distributed System Security Symposium*, 2005.

[25] R. Roemer, E. Buchanan, H. Shacham and S. Savage, Return-oriented programming: Systems, languages and applications, *ACM Transactions on Information and System Security*, vol. 15(1), article no. 2, 2012.

[26] H. Shacham, The geometry of innocent flesh on the bone: `return-into-libc` without function calls (on the x86), *Proceedings of the Fourteenth ACM Conference on Computer and Communications Security*, pp. 552–561, 2007.

[27] G. Suh, J. Lee, D. Zhang and S. Devadas, Secure program execution via dynamic information flow tracking, *Proceedings of the Eleventh International Conference on Architectural Support for Programming Languages and Operating Systems*, pp. 85–96, 2004.

[28] Trusted Computing Group, TCG Specification Architecture Overview, Revision 1.4, Beaverton, Oregon, 2007.

[29] Trusted Computing Group, TNC Architecture for Interoperability, Specification 1.3, Revision 6, Beaverton, Oregon, 2008.

[30] Trusted Computing Group, TPM Main Specification, Level 2, Version 1.2, Revision 116, Beaverton, Oregon, 2011.

[31] N. Vachharajani, M. Bridges, J. Chang, R. Rangan, G. Ottoni, J. Blome, G. Reis, M. Vachharajani and D. August, RIFLE: An architectural framework for user-centric information-flow security, *Proceedings of the Thirty-Seventh International Symposium on Microarchitecture*, pp. 243–254, 2004.

[32] C. Zhang, T. Wei, Z. Chen, L. Duan, L. Szekeres, S. McCamant, D. Song and W. Zou, Practical control flow integrity and randomization for binary executables, *Proceedings of the IEEE Symposium on Security and Privacy*, pp. 559–573, 2013.

Chapter 11

SECURITY CHALLENGES OF ADDITIVE MANUFACTURING WITH METALS AND ALLOYS

Mark Yampolskiy, Lena Schutzle, Uday Vaidya and Alec Yasinsac

Abstract   Cyber-physical systems are under constant and increasing attacks as components of the critical infrastructure. Additive manufacturing systems are a new class of cyber-physical systems that produce three-dimensional objects layer by layer. Agencies and companies such as NASA, the European Space Agency, General Electric and SpaceX have explored a broad range of application areas for additive manufacturing, including creating functional parts of safety-critical systems such as jet engines. The range of application areas and dependence on computerization makes additive manufacturing an attractive target for attackers.

This chapter focuses on attacks that seek to change the physical properties of additive-manufactured components. Such attacks can weaken, damage or destroy manufactured components and, in scenarios where weak or damaged components are used in safety-critical systems, potentially endanger human lives. Attacks intended to damage additive manufacturing equipment and additive manufacturing environments are also discussed.

Keywords: Additive manufacturing, 3D printing, threats, risks

1.   Introduction

Cyber-physical systems are under constant and increasing attack. Examples encountered "in the wild" as well as those considered in the research literature include attacks on industrial control systems [5, 14, 25, 44], automobiles [7, 23] and unmanned vehicles [16, 53].

Additive manufacturing, also known as additive layer manufacturing, solid freeform fabrication and, perhaps most commonly, 3D printing, employs an important class of cyber-physical systems that produce 3D objects. Unlike a traditional subtractive manufacturing process, in which a mold is poured or a solid block of a material is reduced via milling and turning to a desired form,

© IFIP International Federation for Information Processing 2015

M. Rice, S. Shenoi (Eds.): Critical Infrastructure Protection IX, IFIP AICT 466, pp. 169–183, 2015.

DOI: 10.1007/978-3-319-26567-4_11

additive manufacturing creates 3D objects by adding thin layers one at a time to gradually build up an object from two dimensions to three dimensions and, ultimately, to the desired form [50].

The market penetration of additive manufacturing as a manufacturing technology has tremendous potential. The reasons include technical and economic advantages such as just-in-time and on-demand production, the ability to manufacture components closer to assembly lines, shorter design-to-product time and, especially, the ability to produce functional parts with complex internal structures and with complex (task-specific) physical properties. In 2014, Wohlers Associates [50] reported that the additive manufacturing industry had a total revenue of $4.1 billion, with 29% of all manufactured objects used as functional parts. According to NIST reports [46, 47], additive manufacturing revenue will rise to about $50 billion between 2029 and 2031.

However, the economical, geopolitical and other implications of additive manufacturing technology [6] will inevitably draw the attention of adversaries ranging from malicious individuals to state actors. As research in the area of critical infrastructure protection has revealed, attacks will often seek to achieve physical impacts via cyber means [14, 20, 40, 44, 55]. In the case of additive manufacturing, the attacks would likely translate to physical impacts on the manufactured 3D objects, especially in cases where the objects are used as functional parts of safety-critical systems such as jet engines.

This chapter presents a qualitative analysis of attacks that can be executed on additive manufacturing equipment that works with metals and alloys. Special attention is directed at attacks that change the physical properties of additive-manufactured components. Such attacks can contribute to weak and unreliable components and, in scenarios where these components are used in safety-critical systems, endanger human lives. Attacks intended to damage additive manufacturing equipment and additive manufacturing environments are also discussed.

2.   Related Work

Very little research has focused on the security aspects of additive manufacturing. However, a growing body of research discusses the impact of 3D printing, including its socioeconomic [6, 22, 38, 39], geopolitical [6, 33] and environmental [10, 34] aspects. These impacts can motivate a variety of adversaries ranging from malicious individuals to state-sponsored actors and nation states.

Two security threat categories are associated with additive manufacturing [52]: (i) intellectual property theft; and (ii) physical (i.e., kinetic) damage. Recent articles have shown that there is a growing awareness of intellectual property violations in the context of additive manufacturing [4, 49, 51]. However, literature research reveals that the second threat category has not been considered adequately. The only notable exception is the possibility of a 3D printer exploding due to mismanagement [45], which actually occurred in November 2013 at Powderpart Inc. [36]. There is, however, a significant body of literature in materials science and mechanical engineering that provides a basis for analyzing attacks that can inflict physical damage by altering the physical properties of manufactured 3D objects.

The American Society for Testing and Materials (ASTM) International Committee F42 on Additive Manufacturing Technologies has approved a list of seven additive manufacturing process categories [50]. Three of the seven processes are suitable for fusing metals and alloys, materials that are commonly used in safety-critical applications: powder bed fusion, directed energy deposition and sheet lamination [15, 27, 37, 50]. All these processes are strongly dependent on computer control and automation. Depending on the chosen additive manufacturing technique, various manufacturing process parameters can influence the quality of manufactured parts. This section outlines the basic principles of the three additive manufacturing processes. The next section discusses the manufacturing parameters that affect the quality of the produced 3D objects.

In the powder bed fusion process, a layer of material (usually metal or polymer) in powder form is distributed in a chamber. A heat source, typically a laser or electron beam, is then used to selectively melt and fuse regions of the powder bed, thus producing a slice of the 3D object [50]. This process involving powder distribution and melting is repeated layer by layer.

In the directed energy deposition process, wire or powder is distributed via a nozzle [19, 26, 32]. Focused thermal energy, typically produced by a laser, melts and fuses the source material during its deposition [50].

In the sheet lamination process, thin sheets of metal or fiber-reinforced composites are bonded by compressive force and ultrasonic energy supplied by a rolling sonotrobe [18, 50]. A complex 3D part is then created by cutting the fused sheets of metal or composite lamina according to the desired shapes of the layers.

3.   Additive Manufacturing Threat Surface

This section discuss two aspects of attacks involving 3D printers: (i) attack vectors (i.e., how attacks can be launched); and (ii) changes to additive manufacturing process parameters that impact the physical properties of manufactured objects or even damage the additive manufacturing equipment itself. Although the additive manufacturing attack vectors have a significant overlap with traditional cyber attack vectors, several new attack vectors are unique to the additive manufacturing domain. Note that the types of adversaries and their motivation and business models are outside the scope of this research, although they are very important to understand.

3.1   Attack Vectors

Attack vectors should be analyzed in the context of the additive manufacturing workflow. Any actor in the workflow can be malicious and may compromise or circumvent communications channels.

Additive manufacturing equipment is usually obtained from dedicated manufacturers. In 2014, 49 manufacturers in thirteen countries produced and sold industrial-grade additive manufacturing equipment and hundreds of small companies sold desktop 3D printers [50]. The manufacturers, third-party companies and the user community develop and provide software and firmware that execute in the embedded controllers of additive manufacturing equipment as well as in the personal computers (control computers) that are used to submit manufacturing jobs. The control computers are also used to apply firmware updates to additive manufacturing equipment. The specification of a 3D object is provided using the Surface Tessellation Language (STL) [21] or the Additive Manufacturing File (AMF) format [1, 8, 28, 29], both of which specify "sliced" versions of a computer-aided design (CAD) model of the 3D object to be manufactured. Based on the 3D object description stored in an STL or AMF file, the control computer sends commands to the 3D printer that creates the specified object (e.g., positioning the build platform and nozzle, and adjusting the platform temperature). These commands are usually encoded in G-code [11], a language commonly used in computer-aided manufacturing (CAM).

- **Supply Chain Attacks:** Protecting against supply chain attacks is extremely challenging and expensive. Since software and hardware and the tools used for their design and development are commonly provided by third parties, it is impossible to guarantee that they are free from malicious content [48]. In the context of additive manufacturing, supply chain attacks can alter the hardware, firmware and software used in 3D printers and control computers. For example, hardware Trojans, backdoors and other malware can be embedded in 3D printers and control computers, enabling adversaries to alter manufacturing process parameters. Also, modifications of the tools used in additive manufacturing (e.g., to generate STL files) are categorized as supply chain attacks.

  Two types of supply chain attacks on additive manufacturing systems are not encountered in the cyber domain. One category of attacks involves the manipulation of physical components (e.g., mechanical parts used to distribute powder, motors used to move mechanical parts and heat sources); obviously, such attacks can have tremendous effects on the manufactured 3D objects. The second category includes attacks that target the production and distribution of source materials; these attacks result in different properties (e.g., composition, size, form factor and/or consistency) of the materials used in additive manufacturing. These two types of supply chain attacks cause physical manipulations that generally have more serious ramifications than typical cyber attacks.

- **Software and Firmware Updates:** Attacks on software and firmware updates are supply chain attacks that deserve special consideration and treatment. The updates, which are commonly used to fix bugs and vulnerabilities as well as to incorporate new features, can themselves introduce new bugs and vulnerabilities, and may even contain malware. Malicious updates can enable adversaries to manipulate a range of additive manufacturing parameters, affecting the manufacturing processes and, consequently, the physical properties of the manufactured objects. Because of their embedded nature, firmware updates are most commonly updated via device-to-device connections. Vendors distribute updates on media that are directly connected to the equipment by a trusted party in the additive manufacturing environment. Malicious updates can be passed by a malicious supplier that delivers malware as a component of a legitimate update, by a malicious entity that delivers an update that masquerades as a legitimate update, or by a malicious insider with physical access to the device who uses the update facility to install unauthorized firmware.

- **Code Injection:** It has been demonstrated over and over again that program bugs in third-party software can be exploited, as in the case of PDF files and viewers. Although the STL/AMF (and ASCII and binary) file formats are very simple, there is no guarantee that additive manufacturing devices have bugs that cannot be exploited by specially-crafted STL/AMF or other files. These bugs can enable the injection and execution of arbitrary code in additive manufacturing equipment. In fact, code injection attacks on additive manufacturing equipment would be expected to be very common because of the exposure of the equipment to STL and other files submitted by customers.

- **Modification of 3D Models:** Whereas the previously-described attack vectors compromise additive manufacturing equipment and, thus, affect selected or all manufacturing jobs, more targeted attacks are also possible. An important category of attacks are those that modify 3D models. An STL file specifies the geometric properties of an object that is to be manufactured. It also defines how the object should be manufactured, layer by layer; as such, it specifies the orientations involved during manufacturing. Modifications of the internal form (e.g., by creating internal cavities that are larger or smaller than designed, and changing the manufacturing orientation) can be hard to detect, but can have a significant impact on the physical (mechanical) properties of the manufactured object. Like a supply chain attack, the modifications can be performed by a malicious entity in the chain between the customer who designs the 3D object model and the additive manufacturing service provider that creates the object. Such attacks are commonly referred to as man-in-the-middle attacks.

- **Manufacturing Process Specification:** A scenario in which the specifications of manufacturing processes come from third parties is certainly futuristic. However, as discussed in [51], this would create new business opportunities and specialization models for different companies. At the same time, this would create an additional attack vector. Just like the modification of an object model, the modification of a manufacturing process specification would have direct implications on the physical properties of the manufactured objects.

It is clear that the attack vectors determine which attacks are possible. It is also obvious that different attack vectors can be used to launch the same type of attack. For example, multiple attack vectors can affect additive manufacturing parameters in the same way, resulting in the same impact on the manufactured objects.

3.2 Impact of Manufacturing Parameters

Successful attacks can exercise various influences on a manufacturing process. The attack vector determines the possible influences and their impacts on a manufactured 3D object as well on the additive manufacturing equipment. The exact relationship between the influence on the manufacturing process and the impact on the 3D object is extremely complex and depends on multiple parameters. The following qualitative causal relationships involving manufacturing parameters have been derived by analyzing the materials science and mechanical engineering literature related to additive manufacturing.

- **3D Shape:** Probably the most straightforward influence on an additive manufacturing process is a change in the specification of an object, especially its 3D shape. A particular customer or manufacturer could be targeted via a man-in-the-middle attack that intercepts and changes an STL or AMF file as it is transmitted from the customer to the manufacturer. On a broader scale, if the software, firmware or hardware of a 3D printer or control computer have been compromised, then changes to the 3D object description can be performed "on the fly." Modifications to 3D modeling and/or STL/AMF file generation tools have similar impacts.

  Modifications to the shape of an object can have various consequences. The most profound, albeit easy to detect, is a change to the external shape or size of a 3D object. If the manufactured object is a functional part of a complex device (e.g., jet engine), a change to its external shape or size can prevent its integration. One of the biggest advantages of additive manufacturing is its ability to produce objects with complex internal shapes (e.g., with custom shaped cavities) that reduce weight and save source material while ensuring the required structural properties. An attack that changes the shapes and/or sizes of the internal cavities can affect the weight of a 3D object and even its physical properties, affecting the reliability of the device. Furthermore, the exact size, location and form of a cavity can have an immediate impact on various physical properties, including resistance to mechanical and thermal exposure. These properties can greatly affect the lifetime of the functional part as well as that of the entire device.

- **Manufacturing Orientation:** Tensile tests reveal that the material used to manufacture 3D objects exhibits anisotropy – this means that the mechanical properties of a 3D object depend on its orientation when it was printed. An attack that rotates the description of a 3D object (e.g., 90 degrees around an axis) can significantly impact its mechanical properties. Compared with the more obvious changes to the shape or size of an object, a change in the object orientation is much harder to discern. Such an attack can impact the lifetime of the object (e.g., jet engine) and, by extension, the reliability of the larger system in which the object is used (e.g., airplane).

- **Powder Deposition:** When a powder bed fusion process is used, an attack can influence the thickness of the powder layer by manipulating the height of the build platform. To some extent, the thickness of the powder layer is also affected by the height of the powder dispenser platform. Furthermore, a manipulation of the distribution mechanism that levels the powder layer can create irregularities in powder layer thickness. Powder layer thickness has a strong impact on the microstructure. If the thickness of each layer is increased by a constant amount, the exterior dimensions and proportions of the manufactured object are affected. As in the case of a modification to the 3D object specification in an STL or AMF file, this attack can affect the ability to integrate the part in a complex device. Fortunately, the modifications are easily detected by taking measurements of the 3D object. In a more complex attack scenario, the thicknesses of the layers can be varied so that the exterior measurements do not exceed a threshold, which means that the changes would remain undetected even by a sophisticated tool such as a coordinate measuring machine. The varying thicknesses would almost certainly change the object microstructure, affecting the physical properties of the object and the larger device of which it is a component.

- **Wire Feed Speed:** The speed of the heat source in a powder bed process and both the speed of the wire feed and the heat source in a directed energy deposition process affect the quality and the degree of bonding of adjacent layers of material. If the wire feed system (nozzle) runs too fast, the material does not fuse or does not fuse properly due to the lower temperature. On the other hand, the quality of an object may be affected negatively if the heat source moves too slowly. In this case, some portions of an object would be exposed to higher temperature gradients than other portions, which would lead to an uneven microstructure and possibly high pore density. Moreover, the speed of the wire feed system influences the amount of the deposited material. This, in turn, influences the manufactured precision of the 3D object and may render the object non-compliant with the customer's specification.

- **Targeting and Positioning System:** In the directed energy deposition and powder bed fusion processes, a laser or an electron beam target the spot where the source material is supposed to melt (with the help of a scanning mirror in the case of the laser). In the directed energy deposition process, the nozzle and the build platform must be positioned properly in order to add a new droplet at the correct location. In some cases, the build platform moves relative to the nozzle (four- or five-axis-movements). Regardless of which nozzle deposition technology is used, the manipulation of the targeting or positioning systems would have an immediate impact on the shape and precision of the manufactured object. Furthermore, if a particular area is targeted by the heat source for an extended period of time, the resulting melting and uncontrollable material flow could significantly impact the precision as well as the microstructure of the manufactured object.

In an extreme case, selective heat source targeting can damage the additive manufacturing equipment. Furthermore, using a laser or an electron beam as a heat source requires the chamber to contain an inert gas or a high vacuum, respectively [2]; therefore, damage to the chamber can eventually lead to an explosion or implosion, respectively. If combustible metal powders such as titanium or aluminum alloys are used, damage to the containment chamber can lead to a fire or dust explosion [35], like the November 2013 incident at Powderpart Inc. [36]. Last, but not least, secondary explosions can be far more destructive than a primary explosion due to the increased quantity and concentration of dispersed combustible dust [35]. These can potentially cause deaths and injuries, and even the destruction of a manufacturing facility [35].

- **Fusing Material Patterns:** Another factor that greatly influences the temperature gradient is the pattern of the heat source [3]. The manipulation or replacement of this pattern changes the temperature gradient and negatively influences the microstructure and, consequently, the mechanical properties of the manufactured object. In the worst case, an adversary can selectively create weak points in a manufactured object, arbitrarily reducing its lifetime or causing a specific type of damage.

- **Timing:** In additive manufacturing, new layers should be applied over already-solidified underlying layers. Several timing attacks are possible. If the time intervals between the depositions of layers are insufficient, the consequences can be melting and uncontrollable material flow, which negatively impact the shape and physical properties of the manufactured object. If the time periods are too long, the object microstructure can be affected quite severely because of the weak bonding of adjacent layers. In composite parts, weak interfaces can lead to debonding and delamination, leading to premature failure of the manufactured objects. These patterns are often seen when the additive manufacturing process has been interrupted and continued shortly thereafter.

A timing attack can also influence the positioning mechanism. If the speed of the heat source or the depositing nozzle are manipulated, the material is exposed to less heat so that it does not optimally bond to the previous layer. The timing attack can be performed by manipulating the control software or the clock used by the additive manufacturing equipment.

- **Support Material:** If a support structure is necessary during additive manufacturing, then changing the amount of the support material or its physical properties can have an impact on the manufactured object. An attack that reduces the amount of support material can cause portions of the manufactured object to sag, leading to an unacceptable overall 3D shape [24]. Furthermore, the quality of the support material is also important because it enhances heat distribution and increases stiffness. Heat is distributed at the contact points of the support material and part, and is affected by the geometry and properties of the support material. Therefore, manipulations of the support material and its distribution can negatively affect the quality of the manufactured object.

- **Source Material:** Regardless of whether the powder is distributed in a powder bed or via a nozzle, the quality of the manufactured part depends on the powder particle size, shape (spherical/random) and the degree of recycling [43]. Unevenly-distributed particle sizes may lead to a part with higher density whereas evenly-distributed particle sizes may result in greater strength [30, 42]. The powder particle is usually less than 150 μm [12, 43]; the minimum sizes are dependent on the material. The particle size could be reduced further, but for cost and efficiency reasons, 60-150 μm particles are generally used. Some studies indicate that powders with spherical particles have good flow properties and high packing density [41, 42]. Therefore, a supply chain attack that replaces the expected powder with one with different properties can influence the physical properties of the manufactured objects.

- **Powder Recycling:** Powder is recycled to reduce waste. A manipulation of the system that mixes used and new material can have an immediate impact on the manufactured objects. A greater percentage of used powder has a greater negative impact on the microstructure and, consequently, the physical properties of the manufactured objects.

- **Ultrasonic Properties:** In the sheet lamination process (also known as ultrasonic additive manufacturing), thin metal sheets are fused by ultrasonic welding. The ultrasonic horn frequency and amplitude are adjusted by hardware or via a digital card housed in the control computer. An attack can cause the sonotrobe to produce ultrasound with different properties (i.e., frequency or amplitude). For example, high frequency ultrasound provides maximum spatial resolution and is, therefore, effective for bonding thin parts. Varying the frequency negatively impacts the bond strength [12, 18], affecting the mechanical properties of the manufactured objects, with all the possible consequences described above.

- **Temperature Control:** Each additive manufacturing process requires specific temperature conditions. Therefore, an attack that targets the cooling and/or pre-heating system can change the physical properties of the manufactured objects. Of great concern is the microstructure, which depends significantly on the cooling temperature and gradient. In order to reduce the temperature gradient between layers and to reduce the residual stress in the material, a constant temperature below the melting point is often maintained in the chambers of some additive manufacturing devices. Therefore, manipulations of the temperature in the chamber can affect the physical and interfacial properties of the manufactured objects with all the associated consequences.

An attack that manipulates the heating system can reduce the chamber temperature or increase the temperature of the material above its melting point. In the first case, the lower temperature adversely influences the microstructure and, thus, the physical properties of the 3D objects. In the second case, the higher temperature could lead to uncontrollable material flow, affecting the shape, size and microstructure of the manufactured object as well as requiring expensive cleaning of the chamber.

A cooling process is initiated after object printing and/or during post-processing. A high cooling rate may be used to achieve certain microstructure characteristics during post-processing. Manipulating the cooling process can affect the manufactured objects as well as contribute to increased wear of the additive manufacturing equipment and even damage key components.

- **Heat Sources:** Lasers and electron beams serve as heat sources in additive manufacturing processes. An attack that compromises a heat source can affect the temperature profile of the material. Temperature profiles that are higher or lower than normal can affect the microstructure of a manufactured object and negatively affect its physical properties. In addition to the intensity of the laser or electron beam, parameters such as the distance from the material and the speed at which the heat source rides over the powder influence the temperature gradient and, thus, affect the microstructure. The impact of this attack can be increased by combining it with other attacks such as the manipulation of the cooling system.

- **Chamber Atmosphere:** If a laser or electron beam is used as a heat source, the chamber should have an inert gas or a high vacuum, respectively [2]. In the case of a laser heat source, an attack that manipulates the inert gas pressure can impact the temperature profile and, thus, the object microstructure and physical properties [19]. If the vacuum is manipulated, the electron beam intensity decreases because electrons are deflected; the resulting change in the temperature profile affects the object microstructure and its physical properties.

- **Post-Processing:** Post-processing is intended to increase the quality of the end product. High isostatic pressure processing is commonly used

– it involves heating the manufactured object for several hours at high temperature and pressure [43]. An attack on the post-processing system can negatively impact the quality of the manufactured object; moreover, exceedingly high pressures and/or temperatures can damage the post-processing chamber itself. When composites are processed, it is customary to conduct post-cure cycles ranging from a few hours to a few days to relieve residual stresses in the manufactured objects. Malicious variations of key parameters during this phase can cause warping, shrinkage, stresses and possible damage.

4. Conclusions

Additive manufacturing is an emerging technology that builds 3D objects layer by layer. The range of applications and dependence on computerization make additive manufacturing an attractive target for attackers.

This chapter has focused on attacks that seek to change the physical properties of additive-manufactured components. The attacks can lead to weaker and possibly damaged manufactured components, and, in instances where the compromised components are used in safety-critical systems, the attacks can endanger human lives. In particular, this chapter has identified the attack vectors and the key additive manufacturing parameters that can be targeted to alter the physical properties of manufactured parts, damage additive manufacturing equipment and even a manufacturing facility itself. While some of the attack vectors emanate from the cyber domain, the majority of the attacks and influences target the materials science and mechanical engineering aspects of additive manufacturing processes and equipment.

Deep understanding of additive manufacturing and the potential threats is vital to developing protection and mitigation techniques and tools. Future research will attempt to quantify the effort needed to manipulate additive manufacturing processes and assess the severity of the consequences of successful attacks. The analysis of the commonalities of and differences between attacks will be facilitated by describing the attacks and the related effect propagation chains using CP-ADL, a powerful cyber-physical attack description language [54, 55].

References

[1] American Society for Testing and Materials, ISO/ASTM52915-13, Standard Specification for Additive Manufacturing File Format (AMF), Version 1.1, West Conshohocken, Pennsylvania, 2013.

[2] Arcam, Electron Beam Melting – in the Forefront of Additive Manufacturing, Molndal, Sweden (arcam.com/technology/electron-beam-melting), 2014.

[3] A. Bagsik, V. Schoppner and E. Klemp, FDM part quality manufactured with Ultem*9085, *Proceedings of the Fourteenth International Scientific Conference on Polymeric Materials*, 2010.

[4] S. Bradshaw, A. Bowyer and P. Haufe, The intellectual property implications of low-cost 3D printing, *ScriptEd*, vol. 7(1), pp. 5–31, 2010.

[5] E. Byres and J. Lowe, The myths and facts behind cyber security risks for industrial control systems, *Proceedings of the VDE Kongress*, 2004.

[6] T. Campbell and O. Ivanova, Additive manufacturing as a disruptive technology: Implications of three-dimensional printing, *Technology and Innovation*, vol. 15, pp. 67–79, 2013.

[7] S. Checkoway, D. McCoy, B. Kantor, D. Anderson, H. Shacham, S. Savage, K. Koscher, A. Czeskis, F. Roesner and T. Kohno, Comprehensive experimental analyses of automotive attack surfaces, *Proceedings of the Twentieth USENIX Conference on Security*, 2011.

[8] Cornell Creative Machines Lab, Standard Specification for Additive Manufacturing File Format (Draft F XXXX-10), Cornell University, Ithaca, New York (`creativemachines.cornell.edu/sites/default/files/AMF_V0.47.pdf`), 2014.

[9] S. Dadbakhsh and L. Hao, Effect of layer thickness in selective laser melting on microstructure of Al/5 wt.%Fe_2O_3 powder consolidated parts, *Scientific World Journal*, vol. 2014, article id. 106129, 2014.

[10] A. Drizo and J. Pegna, Environmental impacts of rapid prototyping: An overview of research to date, *Rapid Prototyping Journal*, vol. 12(2), pp. 64–71, 2006.

[11] Electronic Industries Association, Interchangeable Variable Block Data Format for Positioning, Contouring and Contouring/Positioning Numerically Controlled Machines, EIA Standard RS-274-D, Washington, DC, 1980.

[12] European Powder Metallurgy Association, Additive Manufacturing Technology, Shrewsbury, United Kingdom (`epma.com/additive-manufacturing-technology`), 2014.

[13] Fabrisonic, Sound 3D Printing, Columbus, Ohio (`fabrisonic.com`), 2014.

[14] N. Falliere, L. O'Murchu and E. Chien, W32.Stuxnet Dossier, Version 1.4, Symantec, Mountain View, California, 2011.

[15] P. Fastermann, *3D-Drucken: Wie die Generative Fertigungstechnik Funktioniert*, Springer-Verlag, Berlin Heidelberg, Germany, 2014.

[16] L. Forbes, H. Vu, B. Udrea, H. Hagar, X. Koutsoukos and M. Yampolskiy, SecureCPS: Defending a nanosatellite cyber-physical system, *Proceedings of the SPIE*, vol. 9085, 2014.

[17] H. Fujii, M. Sriraman and S. Babu, Quantitative evaluation of bulk and interface microstructures in Al-3003 alloy builds made by very high power ultrasonic additive manufacturing, *Metallurgical and Materials Transactions A*, vol. 42(13), pp. 4045–4055, 2011.

[18] A. Gebhardt, *Understanding Additive Manufacturing: Rapid Prototyping, Rapid Tooling, Rapid Manufacturing*, Hanser Publishers, Munich, Germany, 2012.

[19] I. Gibson, D. Rosen and B. Stucker, *Additive Manufacturing Technologies: Rapid Prototyping to Direct Digital Manufacturing*, Springer, New York, 2010.

[20] D. Helbing, Globally networked risks and how to respond, *Nature*, vol. 497(7447), pp. 51–59, 2013.

[21] J. Hiller and H. Lipson, STL 2.0: A Proposal for a Universal Multi-Material Additive Manufacturing File Format, Department of Mechanical and Aerospace Engineering, Cornell University, Ithaca, New York (creativemachines.cornell.edu/sites/default/files/SFF09_Hiller1.pdf), 2009.

[22] S. Huang, P. Liu, A. Mokasdar and L. Hou, Additive manufacturing and its societal impact: A literature review, *International Journal of Advanced Manufacturing Technology*, vol. 67(5-8), pp. 1191–1203, 2013.

[23] K. Koscher, A. Czeskis, F. Roesner, S. Patel, T. Kohno, S. Checkoway, D. McCoy, B. Kantor, D. Anderson, H. Shacham and S. Savage, Experimental security analysis of a modern automobile, *Proceedings of the IEEE Symposium on Security and Privacy*, pp. 447–462, 2010.

[24] T. Krol, M. Zah and C. Seidel, Optimization of supports in metal-based additive manufacturing by means of finite element models, *Proceedings of the International Solid Freeform Fabrication Symposium*, 2012.

[25] M. Krotofil, A. Cardenas, J. Larsen and D. Gollmann, Vulnerabilities of cyber-physical systems to stale data – Determining the optimal time to launch attacks, *International Journal of Critical Infrastructure Protection*, vol. 7(4), pp. 213–232, 2014.

[26] J. Kruth, M. Leu and T. Nakagawa, Progress in additive manufacturing and rapid prototyping, *CIRP Annals – Manufacturing Technology*, vol. 47(2), pp. 525–540, 1998.

[27] G. Lewis and E. Schlienger, Practical considerations and capabilities for laser assisted direct metal deposition, *Materials and Design*, vol. 21(4), pp. 417–423, 2000.

[28] H. Lipson, AMF tutorial: The basics (Part 1), *3D Printing and Additive Manufacturing*, vol. 1(2), pp. 85–87, 2014.

[29] H. Lipson, AMF tutorial: Colors and textures (Part 2), *3D Printing and Additive Manufacturing*, vol. 1(4), pp. 181–184, 2014.

[30] B. Liu, R. Wildman, C. Tuck, I. Ashcroft and R. Hague, Investigation of the effect of particle size distribution on processing parameters optimization in the selective laser melting process, *Proceedings of the International Solid Freeform Fabrication Symposium*, pp. 227–238, 2011.

[31] D. Manfredi, F. Calignano, M. Krishnan, R. Canali, E. Ambrosio and E. Atzeni, From powders to dense metal parts: Characterization of a commercial AlSiMg alloy processed through direct metal laser sintering, *Materials*, vol. 6(3), pp. 856–869, 2013.

[32] J. Mazumder, D. Dutta, N. Kikuchi and A. Ghosh, Closed loop direct metal deposition: Art to part, *Optics and Lasers in Engineering*, vol. 34(4-6), pp. 397–414, 2000.

[33] C. McNulty, N. Arnas and T. Campbell, Toward the printed world: Additive manufacturing and implications for national security, *Defense Horizons*, no. 73, pp. 1–16, 2012.

[34] A. Munoz and P. Sheng, An analytical approach for determining the environmental impact of machining processes, *Journal of Materials Processing Technology*, vol. 53(3), pp. 736–758, 1995.

[35] Occupational Safety and Health Administration, Hazard Alert: Combustible Dust Explosions, OSHA Fact Sheet, Washington, DC, 2014.

[36] Office of Public Affairs, After explosion, U.S. Department of Labor's OSHA cites 3-D printing firm for exposing workers to combustible metal powder, electrical hazards – Powderpart Inc. faces $64,400 in penalties, OSHA Regional News Release, Department of Labor, Washington, DC, May 20, 2014.

[37] G. Ram, Y. Yang and B. Stucker, Effect of process parameters on bond formation during ultrasonic consolidation of aluminum alloy 3003, *Journal of Manufacturing Systems*, vol. 25(3), pp. 221–238, 2006.

[38] M. Ratto and R. Ree, Materializing information: 3D printing and social change, *First Monday*, vol. 17(7), 2012.

[39] P. Reeves, How the socioeconomic benefits of rapid manufacturing can offset technological limitations, *Proceedings of the RAPID Conference and Exposition*, 2008.

[40] S. Rinaldi, J. Peerenboom and T. Kelly, Identifying, understanding and analyzing critical infrastructure interdependencies, *IEEE Control Systems*, vol. 21(6), pp. 11–25, 2001.

[41] Sandvik Materials Technology, Metal Powder for Additive Manufacturing, Sandviken, Sweden (smt.sandvik.com/en/products/metal-powder/add itive-manufacturing), 2015.

[42] C. Schade, T. Murphy and C. Walton, Development of Atomized Powders for Additive Manufacturing, Hoeganaes Corporation, Cinnaminson, New Jersey (www.gkn.com/hoeganaes/media/Tech%20Library/Schade ade-Atomized%20Powders%20for%20Additive%20Manufacturing%20(1) .pdf), 2014.

[43] L. Schutzle, Research on the Impact of Additive Layer Manufacturing for Future Space Missions, Internship Report CDF-STA-009, European Space Agency, Paris, France, 2014.

[44] J. Slay and M. Miller, Lessons learned from the Maroochy water breach, in *Critical Infrastructure Protection*, E. Goetz and S. Shenoi (Eds.), Springer, Boston, Massachusetts, pp. 73–82, 2007.

[45] A. Sternstein, Things can go kaboom when a defense contractor's 3-D printer gets hacked, *Nextgov*, September 11, 2014.

[46] D. Thomas, Economics of the U.S. Additive Manufacturing Industry, NIST Special Publication 1163, National Institute of Standards and Technology, Gaithersburg, Maryland, 2013.

[47] D. Thomas and S. Gilbert, Costs and Cost Effectiveness of Additive Manufacturing, NIST Special Publication 1176, National Institute of Standards and Technology, Gaithersburg, Maryland, 2014.

[48] K. Thompson, Reflections on trusting trust, *Communications of the ACM*, vol. 27(8), pp. 761–763, 1984.

[49] M. Weinberg, It will be awesome if they don't screw it up: 3D printing, intellectual property and the fight over the next great disruptive technology, Public Knowledge, Washington, DC (www.publicknowledge.org/files/docs/3DPrintingPaperPublicKnowledge.pdf), 2010.

[50] Wohlers Associates, Wohlers Report 2015, Fort Collins, Colorado, 2015.

[51] M. Yampolskiy, T. Andel, J. McDonald, W. Glisson and A. Yasinsac, Intellectual property protection in additive layer manufacturing: Requirements for secure outsourcing, *Proceedings of the Fourth Program Protection and Reverse Engineering Workshop*, article no. 7, 2014.

[52] M. Yampolskiy, T. Andel, J. McDonald, W. Glisson and A. Yasinsac, Towards security of additive layer manufacturing, presented at the *Thirtieth Annual Computer Security Applications Conference*, 2014.

[53] M. Yampolskiy, P. Horvath, X. Koutsoukos, Y. Xue and J. Sztipanovits, Systematic analysis of cyber-attacks on the CPS-evaluating applicability of the DFD-based approach, *Proceedings of the Fifth International Symposium on Resilient Control Systems*, pp. 55–62, 2012.

[54] M. Yampolskiy, P. Horvath, X. Koutsoukos, Y. Xue and J. Sztipanovits, Taxonomy for descriptions of cross-domain attacks on CPSs, *Proceedings of the Second ACM International Conference on High Confidence Networked Systems*, pp. 135–142, 2013.

[55] M. Yampolskiy, P. Horvath, X. Koutsoukos, Y. Xue and J. Sztipanovits, A language for describing attacks on cyber-physical systems, *International Journal of Critical Infrastructure Protection*, vol. 8, pp. 40–52, 2015.

Chapter 12

USING INFORMATION FLOW METHODS TO SECURE CYBER-PHYSICAL SYSTEMS

Gerry Howser

Abstract   The problems involved in securing cyber-physical systems are well known to the critical infrastructure protection community. However, the diversity of cyber-physical systems means that the methods used to analyze system security must often be reinvented. The issues of securing the physical assets of a system, the electronics that control the system and the interfaces between the cyber and physical components of the system require a number of security tools. Of particular interest is preventing an attacker from exploiting nondeducibility-secure information flows to hide an attack or the source of an attack. This potentially enables the attacker to interrupt system availability.

This chapter presents an algorithm that formalizes the steps taken to design and test the security of a cyber-physical system. The algorithm leverages information flow security techniques to secure physical assets, cyber assets and the boundaries between security domains.

Keywords: Cyber-physical systems, information flow security, nondeducibility

1.   Introduction

Modern critical infrastructures, which comprise computers, embedded devices, networks and software systems, are vital to day-to-day operations in every sector [6, 28]. A prominent feature of a cyber-physical system (CPS) is that it consists of embedded computers and communications networks that govern physical manifestations and computations, which, in turn, affect how these two major components interact with each other and the outside world [17]. The combined discrete computational and continuous physical nature of a cyber-physical system compounds the difficulty; not only do these systems have different semantics, but the system boundaries are blurred from pure cyber and pure physical systems. The lack of clearly-defined boundaries creates new se-

© IFIP International Federation for Information Processing 2015
M. Rice, S. Shenoi (Eds.): Critical Infrastructure Protection IX, IFIP AICT 466, pp. 185–205, 2015.
DOI: 10.1007/978-3-319-26567-4_12

curity and privacy vulnerabilities, some of which are difficult to detect and correct.

A textbook definition of computer security [4] relies on three fundamental concepts: confidentiality, integrity and availability. In the case of critical infrastructure protection, a unique problem exists from a security perspective – changes in the physical portion of an infrastructure are observable, which inherently violates confidentiality in the infrastructure. Adversaries can potentially derive sensitive internal settings by observing external system changes. This derived knowledge, coupled with the semantic knowledge of the system, can be used against the system in the form of integrity and availability attacks.

The problem of securing physical assets is as old as society itself. The idea of more secure zones completely contained within less secure zones is still one of the most effective ways to secure a physical area. This concept can be adapted to designing security for electronics, computer systems and the cyber portions of cyber-physical systems. Access control methods combined with methods that divide the cyber assets into domains with varying levels of security [2] can produce a reasonably secure cyber system.

However, cyber-physical systems present unique challenges in terms of security. Not only must the cyber and physical components of the system be secured, but the two sets of components are interdependent. This interdependence or coupling leads to complex situations that cannot usually be described by traditional security models. Cyber-physical system security must also address the flow of information between the cyber and physical systems as well as information leaked by the act of observing the physical system. The security domains are intricate in that more secure layers are not completely contained within less secure layers (like an onion) and the security domains frequently overlap in highly complex ways.

What is lacking is a clear methodology for securing cyber-physical system assets despite their inherent complexity. This chapter presents an algorithm that can guide a team of experts who are familiar with a specific cyber-physical system to develop descriptions of physical asset security, cyber asset security, and secure information flows between the various assets. The question is: How can all the parts of a cyber-physical system that cannot be hidden from an observer be secured? Due to its very nature, a cyber-physical system leaks some information that an adversary can use against the system. Unfortunately, it is not enough to secure the physical and cyber systems independently; it is imperative to also secure the flow of information between the two systems.

2.   Background

This section discusses the principal concepts involved in using information flow methods to secure cyber-physical systems. Table 1 describes the nomenclature used in this chapter.

Table 1. Nomenclature.

Symbol	Description
s_x	Boolean state variable; s_x is true or false
$\neg$	Logical NOT
$\wedge$	Logical AND
$\vee$	Logical OR
$\oplus$	Exclusive OR: $\varphi \oplus \psi \equiv (\varphi \vee \psi) \wedge \neg(\varphi \wedge \psi)$
$\rightarrow$	Material implication: $\varphi \rightarrow \psi \equiv \neg\varphi \vee \psi$
φ	Arbitrary logical formula or statement evaluated in $w \in W$
ψ	Arbitrary logical formula or statement evaluated in $w \in W$
wff	Well-formed logical formula
$\Box\varphi$	Modal "must be so" operator ("it is always that...")
$\Diamond\varphi$	Modal "possible" operator ("it is possible that...")
$w \vdash \varphi$	Statement φ is valid in world w ("yields")
$w \models \varphi$	Values from world w cause φ to evaluate to true ("models")
$\mathfrak{F}$	Kripke frame
$\mathfrak{M}$	Kripke model built over a Kripke frame
$_wR_{w'}$	Transition function from world w to $w' : w, w' \in W$
$\mathfrak{R}$	Set of transition functions in a complete Kripke frame
$\mathbb{V}_x^i(\varphi)$	Valuation function of Boolean x in domain i
$B_i\varphi$	Modal BELIEF operator
$I_{i,j}\varphi$	Modal INFORMATION TRANSFER operator
$U_j\varphi$	Modal UTTERANCE (broadcast) operator
$T_{i,j}$	Modal TRUST operator

2.1 Information Flow Security

Two main approaches are available within the context of critical infrastructure system security policies and mechanisms: (i) access control methods; and (ii) information flow methods. Although access control methods are frequently used and are well understood, considerable evidence in the literature suggests that information flow models are the most promising mechanisms for cyberphysical systems [5, 11, 20–23, 26, 29].

The principal focus of information flow security is to prevent unintended high-level (secure/private) domain information disclosures to a low-level (open or public) domain. A security policy may define exactly what low-level users are forbidden to know about a high-level domain, but the enforcement depends on sound implementation and trust. Traditional security models such as the Harrison-Ruzzo-Ullman (HRU) model [12], Bell-LaPadula (BLP) model [1, 2] and Biba model [3] restrict access to information and resources by taking an access control approach to the security problems of assuring confidentiality, integrity and availability.

Access control methods are unable to address the issues of indirect security violations that involve explicit or implicit information flows [13]. Imposing strict rules and restrictions on the assets that can be accessed cannot govern how the assets and data are used after they have been accessed. A high-level process can easily signal information to a low-level process by setting a flag, filling a buffer or writing data to a non-secure location. While this is an indirect violation of the Bell-LaPadula *-property [2], no direct violation of the "write-down" property occurs; yet, the low-level process may have gained sensitive information that resides in a high-level security partition. Access control methods cannot enforce proper security on information flows (nor were they designed to do so) without enforcing severe restrictions on the access to sensitive assets. This issue has been pointed out by many researchers [5, 11, 20–23, 26, 29]. Using access control models to correctly describe and constrain information flows is attempting to do something that they were never designed to do. These models trust that all agents act according to the rules; they cannot guarantee security if an agent is not trustworthy.

While access control models rely heavily on idealized security partitions, cyber-physical systems usually have less well-defined and well-ordered partitioning. A more useful approach is to use information flow security policies to impose restrictions on all known information flows between security partitions with less regard for the high-level/low-level ordering. In short, information flows between security partitions should be viewed from the perspective of various loosely-defined security domains with less regard for security clearances. In information flow security, a violation by an agent in a lower security domain could involve actions such as monitoring an information flow, disrupting an information flow, modifying an information flow or simply detecting the existence of an information flow. The only solution is to prevent information flows between processes that are not allowed to communicate under the security policies of the system [8, 29]. Many information flow models describe these desired and unwanted information flows. Some of the most notable models are noninterference [10], noninference [24], nondeducibility [27] and multiple security domain nondeducibility (MSDND) [14].

The physical assets of a critical cyber-physical system must be thought of as low-level outputs because the assets can be physically viewed by an attacker. Frequently, by monitoring the changes in physical assets, sensitive information about the states and actions of a system can flow to the attacker. These flows can be described using the notions of noninterference, noninference and nondeducibility. Noninterference is most consistent with the popular notion of high security. If a system is noninterference secure, agents in the low level are unaware of any actions in the high level. Noninference-secure systems prevent low-level agents from determining if the actions they observe are due to high-level or low-level events. Nondeducibility-secure systems prevent all low-level agents from determining high-level events no matter how many low-level events are observed. In essence, in a nondeducibility-secure system, low-level events might be the result of many different high-level, or even low-level, events and, therefore, no reliable information is leaked.

2.2   Physical System Security

Fortunately, it is known how to secure physical assets. This has likely been done since before the dawn of recorded history. In essence, securing a physical system such as an electric grid is the same problem as securing any other physical asset. No matter how secure the system is electronically, an attacker who gets to the system can disable it.

2.3   Cyber System Security

While tight physical security is ideal, it makes a cyber-physical system more difficult for users to access. Ideally, a mobile user would access the system only via a network. Indeed, with the advent of cloud computing, the user need not even know where the physically-secured assets are located. Do you really know where your email server is located? Do you know where your Internet service provider connects to the Internet?

Over the past thirty or forty years, an excellent suite of cyber security tools has been developed. It is known how to secure a cyber system and the trade-offs between security and accessibility are well understood. Techniques such as user names and passwords, when combined with common sense and encryption, work well to manage the use of assets. Messages between cyber systems can be kept private by the proper use of encryption in most cases. Indeed, cyber security is almost as well understood as physical security.

2.4   Information Flow as Information Leakage

Too many people believe that combining physical security with cyber security is adequate to secure a cyber-physical system. However, it is not that simple. A cyber-physical system typically leaks information when it is operating normally. For example, many modern cars automatically unlock when the correct key fob is present. The information that the correct key fob is within range is leaked to the driver and to any observers in the vicinity. If an individual enters a locked car without physically unlocking the door, it is safe to assume that the individual has the correct key fob somewhere on his or her person. If not, the door would remain locked. Secure information that "the individual has the key" is leaked by way of noninterference [10, 13, 21]. An information flow has occurred from the secure domain of the car to the unsecured domain of the outside world. Such flows of information could have serious consequences in mission-critical systems.

What is needed is a method – preferably an algorithm – to ensure that a cyber-physical system is properly secured from physical threats and cyber threats, and that all information flows are either eliminated or secured. Algorithm 1 formalizes the steps needed to design and test the security of a cyber-physical system.

Algorithm 1 : Cyber-physical system security.

1: **procedure** CPS SECURITY(status)
2:     Set status to insecure   ▷ Assume the worst
3:     **while** status insecure **do**   ▷ Check physical security
4:         **procedure** PHYSICAL SECURITY(status)
5:             Disallow all access   ▷ Start with no access
6:             Allow limited access   ▷ Only allow as much access as needed
7:             Check known physical threats
8:             **if** physically protected **then**
9:                 Set status to secure
10:            **else**
11:                Refine physical security
12:            **end if**
13:        **end procedure**
14:        **if** status secure **then**
15:            **procedure** CYBER SECURITY(status)
16:                Set status to insecure
17:                Describe CPS using HRU   ▷ Access control model
18:                **if** HRU secure **then**
19:                    Describe CPS using BLP/Lipner   ▷ Similar to "Top Secret"
20:                    **if** BLP/Lipner secure **then**
21:                        Set status to secure
22:                    **else**
23:                        Refine BLP/Lipner security
24:                    **end if**
25:                **else**
26:                    Refine access control matrix security
27:                **end if**
28:            **end procedure**
29:        **end if**
30:        **if** status secure **then**
31:            **procedure** MSDND SECURITY(status)
32:                Set status to insecure
33:                **while** status insecure **do**
34:                    Describe CPS using MSDND
35:                    Test all known information flow threats
36:                    **if** MSDND secure **then**
37:                        Set status to secure
38:                    **else**
39:                        Refine MSDND security
40:                    **end if**
41:                **end while**
42:            **end procedure**
43:        **end if**
44:    **end while**
45: **end procedure**

---

3.   Securing Cyber-Physical Systems

Because a cyber-physical system naturally divides into three main areas (physical system, cyber system and the interactions between the two systems), the cyber-physical system can be secured in three major steps with some adjustments. The steps are really loops in the sense that it is possible to go back to the start frequently because the fundamental understanding of the cyber-physical system may change during the security analysis. For example, it may be determined that some objects are really subjects or that some security domains may have to be reconsidered. Changes made to secure one cyber asset may expose previously-secure cyber assets to attack.

3.1   Physical Security Analysis

The first step in securing a cyber-physical system is to implement physical security. Without physical security there is no point in attempting any cyber security. Physical security can be achieved by following the procedure CPS SECURITY in Algorithm 1. As in the case of configuring a firewall (network firewall or physical firewall), it is best to start by eliminating all access. Should an access path be overlooked, it will have already been closed. After the assets are physically secured, each user is analyzed to see exactly what physical access the user requires in order to use the cyber-physical system. Usually, only the engineering and maintenance staff would require physical access to the cyber-physical system, but there will always be some individuals who think they require the ability to physically touch the equipment. A good rule of thumb is to view any individual with physical access as a physical threat to the system; this includes security personnel as well.

3.2   Cyber Security Analysis

Several tools have been developed for securing the cyber assets of cyber-physical systems. This work will touch on a few that are useful for conducting information flow security analyses. It is still critical to secure the electronics, computing equipment, data and communications channels, but the main thrust is to concentrate on the methods that can help identify the parts of a cyber-physical system that are components of an information flow security analysis.

- **Harrison-Ruzzo-Ullman Access Control Matrix:** The access control matrix introduced by Harrison et al. [12, 21] is analogous to the common permissions in Unix and Linux systems. The Harrison-Ruzzo-Ullman model separates the entities under consideration into two categories that are of interest in an information flow security study. One category comprises objects that can only react to commands and report status, but not initiate any actions. The other category comprises subjects that can initiate actions that affect other subjects or objects, in addition to doing all the things that an object can do.

Table 2.   Harrison-Ruzzo-Ullman model and Linux analog.

	HRU Object	HRU Subject
Linux r	Allows object to report information	Same as for HRU object
Linux w	Allows object to accept commands	Same as for HRU object
Linux x	Not allowed	Subject issues commands

A Linux analogy is useful (Table 2). In Linux, everything is treated as a file and the permissions on the file determine what the file is allowed to do. A file with the x (execute) permission set is analogous to a subject and can initiate actions or be acted upon by other subjects. If the x permission is not set, the file cannot initiate any actions, but can only be acted upon, much like a Harrison-Ruzzo-Ullman object. Unfortunately, the Harrison-Ruzzo-Ullman model is not of much use in describing a cyber-physical system or even in examining the cyber components for vulnerabilities. However, it can be used to quickly identify the entities of the system and assign each entity the role of a subject or object, which are important when performing an information flow security analysis.

- **Bell-LaPadula Model:** The Bell-LaPadula model [1, 21] describes the protection of the confidentiality, integrity and availability of assets by assigning each subject or object to an appropriate security domain. The Bell-LaPadula model also forces an analyst to order the security domains from least secure to most secure; while this is highly appropriate for cyber assets, it is not always appropriate for cyber-physical systems. The domains that result when using the Bell-LaPadula model to describe the system are usually a good starting point for determining the security domains for a multiple security domain nondeducibility (MSDND) information flow analysis.

- **Biba and Lipner Models:** If the security partition analysis performed on a system specified using the Bell-LaPadula model leads to issues related to the trust and integrity between partitions, further granularity may be introduced by using the Biba [3] or Lipner [19] models. The two models allow a form of lattice security, but, unfortunately, while a cyber-physical system may be described in a better manner, it is usually not more secure. The Biba and Lipner models were developed to secure purely cyber assets and attackers have many simple methods to get around the constraints of the models.

3.3   Complications

Complications occur when a cyber system controls a physical system. As noted above, the earlier security models were developed to handle pure cyber assets. However, cyber-physical systems introduce novel vulnerabilities for the following reasons:

- Physical assets can be observed by an attacker.

- Physical and cyber assets are inextricably intertwined and can be exploited easily.

- Cyber-physical systems always leak some information. If detailed information flow security analyses are not performed, then the cyber-physical systems may be highly vulnerable.

For example, if a large data center is hidden underground, an attacker might still find the center by observing the cooling system which is invariably outdoors. Likewise, the security gates and traffic into and out of the center are difficult to hide.

As another example, assume that a cluster of Linux processors is set up to crack the encryption of Internet traffic. While it is relatively simple to remove the rights of a casual employee to monitor the processes on the cluster, it is difficult to mask the changes in the amount of processing that occur at any given time. The high usage of cyber assets leads to an observable increase in the use of physical assets such as fans, power, cooling and blinking lights.

Drive-by-wire automobiles, fly-by-wire airplanes, subway traffic control systems and smart traffic lights can be observed over long periods of time. Their actions cannot be hidden and lead to information about system commands and responses being leaked. If the flows are identified, they may be masked as proposed by Gamage [9] or at least be monitored for possible attacks.

4. Nondeducibility and Security

Several information flow security models, such as noninterference and noninference [8, 10, 21], were developed in the 1980s and 1990s to protect information flow between cyber processes. Flows that can be described accurately by these early models can also be described by multiple security domain nondeducibility (MSDND); this reduces the number of models that need to be considered. Nondeducibility of an information flow is important because, not only can information be leaked without detection, but an attacker can use nondeducibility to hide an attack completely or at least hide the source of the attack.

4.1 Deducibility vs. Nondeducibility

Assume that a network is using a hardware encryption block for all communications. If the hardware encryption block does not draw power when it passes a plaintext message, an adversary would be able to correctly deduce the fact that a message is encrypted when extra power usage is observed. In this case, the encryption of a message is deducible.

On the other hand, if the hardware encryption block were to be changed to encrypt all messages and then send either encrypted or plaintext messages, the power usage would be essentially the same for an encrypted message and a plaintext message. An adversary could not be able to correctly deduce if a message was being sent as encrypted or as plaintext. In this case, the state of the message is nondeducible or nondeducibly secure.

4.2   Definitions

This section provides the definitions of several key concepts.

Kripke Frames and Models.   This work examines information flow security from the viewpoint of Kripke frames and models [14]. It is enough to know that a frame is made up of worlds ($w \in W$ where each world is a unique combination of binary state variables) and the transitions between worlds. A model with valuation functions to evaluate logical questions about the state variable values for a world can be built on the Kripke frame. This model can then be used to describe the information flows and state changes of a cyber-physical system. It is important to note that, if there is no valuation function for a state variable for a given world, then neither the value of the state variable nor the truth value of any query containing the variable can be determined.

This work uses the shorthand $\mathbb{V}_\varphi^i(w)$ to denote the valuation function used by an agent i for a logical query with a number of state variables. If the entity has valuation functions for all the state variables in query φ, then the functions can be composed into a single valuation for the query on the world w.

Nondeducibility.   Multiple security domain nondeducibility (MSDND) [14] was proposed to address situations where information flows in cyber-physical systems are difficult to describe using existing models. If two states are mutually exclusive, i.e., one and only one state may be true and the other must be false, and an agent cannot evaluate either state, then the resulting states are nondeducibility secure. Simply put, if the state of a true/false variable cannot be deduced, then the variable is nondeducibility secure.

Multiple Security Domain Nondeducibility (MSDND).   MSDND is defined over a set of state changes of a cyber-physical system. Suppose $x_i \in X$ is a set of state variables. In order to know the state of any $x_i \in X$, the model must have some valuation function that returns the truth value of the variable. This is denoted by $\mathbb{V}_i^j(w)$, which returns the truth value of x_i as seen by entity j. It is entirely possible that one entity can evaluate x_i and another cannot. For example, a systems administrator may be able to see that file `fred` exists while user Sam might not. Suppose $\varphi = x_i$ is a logical expression. Then, the expression must be either true or false on every world; there is no other choice.

Therefore, φ is MSDND secure on world w if and only if Equation (1) or Equation (2) is true as in Figure 1. In other words, if for every possible combination of events, an entity cannot evaluate a logical expression, then the expression is MSDND secure.

$$MSDND = \forall w \in W : w \vdash \Box\,[s_x \oplus s_y] \wedge \left[w \models (\,\not\exists\mathbb{V}_x^i(w) \wedge\,\not\exists\mathbb{V}_y^i(w))\right] \qquad (1)$$

When s_x is $\varphi = \top$ and s_y is $\neg\varphi = \top$:

$$MSDND = \forall w \in W : \left[w \models (\,\not\exists\mathbb{V}_\varphi^i(w))\right] \qquad (2)$$

Figure 1. Formal definition of MSDND.

5. Nondeducibility Secure Attacks

This section discusses two examples of nondeducibility secure attacks, one involving a drive-by-wire car and the other involving a cream separator at an ice cream plant. As a matter of fact, the modeling and analysis of the cream separator formally shows how the Stuxnet virus operated [15].

Table 3. HRU analysis of the drive-by-wire car.

Entity	HRU	Actions
car	Subject	Can initiate and respond to actions
corp	Subject	Can initiate and respond to actions
driver	Subject	Can initiate and respond to actions
tc	Object	Can respond to commands

5.1 Drive-by-Wire Car

A drive-by-wire car equipped with remote assistance such as OnStar or Toyota Connect is a good example of a cyber-physical system with complex security domains [13]. The model comprises a (*corp*) that provides an automobile (*car*) with onboard drive-by-wire functionality and traction control (*tc*) and service to the driver of the automobile (*driver*) in the form of remote assistance (navigation, remote unlock, remote shutdown, etc.). Table 3 shows the results of a Harrison-Ruzzo-Ullman analysis of the system.

Table 4 presents the results of a Bell-LaPadula (BLP) analysis, which yields increasingly secure domains with *tc* being the most secure. However, these results do not reflect the reality of the drive-by-wire car. As will be shown later, in some modes of operation, the driver is unable to issue commands and essentially becomes a passenger in the car [13]. In reality, the security domains are overlapping and complex (Figure 2). What is more, the relationships between the *car*, *corp*, *driver* and *tc* change depending on the mode of operation. The Bell-LaPadula model is simply not designed to handle this situation.

The security of this cyber-physical system depends on more than access control or security domains. The operation of the car leads to complex information

Table 4.   Bell-LaPadula domains of the drive-by-wire car.

Entity	BLP Domain	Security Level
driver	SD^{driver}	4
car	SD^{car}	2
corp	SD^{corp}	3
tc	SD^{tc}	1

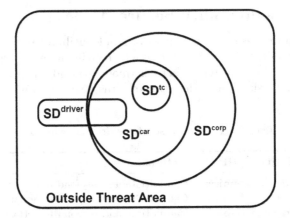

Figure 2.   Security domains of the car.

flows between the entities and these flows must be secured from interruption and modification. The MSDND model was developed to accurately describe such information flows. Some flows may need to be made MSDND secure from outside observation; these flows can be made even more secure. Other flows may be critical to the operation of the car and open to an MSDND-secure attack that allows an attacker to hide his actions or at least hide the source of the attack. In this case, steps should be taken to make the information flow not MSDND secure using a separate physical indicator or measurement.

The following three modes of operation are relevant to the discussion:

- **Normal Operation:** The *driver* can operate the *car*. From this, the *driver* knows he/she controls the *car*.

- **Hazardous Road Conditions:** Most modern automobiles are equipped with traction control systems that automatically correct when there is a loss of traction. When traction control (*tc*) is active, the *car* will attempt to correct a skid and counter anything the *driver* does that would make the skid worse.

- **Corporate Remote Operations:** If the *car* is equipped with a service such as OnStar, the corporation (*corp*) can issue commands to the *car*.

The *driver* must trust the corporation to act in his best interests [13, 14]. Television commercials present the benefits of access to a car via a network such as the Internet or a corporate connection, but is this a good thing? It may be fun to lock or unlock car doors from a cell phone [30], but what happens when the cell phone is hacked or stolen? What if the corporation or car network is hacked and the hacker decides to simply power off as many cars as possible [25]?

The fundamental question is: Who is in control when the *car* refuses to respond? It is obvious that the *car* will only respond to one set of commands from either the *driver*, traction control (*tc*) or the corporate network (*corp*). Depending on which mode the *car* is in, the *driver* may be unable to distinguish who or what is actually in control. Of particular interest is remote operation by *corp*, which exists in one security domain, versus operation by *driver*, which is in another security domain (see Figure 2). What the *driver* can and cannot ascertain is governed by the information flow that exists between domains – the cyber domain as well as the physical domain. The ensuing discussion shows how classical models of information flow and deducibility break down in the cyber-physical environment.

If traction control takes control of the *car*, the *driver* notices a complete lack of response to *driver* commands. While this is disconcerting at first, the traction control (*tc*) reacts to more accurate and timely knowledge of the road conditions and any lack of traction by the tires than the *driver*.

But what if someone uses the network to take control of the car? In this case, the *car* will not respond to *driver* commands, but will only respond to the network commands.

There are two questions of interest here. First, who is in control of the *car*? Second, can the *driver* correctly deduce who is in control?

Obviously, the *car* will only respond to commands from one source at a time. The highest level of commands are from the corporation network (*corp*) such as OnStar, then the traction control module (*tc*) and finally the *driver*. If the commands come from the *driver*, all is well and the *driver* can correctly deduce who is in control. However, the *driver* sees the same loss of control and unexpected actions if either *tc* or *corp* is in control, but cannot determine which entity is in control.

Mathematically, the question of who is in control of the car is expressed as:

$$\forall w \in W : w \vdash [tc \oplus corp] \wedge \left[\not\exists \mathbb{V}_{corp}^{driver}(w) \wedge \not\exists \mathbb{V}_{tc}^{driver}(w) \right] \qquad (3)$$

This is exactly what is required to show that the control of the *car* is MSDND secure from the *driver*. In this case, MSDND has been turned against the *driver* to hide a possible attack. Moreover, because a failure of the *tc* would act in the same way, the source of the attack is also MSDND secure by the same reasoning. Indeed, it is quite possible that, in the case of a cyber-physical system, security tools and methods may be turned against the system itself. In

Table 5.   Harrison-Ruzzo-Ullman analysis of the cream separator.

Domain	Name	Type
0	Cream Separator	Object
1	Virus	Subject
2	Controller	Subject
3	Monitor System	Subject
4	Human Operator	Subject

fact, when attacking a cyber-physical system, it is often enough to disrupt the normal flow of commands to damage or destroy the system.

5.2   Cream Separator

Assume that an ice cream company has discovered the exact butterfat content to make perfect ice cream. The process employs a centrifuge connected to a programmable logic controller (PLC) to act as a cream separator.

Table 6.   Process control system security domains.

Domain	Valuation	Name
SD^0	$\mathbb{V}^0$	Cream Separator
SD^1	$\mathbb{V}^1$	Virus
SD^2	$\mathbb{V}^2$	Controller
SD^3	$\mathbb{V}^3$	Monitor System
SD^4	$\mathbb{V}^4$	Human Operator

A cursory Harrison-Ruzzo-Ullman analysis results in the identification of subjects and objects shown in Table 5. However, an attempt to describe the system using the Bell-LaPadula model produces a less than satisfactory set of security domains. The cream separator does not easily divide into the security partitions expected when using the Bell-LaPadula model. The security domains are not hierarchical as would be expected, although there is a logical structure, the Bell-LaPadula model simply fails for this system. However, the Bell-LaPadula model does assist in decomposing the cyber-physical system into security domains. As such, there are five separate security domains as defined in Table 6 and illustrated in Figure 3. In this case, an information flow security analysis yields a more useful description.

The plant can use an MSDND-security analysis to spot this possibility where other methods will not. At the separator, the speed is not MSDND secure because the sensors on the separator correctly read the speed. However, when the speed reading is reported to the controller, the virus intercepts the reading

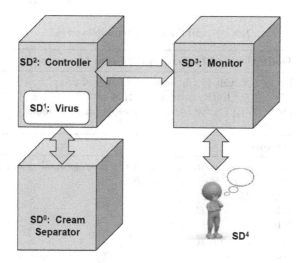

Figure 3. Abstract plant model with security domains.

and reports to the controller that the separator is operating at the correct speed regardless of its actual speed. Likewise, the virus intercepts messages from the controller to speed up or slow down the separator. Eventually, the separator spins at the wrong speed and poor quality ice cream is produced. To assist in this analysis, Liau's BIT logic [18] presented in Table 7 is employed. Interested readers are referred to [15] for the complete axiomatic system.

The separator makes cream under the control of a programmable controller. A monitor reads what the controller senses from the physical process and displays the results to a human. Consider a portion of the controller to be a program that is not functioning as anticipated. This could be due to many reasons ranging from a software bug to an actual virus. In this model, multiple security domains exist, but the notions of high and low security are not relevant. In the remainder of the discussion, let φ denote "cream is being separated properly." Obviously, either φ or $\neg\varphi$ must be true at all times. Under normal conditions, the controller/monitor system oversees the cream separator and makes adjustments to ensure that φ is true.

If the system is operating correctly (without the virus), all operations performed by the controller are successfully carried out and reported back to the monitor deducibly. In other words, every action in a domain is uniquely identifiable in another domain; the cream separation process is reported correctly to the operator, operator commands are carried out by the controller on the cream separator, etc.

The key to demonstrating the integrity of the system is to show that the desired information flow cannot be disrupted. If the system is not MSDND secure, then each observation or command can be uniquely attributed to its corresponding command and observation. To start with, it is necessary to

Table 7. BIT logic axiomatic system.

---

1. Definitions of Logical and Modal Operators

D6:	$B_i\varphi$ Entity i believes the truth of φ
D7:	$I_{i,j}\varphi$ Entity j informs i that $\varphi \equiv \top$
D8:	$T_{i,j}\varphi$ Entity i trusts the report from j about φ

---

2. Axioms

P:	All the tautologies from the propositional calculus
B1:	$[B_i\varphi \wedge B_i(\varphi \to \psi)] \to B_i\psi$
B2:	$\neg B_i\bot$
B3:	$B_i\varphi \to B_iB_i\varphi$
B4:	$\neg B_i\varphi \to B_i\neg B_i\varphi$
I1:	$[I_{i,j}\varphi \wedge I_{i,j}(\varphi \to \psi)] \to I_{i,j}\psi$
I2:	$\neg I_{i,j}\bot$
C1:	$B_iI_{i,j}\varphi \wedge T_{i,j}\varphi \to B_i\varphi$
C2:	$T_{i,j}\varphi \equiv B_iT_{i,j}\varphi$

---

3. Rules of Inference

R5:	From $\vdash \varphi \equiv \psi$ infer $\vdash T_{i,j}\varphi \equiv T_{i,j}\psi$

---

4. Logical Statement Formulation Rules

F1:	If φ is a wff, so are $\neg\varphi, \Box\varphi,$ and $\Diamond\varphi$
F2:	If φ and ψ are wff, so is $\varphi \vee \psi$
F3:	If φ and ψ are wff, so is $\varphi \wedge \psi$
F4:	If φ is a wff, so are $B_i\varphi,$ and $\neg B_i\varphi$
F5:	If φ is a wff, so are $I_{i,j}\varphi,$ and $\neg I_{i,j}\varphi$
F6:	If φ is a wff, so are $T_{i,j}\varphi,$ and $\neg T_{i,j}\varphi$

---

establish that the cream separator correctly reports its status and dutifully follows the commands sent to it by the controller.

Using BIT logic [18], information transfer is represented by $I_{i,j}\varphi$, which clearly states how i gains knowledge of φ (see Table 7). The information transfer operator inherently assumes j will not lie to i; however, this restriction allows liars to lie to trusting agents. Note that the information is transferred directly to an agent who has no direct way to evaluate whether or not j is a liar. As such, the status of the cream is not MSDND secure at the cream separator. The physical cream separator correctly reports the status of its cream.

Theorem 1. *The cream status is not MSDND secure at the cream separator.*

Proof. Clearly, $(\varphi \oplus \neg\varphi) = $ true, so the first condition for MSDND is met by the definition. However, the separator directly measures the cream and, therefore, both $\mathbb{V}_\varphi^0(w)$ and $\mathbb{V}_{\neg\varphi}^0(w)$ are correctly evaluated for any w and the conditions for MSDND are not met. □

In order to cause the maximum amount of disruption, the virus can completely block information flow from the cream separator to the controller. However, this is a trivial case that is easily detected via timeouts on readings from the cream separator. Instead, the focus is on the more insidious case where the virus fabricates readings to create a false information flow. The fabricated readings cause an observation at the monitor to be consistent with multiple possibilities in the physical system, essentially making the system nondeducible from the perspective of the human operator.

Theorem 2. *The speed of the separator is MSDND secure for SD^2 during the attack phase for the infected systems and any agent i in SD^2 will believe all is well or φ.*

Proof. By definition, $(\varphi \oplus \neg\varphi) = \text{true}$, so the first condition for MSDND is met. If φ cannot be correctly evaluated in SD^2, then both conditions are met.

Case (i): Separator speed is nominal and $\varphi = \text{true}$

1.	φ	Separator speed is nominal
2.	$w \vDash \mathbb{V}_\varphi^0(w) = \text{true}$	Definition of $w \vDash \mathbb{V}_\varphi^0(w)$
3.	$I_{1,0}\varphi$	Sensor reports to virus
4.	$B_1 I_{1,0}\varphi$	Virus believes sensor report
5.	$T_{1,0}\varphi$	Virus trusts the sensors
6.	$B_1 I_{1,0}\varphi \wedge T_{1,0}\varphi \to B_1\varphi$	Axiom C1, Virus believes status
7.	$I_{2,1}\varphi$	Virus reports all is well
8.	$B_2 I_{2,1}\varphi$	PLC believes interface report
9.	$T_{2,1}\varphi$	PLC trusts reports
10.	$B_2 I_{2,1}\varphi \wedge T_{2,1}\varphi \to B_2\varphi$	Axiom C1, PLC believes φ
11.	$w \vDash \mathbb{V}_\varphi^2(w) = \text{true}$	$\mathbb{V}_\varphi^2(w)$ always returns true

Case (ii): Separator speed is not nominal and $\neg\varphi = \text{true}$

1.	$\neg\varphi$	Separator speed is not nominal
2.	$w \vDash \mathbb{V}_\varphi^0(w) = \text{false}$	Definition of $w \vDash \mathbb{V}_\varphi^0(w)$
3.	$I_{1,0}\neg\varphi$	Sensor reports problem to virus
4.	$B_1 I_{1,0}\neg\varphi$	Virus believes sensor report
5.	$T_{1,0}\neg\varphi$	Virus trusts the sensors
6.	$B_1 I_{1,0}\neg\varphi \wedge T_{1,0}\neg\varphi \to B_1\neg\varphi$	Axiom C1, Virus believes status
7.	$I_{2,1}\varphi$	Virus reports all is well
8.	$B_2 I_{2,1}\varphi$	PLC believes interface report
9.	$T_{2,1}\varphi$	PLC trusts reports
10.	$B_2 I_{2,1}\varphi \wedge T_{2,1}\varphi \to B_2\varphi$	Axiom C1, PLC believes φ
11.	$w \vDash \mathbb{V}_\varphi^2(w) = \text{true}$	$\mathbb{V}_\varphi^2(w)$ always returns true

Since $T_{2,1}\varphi \wedge B_2 I_{2,1}\varphi \rightarrow B_2\varphi$, the programmable logic controller believes the lie told in Step 7 in all cases. Therefore, unknown to the entities in SD^2, $\mathbb{V}^2_\varphi(w)$ and $\mathbb{V}^2_{\neg\varphi}(w)$ cannot be evaluated. These are the requirements to conclude that φ is MSDND secure from SD^2. $\square$

Theorem 3. *If the system is MSDND secure for SD^2, then any entity i within SD^2, SD^3 and SD^4 will believe all is well.*

Proof. Obviously, $(\varphi \oplus \neg\varphi) =$ true, so the first condition for MSDND is met. If φ cannot be correctly evaluated in SD^2, then both conditions are met. The virus always reports to SD^2 that $\varphi =$ true, so regardless of the status of the cream separator, the infected system reports to SD^2 that all is well. Any entity in SD^2 will report all is well all the way up to SD^4. No matter what, the trusting human will suspect nothing and the cream will be ruined. $\square$

But what if the human is not so trusting? If the human walks over periodically to check the speed gauge on the cream separator, he or she will know instantly that something is wrong and the MSDND security of the virus attack would be broken. Thus, an analysis of the information flows to find MSDND-secure flows could save the ice cream company, but measures must be taken to ensure that all the information flows are not MSDND secure. This leads to the odd result that breaking the security of an attack effectively spoils that attack. Nevertheless, the approach has made it impossible for the attacker to use security against the ice cream company.

Interested readers should note that the modeling and analysis of the cream separator formally shows how the Stuxnet virus operated [15].

6.   Conclusions

This chapter has demonstrated the advantages of conducting a formal security analysis of a cyber-physical system that includes the security of the physical assets, the cyber assets and the information flows that are inherent to interdependent cyber-physical systems. Indeed, information flow analysis is most critical because the other aspects of security are well understood.

It is important to examine all the information flows in a cyber-physical system and modify the nondeducible flows to eliminate nondeducibility. This prevents an agent from using nondeducibility against the system. While attacks may not be prevented, all attacks that are not nondeducibility secure can at least be detected early. Additionally, because MSDND is not trace-based like many other information flow security models, it is possible to use MSDND techniques to monitor the security of information flows in real time.

Cyber-physical systems present serious challenges to security professionals. If a cyber-physical system is viewed only as a set of physical things controlled by secure electronics, there is a good chance an adversary could observe the physical actions of the system and deduce the secure actions that must be hidden to protect the cyber-physical system. The complex intertwining or coupling of the two sides of a cyber-physical system produces ample opportunities for information flows that can be used as attack vectors. Because of the collateral damage that can occur when a cyber-physical system is not properly controlled, an attack could lead to unacceptable property damage and even the loss of human life.

While access control models are inadequate for securing cyber-physical systems, the models help determine the subjects and objects of the cyber side of cyber-physical systems. The Bell-LaPadula model is especially useful for determining the security domains of a system while the Lipner model may help determine the trust roles between subjects. However, access control makes little sense when the security domains of a cyber-physical system are not well defined or overlap in unexpected ways.

Information flow security models are of greatest use in protecting cyber-physical systems. Noninterference and noninference are very useful for discovering the more obvious information flows that can be observed by an adversary, but nondeducibility methods must be used to discover more subtle information flows. MSDND is a very powerful tool for modeling subtle leaks of information that are critical to the operation of cyber-physical systems and can easily be used to find attack vectors that are MSDND secure. A cyber-physical system can then be modified to reduce or eliminate the attacks. This is a necessary step in the race to secure a system before it is attacked.

Acknowledgement

The author wishes to thank the reviewers for their helpful suggestions that have improved this chapter.

References

[1] D. Bell and L. LaPadula, Secure Computer Systems: Mathematical Foundations, Technical Report 2547, Volume 1, MITRE, Bedford, Massachusetts, 1973.

[2] D. Bell and L. LaPadula, Computer Security Model: Unified Exposition and Multics Interpretation, Technical Report ESD-TR-75-306, MTR-2997, Rev. 1, MITRE, Bedford, Massachusetts, 1976.

[3] K. Biba, Integrity Considerations for Secure Computer Systems, Technical Report ESD-TR-76-372, MTR-3153, Rev. 1, MITRE, Bedford, Massachusetts, 1977.

[4] M. Bishop, *Computer Security: Art and Science*, Addison-Wesley, Boston, Massachusetts, 2003.

[5] C. Bryce, J. Banatre and D. LeMetayer, An approach to information security in distributed systems, *Proceedings of the Fifth IEEE Workshop on Future Trends in Distributed Computing Systems*, pp. 384–394, 1995.

[6] J. Butts and S. Shenoi, Preface, in *Critical Infrastructure Protection VI*, J. Butts and S. Shenoi (Eds.), Springer, Heidelberg, Germany, pp. xv–xvi, 2012.

[7] I. Copi, *Introduction to Logic*, Macmillan, New York, 1972.

[8] T. Fine, J. Haigh, R. O'Brien and D. Toups, Noninterference and unwinding for LOCK, *Proceedings of the Computer Security Foundations Workshop*, pp. 22–28, 1989.

[9] T. Gamage, B. McMillin and T. Roth, Enforcing information flow security properties in cyber-physical systems: A generalized framework based on compensation, *Proceedings of the Thirty-Fourth IEEE Computer Software and Applications Conference Workshops*, pp. 158–163, 2010.

[10] J. Goguen and J. Meseguer, Security policies and security models, *Proceedings of the IEEE Symposium on Security and Privacy*, pp. 11–20, 1982.

[11] J. Goguen and J. Meseguer, Unwinding and inference control, *Proceedings of the IEEE Symposium on Security and Privacy*, p. 75–87, 1984.

[12] M. Harrison, W. Ruzzo and J. Ullman, Protection in operating systems, *Communications of the ACM*, vol. 19(8), pp. 461–471, 1976.

[13] G. Howser and B. McMillin, Modeling and reasoning about the security of drive-by-wire automobile systems, *International Journal of Critical Infrastructure Protection*, vol. 5(3-4), pp. 127–134, 2012.

[14] G. Howser and B. McMillin, A multiple security domain model of a drive-by-wire system, *Proceedings of the Thirty-Seventh IEEE Computer Software and Applications Conference*, pp. 369–374, 2013.

[15] G. Howser and B. McMillin, A modal model of Stuxnet attacks on cyber-physical systems: A matter of trust, *Proceedings of the Eighth International Conference on Software Security and Reliability*, pp. 225–234, 2014.

[16] S. Kripke, A completeness theorem in modal logic, *Journal of Symbolic Logic*, vol. 24(1), pp. 1–14, 1959.

[17] E. Lee, Cyber-physical systems – Are computing foundations adequate? presented at the *NSF Workshop on Cyber-Physical Systems: Research Motivation, Techniques and Roadmap* (`ptolemy.eecs.berkeley.edu/pub lications/papers/06/CPSPositionPaper`), 2006.

[18] C. Liau, Belief, information acquisition and trust in multi-agent systems – A modal logic formulation, *Artificial Intelligence*, vol. 149(1), pp. 31–60, 2003.

[19] S. Lipner, Non-discretionary controls for commercial applications, *Proceedings of the IEEE Symposium on Security and Privacy*, pp. 2–10, 1982.

[20] S. McCamant and M. Ernst, Quantitative information flow as network flow capacity, *ACM SIGPLAN Notices*, vol. 43(6), pp. 193–205, 2008.

[21] J. McLean, Security models and information flow, *Proceedings of the IEEE Symposium on Security and Privacy*, pp. 180–187, 1990.

[22] A. Myers and B. Liskov, Protecting privacy in a decentralized environment, *Proceedings of the DARPA Information Survivability Conference and Exposition*, vol. 1, pp. 266–277, 2000.

[23] N. Nagatou and T. Watanabe, Run-time detection of covert channels, *Proceedings of the Seventh International Conference on Availability, Reliability and Security*, pp. 577–584, 2006.

[24] C. O'Halloran, A calculus of information flow, *Proceedings of the First European Symposium on Research in Computer Security*, pp. 147–159, 1990.

[25] K. Poulsen, Hacker disables more than 100 cars remotely, *Wired*, March 17, 2010.

[26] A. Sabelfeld and A. Myers, Language-based information-flow security, *IEEE Journal on Selected Areas in Communications*, vol. 21(1), pp. 5–19, 2003.

[27] D. Sutherland, A model of information, *Proceedings of the Ninth National Computer Security Conference*, pp. 175–183, 1986.

[28] U.S. Department of Homeland Security, Cyber Security Overview, Washington, DC (`www.dhs.gov/cybersecurity-overview`), 2015.

[29] J. Wittbold and D. Johnson, Information flow in nondeterministic systems, *Proceedings of the IEEE Symposium on Security and Privacy*, pp. 144–161, 1990.

[30] C. Woodyard, Start, unlock or honk horn of your GM car from a cellphone, *USA Today*, July 22, 2010.

IV

INFRASTRUCTURE SECURITY

Chapter 13

EVALUATING ITU-T G.9959 BASED WIRELESS SYSTEMS USED IN CRITICAL INFRASTRUCTURE ASSETS

Christopher Badenhop, Jonathan Fuller, Joseph Hall, Benjamin Ramsey and Mason Rice

Abstract   ITU-T G.9959 wireless connectivity is increasingly incorporated in the critical infrastructure. However, evaluating the robustness and security of commercially-available products based on this standard is challenging due to the closed-source nature of the transceiver and application designs. Given that ITU-T G.9959 transceivers are being used in smart grids, building security systems and safety sensors, the development of reliable, open-source tools would enhance the ability to monitor and secure ITU-T G.9959 networks. This chapter discusses the ITU-T G.9959 wireless standard and research on ITU-T G.9959 network security. An open-source, software-defined radio implementation of an ITU-T G.9959 protocol sniffer is used to explore several passive reconnaissance techniques and deduce the properties of active network devices. The experimental results show that some properties are observable regardless of whether or not encryption is used. In particular, the acknowledgment response times vary due to differences in vendor firmware implementations.

Keywords: ITU-T G.9959, Z-Wave, vulnerabilities, wireless sniffing

1.   Introduction

The prevalence of wireless connectivity in industrial control and sensor systems is increasing because it extends communications ranges at lower cost than wired alternatives. A 2011 survey of industrial control system operators reported that wireless networks were deployed in 43% of industrial control systems and numerous additional deployments were projected [3]. The survey respondents reported the use of IEEE 802.11, WirelessHART, Bluetooth and ZigBee as well as proprietary wireless systems [3]. An analysis of vulnerabilities

© IFIP International Federation for Information Processing 2015 (outside the US)
M. Rice, S. Shenoi (Eds.): Critical Infrastructure Protection IX, IFIP AICT 466, pp. 209–227, 2015.
DOI: 10.1007/978-3-319-26567-4_13

and suggestions for mitigation have been published for these protocols, with the exception of the proprietary systems [15].

The growing use of proprietary systems makes it necessary to analyze and discuss their security implications, especially when considering these systems for use in critical infrastructure assets. Of the numerous proprietary systems, wireless systems based on the ITU-T G.9959 recommendation, which specifies a short range narrow-band digital radio communications transceiver operating in the sub-GHz spectrum, have significant potential for growth in the critical infrastructure. The most common commercial instantiation of ITU-T G.9959 is Z-Wave, which is standardized and marketed by the Z-Wave Alliance. The Z-Wave Alliance comprises more than 300 companies and is actively working to increase the adoption of Z-Wave products around the globe.

IEEE 802.15.4 networks (e.g., WirelessHART and ZigBee) fulfill low-rate communications roles similar to those of Z-Wave in the critical infrastructure. Recent research efforts (see, e.g., [4, 12, 14]) have proposed novel security strategies for these networks. However, Z-Wave product development has been significantly restricted by nondisclosure and confidentiality agreements that stifle open-source security and resilience research. As a result, the security implications of the use of Z-Wave networks in the critical infrastructure are not well understood. In order to address this issue, this chapter introduces open-source techniques and tools for evaluating the security of ITU-T G.9959 wireless networks (including Z-Wave products) used in critical infrastructure assets.

2.   ITU-T G.9959-Based Z-Wave Protocol

The ITU-T G.9959 recommendation specifies the physical (PHY) and media access control (MAC) layers for short-range, narrow-band digital radio communications transceivers. All manufactures adhere to the PHY/MAC specifications to ensure interoperability, but market their devices based on the network and application layers.

ITU-T G.9959-based networks operate in unlicensed frequency bands (e.g., 908.4 MHz in North America, 860.4 MHz in Europe and additional frequencies in other regions). Data rates of 9.6 Kbps (Rate 1), 40 Kbps (Rate 2) and 100 Kbps (Rate 3) are supported, depending on the transceiver type. Networks have two basic types of nodes: (i) control nodes; and (ii) end device nodes. Control nodes initiate commands while end device nodes respond to commands. Leveraging mesh topologies, end device nodes also forward commands to other nodes that are not directly reachable by a control node. The protocol allows a maximum of four hops between nodes and a maximum of 232 nodes in one network.

Each Z-Wave network is identified by a unique 32-bit Home ID, which is programmed by the manufacturer on each control node. The Home ID allows multiple networks to operate in close proximity without overlap. While a network may contain multiple control nodes, only one control node may be designated as the primary controller and its Home ID uniquely identifies the

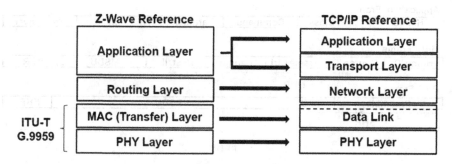

Figure 1. ITU-T G.9959/Z-Wave model mapped to the TCP/IP reference model.

network. During the network inclusion process, the primary control node assigns the new node an 8-bit Node ID, which is only unique in the local network.

The Z-Wave protocol consists of four layers. Figure 1 shows the four-layer ITU-T G.9959/Z-Wave reference model mapped to the five-layer TCP/IP reference model. The PHY layer controls access to the radio frequency medium, the MAC layer handles transmission and reception of frames between adjacent nodes, the routing layer controls the flow of messages throughout the mesh and the application layer executes commands associated with the end device.

2.1   PHY Layer

The PHY layer uses carrier sense multiple access with collision avoidance to control access to the wireless medium. As mentioned above, Z-Wave utilizes unlicensed frequency bands, which differ according to the region. The protocol offers three data rates: (i) 9.6 Kbps using frequency-shift keying with Manchester encoding; (ii) 40 Kbps using frequency-shift keying with non-return-to-zero encoding; and (iii) 100 Kbps using Gaussian frequency-shift keying with non-return to zero encoding.

As shown in Figure 2, the PHY protocol data unit (PPDU) consists of three main parts. The frame begins with a start header (SHR), which contains a preamble for symbol and bit synchronization, followed by a start of frame delimiter (SFD). The frame payload or PHY service data unit (PSDU) follows. Finally, for 9.6 Kbps data rate transmissions only, the frame concludes with an end header (EHR).

2.2   MAC Layer

The MAC layer (sometimes referred to as the transfer layer) is also detailed by ITU-T G.9959. The layer controls the transfer of data between two nodes and is responsible for frame acknowledgment, retransmission, data validation and notifying battery-operated devices to stay awake pending incoming transmissions.

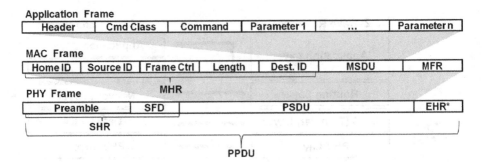

Figure 2. ITU-T G.9959 and Z-Wave frame formats.

There are three basic types of MAC frames: singlecast, acknowledgment and multicast. Each frame type follows the same general layout shown in Figure 2 with a MAC header (MHR), MAC service data unit (MSDU) and a MAC footer (MFR). Singlecast frames are transmitted to only one destination address (including the broadcast address). Acknowledgement frames are structured identically to singlecast frames, but have a MAC service data unit of zero length. Acknowledgement frames are sent in response to singlecast frames. Retransmissions occur when the sending node does not receive an acknowledgment from the receiving node. Multicast frames are sent to multiple destination nodes without acknowledgments.

The MAC header contains the Home ID, Source ID, frame control field, frame length and Destination ID (or bitmask in the case of a multicast frame). The MAC footer contains either an 8-bit checksum or a 16-bit cyclic redundancy check depending on the data rate used.

2.3   Routing Layer

Z-Wave mesh network topologies are managed by the routing layer to ensure that messages are successfully routed among control and end device nodes. The protocol specifies a maximum of 232 nodes and only one primary control node, although multiple secondary control nodes may exist in order to partition a network. Every node, with the exception of battery-operated devices, participates in routing by forwarding frames between nodes outside of direct wireless transmission range. The protocol also specifies a maximum of four hops between the primary control node and any other node.

The routing layer is responsible for scanning the network topology and maintaining a routing table in the primary control node. The routing table is built by the primary control node based on information received, upon inclusion or request, from each end device node about the neighbors of each node. The Z-Wave protocol stack supports automatic topology discovery and healing to optimize routing tables when the location of a node has changed or a node has been removed from the network (exclusion).

2.4   Application Layer

The majority of the application layer is implementation-specific depending on the Z-Wave developer. For brevity, this section discusses only what is applicable to all Z-Wave devices.

The application layer frame consists of the header, command class information and command parameters (see Figure 2). The application layer is responsible for executing the commands passed to it. Commands are broken into two classes: command class and device class.

A command class is related to a specific function or device. An example is the binary switchcommand class. The binary switch uses three commands: (i) SET to turn a device on or off; (ii) GET to request the status of a device; and (iii) REPORT to respond to the request. These three commands are foundational to all Z-Wave devices.

The device class is subdivided into the basic, generic and special device classes. The basic device class distinguishes between controllers, end devices and end devices that are capable of routing. The generic device class defines the function that the device performs as a controller or end device. The special device class allows for more specificity in device functionality.

It is important to note that the Z-Wave protocol supports encryption using the Advanced Encryption Standard (AES) with 128-bit keys. When implemented, the application frame is encrypted and an 8-byte authentication frame header is appended to the end of the MAC service data unit. While data encryption is supported by the protocol, its implementation is left to the manufacturer to decide if the device transmission is sensitive enough to warrant encryption. In wireless sensor networks, memory and power are scarce resources, which discourages developers from implementing encryption "unless required" [6]. Surveys of similar low-rate networks have demonstrated that the use of encryption or other security measures are far from ubiquitous [13].

3.   ITU-T G.9959/Z-Wave Attack Classes

While Z-Wave is a proprietary protocol, vendors may purchase software development kits to produce Z-Wave certified products. Given the nature of hardware and software development, certain vulnerabilities are introduced by developer-specific implementation faults as illustrated in [5]. This section focuses on vulnerabilities of the underlying ITU-T G.9959 recommendation, which are common to all devices and attack classes that exploit the vulnerabilities.

Three classes of attacks are considered: (i) reconnaissance; (ii) denial-of-service; and (iii) packet injection. The three classes of attacks undermine network confidentiality, availability and integrity, respectively. A reconnaissance attack involves the passive collection of traffic or the active probing of a target network to gain information without interfering with normal operations. A denial-of-service attack prevents wireless system access and causes varying degrees of system unavailability. A packet injection attack involves the transmission of specially-crafted packets to manipulate network or device behavior.

3.1   Reconnaissance Attacks

Reconnaissance lays the foundation for sophisticated follow-up attacks. The information acquired includes the protocols in use, device types, traffic flow patterns and even encryption keys if they are not handled properly. Information received from reconnaissance can help an attacker obtain accurate mappings of a system, services and/or vulnerabilities, enabling more significant attacks to be conducted in the future. Using a high-gain antenna, observations can be made at long distances, allowing an attacker to remain inconspicuous while gathering information. Apa and Hollman [1] have presented a proven exploitation of a wireless sensor network used in critical infrastructure assets. In particular, they demonstrated the exploitation of three devices from a maximum distance of 64 km.

An attacker armed with a directional antenna can capture ITU-T G.9959 transmissions for further analysis. Information gathered that might be useful to an attacker includes: (i) traffic patterns; (ii) use of encryption during transmission; and (iii) frame header content, which includes the unique Home ID of an ITU-T G.9959 network, Source ID of the device being sniffed and Destination ID.

Two demonstrations of ITU-T G.9959 exploitation have been published to date, both of them relied heavily on the ability to conduct reconnaissance to gain the knowledge required to craft follow-up attacks. Fouladi and Ghanoun [5] showed how to obtain a detailed understanding of the manner in which a secure door lock implements encryption and authentication; using this knowledge, they were able to discover a flaw that could be exploited. Picod et al. [11] were able to discern the specific commands and associated bit values that could be used to turn an alarm on and off. Follow-on attacks of these example attacks are discussed later in this chapter.

Several entities have developed sniffers for intercepting and transmitting Z-Wave frames. Sigma Designs [17] markets a closed-source development kit for Z-Wave device developers. The kit incorporates several hardware development platforms, technical documentation, software tools and a Z-Wave protocol sniffer. However, the kit comes with a non-disclosure agreement, which restricts the use of the tools.

A second sniffer project is z-force [5]. The sniffer includes custom firmware hosted on a CC1110 development board [20] and a z-force personal computer application. At the time of this writing, z-force has only been demonstrated on European Z-Wave frequency bands. The closed-source nature of z-force makes it difficult to evaluate and extend.

A third Z-Wave sniffer is Scapy-Radio, part of the open-source `hackrf` project [11]. Scapy-Radio integrates Scapy, a Python environment for manipulating network traffic and GNU Radio, an open-source signal processing toolbox. The tool includes GNU Radio companion implementations of Z-Wave,

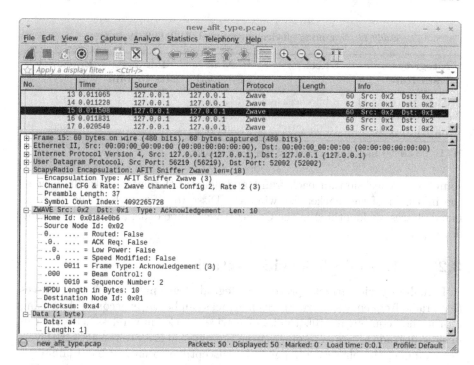

Figure 3. Wireshark Z-Wave dissection.

Bluetooth and ZigBee transceivers. The Z-Wave implementation receives samples from a software-defined radio, demodulates, synchronizes and decodes NRZ or Manchester encodings. As with z-force, the implementation is tuned to European bands, but can be modified for other bands using GNU Radio tools.

Application layer sniffers are available from OpenZWave. OpenZWave is an open-source project that provides libraries and drivers to communicate with USB-based Z-Wave controllers (e.g., Z-Stick S2 from Aeon Labs). OpenZWave provides a network querying tool to demonstrate its MinOZW library API. The python-openzwave package, an open-source wrapper for OpenZWave, provides a Python version of MinOZW and a Z-Wave shell interface to interact with a Z-Wave controller.

While Scapy or a netcat listener could be used to collect the encapsulated UDP frames sent over a local loopback device, future work will support the capture and analysis of Z-Wave frames using Wireshark. Wireshark is capable of intercepting UDP datagrams, but is unable to decode the encapsulation header, MAC header or Z-Wave payloads.

As part of this research, a packet dissector was developed for the encapsulation header and Z-Wave MAC header. Figure 3 shows a Z-Wave frame dissection. The dissector also decodes the first byte of the PHY service data unit payload to identify the application payload command class. The remaining payload bytes depend on the value of the command class field. The dissector

Table 1.   Jamming efficiency against ITU-T G.9959 frames.

Integrity Data Rate	Check*	Max Payload	Jammer Bits to Jam	Efficiency
9.6 Kbps (Rate 1)	8-bit checksum	512 bits	1	512
40 Kbps (Rate 2)	8-bit checksum	512 bits	1	512
100 Kbps (Rate 3)	16-bit CRC	1,360 bits	1	1,360

*ITU-T G.9959 uses non-correcting integrity checks.

computes a checksum for each frame and denotes the outcome to the user in the info field of the packet list window. Dissectors for each of the 49 command classes, as identified in the OpenZWave source code, are currently being developed.

3.2   Denial-of-Service Attacks

Denial-of-service attacks prevent or degrade legitimate access to resources (e.g., radio frequency spectrum). Such attacks can be easily accomplished using off-the-shelf equipment [10]. Denial-of-service attacks on wireless networks can deny or degrade access to resources from the physical layer to the network layer. For example, the physical layer may be susceptible to narrow-band jamming, the carrier sense algorithms may be exploited to deny access to the medium [22] and routers can be consumed with overflowing interface queues.

Constant and deceptive jamming are effective for conducting denial-of-service attacks due to the MAC layer collision avoidance characteristics of ITU-T G.9959. When an attacker is operating a constant or deceptive jammer, any node within range will sense the channel as busy and wait to transmit. Even more effective and efficient is reactive jamming [8], which is difficult to detect [18]. A reactive jammer, that only transmits after the preamble and start of a frame delimiter of an ITU-T G.9959 PHY frame are detected, merely has to corrupt one bit of the PHY service data unit in order to cause an integrity check error and the complete loss of the frame. The non-correcting integrity checks used by Z-Wave are capable of detecting, but not correcting, single-bit errors. Even worse, the corruption of a single bit in the Z-Wave PHY layer, unlike a PHY layer that uses a spreading technique such as direct-sequence spread spectrum (DSSS), is achievable using narrow-band jamming. The use of error correction codes, as in IEEE 802.11a, is more robust to bitwise jamming [9]. Table 1 presents an estimate of jammer efficiency in terms of bits jammed per bit transmitted against ITU-T G.9959 (i.e., ratio of communications effort to jammer effort) based on the results in [9].

Depending on the objective, an attacker may use any of the methods described above to impact the availability of one or more nodes in a wireless network. For example, a Z-Wave network containing a thermostat (sensor) and water valve (actuator) could be subjected to a denial-of-service attack that prevents the thermostat from reporting the current temperature or obstructs a command to activate the water valve. A similar scenario was successfully demonstrated in [15] with a gas pipeline remote terminal unit that included a wireless pressure sensor, pump and relief valve.

3.3 Packet Injection Attacks

Due to the broadcast nature of wireless networks, an attacker armed with information gained via reconnaissance may be able to inject forged packets into a network. The ability to conduct packet injection enables the attacker to masquerade as a legitimate network device while transmitting messages to manipulate system operation. Badenhop and Mullins [2] have investigated network degradation attacks against wireless routing protocols similar to those used in Z-Wave.

Using publicly-available hardware and software, researchers have reported the ability to conduct packet injection attacks to manipulate ITU-T G.9959 devices. Fouladi and Ghanoun [5] have developed a packet inspection/injection tool using a Texas Instruments radio transceiver and custom software (now publicly-available, albeit not open source). Using the tool, Fouladi and Ghanoun were able to inject traffic to exploit a vulnerability in a device-specific encryption implementation at the application layer that enabled them to send encrypted commands to perform unauthorized actions.

Picod et al. [11] have also demonstrated a packet injection attack against ITU-T G.9959 devices. Their packet inspection/injection tool uses a software-defined radio and open-source software packages. They demonstrated the ability to sense legitimate SWITCH_BINARY_ON commands and automatically inject subsequent SWITCH_BINARY_OFF commands, which effectively nullified legitimate messages.

These preliminary case studies demonstrate the attack possibilities when a malicious entity has the ability to inject forged ITU-T G.9959 traffic. In addition to these examples, an attacker may be able to: (i) flood a network with traffic causing a denial of service at the routing or application layers; (ii) send false status messages; or (iii) provide a control node with false routing information to poison the network routing table.

If the target ITU-T G.9959-based network is used in a critical infrastructure asset, the ability to inject commands and report false state information could prove disastrous. For example, an attacker may choose to send a close command to a water valve in a cooling system immediately following every open command sent by the master terminal unit while falsely reporting to the human-machine interface that the valve is open.

4. Passive Reconnaissance Techniques

Several high-level attack classes for Z-Wave systems have been presented above. A basic, invariant system threat from which other threats originate is passive reconnaissance. In the remainder of this chapter, the focus is on

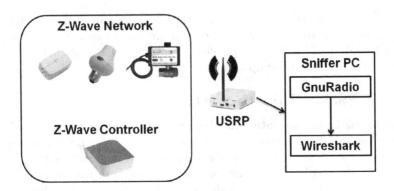

Figure 4. Sniffer architecture.

identifying several low-complexity passive reconnaissance techniques to further the exploration of Z-Wave security.

To capture arbitrary Z-Wave frames, a receiver chain was constructed using a USRP N210, GNU Radio, Scapy-Radio and a Z-Wave Wireshark packet dissector. Figure 4 shows the sniffer architecture. The USRP was tuned to a center frequency of 908.40 MHz to collect frequency-shift-keyed symbols at ±20 KHz deviation from the center frequency. An Ettus VERT900 dipole antenna was connected directly to the USRP and sampling was performed at 800 Kbps with 20 MHz bandwidth. Filtering, demodulation and symbol synchronization were performed by GNU Radio. Scapy-Radio, a subsystem within GNU Radio, provided preamble detection, byte synchronization, NRZ decoding and frame extraction operations. The extracted frames were transmitted over the `localhost` interface encapsulated as UDP datagrams to port 52002. Wireshark captured traffic over the `localhost` interface to intercept the datagrams. A custom Z-Wave packet dissector was used to decode the encapsulated Z-Wave frames, which were preserved in the PCAP format for later analysis. The experimental setup in Figure 4 permitted the passive collection of Z-Wave frames. Unlike application level sniffers, Z-Wave frames were captured regardless of the frame Home-ID. Moreover, the PHY and MAC layers were retained rather than stripped in order to provide insights into system behavior.

4.1   Controller-Device Pairing

Observations of the responses of the included device to the controller revealed significant details about the hardware, software and current state. At the end of an inclusion process, the controller interrogates the included device to learn about it. This information is used by the controller to present accurate control options and device information to the user.

Figure 5 shows a frame capture of an Aeon Labs Z-Stick controller using a Jasco JS-45603 smart dimmer. The data in the application payloads, which was reversed by referencing the Open-ZWave command class source code, is summarized to the right of Figure 5. The figure shows a sequence of GET commands

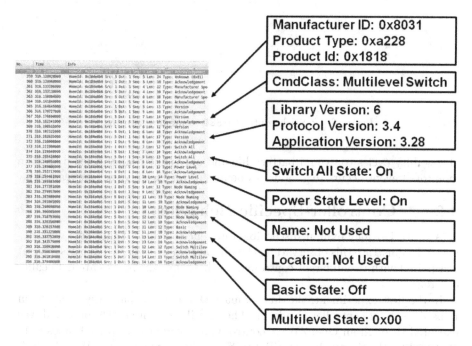

Figure 5. Pairing between a Jasco smart dimmer and an Aeon Z-Stick controller.

from the controller to the dimmer. The dimmer responds to each request with a REPORT message that reveals information. Device-level information, such as the vendor, device type and ID are provided in a manufacturer-specific REPORT message. The controller requests software version information, to which the dimmer device replies with a Z-Wave library, protocol and application version. After the device and software level information is gathered, the controller queries the device on the current state of each configuration and control item. This state information can be used by an observer to determine the set of messages that the device services, which is especially useful when the device-specific data refers to an unknown product type or manufacturer ID. The location state is of particular interest. While location information was not initialized in the capture shown in Figure 5, it is still possible for a device to reveal some information about its configured location. The location information is in the form of a grouping index that corresponds to a user-defined label assigned at the controller interface. A user may group devices by room, floor or functionality, so additional information is required to understand the semantics of this value.

If the pairing is not observable, passive reconnaissance may still capture the interactions between the controller and end devices. As with the latter portion of the pairing process, the command classes of observed messages provide information about the device function. The drawback is that the observation period is significantly longer than if observed during the pairing process. This is especially true for low-power event triggered devices. These devices operate

No.	Time	Protocol	Length	Info
52	2.344342000	Zwave	63	HomeId: 0x184e0b6 Src: 1 Dst: 5 Seq: 8 Len: 13 Type: Switch Multilevel
54	2.353639000	Zwave	60	HomeId: 0x184e0b6 Src: 5 Dst: 1 Seq: 8 Len: 10 Type: Acknowledgement
56	2.366168000	Zwave	62	HomeId: 0x184e0b6 Src: 1 Dst: 5 Seq: 9 Len: 12 Type: Switch Multilevel
58	2.368858000	Zwave	60	HomeId: 0x184e0b6 Src: 5 Dst: 1 Seq: 9 Len: 10 Type: Acknowledgement
60	2.375081000	Zwave	63	HomeId: 0x184e0b6 Src: 5 Dst: 1 Seq: 6 Len: 13 Type: Switch Multilevel
62	2.380123000	Zwave	60	HomeId: 0x184e0b6 Src: 1 Dst: 5 Seq: 6 Len: 10 Type: Acknowledgement

Figure 6. Z-Stick controller **SET** command capture.

at low duty cycles to extend battery life and only emit frames when a specific monitored event occurs (e.g., a door opening or an excessive sensor reading).

4.2 Controller-Specific Behavior

A controller may exhibit discernible differences in how it interacts with devices. To illustrate this observation, the dimmer (multilevel switch class device) was paired with two different controllers to show that the frames are noticeably different.

In the first experiment, the Jasco Smart Dimmer was paired with an Aeon Labs Z-Stick S2 controller (Node 1). The multilevel switch **SET** command was executed through an OpenZWave control panel while the Z-Wave frames were captured by the Scapy-Radio USRP sniffer and processed by the Wireshark Z-Wave dissector. Note that the Z-Stick controller has an ID of 1 and the dimmer has a node ID of 5. The Z-Stick controller sends a multilevel dimmer command to set the dimmer to a value, shown as frame 52, which is acknowledged by the device. After receiving the acknowledgment (ACK), the controller requests an update of the current dimmer state (output voltage) by sending frame number 56 in Figure 6. The dimmer complies by sending its current value to the controller in frame 60 in Figure 6. This results in six frames being exchanged per transaction. The same pattern occurs when the Aeon Z-Stick controller sends commands to other devices. Essentially, the controller issues a **SET** command, followed by a **GET** command on the same value to confirm that the device complied with the command. The targeted device responds to the command with a **REPORT** command.

No.	Time	Protocol	Length	Info
63	8.171197000	Zwave	63	HomeId: 0x17b784d Src: 1 Dst: 5 Seq: 3 Len: 13 Type: Switch Multilevel
65	8.272984000	Zwave	63	HomeId: 0x17b784d Src: 1 Dst: 5 Seq: 4 Len: 13 Type: Switch Multilevel
67	8.279402000	Zwave	60	HomeId: 0x17b784d Src: 5 Dst: 1 Seq: 4 Len: 10 Type: Acknowledgement

Figure 7. VeraLite controller **SET** command capture.

In the second experiment, the same dimmer device was paired with a VeraLite controller. Using the VeraLite controller web interface, the multilevel switch **SET** command was invoked while capturing Z-Wave frames. Figure 7 shows the results of the capture. Coincidentally, the node IDs are once again one and five. The VeraLite controller sends two versions of the same multilevel switch SET command. In frame 63, the ACK-required bit in the frame control field is not set; however, it is set in frame 65. After the dimmer device receives frame 65, it acknowledges receipt to the controller, which is shown in Figure 7 by the matching sequence numbers. The controller initiates the same command with and without the ACK-required bit set is very likely because the controller is compatible with devices that are not able to reply. Devices that are unable to transmit may ignore frames that require an ACK. As with the Z-Stick controller, this pattern is observable when the VeraLite controller issues SET commands to devices. The SET command is sent both with and without the ACK and does not necessarily expect a reply.

The results show that there is more than one way to execute a switch SET transaction. While it cannot be concluded that the observed patterns are unique to the controllers, it can be deduced that a given command pattern reduces the possible identities of the target controller. For example, when an unknown controller exhibits a pattern consistent with that of a Z-Stick controller, this would imply that the unknown device is not a VeraLite controller.

4.3   Device-Specific ACK Times

When the application layer of Z-Wave frames are encrypted, passive reconnaissance of a device using the previously-identified methods may prove ineffective. Application layer encryption obscures the command class fields, making it more difficult to identify controller-specific command patterns. An outside observer must turn to non-encrypted observations to deduce properties of the devices. Implementation differences between hardware, software and the physical environments of devices may result in observable differences outside of the encrypted traffic. Existing techniques such as traffic analysis and side channel analysis have been shown to be effective at thwarting confidentiality mechanisms like encryption [21].

A fingerprinting technique known as preamble manipulation may be applicable to Z-Wave devices [14]. Unfortunately, it was difficult to find a Z-Wave device that uses a transceiver other than the ZM3102N to verify this technique. Since the experimental hardware was homogeneous, firmware implementations could be examined behaviorally to identify implementation and functionality differences. As a matter of fact, the 32 KB of flash memory available in the ZM3102N provides ample opportunities for vendors to customize their implementations.

One ubiquitous observable behavior below the application layer is the time taken by a node to send an ACK upon receiving a request. Time-of-flight fingerprinting metrics are explored in [16], where the authors report that measurement variance is due to hardware and environmental factors. In their experiments, laptop computers were used to perform packet injection, ACK response and time measurements. Each had an operating system that managed independent operations, but also competed for CPU clock cycles, resulting in variations in the time-of-flight measurements. While this is a valid issue, Z-Wave devices are far more specialized than laptop computers, having application-specific I/O and fewer, if any, concurrent tasks. This suggests that an ACK response of a Z-Wave device is more deterministic than a general purpose laptop. If this is true, ACK-based fingerprinting would be a valid approach for identifying Z-Wave devices.

The experiments described in the remainder of this section demonstrate that ACK-based fingerprinting of Z-Wave devices shows promise. While the Z-Wave devices used in the experiments were all embedded systems, the sniffer ran on a Dell Latitude E6520 laptop. The laptop incurred a degree of the dynamics identified in [16]. The ACK delay time was measured using the packet arrival times observed by the Wireshark Z-Wave dissector. The time values were determined by the Wireshark process when an encapsulated Z-Wave frame was observed on the `localhost` interface. Encapsulated frames were sent over the `localhost` interface by the GNU Radio process. The GNU Radio process received samples from the USRP FPGA via a gigabit Ethernet interface. In the experiments, each process, interface and device driver contended with other resources on the sniffer laptop and were subject to contention dynamics. Regardless of the dynamics, adequate sampling of ACK delays eliminated the confounding effects from the measurements. Seventy ACK response times were collected for each device under test to mitigate sampling bias and to facilitate observational comparisons.

ACK Times for Different Vendor Devices. In the first experiment, a VeraLite controller was used to repeatedly issue commands to a FortrezZ water valve. Each command generated several acknowledged frames from the controller and valve. The ACK response to a particular singlecast frame could be identified by the matching four-bit sequence numbers. After carefully pairing the singlecast frames with their associated ACKs, the response time was measured as the difference in time of between the observation of the singlecast frame being sent and the observation of the ACK being sent. The distances between the water valve, VeraLite controller and the Z-Wave sniffer were all within one meter of one another, implying that signal propagation delays were negligible.

Figure 8 shows the 99% confidence intervals estimating the true mean ($n = 70$) of the ACK response times for the VeraLite controller and FortrezZ water valve. The mean response times are different with a two-sample t-test p-value of 0.00; clearly, the response time of the water valve is greater than that of the VeraLite controller. Moreover, the difference in the response times is an order of magnitude more than variations due to thermal effects [23]. Since both devices use the same hardware, the differences may be due to firmware implementation differences.

ACK Times for Same Vendor Devices. The same experiment was repeated, except that the selected controller and device originated from the same vendor. The Aeon Labs Z-Stick S2 controller was used as the controller and an Aeon Labs Appliance Switch was used as the device. A total of 70

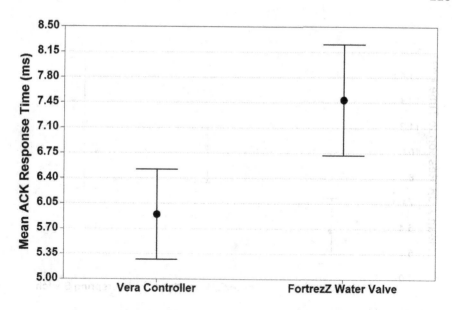

Figure 8. Mean ACK response times for devices from two different vendors.

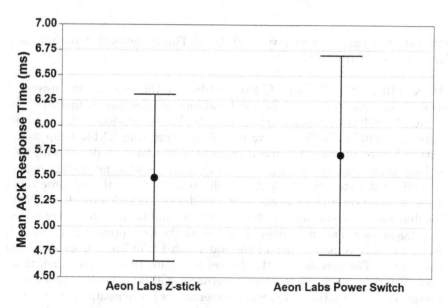

Figure 9. Mean ACK response times for devices from the same vendor.

ACKs were recorded for both systems by repeatedly issuing commands from the controller. Figure 9 shows the observed mean ACK response times for the two devices ($n = 70$ and a confidence interval of 99%). In this case, the mean ACK response times of the two Aeon Labs devices are not statistically

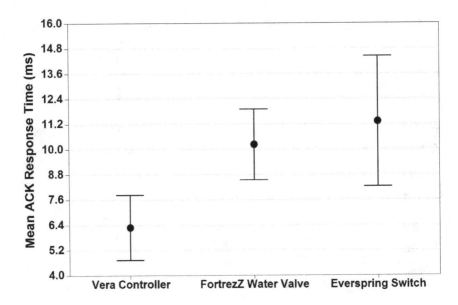

Figure 10. Mean ACK response times for a 60-second polling interval.

different (two-sample t-test p-value = 0.64). This suggests that both devices have similar ZM3102N implementations.

ACK Times for Polling Commands. In this experiment, instead of manually creating Z-Wave traffic, the VeraLite controller was configured to automatically poll two devices every 60 seconds. The two devices polled were the FortrezZ WV01LFUS075 water valve and an Everspring AN145 lamp socket switch. Figure 10 shows the mean response delays for each device with 99% confidence intervals ($n = 70$). The figure reveals several interesting points. First, there is a statistically significant difference between the response times of the VeraLite controller and the other two devices (ANOVA p-value = 0.00). The difference of means between the water valve and lamp switch is not statistically significant, but the variance is higher for the Everspring switch. Second, the mean ACK response time of the water valve is different from that seen in Figure 8. The variances of the devices in Figure 10 are larger than those reported in Figures 8 and 9. This experiment had 60 seconds between each transaction, whereas the two previous experiments had repetitions at intervals of one or two seconds. During the 60-second period of inactivity, it is hypothesized that the devices went into a lower power state, which increased their ACK response times.

Differences in Mean ACK Response Times. The experimental data suggests that the differences in means are due to implementation differences in how ACKs are handled by the devices. Upon receiving a frame, a checksum is performed. If the checksum passes and the frame has either requested an ACK or the protocol requires it, the recipient generates an ACK using the sequence number of the received frame and sends the response to the originator. The differences arise depending on when these steps are taken during the transceiver chains. The ACK response may be initiated immediately upon receiving the frame or after the frame is queued so that the receiver may quickly return to search for the next frame. This option, for example, is provided by the CC2420 transceiver [19].

After the ACK is generated, another implementation decision involves the transmission of the ACK frame. If the ACK is given priority, it is either placed at the front of the send queue or an interrupt is generated to force the transceiver to immediately transmit the ACK. Other design choices include the sizes of the receive and send queues, buffer exception handling and the queue service rates. In a delay-prone scenario, ACKs are handled by an attached microprocessor via the SPI bus.

Another source of differences may be the ZM3102N configuration settings. The ITU-T G.9959 specification lists parameters relevant to ACK response times such as *MacMinAckWaitDuration*, *TurnaroundTimeRXTX* and *MacMin CCARetryDuration*. The three parameters specify the minimum frame spacing between receiving a packet and transmitting its ACK, the time penalty for switching from the receive mode to the transmit mode and the minimum time to wait between clear channel assessments, respectively. It is not clear which, if any, of these parameters are configurable on the ZM3102N; however, each may impact the ACK response time.

5. Conclusions

This chapter has examined the security implications of using ITU-T G.9959 wireless networks with Z-Wave devices in critical infrastructure assets. Several techniques for passively discriminating between Z-Wave devices based on functionality and vendor were investigated. Experiments involving passive observations of ACK response times demonstrate that it is possible to identify implementation differences in ZM3102N firmware. In particular, the experimental results reveal that a VeraLite controller and FortrezZ water valve have different mean ACK response times, while an Z-Stick controller and appliance switch from the same vendor (Aeon Labs) have equivalent response times. These results suggest intra-vendor similarities.

Future research will focus on developing new passive techniques and refining existing techniques for use with other types of devices. Additionally, research will attempt to understand the reasons for the differences in the mean ACK response times. Efforts will also explore active fingerprinting techniques. One such technique will involve sending messages corresponding to all the command classes to a target device to discern its capabilities. The ultimate goal is to develop a tool that leverages passive and active techniques in device fingerprinting, with functionality similar to the popular `nmap` operating system fingerprinting tool.

Note that the views expressed in this chapter are those of the authors and do not reflect the official policy or position of the U.S. Air Force, U.S. Army, U.S. Department of Defense or U.S. Government.

References

[1] L. Apa and C. Hollman, Compromising industrial facilities from 40 miles away, presented at the *Black Hat USA Conference*, 2013.

[2] C. Badenhop and B. Mullins, A black hole attack model using topology approximation for reactive ad-hoc routing protocols, *International Journal of Security and Networks*, vol. 9(2), pp. 63–77, 2014.

[3] W. Boyes, All quiet on the wireless front, Control Global, Schaumburg, Illinois (www.controlglobal.com/articles/2011/all-quite-on-the-wireless-front), August 9, 2011.

[4] C. Dubendorfer, B. Ramsey and M. Temple, ZigBee device verification for securing industrial control and building automation systems, in *Critical Infrastructure Protection VII*, J. Butts and S. Shenoi (Eds.), Springer, Heidelberg, Germany, pp. 47–62, 2013.

[5] B. Fouladi and S. Ghanoun, Security evaluation of the Z-Wave wireless protocol, presented at the *Black Hat USA Conference*, 2013.

[6] Freescale Semiconductor, Freescale Beestack: Application Development Guide, Document Number: BSADG Rev. 1.1, Chandler, Arizona, 2008.

[7] InGuardians, Converting Radio Signals to Data Packets: Examination of Using GNU Radio Companion for Security Research and Assessment, Washington, DC (www.inguardians.com/pubs/GRC_signal_analysis_InGuardians_v1.pdf), 2014.

[8] M. Li, I. Koutsopoulos and R. Poovendran, Optimal jamming attack strategies and network defense policies in wireless sensor networks, *IEEE Transactions on Mobile Computing*, vol. 9(8), pp. 1119–1133, 2010.

[9] G. Noubir, Robust wireless infrastructure against jamming attacks, in *Handbook on Securing Cyber-Physical Critical Infrastructure: Foundations and Challenges*, S. Das, K. Kant and N. Zhang (Eds.), Morgan Kaufmann, Waltham, Massachusetts, pp. 123–145, 2012.

[10] K. Pelechrinis, M. Iliofotou and S. Krishnamurthy, Denial-of-service attacks on wireless networks: The case of the jammers, *IEEE Communications Surveys and Tutorials*, vol. 13(2), pp. 245–257, 2011.

[11] J. Picod, A. Lebrun and J. Demay, Bringing software defined radio to the penetration testing community, presented at the *Black Hat USA Conference*, 2014.

[12] B. Ramsey and B. Mullins, Defensive rekeying strategies for physical-layer-monitored low-rate wireless personal area networks, in *Critical Infrastructure Protection VII*, J. Butts and S. Shenoi (Eds.), Springer, Heidelberg, Germany, pp. 63–79, 2013.

[13] B. Ramsey, B. Mullins, R. Speers and K. Batterton, Watching for weakness in wild WPANs, *Proceedings of the IEEE Military Communications Conference*, pp. 1404–1409, 2013.

[14] B. Ramsey, T. Stubbs, B. Mullins, M. Temple and M. Buckner, Wireless infrastructure protection using low-cost radio frequency fingerprinting receivers, *International Journal of Critical Infrastructure Protection*, vol. 8, pp. 27–39, 2015.

[15] B. Reaves and T. Morris, Analysis and mitigation of vulnerabilities in short-range wireless communications for industrial control systems, *International Journal of Critical Infrastructure Protection*, vol. 5(3-4), pp. 154–174, 2012.

[16] L. Schauer, F. Dorfmeister and M. Maier, Potentials and limitations of WiFi-positioning using time-of-flight, *Proceedings of the International Conference on Indoor Positioning and Indoor Navigation*, 2013.

[17] Sigma Designs, Z-Wave Products, Fremont, California (`z-wave.sigma designs.com/products`), 2015.

[18] M. Strasser, B. Danev and S. Capkun, Detection of reactive jamming in sensor networks, *ACM Transactions on Sensor Networks*, vol. 7(2), article no. 16, 2010.

[19] Texas Instruments, 2.4 GHz IEEE 802.15.4/ZigBee-Ready RF transceiver, CC2420, SWRS041c, Dallas, Texas (`www.ti.com/lit/ds/symlink/cc24 20.pdf`), 2014.

[20] Texas Instruments, Low-Power Sub-1 GHz RF Transceiver, CC1101, SWRS061l, Dallas, Texas (`www.ti.com/lit/ds/symlink/cc1101.pdf`), 2015.

[21] C. Wright, L. Ballard, S. Coull, F. Monrose and G Masson, Uncovering spoken phrases in encrypted voice-over-IP conversations, *ACM Transactions on Information and System Security*, vol. 13(4), article no. 35, 2010.

[22] W. Xu, W. Trappe, Y. Zhang and T. Wood, The feasibility of launching and detecting jamming attacks in wireless networks, *Proceedings of the Sixth ACM International Symposium on Mobile Ad Hoc Neworking and Computing*, pp. 46–57, 2005.

[23] Zensys, ZM3102N Z-Wave Module Datasheet, Document No. DSH10756, version 6, Fremont, California (`media.digikey.com/pdf/Data%20She ets/Zensys%20PDFs/ZM3102N.pdf`), 2007.

Chapter 14

IMPLEMENTING CYBER SECURITY REQUIREMENTS AND MECHANISMS IN MICROGRIDS

Apurva Mohan and Himanshu Khurana

Abstract   A microgrid is a collection of distributed energy resources, storage and loads under common coordination and control that provides a single functional interface to enable its management as a single unit. Microgrids provide several advantages such as power quality control, uninterrupted power supply and integration of renewable resources. However, microgrids are increasingly connected to the Internet for remote control and management, which makes them susceptible to cyber attacks. To address this issue, several pilot deployments have implemented bolt-on security mechanisms, typically focused on securing the protocols used in microgrids. Unfortunately, these solutions are inadequate because they fail to address some important cyber security requirements.

This chapter describes the μGridSec methodology, which is intended to provide comprehensive cyber security solutions for microgrid deployments. First, cyber security requirements are derived from relevant industry standards and by studying pilot microgrid deployments. Next, the μGridSec methodology is applied to ensure that appropriate mechanisms are applied to microgrid architectures to meet the cyber security requirements. Finally, a high-level threat model for a representative microgrid architecture is used to identify security threats and demonstrate how μGridSec can address the threats.

Keywords: Microgrids, cyber security, NERC-CIP standards, threat modeling

1.   Introduction

A microgrid is a collection of local electricity generation and energy storage systems, and electrical loads that are under common coordination and control. Although a microgrid consists of multiple entities, it can be controlled as if it were a single entity. The integration of distributed energy resources (DERs), storage and loads increases the efficiency of the entire system. It also makes it

© IFIP International Federation for Information Processing 2015
M. Rice, S. Shenoi (Eds.): Critical Infrastructure Protection IX, IFIP AICT 466, pp. 229–244, 2015.
DOI: 10.1007/978-3-319-26567-4_14

possible to connect multiple microgrids to create a "power enclave" with high voltage capacity [21]. A single microgrid can function in the "grid connected" mode in which the microgrid is connected to the main power grid and jointly provides power. Alternatively, a microgrid can operate in the "islanded" mode where the microgrid functions autonomously as a self-contained system that provides power to a local site.

Microgrids offer advantages such as enhanced power quality via voltage sag correction, increased power factors, enhanced reliability for critical loads, greater energy security, higher local power distribution efficiency due to shorter distances, better sustainability by integrating renewable resources and clean fuel sources, and the potential for greater physical and cyber security. Due to these advantages, microgrids are being hailed as critical components of future energy systems. Microgrids are in operation around the world and the adoption and deployment of microgrids is increasing [18].

Microgrids are currently deployed at a variety of organizations, including university campuses, military bases, hospitals, residential communities and rural areas. They provide energy security and constitute an important part of the critical energy infrastructure. At sensitive sites such as military bases, hospitals and safety-critical facilities, it is vital to ensure that the power supply is not disrupted by adversaries. For example, a military base may rely on a microgrid for uninterrupted power supply during periods of grid downtime or grid peak loads, and its operational capability can be significantly affected by physical or cyber attacks on the microgrid. This chapter focuses on the cyber security of microgrids; securing microgrids from physical attacks is outside the scope of this work.

This chapter formulates cyber security requirements for microgrids. Some of the relevant standards that can be used to derive smart grid cyber security requirements are: NIST IR 7628 [19], NERC-CIP-002 to CIP-009 [14], NIST 800-53 [12], NIST 800-82 [20], ISO 27002 [7] and the Department of Homeland Security (DHS) Catalog of Control Systems Security [3]. In this chapter, the NERC-CIP Standards CIP-002-1 through CIP-009-2 [14] are used to derive the cyber security requirements. Although the NERC-CIP standards are widely used in the bulk electricity generation infrastructure and are not directly applicable to microgrids, they are, nevertheless, among the most relevant standards for electrical systems. Additional cyber security requirements are derived by considering microgrid pilot project deployments [18]. This chapter presents the μGridSec methodology, which ensures that appropriate mechanisms are applied to microgrid architectures to meet the cyber security requirements. A high-level threat model for a representative microgrid architecture is used to identify security threats and demonstrate how μGridSec can address the threats.

2.   Security Requirements for Microgrids

This section articulates the cyber security requirements for microgrids. The requirements are derived from the North American Electric Reliability Corporation – Critical Infrastructure Protection (NERC-CIP) Standards CIP-002-1 through CIP-009-2 [14] and from pilot microgrid deployments [18]. Note that the NERC-CIP requirements are formally defined for electric power infrastructure assets such as utilities, but they are re-interpreted for microgrids in this work. In particular, each requirement was formally analyzed and applied to a microgrid environment. A number of NERC-CIP requirements are administrative in nature and only the technical requirements are considered in this work. An analysis of pilot microgrid deployments revealed that the NERC-CIP requirements do not completely cover the cyber security requirements for microgrids. To address this gap, additional cyber security requirements for microgrids were formulated by studying some pilot microgrid deployments [18].

The enhanced set of cyber security requirements for microgrids includes:

1. **Critical Asset Identification:** The critical assets related to microgrid operations and communications should be identified. This is done to ensure adequate protection of critical assets.

2. **Cyber Vulnerability Assessment:** Cyber vulnerability assessments should be performed for: (i) electronic access points; (ii) electronic security perimeters; and (iii) critical assets. A comprehensive architectural risk analysis should be performed to identify the cyber security threats in the architecture and the security controls to address the threats.

3. **Electronic Security Perimeter:** Every critical cyber asset should be within the electronic security perimeter.

4. **Identity Management:** The microgrid system should provide digital identity management to all internal and external entities. This is important for all communications, coordination and control activities in a single microgrid and when multiple microgrids interact.

5. **Access Control:** Appropriate access control should be enforced to mediate access to: (i) all critical assets; and (ii) all electronic access points at the perimeter. This includes the implementation of secure authentication mechanisms.

6. **Information Protection:** Appropriate measures should be taken to identify, classify and protect sensitive information associated with microgrid operations and communications.

7. **Anomaly Detection:** Remote entities should be allowed to perform only a well-defined set of actions associated with their accounts or roles. The sets of actions may be further broken down into sequences of commands that can be executed by remote entities. Any deviation from a sequence should be rejected and the anomaly should be logged.

8. **Critical Asset Protection:** Critical assets should be identified and protected from damage due to the actions of remote entities. The mechanisms should work in conjunction with the safety features of the identified critical assets.

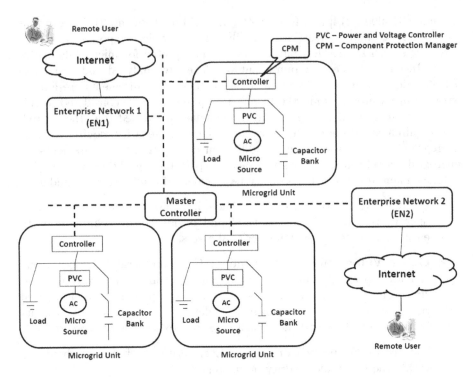

Figure 1. Architecture with coupled microgrids.

3. μGridSec Methodology

This section discusses some representative microgrid architectures and provides details about their operation along with their information and communication components. Following this, the μGridSec methodology is described in detail.

3.1 Information and Communications

Figures 1 and 2 show two microgrid architectures. Figure 1 shows an architecture where multiple microgrids are coupled together in a large deployment. Figure 2 shows a microgrid bank with multiple microgrid campuses connected together to create an energy farm along the lines of the architecture proposed in [2]. These large and complex deployments are considered because the proposed methodology is intended to cover the security requirements for large, complex, current and future architectures.

Figure 1 shows a large deployment with multiple microgrids coupled together to meet the demands of a large campus. EN1 and EN2 are enterprise networks that provide electronic entry points to the microgrid. EN1 and EN2 are connected to the Internet and host a range of enterprise services for campus users.

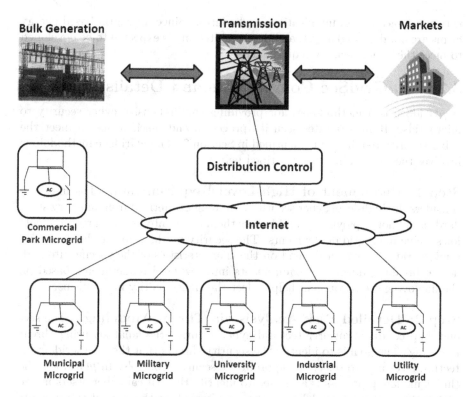

Figure 2. Architecture with an energy bank comprising independent microgrids.

They also host control centers that enable users such as operators, technicians and administrators to control and manage the microgrids. The microgrids have two types of connections: (i) electrical wires for power flow; and (ii) network cables for communications and control. The network cables, which connect the microgrid controllers (Figure 1), typically use smart grid protocols such as DNP3 or IEC 61850. Information flowing along the channels is rarely encrypted and access control mechanisms are rarely used to access information and resources in the microgrids. The enterprise networks host control centers, which typically implement weak or no authentication mechanisms. The controllers execute the commands they receive without any authentication and a requestor can see information or access any component without any access control checks.

Figure 2 shows a futuristic energy farm in which multiple microgrid deployments coordinate to supply power to a utility by connecting to its distribution system. At this time, several technical limitations exist related to the power engineering aspects of such a deployment; however, research efforts are underway to address the challenges. The microgrids in Figure 2 connect to each other and to the utility distribution system using electrical wires for power flow and network cables for communications and control. Since microgrid based energy farms are not deployed as yet, an initial architecture is expected to be developed to meet the cyber security requirements.

3.2   μGridSec Components and Details

μGridSec is a methodology for providing comprehensive cyber security to microgrids. It incorporates security processes and mechanisms to meet the cyber security requirements identified in Section 2. The μGridSec methodology involves the four main steps described below.

Step 1: Refinement of High-Level Requirements. The first step considers the high-level cyber security requirements derived from industry standards and pilot deployments and breaks them down into low-level requirements for specific microgrid deployments. The security mechanisms needed to secure a microgrid deployment depend on the characteristics of the specific site and, hence, breaking down the requirements into low-level requirements based on the deployment environment helps select the right security mechanisms.

Step 2: Detailed Risk Analysis via Threat Modeling. The second step conducts an architectural cyber security risk analysis using threat modeling. The goal is to identify the security threats that the microgrid architecture faces and to select the appropriate security controls. In μGridSec, the threat modeling process is also used to identify the critical cyber assets in the architecture. Threat modeling is then performed on the critical cyber assets to identify the threats and vulnerabilities in the architecture that an adversary can exploit to attack the system. Finally, security controls are selected and implemented to effectively address the security threats and vulnerabilities. Threat modeling can be performed using the Microsoft SDL tool [9] or other popular threat modeling tools. The next section presents a threat modeling process assuming that the SDL tool is used to achieve Requirements 1 and 2 listed in Section 2.

Threat modeling involves the following steps:

- Identify the main components responsible for microgrid operation and communications. For example, in Figure 1, the components are the power generation resources, storage and loads. The communications and control components are the controllers, communications channels and master controller. These components can be modeled using a threat modeling tool such as SDL [9].

- Draw the trust boundaries. Boundaries are drawn for the security zones and conduits model, which creates trust zones in the system architecture that communicate through channels called conduits.

- Execute the threat modeling tool and work on the STRIDE questions that explore the security threats in the architecture. The STRIDE threat model was developed by Microsoft to help categorize security threats. STRIDE refers to six threat categories: (i) spoofing; (ii) tampering; (iii) repudiation; (iv) information disclosure; (v) denial of service; and (vi) privilege escalation.

- (Optional) Prioritize the threats using the CVSS2 system [13].

- Select security controls that address the identified threats. Standards such as NIST SP 800-53 [12], NIST SP 800-82 [20] and ISA-99 [6] can be used to select the appropriate security controls.

Step 3: Information Protection Mechanisms. The third step in the μGridSec methodology defines security mechanisms for information protection. These mechanisms, which help comply with Requirements 3 through 6, protect information in transit and at rest, and implement network security, identity management, and authentication and access control to secure information and critical assets.

The first mechanism defines the trust domains in the architecture. The zones in Figure 1 represent different trust domains. Each trust domain is protected by systems such as firewalls and access control lists. The level of perimeter protection depends on the level of trust associated with each domain. For example, in Figure 1, each microgrid is at the same trust level, therefore, some access-control-list-based perimeter protection should suffice. For conduits that connect microgrid trust domains to the enterprise network, firewalls with advanced capabilities are recommended. This architecture provides a layered approach with strong perimeter protection and additional layers of protection within the main perimeter.

The second mechanism enforces strong authentication and access control in a microgrid system. Strong authentication is enforced for users who access information and/or resources. Several authentication technologies can be used as outlined in NIST SP 800-53 [12]. Role-based access control [17] is recommended for access control. Since a small number of roles exist in microgrid systems, the management of access control policies would be efficient and less prone to errors. Authenticated subjects are mapped to one or multiple roles. The access control policy defines each role and its level of access to the information and microgrid components.

The third mechanism protects information at rest and in transit. μGridSec engages standard cryptographic mechanisms to protect information. The networks are protected using TLS 1.2 for channel encryption and AES-256 for message encryption; AES-256 is used to encrypt all data at rest. Messages incorporate sequence numbers to guarantee message freshness. Public-key certificates based on the X.509 v3 standard are used; depending on the deployment, the certificates are either self-signed or certificate-authority-provided. Certificate management and key management are performed according to best practices [1]. Digital signatures can be used optionally for messages to ensure non-repudiation. The ability to affix and verify digital signatures is provided, but is not mandatory. Also, hash message authentication codes may be used to provide message authenticity at the application level.

The fourth and final mechanism provides digital identity management in μGridSec. Each component that is addressable by a communication has a unique identity in a microgrid and the corresponding mapping is stored in a database. Each microgrid has a unique identifier that is appended to the component identity in the case of multiple connected microgrids to resolve namespace clashes. The database also contains other information about microgrid components that might aid in providing identity management services.

Step 4: Anomaly Detection and Component Protection Mechanisms. The fourth and final step of the methodology provides anomaly detection and microgrid component protection. This involves two phases. In the first phase, μGridSec proposes command validation such that only validated commands can be executed on critical assets. This functionality can be achieved by command whitelisting. The access control engine can perform whitelist checking or a commercial whitelisting product may be integrated with μGridSec to assist with command whitelisting. Whitelisting of commands can be performed per role to enhance its effectiveness. The access control engine can also track entities (and roles) that repeatedly send commands that are prohibited and raise alarms. Logs should be analyzed to identify entities that display erroneous or potentially malicious behavior.

In the second phase, the component protection manager (CPM), which is inside the controller, communicates with the power and voltage controller (PVC) (Figure 1). A command to a microsource is executed only after the power and voltage controller verifies that it does not violate the safety limits of the microsource. The component protection manager along with the whitelist manager in the access control engine ensure that the setpoints of the power and voltage controller are not modified by unauthorized entities. These two steps guarantee the integrity of setpoints and that microsources are not damaged by adversaries who execute arbitrary commands on the microsources.

4.   Implementing μGridSec

This section discusses some widely-available commercial and open-source technologies that can be used to implement the security controls listed above.

Threat modeling for a microgrid architecture can be performed using a manual approach or an automated tool. The popular Microsoft SDL tool [9] may be used for modeling the threats to a microgrid architecture or system.

μGridSec recommends the use of network firewalls for perimeter protection. Several vendors provide network firewalls with advanced features that can be used for microgrid deployments. While it is important to find the right vendor to meet the deployment requirements, it is even more important to maintain secure configurations of the firewalls. Most firewalls allow remote configuration and maintenance by administrators; this feature should be protected very carefully if it is employed.

Authentication and access control are two other features that can be deployed using a combination of commercial technologies and custom implementation. Authentication is supported by protocols such as IEC 62351 [5] and OLE for Process Control Unified Architecture (OPC UA) [15]. Standard username-password based authentication is provided by these protocols. Secure authentication can be implemented for privileged users such as administrators via two-factor authentication mechanisms. The second factor can be implemented using a commercial solution.

Access control should be implemented on microgrid devices and in the network. In the case of microgrid devices, access control lists on Linux platforms can be leveraged to provide fine-grained access control to resources and operations. In the case of a network, role-based access control may be implemented to provide strong access control. One solution is OpenRBAC, an open-source implementation of the ANSI/INCITS Standard 359-2004 (Role Based Access Control) [4]. This solution is flexible, configurable and easily integrated into microgrid networks.

μGridSec proposes TLS 1.2 for channel protection and AES-256 for message protection. The popular OpenSSL library [16] may be integrated in a microgrid system to provide TLS 1.2 and AES-256 mechanisms.

Finally, command validation may be implemented via command whitelisting. This can be performed by custom software integrated with the access control engine or by a commercial whitelisting product. Whitelisting of commands can be performed per role to enhance its effectiveness. Command validation provides protection from command injection attacks and also limits the invocation of sensitive executables to certain roles.

5.   Cyber Security Requirements

This section revisits the cyber security requirements laid out in Section 2 and discusses how they are met by different μGridSec components.

1. **Critical Asset Identification:** This requirement is met by the threat modeling process in μGridSec, where the first step is to identify the critical assets in a microgrid.

2. **Cyber Vulnerability Assessment:** This requirement is also met by the threat modeling process in μGridSec, where the potential cyber vulnerabilities and threats are identified in a microgrid architecture after the critical assets have been identified. The vulnerability assessment is performed using the SDL tool, which engages an attack library based on the STRIDE model.

3. **Electronic Security Perimeter:** A strong electronic security perimeter is built into a microgrid system using external firewalls with advanced features and secure configurations. Additionally, trust domains are created within the perimeter for additional defense. The internal trust domain boundaries can be based on access control lists.

4. **Identity Management:** The digital identity of each resource in a micro-grid is stored in a database and is used whenever the resource is referred to by a communications or control message. When multiple microgrids are integrated in a microgrid bank, the domain name of a specific microgrid is appended before an asset name to avoid namespace clashes. This identity is used as the primary username by the authentication mechanism.

5. **Access Control:** Strong authentication and access control are enforced in a microgrid system. Role-based access control is prescribed for access-ing all sensitive information and critical physical assets.

6. **Information Protection and Authenticity:** Strong mechanisms are in place to protect sensitive information in transit or at rest. μGridSec uses a combination of standard symmetric and asymmetric cryptographic algorithms such as AES-256 and ECC/RSA with strong key management to provide the required functionality. Hash message authentication codes are proposed to ensure message-level authenticity and digital signatures are used to achieve non-repudiation. A public-key infrastructure is em-ployed to enable trust based on digital signatures.

7. **Anomaly Detection:** Anomaly detection is implemented at the com-mand interface based on whitelisting. The whitelist is manually populated by the administrator and is used to verify that each role is only allowed to execute authorized commands. An anomaly is reported if a role attempts to execute unauthorized commands repeatedly.

8. **Critical Asset Protection:** A component protection manager is imple-mented on controllers. The component protection manager ensures the integrity of setpoints in power and voltage controllers and that the safety limits of microsources are not violated. The component protection man-ager and access control lists prevent unauthorized access to configuration and safety data, and, even in the case of authorized access, ensure that the safety limits of the microsources are not violated.

6.   Threat Model

This section presents a cyber security threat model for the microgrid ar-chitectures presented in Figures 1 and 2. The threats are divided into seven categories. The manner in which μGridSec protects a microgrid against each of the identified threat categories is also discussed.

6.1   Unauthorized Access

In this threat category, the attacker can:

- Access the setpoints in a power and voltage controller in an attempt to violate the safety limits and damage equipment.

- Access the energy manager and send malicious messages to microgrid components in order to consume resources or damage the components.

- Access sensitive information in transit or at rest, and remove traces from the system by deleting entries from the access log.

Mitigation: The μGridSec methodology uses strong authentication to determine the identity of a remote user and to map the user identity to the associated roles. A user can only assume roles that are associated with his/her identity. Each asset in the system has an access control list that determines the access rights of a given role for the asset (an asset is any physical component of a microgrid or any information that is protected). This prevents unauthorized access to assets. Since the number of assets and the number of roles in a microgrid are limited, the access control lists would be limited in size and easily manageable by system administrators.

6.2   Privilege Escalation

In this threat category, the attacker can:

- Gain higher privileges in the system. For example, an attacker can leverage implementation weaknesses or lenient access control lists to elevate his/her privilege level and abuse the new access rights gained as a result.

- Gain access to privileged information. For example, an attacker can launch an SQL injection attack on a controller that uses an SQL database to access privileged information stored in the database.

Mitigation: The μGridSec methodology uses role-based access control and implements a least-privilege access control architecture. Thus, each role is granted the minimum privileges to perform the required tasks; this prevents unauthorized or unintended access. It is still necessary to protect against other implementation weaknesses such as those exploited by SQL injection attacks. However, using a least-privilege architecture ensures that higher privileges than are absolutely necessary are not provided by default.

6.3   Spoofing

In this threat category, the attacker can:

- Spoof accounts by stealing credentials or exploiting storage, guessing credentials by exploiting weak account management, brute-forcing user passwords and recovering passwords by exploiting weak password policies.

Mitigation: The μGridSec methodology defines secure account and password management policies. Some of the principal features are:

- Strong and secure authentication mechanisms that always use secure channels to perform authentication.

- Strong password policies covering password entropy, password resets, password expiry, etc.

- Passwords are stored as hashes generated by the PBKDF2 function.

6.4   Denial-of-Service

In this threat category, the attacker can:

- Launch denial-of-service attacks on a microgrid system. A common example is a network flooding attack using SYN or ICMP packets. Another common denial-of-service attack (at the application layer) is flooding an application with service requests that cannot be filtered at the network layer.

Mitigation: The μGridSec methodology enforces firewalls with advanced features at the network perimeter for effective perimeter protection. Also, the various trust domains are protected by firewalls and access control lists that provide an additional layer of defense. Additionally, access control lists restrict the roles that can send requests to an asset. Note that applications typically use additional mechanisms such as rate limitation or context-based request processing to handle flooding attacks at the application layer.

6.5   Software and Firmware Integrity

In this threat category, the attacker can:

- Download malware-infected firmware on a device such as a controller and gain complete control of the device.

Mitigation: The μGridSec methodology uses a public-key infrastructure to enforce digital signatures on hashes of firmware. Each device verifies the integrity of the firmware before it is downloaded.

6.6   Unauthorized Network Access

In this threat category, the attacker can:

- Access confidential information in the absence of adequate transport layer protection.

Mitigation: The μGridSec methodology uses TLS 1.2 for transport layer protection. This ensures strong network level protection for communications both within and outside a microgrid system.

6.7   Repudiation

In this threat category, the attacker can:

- Deny sending or receiving certain messages. This can be critical for financial transactions (e.g., market price data and units of electricity sold or purchased). This type of attack can be launched by compromising a microgrid component or by relying on a dishonest or compromised employee.

Mitigation: The μGridSec methodology mandates the use of digital signatures for financial and other sensitive transactions. The use of digital signatures is optional for non-sensitive transactions, but they can be used at the discretion of an administrator. μGridSec supports a public-key infrastructure in which each entity has a public-key certificate and a corresponding private key. The private key is used to sign the hash of a sensitive message or transaction.

7.   Related Work

The Smart Power Infrastructure Demonstration for Energy Reliability and Security (SPIDERS) Project is executed jointly by the Department of Energy, Department of Defense and Department of Homeland Security [18]. The goal of the SPIDERS microgrid demonstration project is to provide secure control of electricity generation at U.S. military bases. This will be achieved by building smart, secure and robust microgrids that incorporate renewable resources. The SPIDERS Project is the first of its kind to provide cyber security for microgrid control and operations. Cyber security is provided by commercially-available technologies and, therefore, the SPIDERS cyber security technology itself is not novel. Also, SPIDERS does not provide a methodology that comprehensively addresses the possible attack vectors as in the case of μGridSec.

The CERTS MicroGrid concept integrates distributed energy resources in a microgrid to seamlessly separate or island them from the grid and reconnect them to the grid [8]. To the external entity, the entire microgrid appears as a single entity instead of a collection of distributed energy resources. The traditional method has been to integrate a small number of distributed energy resources and to shut down a microgrid when a problems arises, as detailed in the IEEE P1547 standard. The CERTS MicroGrid architecture serves as the base model for μGridSec with respect to microgrid architecture and operations. However, the CERTS model does not consider cyber security issues whereas μGridSec is focused on entirely on cyber security for microgrids.

Wang and Lemmon [21] have proposed a method for coupling low voltage microgrids into mid-voltage distribution systems. They propose a hierarchical control architecture to maximize the real power exported to a mid-voltage distribution network by coupling low voltage microgrids. Their architecture is similar to the microgrid coupling architecture considered in this work. However, Wang and Lemmon consider the electrical architecture of microgrids whereas μGridSec is focused on cyber security for microgrids. Note that the work of Wang and Lemmon as well as other efforts related to microgrid infrastructures could serve as platforms on which μGridSec could be deployed.

Mueller [11] has published details of the NSF ERC FREEDM Project on microgrids. This project investigates the challenges of the cyber-physical aspects of microgrids and highlights novel opportunities for selective power delivery during power outages. It also recognizes the need to secure microgrids because distributed control systems are highly vulnerable to cyber attacks. Mueller makes a case for securing microgrids, but does not propose any solutions. In contrast, μGridSec recognizes the need and challenges involved in implementing cyber security for microgrids. μGridSec also derives requirements from established standards and deployments and presents a comprehensive methodology that meets the requirements.

8. Conclusions

Microgrids are an important component of current and future energy systems. They provide several benefits, including enhanced power quality, uninterrupted power supply and integration of renewable sources in the power distribution system. Since microgrids are a key component of the energy critical infrastructure, it is important that they are not disrupted or damaged by cyber attacks. The μGridSec methodology presented in this chapter is an architecture-agnostic approach that provides standards-based high security for microgrid deployments. In particular, the methodology can be applied to ensure that appropriate mechanisms are applied to microgrid architectures in order to meet cyber security requirements derived from the NERC-CIP standards and pilot microgrid deployments. A security evaluation of a representative microgrid architecture demonstrates that the μGridSec methodology can comprehensively address the identified threats. In cases where legacy devices in a microgrid do not support cryptographic mechanisms such as TLS or integrity validation, security can be implemented in the form of bump-in-the-wire hardware solutions; this concept is illustrated in a companion chapter in this volume [10]. The μGridSec methodology can enable the wider adoption of microgrids, especially in sensitive installations such as military bases and hospitals, thus enhancing energy security.

Future research will explore other relevant standards and derive additional cyber security requirements that will extend the μGridSec methodology. Although the threat modeling and architectural risk analysis presented in this chapter demonstrate that μGridSec effectively addresses cyber threats, the incorporation of requirements from additional standards will render the methodology more comprehensive and will help achieve compliance with smart grid standards.

References

[1] E. Barker, W. Barker, W. Burr, W. Polk and M. Smid, Recommendation for Key Management, NIST Special Publication 800-57 (Part 1, Revised), National Institute of Standards and Technology, Gaithersburg, Maryland, 2007.

[2] S. Bossart, DoE perspective on microgrids, presented at the *Advanced Microgrid Concepts and Technologies Workshop*, 2012.

[3] Department of Homeland Security, Catalog of Control Systems Security: Recommendations for Standards Developers, Washington, DC, 2011.

[4] Directory Applications and Advanced Security and Information Management International, OpenRBAC, Tubingen, Germany (daasi.de/en/daasi-knowledge-base/openrbac), 2014.

[5] International Electrotechnical Commission, IEC/TS 62351-1 to 62351-7, Power Systems Management and Associated Information Exchange – Data and Communications Security, Geneva, Switzerland, 2012.

[6] International Society of Automation, ISA99: Industrial Automation and Control Systems Security, Research Triangle Park, North Carolina (www.isa.org/isa99), 2015.

[7] International Standards Organization, ISO 27002:2013, Information Technology – Security Techniques, Code of Practice for Information Security Controls, Geneva, Switzerland, 2013.

[8] R. Lasseter, A. Akhil, C. Marnay, J. Stephens, J. Dagle, R. Guttromson, A. Meliopoulous, R. Yinger and J. Eto, Integration of Distributed Energy Resources: The CERTS MicroGrid Concept, P500-03-089F, California Energy Commission, Sacramento, California (certs.lbl.gov/pdf/50829.pdf), 2003.

[9] Microsoft, SDL Threat Modeling Tool, Redmond, Washington (www.microsoft.com/en-us/sdl/adopt/threatmodeling.aspx), 2014.

[10] A. Mohan, G. Brainard, H. Khurana and S. Fischer, A cyber security architecture for microgrid deployments, in *Critical Infrastructure Protection IX*, M. Rice and S. Shenoi (Eds.), Springer, Heidelberg, Germany, pp. 245–259, 2015.

[11] F. Mueller, Cyber-Physical Aspects of Energy Systems for the 21st Century: A Perspective from the NSF ERC FREEDM Project, Department of Computer Science, North Carolina State University, Raleigh, North Carolina (moss.csc.ncsu.edu/~mueller/ftp/pub/mueller/papers/cps09.pdf), 2009.

[12] National Institute of Standards and Technology, Security and Privacy Controls for Federal Information Systems and Organizations, NIST Special Publication 800–53 (Revision 4), Gaithersburg, Maryland, 2013.

[13] National Institute of Standards and Technology, NVD Common Vulnerability Scoring System Support v2, Gaithersburg, Maryland (nvd.nist.gov/cvss.cfm), 2014.

[14] North American Electricity Reliability Corporation, Standards, Washington DC (www.nerc.com/pa/stand/Pages/default.aspx), 2014.

[15] OPC Foundation, Unified Architecture, Scottsdale, Arizona (opcfoundation.org/developer-tools/specifications-unified-architecture), 2015.

[16] OpenSSL Project, Welcome to the OpenSSL Project (www.openssl.org), 2014.

[17] R. Sandhu, D. Ferraiolo and R. Kuhn, The NIST model for role-based access control: Towards a unified standard, *Proceedings of the Fifth ACM Workshop on Role-Based Access Control*, pp. 47–63, 2000.

[18] Sandia National Laboratories, SPIDERS Microgrid Project secures military installations, Sandia Labs News Release, Albuquerque, New Mexico (share.sandia.gov/news/resources/news_releases/spiders/#.V W2kCq3bKEJ), February 22, 2012.

[19] Smart Grid Interoperability Panel, Cyber Security Working Group, Introduction to NISTIR 7628 Guidelines for Smart Grid Cyber Security, National Institute of Standards and Technology, Gaithersburg, Maryland, 2010.

[20] K. Stouffer, J. Falco and K. Scarfone, Guide to Industrial Control Systems (ICS) Security, NIST Special Publication 800-82, National Institute of Standards and Technology, Gaithersburg, Maryland, 2011.

[21] Z. Wang and M. Lemmon, Task 1: Coupling Low-Voltage Microgrids into Mid-Voltage Distribution Systems, Department of Electrical Engineering, University of Notre Dame, Notre Dame, Indiana (www3.nd.edu/~lemmon/projects/GE-project-2010/Vault/Publicati ons/algorithm_develop_report_01302012.pdf), 2012.

Chapter 15

A CYBER SECURITY ARCHITECTURE FOR MICROGRID DEPLOYMENTS

Apurva Mohan, Gregory Brainard, Himanshu Khurana and Scott Fischer

Abstract   Microgrids enable the aggregation of various types of generating and non-generating sources as a unified control unit. Microgrid control networks are connected to external networks – SCADA networks for demand-response applications, enterprise networks and the Internet for remote monitoring and control. These external connections expose microgrids to serious threats from cyber attacks. This is a major concern for microgrids at sensitive installations such as military bases and hospitals. One of the challenges in protecting microgrids is that control networks require very low latency. Cryptographic protection, which adds additional latency to communications, is unacceptable in real-time control, especially with regard to synchronization and stability. Also, a complex network at a microgrid site with interconnected control and SCADA networks makes the process of acquiring security certifications (e.g., DIACAP) extremely difficult. To address these challenges, this chapter presents the SNAPE cyber security architecture, which segregates communications networks needed for fast, real-time control from networks used for external control signals and monitoring, thereby drastically reducing the attack surface of a microgrid control network. Network segregation is achieved by hardware devices that provide strong cryptographic separation. The segregation isolates control networks so that they can use lightweight cryptography to meet the low latency requirements. The novel approach minimizes the cyber security certification burden by reducing the scope of certification to a subset of a microgrid network.

Keywords: Microgrids, cyber security architecture, threat modeling

1. Introduction

A microgrid is a collection of distributed energy resources (DERs), storage and loads under common coordination and control that provides a functional

© IFIP International Federation for Information Processing 2015
M. Rice, S. Shenoi (Eds.): Critical Infrastructure Protection IX, IFIP AICT 466, pp. 245–259, 2015.
DOI: 10.1007/978-3-319-26567-4_15

interface to enable its management as a single unit. The U.S. Department of Energy defines a microgrid as: "[A] group of interconnected loads and distributed energy resources within clearly defined electrical boundaries that acts as a single controllable entity with respect to the grid. A microgrid can connect and disconnect from the grid to enable it to operate in the grid-connected or island-modes" [1]. A microgrid acts as a single point of integration for generating (renewable and non-renewable) and non-generating sources. A microgrid accumulates all the generation capacity at a site and provides power to a local site not only in cases of blackouts, but also as ancillary capacity to lower energy usage from the main electric power grid. Microgrids are currently deployed at military bases, hospitals, universities, residential communities and government buildings to enhance energy efficiency and energy security. Microgrids can be deployed in a variety of architectures – as a single microgrid that provides power to a site, as multiple microgrids that function in isolation at a site, or as multiple microgrids deployed as power enclaves, where each enclave is served by a single microgrid unit, but all the units are connected via electrical power lines for load balancing and via communications lines for common control and coordination.

In many critical infrastructures, operations sites are often distributed and multiple sites are connected to a common control center. Also, the control center needs to communicate with the enterprise network. To enable all the required communications, microgrids/control centers are often connected to the Internet directly or via a control center. Typically, the control center to microgrid communications use distributed control system (DCS) protocols such as DNP3 and Modbus; IP-based protocols such as DCS IP or TCP/IP are typically used for longer distances. The Internet connectivity exposes microgrids to numerous cyber threats. Cyber attackers could target microgrid operations and potentially disrupt the power supply. Attacks on microgrids installed at sensitive sites such as military bases, hospitals or government buildings could have serious consequences.

This chapter describes the novel Secure Network of Assured Power Enclaves (SNAPE) cyber security architecture, which enforces network separation in microgrid communications to reduce the attack surface while enhancing communications efficiency and security. In particular, SNAPE segregates the communications networks needed for fast, real-time control from networks used for external control signals and monitoring. The SNAPE architecture was created for a large U.S. Army base where multiple power enclaves with secure communications were envisioned. A deployed microgrid system based on the SNAPE architecture would contribute to the energy security and net-zero goals of the U.S. Department of Defense. The architecture uses cryptographic mechanisms to enforce network separation and provide strong cyber security.

The research described in this chapter has three main contributions. The first is the development of a conceptual cyber security architecture for microgrids with a cryptographic network separation strategy that minimizes control network latency and the control network attack surface. The second is a practical deployment architecture for microgrids that provides security and scalability. The third contribution is the use of certified hardware devices for cryptographic network separation, which significantly reduces the certification burden for microgrid deployments at U.S. military bases.

2.   Problem Description

Current distributed control system and SCADA environments typically rely on the IEC 61850 standard for communications between power substations. It is also a natural choice for connecting power enclaves defined in the SNAPE architecture, where multiple microgrids coordinate command and control. This environment has a very strict timeframe of a few milliseconds for command-response messages and any additional latency adversely impacts system performance in terms of the established requirements.

As mentioned above, microgrid systems are being connected to external networks such as enterprise networks and the Internet, which significantly increases cyber threats. Cyber attackers can attack microgrid power enclaves and compromise critical operations by exploiting vulnerabilities at the network, system and/or application levels. Microgrid deployments are being planned with network and information technology security postures that are not compliant with standards such as NIST 800-53 [12] or IEC 62443 [5]. Most systems rely on perimeter protection with the internal systems designed with lower security because they were intended to be part of a closed network. As such, achieving defense-in-depth in these microgrid systems and networks is a major challenge.

Another related problem in power networks is that communications protocols (e.g., IEC 61850) were not designed for security and they do not inherently support security features. As a result, providing communications security for these protocols requires considerable ad hoc and ancillary security mechanisms. These mechanisms inadvertently introduce security vulnerabilities that are easily exploited by cyber attacks. Recent standards such as IEC 62351 focus on securing IEC 61850 based communications [4], but even IEC 62351 does not cover the entire gamut of security vulnerabilities in networked microgrid deployments. OLE for Process Control – Unified Architecture (OPC UA) [13] presents a framework with a standards-based communications backbone and built-in security that covers a larger set of cyber security threats. However, it does not address microgrid-specific threats such as the exposure of sensitive control networks, the integration of legacy components and the complexities involved in achieving cyber security certifications.

This chapter focuses on three problems. First, the internal networks in a microgrid deployment comprise several sub-networks such as the SCADA network and microgrid control network, and maintain connections to the enterprise network. Since these networks are interconnected, the exposure of microgrid control networks to attacks is increased. A malicious entity could exploit an attack vector to break into any one of the sub-networks and then attempt to disrupt operations elsewhere in the microgrid control network. Second, many legacy devices are unable to implement security mechanisms such as encryp-

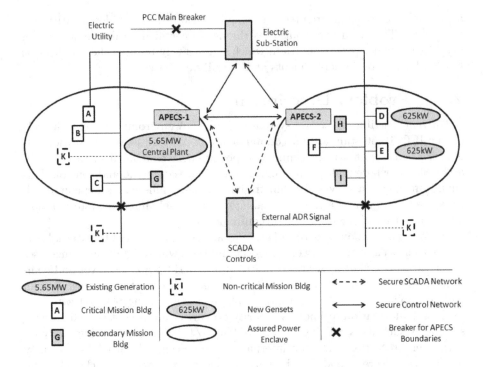

Figure 1. Conceptual architecture of a SNAPE microgrid.

tion, message signing and message hashing. This makes it difficult to enforce a strong and uniform security policy in the system. If the security policy is chosen for varying levels of security based on device capabilities, then attackers could compromise the lower-end devices with weaker security and then pivot to other networked devices. Third, in the case of microgrids at U.S. Department of Defense installations, the deployments have to obtain DIACAP or the more recent DIARMF (Department of Defense Information Assurance Risk Management Framework) certifications. Since a microgrid network comprises several sub-networks, the task of security assessment and certification of the microgrid control network becomes very complex and challenging.

3. SNAPE Cyber Security Architecture

The SNAPE architecture enables secure communications and control for multiple microgrid systems at a site, where each microgrid corresponds to a power enclave. A SNAPE microgrid can function in the grid connected mode or in the islanding mode to provide power to a local site. SNAPE SCADA control systems accept external automated demand response (ADR) signals and participate in automated demand response programs for energy efficiency.

Figure 1 presents a conceptual architecture of the SNAPE system. The system has two power enclaves, APECS-1 and APECS-2. Each enclave is attached to critical and non-critical mission buildings. An enclave may have one or more diesel generators powering it. The microgrid has a point of common coupling (PCC) main breaker that can disconnect the microgrid from the main grid to bring it into the islanding mode. The lines connecting the substation to APECS-1 and APECS-2 correspond to the secure control network, whereas the lines connecting the SCADA controls to APECS-1 and APECS-2 correspond to the secure SCADA network. The control and SCADA networks are isolated from each other. The isolation can be physical or logical in nature.

3.1 Security Properties

The SNAPE architecture provides a number of security properties to address the cyber security concerns discussed above. The main security properties are:

- Confidentiality of information, command-response and power system operations.

- Channel integrity – integrity of data and communications flowing in and out of the microgrid.

- Message integrity – message level integrity protection in addition to channel protection.

- Application integrity – protection of the integrity of applications installed in the microgrid system.

- Availability of communication channels and microgrids to participate in command-response communications.

- Authenticity of information sources.

- Protection and isolation from the enterprise network and external networks.

- Auditing and forensic analysis capabilities.

- Reduction of the cyber attack surface.

3.2 Architecture

This section presents the details of the SNAPE cyber security architecture and describes its functioning via some use cases. Also, it discusses how the architecture acquires the security properties listed above.

The secure control network in Figure 1 is isolated from the secure SCADA network. This isolates the control network from access from the enterprise network and other external networks, including the Internet. The isolation also improves the response time in the control network, which is critical to synchronizing microgrids. Additionally, it reduces the attack surface of the control network because no direct communications path exists.

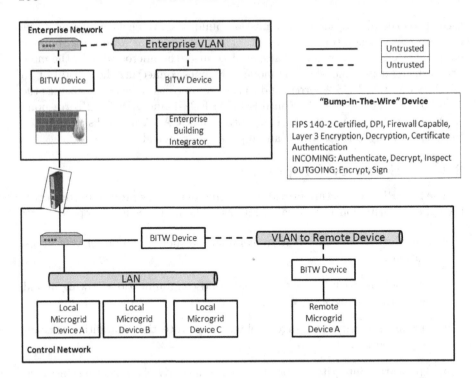

Figure 2. Communications security architecture based on the SNAPE concept.

Figure 2 presents the SNAPE architecture from the communications, network and system security point of view. It shows the external communications with the enterprise network and the local network that connects to the microgrid. "Bump-in-the-wire" devices are used to integrate legacy equipment or microgrid devices that cannot perform cryptographic operations required by secure communications networks. The bump-in-the-wire devices have the ability to encrypt communications using standard protocols. They also provide cryptographic isolation of the networks.

In the SNAPE architecture, OLE for Process Control – Unified Architecture (OPC UA) is used to implement the communications backbone. OPC UA is backward compatible with distributed control system protocols such as IEC 61850. OPC UA provides authentication and authorization services at the application layer. Availability in a network is provided by two mechanisms. First, the isolation of the control network from external networks ensures that the control network communications can meet the low latency requirement and critical infrastructure components are not unavailable due to large latencies or disruptions caused by microgrid components being out of sync. Second, cryptographic protection of messages and the network, as well as network firewalls, ensure that attackers cannot compromise the network or launch denial-of-service attacks against network components. It is important to emphasize

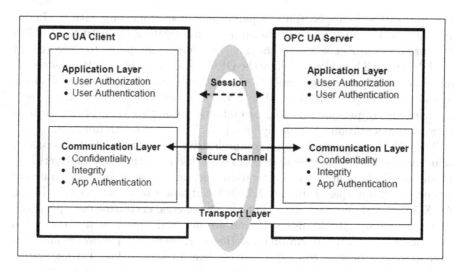

Figure 3. OPC UA security model [13].

that the closed loop control network is enclosed within the secure enclaves and the control network is physically isolated, hence it cannot be reached from the communications network. The communications network uses high-end crypto-graphic protection to enforce cyber security without adding additional latency to the control network due to its isolation.

Finally, important events, accesses and messages are logged to enable auditing and forensic analysis. This helps identify anomalous behavior and perform root cause analysis if an attack is suspected.

3.3 OPC UA Integration

This section describes how OPC UA is integrated with the SNAPE architecture to provide a secure communications backbone. Details of the OPC UA security model are provided to demonstrate that the SNAPE architecture has the security properties listed above.

The OPC UA standard was created by the OPC Foundation [13]. It improves on the earlier OPC Classic standard, which was restricted to the Windows operating system. OPC UA builds on OPC Classic with several significant updates, including an open platform architecture, a built-in security model and a feature-rich data model. It is also backward compatible with standards such as IEC 61850. This makes OPC UA an excellent choice for integration within the SNAPE architecture.

Figure 3 shows the OPC UA security model. The model has two layers, the communications layer and the application layer. In the communications layer, a secure channel provides confidentiality and integrity of the communications. Another feature that is supported is application authentication, which allows only authenticated applications to participate in microgrid operations. In the application layer, user authentication and authorization are used to establish a secure session over a secure channel. An important point to note is that availability itself is not provided by the OPC UA security model. It relies on the minimal processing of messages prior to authentication and defers availability to the server implementation. The SNAPE architecture complements these mechanisms by providing strong availability properties via features such as network segmentation, cryptographic separation and network firewalls.

The OPC UA security model is comprehensive and offers multiple options for achieving security properties in the communications and application layers [13]. In the application layer, authentication may be achieved by three different means: username/password, an X.509v3 certificate or a WS-SecurityToken. An X.509v3 certificate involves multiple asymmetric cryptographic operations that are computationally intensive and are not well suited for authentication in resource-constrained environments. However, username/passwords and WS-security tokens provide comparatively efficient authentication. During system implementation, it would be necessary to compare the different mechanisms against the real-time system requirements and select the most efficient form of authentication for the SNAPE architecture. Authorization in the OPC UA security model is more open ended and can integrate already-deployed authorization solutions. Since the SNAPE architecture targets microgrids, existing authorization mechanisms in the form of access control lists are integrated to provide fine-grained authorization for microgrid resources.

In the communications layer, confidentiality is provided by encryption within a secure channel, message signatures for message integrity and digital signatures for application authentication. Like the application layer, the OPC UA stack provides multiple options to implement each security mechanism. The optimal combination of asymmetric and symmetric cryptographic algorithms was selected for the SNAPE architecture to meet microgrid performance requirements. OPC UA is flexible and allows any combination of the mechanisms to be selected to suit a specific deployment. For example, a combination of mechanisms such as transport layer security (TLS) for channel protection and symmetric algorithms for message integrity may suit a microgrid deployment environment. This would allow SNAPE to leverage the benefits of TLS for channel protection and the advantages of symmetric algorithms such as AES256 and HMAC(SHA1) for improved real-time performance with regard to message integrity protection.

4.   SNAPE Threat Model Analysis

This section identifies the potential cyber threats that exist in the microgrid deployment scenarios presented in Figures 1 and 2, and demonstrates that the SNAPE architecture mitigates the threats.

Remote Sabotage:

- **Threat:** An adversary can remotely access the microgrid and launch a privilege elevation attack to gain higher rights. The adversary can then perform unauthorized operations to disrupt the microgrid system and potentially the power supply.

- **Mitigation:** The SNAPE architecture implements a number of security controls to mitigate this threat. Secure network communications protects against threats such as session hijacking. Identity management with strong account management protects against account spoofing attacks. The access control implementation in the microgrid system prevents unauthorized access to microgrid resources and operations.

Tampering with Power Enclave Synchronization:

- **Threat:** The adversary can disrupt power enclave synchronization by reporting incorrect power measurements to other entities. This could potentially destabilize the power enclaves and disrupt their operations.

- **Mitigation:** In the SNAPE architecture, the control network and the SCADA network are isolated from each other. This isolation drastically reduces the attack surface from the SCADA network to the energy network. Moreover, authentication and access control protection in the microgrid system prevent unauthorized access. As such, it is highly unlikely that an adversary could reach the control network and disrupt its operation.

Sensitive Information Disclosure:

- **Threat:** An attacker can view sensitive microgrid information that is at rest or in transit.

- **Mitigation:** The SNAPE architecture implements authentication and access control in the microgrid system, so that only authorized entities can view or operate on sensitive data. Additionally, information in transit is protected by strong network security involving encrypted communications channels using TLS. Thus, sensitive information at rest or in transit is protected from unauthorized disclosure.

Denial of Service:

- **Threat:** An attacker can launch a denial-of-service attack by flooding a network to disrupt microgrid operations and potentially the power supply.

- **Mitigation:** The SNAPE architecture uses secure network topologies derived from reports and standards such as NIST SP 800-53 and IEC 62443 to deploy firewalls and demilitarized zones to isolate the SCADA and control networks from the enterprise network. The firewalls protect against network flooding attacks. Also, the SCADA and control networks are isolated, which further reduces the control network attack surface. Additionally, the OPC UA communications backbone performs minimal processing of unauthenticated messages to mitigate the denial-of-service threat.

Targeting Legacy Devices:

- **Threat:** Legacy devices in the microgrid system are unable to implement encryption for secure communications channels. An attacker can target these channels to view sensitive information or to inject or manipulate commands.

- **Mitigation:** The SNAPE architecture positions bump-in-the-wire hardware in front of legacy devices to implement secure communications. The bump-in-the-wire devices provide network security via TLS, which makes legacy devices compatible with other devices and provides uniform and strong network security. The bump-in-the-wire devices can be DIACAP- or DIARMF-certified to provide strong, standards-compliant network security regardless of end device capabilities.

Malware Installation:

- **Threat:** An attacker can install malware on microgrid devices.

- **Mitigation:** The SNAPE architecture provides two types of protection against malware installation. First, software or firmware installation on a device is a privileged action that can only be performed by an administrator; it would be very difficult for an attacker to compromise a highly-secure administrator account to install malware. Second, software and firmware integrity checks are performed by validating their digital signatures; only firmware and software that pass the validity checks can be installed. These security mechanisms protect against the installation of malware on the microgrid system.

5.   Discussion

Whenever security considerations are included in an architecture, certain trade-offs have to be made to balance security versus performance, cost, development time and usability. The SNAPE architecture uses bump-in-the-wire devices to support the secure integration of legacy devices. This provides uniform security in a microgrid network by enabling legacy devices to communicate using strong encryption algorithms. The downside, however, is that these devices can be expensive, depending on their functionality and the desired level of security. However, this is an optional feature in the SNAPE architecture, although it may be mandatory for microgrids at sensitive locations such as military bases.

Another trade-off is that network separation using bump-in-the-wire devices may increase network complexity and latency. However, the separation offers the choice of cryptographic algorithms for network protection. The bump-in-the-wire devices are DIACAP-certified and perform cryptographic operations end-to-end. The added latency is very low and is only introduced in the communications network. The control network is part of the secure enclaves where there is no additional latency related to cryptographic operations.

The SNAPE architecture proposes the use of TLS for strong network protection. The architecture also provides end device authentication, which is especially useful in sensitive installations and helps achieve DIACAP or DIARMF compliance. The downside of using TLS is that public-key infrastructure certificates must be installed and managed by the network. Using symmetric encryption is possible with TLS, but this is a non-standard mode of operation that is not recommended for regular deployments.

The final trade-off is related to the integration of OPC UA in SNAPE. The integration increases complexity and the cost of system development. However, on the positive side, it provides standards-based communications security. Also, it inherits a versatile and feature-rich communications backbone from SNAPE.

Massie [9] has presented a proposal for microgrid cyber security based on a distributed control approach that uses IPv6 for communications. IPv6 provides some benefits such as making host scanning and identification more difficult from outside a network because of the large number of possible IP addresses, and supporting end-to-end encryption and secure name resolution that helps counter attacks such as ARP poisoning. The SNAPE architecture provides all the benefits of an IPv6-based network. Indeed, the SNAPE architecture was developed by performing threat modeling and risk analysis, and security controls and mechanisms were subsequently incorporated to address the identified threats. In the SNAPE architecture, a microgrid deployment uses a private network with strong perimeter protection. Secure firewalls disable network scanning and identification. End-to-end encryption is implemented using TLS. Also, TLS used for network-level authentication can be configured for the mutual authentication of clients and servers; this eliminates ARP attacks. Additionally, SNAPE uses bump-in-the-wire devices to provide end-to-end authentication of legacy devices.

Massie's approach [9] suffers from several security issues compared with the SNAPE architecture. First, a decentralized peer-to-peer control architecture means that every node is trusted equally and can even take over the functionality of other nodes, especially during automated recovery. In addition to introducing complexity, this approach potentially opens new attack vectors. The adversary needs to compromise just one node and then pivot to sabotage the system. In a centralized model, a server has much stronger security than a client node. Maintaining trust in an open decentralized peer-to-peer system is a hard problem [6, 10] and even controlled system deployments would inherit some of its threats if they are connected to the Internet. Second, since control and coordination are distributed to every node, it is not possible to segment the network and isolate it for higher security and performance, something that is inherently supported and demonstrated in the SNAPE architecture. Third, Massie's approach assumes that all control devices are deployed with the peer-to-peer functionality and there are no legacy devices (actually, the approach is unable to integrate legacy devices). On the other hand, SNAPE has a method to integrate legacy devices; this is important because most network deployments are incremental in nature and it is exceedingly rare not to encounter legacy devices in a deployment.

Additionally, deploying IPv6-based networks potentially opens a number of security holes. If IPv6 and IPv4 are being run simultaneously, then IPv6 should be tunneled over IPv4 or run independently. In the tunneling mode, configuration problems can create security holes in the system [8]. If the two protocols are run in parallel, then firewalls have to be configured to filter the IPv6 traffic, which is not very common. A normal firewall does not filter IPv6 traffic; this insecure channel can be leveraged by an attacker to enter the system. Also, administrators must employ new (and better) ways to deploy, configure and monitor networks. Important tasks include troubleshooting networks, configuring firewalls, enforcing secure configurations, monitoring security logs, analyzing real-time behavior and performing network audits. Most intrusion detection/prevention systems are still not very effective at handling IPv6 traffic, which increases the potential of attacks.

6.   Related Work

Strickland [16] has presented an approach for protecting military microgrids from cyber attacks. However, the approach relies primarily on security best practices and does not consider some key issues that are addressed in the SNAPE architecture such as the vulnerabilities originating from SCADA networks and legacy devices.

The CERTS MicroGrid is a novel approach for integrating distributed energy resources in a microgrid to seamlessly island it from and reconnect it to the power grid [7]. To the control center, all the distributed energy resources appear to be a single entity for coordination and control. The traditional method has been to integrate a small number of distributed energy resources and to shut down the microgrid when problems arise (according to the IEEE P1547 standard). However, unlike the SNAPE architecture, the CERTS model does not specifically focus on cyber security for microgrids.

The Smart Power Infrastructure Demonstration for Energy Reliability and Security (SPIDERS) Project is conducted jointly by the Department of Energy, Department of Defense and Department of Homeland Security [14, 15]. The project goal is to provide secure control of on-base generation at military bases by building secure and robust microgrids that incorporate renewable energy resources. Cyber security is provided by commercially-available technologies, so the technology itself is not novel. Unlike SNAPE, SPIDERS does not provide a comprehensive architecture to address all possible attack vectors.

Mueller [11] discusses research undertaken under the NSF ERC FREEDM Project [11]. The project investigates the challenges of the cyber-physical nature of microgrids and highlights novel opportunities for providing selective power delivery during power outages. Mueller recognizes the need to secure microgrids from cyber attacks. However, the FREEDM Project does not propose any security solutions. SNAPE stands out because it recognizes the need to secure microgrids and presents a comprehensive cyber security architecture that adheres to industry standards and satisfies actual microgrid requirements.

Massie [9] presents a distributed control framework for microgrids to enhance coordination, communications and security. The framework, which uses IPv6-based communications, attempts to leverage security from IPv6 and the peer-to-peer distributed model, but it also inherits their problems. SNAPE provides all the security features provided by the framework and introduces many additional security mechanisms.

7.   Conclusions

Microgrids are being deployed at military bases and other mission-critical facilities to reduce the dependence on the power grid, to provide power during outages and to achieve the net-zero goal imposed by the U.S. Department of Defense. The SNAPE architecture is designed specifically for the secure deployment of military microgrids. It introduces several key concepts such as the physical or logical separation of microgrid control networks from SCADA networks, bump-in-the-wire devices that integrate legacy devices in a secure manner and standards-based security controls for microgrid network protection.

Current efforts are focused on realizing the SNAPE architecture in a microgrid facility under construction at a U.S. military base. The design divides the power network into several power enclaves, each served by a microgrid unit. These units will be connected using the SNAPE architecture to support common control and coordination. An OPC UA based communications backbone will be implemented along with the additional security mechanisms described in Section 3. An architectural risk analysis of the system has revealed that SNAPE effectively addresses all the identified risks. During the microgrid design phase, security threat use cases will be evaluated using the SNAPE architecture to verify that the threats are comprehensively addressed. During the deployment phase, strong efforts will be taken to ensure that all the architectural and design considerations will be implemented and tested.

References

[1] S. Bossart, DoE perspective on microgrids, presented at the *Advanced Microgrid Concepts and Technologies Workshop*, 2012.

[2] N. Hatziargyriou, H. Asano, R. Iravani and C. Marnay, Microgrids, *IEEE Power and Energy*, vol. 5(4), pp. 78–94, 2007.

[3] F. Hohlbaum, M. Braendle and F. Alvarez, Cyber security practical considerations for implementing IEC 62351, presented at the *PAC World Conference*, 2010.

[4] International Electrotechnical Commission, IEC/TS 62351-1 to 62351-7, Power Systems Management and Associated Information Exchange – Data and Communications Security, Geneva, Switzerland, 2012.

[5] International Electrotechnical Commission, IEC 62443, Industrial Communications Networks – Network and System Security, Geneva, Switzerland, 2013.

[6] S. Kamvar, M. Schlosser and H. Garcia-Molina, The Eigentrust algorithm for reputation management in P2P networks, *Proceedings of the Twelfth International Conference on World Wide Web*, pp. 640–651, 2003.

[7] R. Lasseter, A. Akhil, C. Marnay, J. Stephens, J. Dagle, R. Guttromson, A. Meliopoulous, R. Yinger and J. Eto, Integration of Distributed Energy Resources: The CERTS MicroGrid Concept, P500-03-089F, California Energy Commission, Sacramento, California (`certs.lbl.gov/pdf/50829.pdf`), 2003.

[8] J. Lyne, Why IPv6 matters for your security, Sophos, Oxford, United Kingdom (`www.sophos.com/en-us/security-news-trends/security-trends/why-switch-to-ipv6.aspx`), 2014.

[9] D. Massie, Implementation of a cyber secure microgrid control system, presented at the *SPIDERS JCTD Industry Day*, 2014.

[10] A. Mohan and D. Blough, AttributeTrust – A framework for evaluating trust in aggregated attributes via a reputation system, *Proceedings of the Sixth Annual Conference on Privacy, Security and Trust*, pp. 201–212, 2008.

[11] F. Mueller, Cyber-Physical Aspects of Energy Systems for the 21st Century: A Perspective from the NSF ERC FREEDM Project, Department of Computer Science, North Carolina State University, Raleigh, North Carolina (`moss.csc.ncsu.edu/~mueller/ftp/pub/mueller/papers/cps09.pdf`), 2009.

[12] National Institute of Standards and Technology, Security and Privacy Controls for Federal Information Systems and Organizations, NIST Special Publication 800-53 (Revision 4), Gaithersburg, Maryland, 2013.

[13] OPC Foundation, Unified Architecture, Scottsdale, Arizona (`opcfoundation.org/developer-tools/specifications-unified-architecture`), 2015.

[14] Sandia National Laboratories, SPIDERS Microgrid Project secures military installations, Sandia Labs News Release, Albuquerque, New Mexico (`share.sandia.gov/news/resources/news_releases/spiders/#.VW2kCq3bKEJ`), February 22, 2012.

[15] J. Stamp, The SPIDERS Project – Smart power infrastructure demonstration for energy reliability and security at U.S. military facilities, *Proceedings of the IEEE PES Conference on Innovative Smart Grid Technologies*, 2012.

[16] T. Strickland, Microgrid security considerations in military base deployments, DNV KEMA, Arnhem, The Netherlands (`smartgridsherpa.com/blog/microgrid-security-considerations-in-military-base-deployments`), 2014.

V

INFRASTRUCTURE MODELING AND SIMULATION

Chapter 16

ALLOCATION AND SCHEDULING OF FIREFIGHTING UNITS IN LARGE PETROCHEMICAL COMPLEXES

Khaled Alutaibi, Abdullah Alsubaie and Jose Marti

Abstract   Fire incidents in large petrochemical complexes such as oil refineries cause heavy losses. Due to the strong interdependencies that exist among units in these industrial complexes, planning an efficient response is a challenging task for firefighters. The task is even more challenging during multiple-fire incidents. This chapter describes a firefighting decision support system that helps conduct efficient responses to fire incidents. The decision support system optimizes the allocation of firefighting units in multiple-fire incidents with the objective of minimizing the economic impact. In particular, the system considers infrastructure interdependencies in estimating the damage associated with a given fire scenario, calculates the resulting economic losses and determines the optimal assignment of available firefighters. The decision support system can be used before an incident for training and planning, during an incident for decision support or after an incident for evaluating suppression strategies.

Keywords: Firefighting, industrial fires, decision support system

1.   Introduction

The principal goals of firefighting are to save lives, contain the fire to reduce the risk of a wider impact and balance the risk of environmental impact versus putting out the fire. Decisions about allocating resources such as firefighters, bulldozers, fire trucks, helicopters and air tankers are essential during fires as well as extreme events such as earthquakes and floods. These events can cause large numbers of deaths and injuries, huge economic losses and interruptions of basic services. Mihailidou et al. [24] have examined 319 industrial accidents, about 30% of which were fires. The 319 accidents occurred in 52 countries; 39% of the accidents occurred in the United States.

© IFIP International Federation for Information Processing 2015
M. Rice, S. Shenoi (Eds.): Critical Infrastructure Protection IX, IFIP AICT 466, pp. 263–279, 2015.
DOI: 10.1007/978-3-319-26567-4_16

During a fire incident, the principal objective of firefighters – after saving lives – is to minimize incident losses. According to Hall [11], the "total cost" of a fire is defined as the direct and indirect losses due to the fire plus the cost of provisions to mitigate the losses. The U.S. National Fire Protection Association (NFPA) reported that the estimated fire-related economic loss in 2011 was $14.9 billion. These losses include property damage (direct losses) and business interruption (indirect losses); 65% of the business interruption cost ($9.7 billion) was due to fires in industrial properties [11]. Due to the difficulty of pre-calculating the indirect losses, current firefighting practices target the size of a fire to reduce property damage. However, the analysis of fires reveals that a low correlation exists between the property damage cost and the business interruption cost [11]. In many cases, the business interruption cost far exceeds the direct property loss. Hall [11] states, "Sometimes, though, it can be difficult to determine what the true net loss due to business interruption is." The research described in this chapter considers the indirect loss resulting from business interruption as a significant factor when allocating firefighting resources.

According to the National Fire Protection Association [26], the number of units assigned to respond to a fire incident should be determined by risk analysis and/or pre-fire planning. Typically, unit allocation decisions are made by fire department experts based on the available information about the incident and their incident handling experience. The size of a fire is usually the major factor in assigning the number of units. In the case of industrial incidents, other factors such as economic impact and the criticality of the site are often not taken into account. Better incident response can be achieved by allocating an optimum number of firefighting units to a critical site.

In multiple-fire incidents, as opposed to single-fire incidents, fire department officials must necessarily alter their normal response assignments [30]. The special assignments require deep understanding of the infrastructure systems and their interdependencies. Fire department officials can benefit greatly from a decision support system that can help them plan better responses to large fire incidents that affect critical facilities.

This chapter describes a firefighting decision support system (FFDSS) that is designed to enable fire departments to optimize the allocation of firefighting units in multiple-fire incidents. The system takes into account infrastructure interdependencies in evaluating the economic impacts of incidents. The system uses infrastructure interdependency modeling to evaluate the economic impact of a fire incident and determines the assignment of firefighting units using an optimization agent that leverages a reinforcement learning algorithm. The decision support system can be used before a fire incident for training and planning, during a fire for optimizing the response or after a fire for evaluating suppression strategies.

This research uses a case study involving a petrochemical complex, which is an excellent example of an interdependent system. Petrochemical production processes are modeled and multiple-fire incidents are simulated by the decision support system. After computing the economic loss, a software agent is used to optimize the global objective by dynamically assigning firefighting units to the most critical fires. The decision support system can be extended to other resource allocation problems such as maintenance crew dispatching, warehouse location placement and other applications in similar interdependent environments.

2. Related Work

The key challenge in firefighting operations during a large incident is to efficiently utilize the available resources to reduce the impact of the fire. Over the years, researchers have addressed this challenge by designing fire decision support systems that model fire behavior and facilitate dispatch decisions, impact assessment and process optimization. Prominent fire decision support systems include LANIK [21], DEDICS [28] and WFDSS [7]. However, most of the systems focus on wildfires and offer limited intelligent decision making support for allocating the available resources [2, 10].

Several models have been developed for fire behavior prediction, including BEHAVE [1], FARSITE [6], HFire [25] and Prometheus [32]. However, the models only focus on fire behavior simulation using heat and smoke sources [4]. Moreover, the optimization of firefighting resources and the simulation of firefighting operations are developed separately and are not integrated [13]. In contrast, the decision support system described in this chapter integrates these components in a unifying framework.

Most of the existing fire decision models focus on the initial assignment of resources without dynamically adjusting the assignment [3]. The proposed decision support system, on the other hand, makes assignment decisions dynamically in line with the expected losses, thereby reflecting the long-term consequences of fire incidents. The system is also designed to deal with all types of fires, including wildfires. Moreover, its open architecture facilitates integration with other fire simulators and models.

A survey of the recent literature reveals that several simulation and optimization models have been integrated to support dispatching decisions in firefighting operations. Petrovic et al. [29] have developed a simulation-based model using stochastic processes and queuing theory to represent wildfire dynamics and allocate limited resources during fire suppression. Fried et al. [8] have proposed an integrated model for allocating firefighter resources and evaluating dispatching rules. Other researchers [5, 14, 27] have also integrated fire behavior simulation and optimization to help allocate firefighting resources. Hu and Ntaimo [13] have developed an agent-based discrete event simulation model that simulates fire suppression based on dispatching plans from a stochastic optimization model. Lee et al. [20] have developed a model that combines optimization with stochastic simulation to assign resources (by type) that must arrive at a fire within a specified time and a given budget.

Finally, HomChaudhuri [12] has developed an intelligent resource allocation system that minimizes the damage due to wildfires. The system uses a genetic

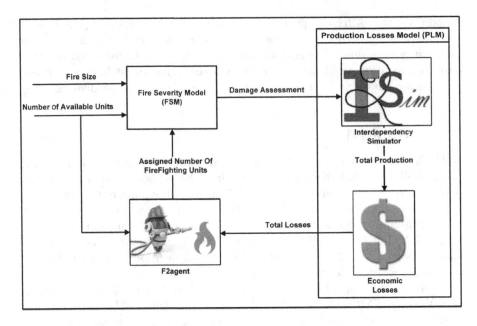

Figure 1. Firefighting decision support system architecture.

algorithm to determine the optimal placement of firefighting crews. However, this system, like other firefighting decision support systems, is limited to a specific type of fire and cannot handle interdependent infrastructures. In contrast, the firefighting decision support system described in this work considers the interdependencies underlying firefighting operations. This assists decision makers in allocating the optimal number of firefighting units during single- or multiple-fire incidents to minimize the overall cost (direct and indirect) as well as the long-term consequences.

3.   Proposed Decision Support System

This section describes the proposed firefighting decision support system, which is designed to assist decision makers in allocating the optimal number of firefighting units during multiple-fire incidents in interdependent infrastructure environments. The system can be used before an incident for training and planning, during an incident for decision support or after an incident for evaluating suppression strategies.

The proposed firefighting decision support system has three main components: (i) a fire severity model (FSM) for simulating fire behavior and damage to an industrial complex; (ii) a production loss model for evaluating the economic impact of each decision on the production output of the industrial complex; and (iii) an optimization agent (F2agent) for optimizing the assignment of firefighting units. Figure 1 presents the architecture of the decision support system.

Table 1. Firefighter assessment matrix.

	Work Hours	Assigned Firefighters (man-hours)				
No. Units		4	8	12	16	20
Man-Hours		20	40	60	80	100
Work Hours		Fire Duration (hh:mm:ss)				
Catastrophic	600	$30{:}00{:}00^5$	$15{:}00{:}00^5$	$10{:}00{:}00^4$	$07{:}30{:}00^3$	$06{:}00{:}00^2$
Critical	300	$15{:}00{:}00^5$	$07{:}30{:}00^4$	$05{:}00{:}00^3$	$03{:}45{:}00^2$	$03{:}00{:}00^1$
Marginal	150	$07{:}30{:}00^4$	$03{:}45{:}00^3$	$02{:}30{:}00^2$	$01{:}50{:}00^1$	$01{:}30{:}00^1$
Negligible	75	$03{:}45{:}00^3$	$01{:}50{:}00^2$	$01{:}15{:}00^1$	$01{:}00{:}00^1$	$00{:}45{:}00^1$

3.1 Fire Severity Model

The fire severity model is used to estimate the man-hours required to suppress a fire. The ability to predict the expected development of a fire incident would assist decision makers in allocating firefighting units.

Various fire severity definitions have been used in the literature. For example, Keeley [17] defines fire severity as the degree of post-fire losses and damage. In this work, fire severity is related to the man-hours required for the suppression operation. The fire severity model is also used to create scenarios for multiple fires and classify the impacts. The model inputs are the fire type and the number of assigned firefighting units; the output is the damage level to the facility. The damage level uses an index called the physical mode, which is used by the i2Sim infrastructure interdependencies simulator. i2Sim, which captures the interdependencies existing between infrastructures, is used to model and simulate the physical infrastructure.

The fire severity model is based on the firefighter assessment matrix shown in Table 1. Note that the superscripts for the duration values correspond to the physical modes and color codes in Table 2 (e.g., the superscript 1 corresponds to PM 1 and color code green while the superscript 5 corresponds to PM 5 and color code red). The model has three components: (i) fire type, which classifies fires into four levels based on their severity (catastrophic, critical, marginal and negligible); (ii) required firefighters, which specifies the man-hours required to suppress each type of fire; and (iii) i2Sim physical mode, which expresses the damage level caused by a fire using a color code. Table 2 describes the five color codes used to express the results of firefighter assignments during the simulation.

As an example, consider a scenario with two fire incidents, one critical and one marginal. According to Table 1, critical and marginal fires need 300 and 150 man-hours to be suppressed, respectively. If 20 firefighter units (each with five firefighters) are assigned to each fire, the critical fire is suppressed in 3 hours ($= 300 \div (20 \times 5)$) while the marginal fire is suppressed in 1 hour and 30 minutes

Table 2.   Physical mode color codes.

Physical Mode	Color Code	Unit Functionality
PM 1	Green	85–100%
PM 2	Blue	70–84%
PM 3	Yellow	45–69%
PM 4	Orange	26–44%
PM 5	Red	0–25%

Table 3.   Damage assessment table.

Physical Mode	Color Code	Level of Damage	Schedule	Description
PM 1	Green	Negligible	Minimal	No damage but light maintenance is required for safety
PM 2	Blue	Normal	1 month	Heavy maintenance and some equipment repair is required
PM 3	Yellow	Marginal	3 months	Minor damage and some equipment replacement is required
PM 4	Orange	Critical	6 months	Major damage and short-term reconstruction is required
PM 5	Red	Catastrophic	12 months	Significant damage and major reconstruction is required

$(= 150 \div (20 \times 5))$. The result is a code green for both fires, which from the damage assessment table (Table 3), corresponds to negligible damage with light maintenance required for safety.

In the real scenario, a limited number of firefighting units are available. In particular, assume that a total of 20 units of firefighters are available for both fires. If 16 units are assigned to the critical fire, only four units can be assigned to the marginal fire. As a result, the critical fire is suppressed in 3 hours and 45 minutes $(= 300 \div (16 \times 5))$ and the marginal fire in 7 hours and 30 minutes $(= 150 \div (4 \times 5))$. The impacts on the production facilities are now code blue and code orange, where code blue implies a normal level of damage with one month of maintenance and code orange means a critical level of damage with six months of maintenance.

3.2 Production Loss Model

The goal of the production loss model is to predict the economic impact of a fire incident based on the firefighter assignments. The model has two components: (i) i2Sim infrastructure interdependencies simulator; and (ii) economic loss model.

Infrastructure Interdependencies Simulator. The i2Sim infrastructure interdependencies simulator provides an environment for representing multiple interdependent critical infrastructures (or production units) [22]. It simulates the effects of resource allocation decisions in real time. i2Sim is an event-driven, time-domain simulator that uses a cell-channel approach to correlate infrastructure interdependencies. It was selected as the simulator for four main reasons: (i) ability to choose the global simulation objective (e.g., economic, environmental or security); (ii) ability to simulate and produce reasonable results even when data is limited; (iii) ability to simulate multiple infrastructure interdependencies (e.g., water, power and oil) without the assistance of infrastructure experts; and (iv) ability to integrate other simulators and assess the impacts of decisions made in one infrastructure on other infrastructures.

The i2Sim model has three main entities: (i) cells; (ii) channels; and (iii) tokens. Infrastructure components are defined as cells and the connections between them, such as transmission lines and oil pipelines, are defined as channels. Resources and services, such as oil, water and power, are defined as tokens that move between cells (i.e., through channels). The relationship between the input and output of a cell is described by a lookup table. The combinations of cells and channels in the i2Sim model set up a mathematical formulation of the relationships between the infrastructures. A system of discrete time equations is created, which is solved simultaneously for all components at every time step along the timeline to find the operating point of each production cell. The operating states of cells and channels are expressed by their physical modes (PMs) associated with damage levels and resource modes (RMs) associated with the availability of input resources. Each physical mode and resource mode is discretized into five levels, where level 1 is the highest and level 5 is the lowest [22, 23].

Economic Loss Model. The plant output corresponds to the materials and/or services produced by the plant. The output of the economic loss model is the economic loss associated with the current operating state of the plant while the fire is evolving dynamically. The production of materials or services is reduced by the fire according to the damage assessed by the fire severity model described above. i2Sim simulates the functionality of the interdependent infrastructures and computes the outputs of all the production facilities. These outputs become the input to the economic loss model, which calculates the projected losses based on the market price.

In this work, the economic impact is calculated using the business interruption cost. This is the cost of the total production loss in a facility due to the fire evaluated according to the market value. The overall economic loss is given by:

$$Overall\ Economic\ Loss = \sum_{t=1}^{T}\sum_{i=1}^{n}\sum_{j=1}^{m}(PLij(t) \times Vj) \tag{1}$$

where t is the time of interruption in T time intervals, n is the number of facilities in the infrastructure, m is the number of produced materials and services in each facility, PL is the total lost production of materials and services j in facility i, and V_j is the market value of materials and services j.

Given U firefighting units and Z fire incidents, the problem can be formulated as minimizing the loss in Equation (1) by distributing the firefighting units among the fire incidents. The primary decision variable in this problem is $u_k(t)$, which is the number of units assigned to fire k during time interval t. Thus, the problem can be formulated as:

$$Minimize \sum_{t=1}^{T}\sum_{i=1}^{n}\sum_{j=1}^{m}(PLij(t) \times Vj) \tag{2}$$

subject to

$$\sum_{k=1}^{Z}(t) \leq U \quad \forall t = 1, 2, \ldots, T \tag{3}$$

$$u_k(t) \leq U \quad k \in Z \quad \forall t = 1, 2, \ldots, T \tag{4}$$

The first constraint ensures that the total assigned units at every time step is less than or equal to the maximum number of available units. The second constraint ensures that all the assignments are positive integers.

3.3   Optimization Agent

Finding the optimal actions to control the behavior of interdependent systems is crucial in many critical infrastructures. In some critical situations, the dynamics of the systems are not completely predictable and it is necessary to quickly find new optimal actions as incidents evolve. Simulation gives a decision maker time to evaluate the options for action. A learning agent F2agent, based on reinforcement learning, was developed and integrated with i2Sim and the fire severity model to create the proposed firefighting decision support system.

In a reinforcement learning algorithm, an agent interacts with its environment to acquire knowledge. The agent decides which action to take and maps each action to a specific situation or state. The agent must maximize a numerical reward signal by choosing among several actions based on the information it receives about its environment at each time step. Often, the agent needs to take a particular sequence of actions to maximize the reward [31]. Reinforcement learning has been applied to solve problems in a variety of disciplines, including scheduling in sensor networks [9], robot learning [19], resource allo-

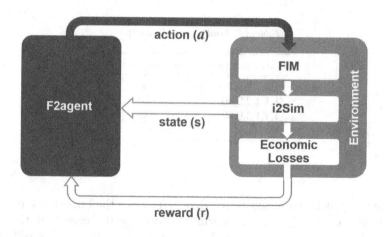

Figure 2. F2agent structure.

cation in business process management [15], learning user behavior in social networks [16] and spacecraft payload processing [33].

Figure 2 shows the structure of F2agent. The objective of F2agent is to minimize the cost of business interruption. The physical mode and resource mode values in the i2Sim model define the state space, which is the set of all states that are reachable from the initial state by a sequence of actions. For example, the state list for two simultaneous fire incidents at two different locations (x and y) is represented as (PM_x, RM_x, PM_y, RM_y) where PM and RM reflect the physical state and the functionality of each entity. As mentioned above, PM and RM are discretized into five levels. Therefore, the total number of states is $5 \times 5 \times 5 \times 5 = 125$. The output of the economic loss model represents the reward for the different assignments of available firefighting units by the fire severity model.

In this example, it is assumed that the number of available firefighters is 100, which enables the formation of 20 units of five firefighters each. Based on the number of fire incidents, the fire severity model creates a list of possible actions from $A = \{0, 20, 40, 60, 80, 100\}$. For example, the available actions for each state in the two simultaneous fire incidents are $\{(0,20), (0,40), (0,60), (0,80), (0,100), (20,0), (20,20), \dots\}$, corresponding to a total of 21 actions.

F2agent begins learning by sensing the current state of the environment reflected by the physical and resource modes of the i2Sim model. It then searches for the current state in a look-up table and stores a Q-value, $Q(s, a)$, for each state-action pair (s, a). Table 4 shows a look-up table sample. The Q-values are initialized randomly. When the agent in state s_t takes an action a_t, it receives a reward r, ending up in state s_{t+1}, and it then takes an action a_{t+1}. The following update is performed [31]:

$$Q(s, a) \leftarrow (1 - \alpha_t)Q(s, a) + \alpha_t(r + \gamma Q(\acute{s}, \acute{a})) \qquad (5)$$

Table 4. Look-up table sample.

(state, action)	Q(state,action)
(1,1,1,1,0,20)	51
(1,1,1,2,0,40)	620
(1,1,1,3,0,60)	422
...	...

where $0 \leq \gamma \leq 1$ is a discount factor that determines the importance of future rewards and $0 \leq \alpha \leq 1$ is the learning rate ($\alpha = 0$ means that the agent does not learn anything while $\alpha = 1$ means that the agent only considers the most recent information). The updates continue until the optimal assignment is reached or the stopping criteria is met.

4. Case Study

This section describes a case study involving a large petrochemical facility, which is used to demonstrate the utility of the proposed firefighting decision support system.

4.1 Framework Description

The petrochemical industry is used as an example of an interdependent infrastructure. It uses oil and natural gas as major raw materials to produce plastics, rubber and fiber materials and other intermediates. The intermediates are converted into thousands of industrial and consumer products that serve as raw materials for other industries. According to Kuwait Finance House (KFH) Research [18], the global petrochemicals market was valued at $472.06 billion in 2011 and is expected to reach $791.05 billion by 2018. In terms of volume, the global petrochemicals consumption is expected to reach 627.51 million tons by 2018 [18].

In the petrochemical industry, production processes typically involve a series of physical and chemical reactions. The processes often involve high temperatures and pressures, and other complex technical operations. Due to the large amounts of flammable gases and liquids involved, the petrochemical industry is continuously exposed to the risk of fires, explosions and other accidents.

One of the measures taken to reduce the risk is to restrict the storage of flammable materials. Therefore, these materials flow from one plant to another. The output of a plant becomes the raw material for other plants. This creates strong physical interdependencies between plants. Due to these physical interdependencies, the states of any two plants, Plant A and Plant B, are interrelated. If Plant A supplies Plant B with its required materials, an interruption of a production process in Plant A could result in an interruption

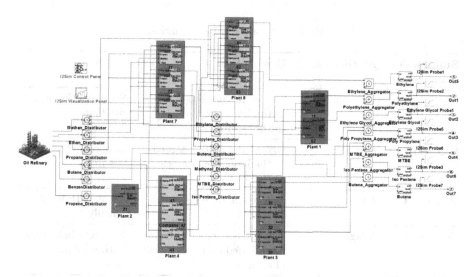

Figure 3. i2Sim model of the petrochemical complex.

in Plant B, Moreover, Plant A might stop producing materials if Plant B is unable to receive the materials as a result of an interruption.

This case study considers an industrial city that has a petrochemical complex comprising fourteen chemical plants that produce a variety of petrochemical materials and 36 pipelines that distribute materials between the plants. The petrochemical complex is modeled based on real data. Figure 3 shows the structure of the complex and the connections between the plants. Only six of the fourteen plants are considered in the model. The industrial city has 100 firefighters, forming 20 units allocated to five fire stations, each station with four firefighting units.

In the case study, two fire incidents, one catastrophic and the other critical, were simulated in Plant 3 and Plant 4, respectively. Table 5 lists the four fire suppression scenarios considered in this work. Scenarios 1 and 2 represent common actions during multiple-fire incidents, which are to allocate firefighting units based on fire size, giving more units to larger fires. Scenario 3 corresponds to a situation where neither fire size nor the optimization agent F2agent are taken into account. Scenario 4 corresponds to a situation where the allocation of units is based on optimized decisions by F2agent. The simulations involved fifteen hours of concurrent suppression operations for the two fire incidents. New assignments of the firefighting units were determined every hour.

The following assumptions were made in the case study:

- No humans were in danger during the incidents, otherwise they would have had priority.

- The environmental impact was not taken into account.

- All the plants had the same level of flammability.

Table 5. Fire suppression scenarios.

Suppression Scenarios	Methodology	Description	Objective
Scenario 1	70%–30%	70% of the units assigned to the large fire, 30% to the other fire	Suppress the large fire first
Scenario 2	60%–40%	60% of the units assigned to the large fire, 40% to the other fire	Suppress the large fire first
Scenario 3	50%–50%	50% of the units assigned to each fire	Treat both fires equally
Scenario 4	F2agent	Agent-based model assigns units based on the criticality of each fire	Suppress both fires with minimum loss

- No other organizations (e.g., police and ambulance services) were involved.

- The wind speed and wind direction were uniform in both fire incidents.

4.2   Results and Analysis

Simulations were conducted for the four fire suppression scenarios listed in Table 5. Each scenario involved a different assignment sequence of firefighting units to the two fire incidents.

Table 6 shows the simulation results. The proposed firefighting decision support system was able to recognize the critical fire based on the existing interdependencies and suppressed both fires in the least amount of time (Scenario 4) compared with the other three suppression scenarios. Note that Scenario 1 corresponds to the "business as usual" case in firefighting operations, where the majority of available units are assigned to the larger fire. However, the results show that this is the worst decision because it has the longest suppression time.

Effective decisions in response to fire incidents can significantly reduce economic losses. In order to evaluate the impacts of the four fire suppression scenarios on the economic loss, the daily reduction in production of the simulated portion of the petrochemical complex was examined over a one-year period. The daily production income of the complex is about $41 million per day during normal operations. Upon comparing this level of income with the income after the two fires were suppressed, it is clear that the decision support system (Scenario 4) achieved the minimum economic loss. Figure 4 shows that the total economic loss in Scenario 4 was just $800 million compared with $5,800 million for Scenario 1, $3,000 million for Scenario 2 and $1,500 million

Table 6. Results for the fire suppression scenarios (U: no. units; T: time).

Time	Scenario 1				Scenario 2				Scenario 3				Scenario 4			
	Fire 1		Fire 2		Fire 1		Fire 2		Fire 1		Fire 2		Fire 1		Fire 2	
	U	T	U	T	U	T	U	T	U	T	U	T	U	T	U	T
1	6	300	14	600	8	300	12	600	10	300	10	600	16	300	4	600
2	6	270	14	530	8	260	12	540	10	250	10	550	16	220	4	580
3	6	240	14	460	8	220	12	480	10	200	10	500	16	140	4	560
4	6	210	14	390	8	180	12	420	10	150	10	450	12	60	6	540
5	6	180	14	320	8	140	12	360	10	100	10	400	0	X	20	500
6	6	150	14	250	8	100	12	300	10	50	10	350			20	400
7	6	120	14	180	8	60	12	240	0	X	20	300			20	300
8	6	90	14	110	8	20	12	180			20	200			20	200
9	6	60	14	40	0	X	20	120			20	100			20	100
10	20	30	0	X			20	20			0	X			0	X
11	0	X					0	X								
12																
13																
14																
15																

X: Fire suppressed.

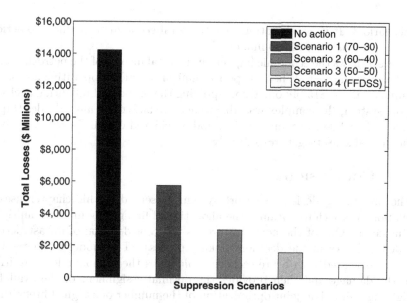

Figure 4. Total losses for the fire suppression scenarios.

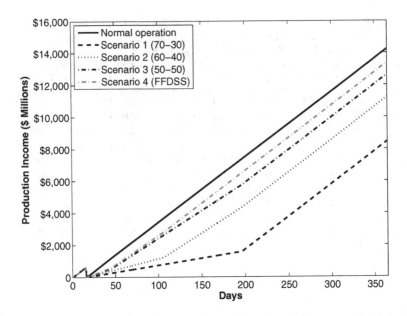

Figure 5.   Economic impact on annual production for the suppression scenarios.

for Scenario 3. It is worth noting that the total economic loss when no action is taken is a massive $14,200 million.

Figure 5 shows the economic impact on the total income of the petrochemical complex over one year. When the petrochemical complex is operating normally, the annual sales is $15 billion. Upon applying the proposed firefighting decision support system, the complex was able to achieve 95% of its annual sales target (Scenario 4), while the Scenarios 1, 2 and 3 achieved only 61%, 80% and 89% of the annual sales target, respectively.

5.   Conclusions

The firefighting decision support system presented in this chapter uses a simulation approach to optimize the allocation of firefighting units in multiple-fire incidents. One of the novel features is the consideration of infrastructure interdependencies in the decision making process. The model estimates the damage associated with a fire scenario, calculates the economic loss resulting from the damage and then provides the optimal assignment of the available firefighting units. The joint optimization of the number of assigned firefighting units and the estimated damage significantly reduces the economic loss. The firefighting decision support system can be used before an incident for training and planning, during an incident for decision support or after the incident for evaluating fire suppression strategies.

Acknowledgements

The authors wish to thank Dr. Sarbjit Sarkaria for his insightful comments and suggestions. The first author wishes to thank the Ministry of Interior (Civil Defense), Saudi Arabia for its financial support.

References

[1] P. Andrews, BEHAVE: Fire Behavior Prediction and Fuel Modeling System – BURN Subsystem, Part 1, General Technical Report INT-194, Forest Service, U.S. Department of Agriculture, Washington, DC, 1986.

[2] D. Butry, J. Prestemon, K. Abt and R. Sutphen, Economic optimization of wildfire intervention activities, *International Journal of Wildland Fire*, vol. 19(5), pp. 659–672, 2010.

[3] D. Calkin, M. Thompson, M. Finney and K. Hyde, A real-time risk assessment tool supporting wildland fire decision making, *Journal of Forestry*, vol. 109(5), pp. 274–280, 2011.

[4] R. Carvel, Fire Size in Tunnels, Ph.D. Dissertation, Division of Civil Engineering, Heriot-Watt University, Edinburgh, United Kingdom, 2004.

[5] J. Figueras-Jove, A. Guasch-Petit, P. Fonseca-Casa and J. Casanovas-Garcia, Simulation and optimization for an experimental environment to wildfire resource management and planning: Firefight project modeling and architecture, *Proceedings of the Winter Simulation Conference*, pp. 1950–1960, 2013.

[6] M. Finney, FARSITE: A fire area simulator for fire managers, *Proceedings of the Biswell Symposium: Fire Issues and Solutions in Urban Interface and Wildland Ecosystems*, pp. 55–56, 1995.

[7] Fire and Aviation Management, Fire and Aviation Management Fiscal Year 2006 in Review, FS-885, Forest Service, U.S. Department of Agriculture, Washington, DC, 2007.

[8] J. Fried, J. Gilless and J. Spero, Analyzing initial attack on wildland fires using stochastic simulation, *International Journal of Wildland Fire*, vol. 15(1), pp. 137–146, 2006.

[9] O. Gul and E. Uysal-Biyikoglu, A randomized scheduling algorithm for energy harvesting wireless sensor networks achieving nearly 100% throughput, *Proceedings of the IEEE Wireless Communication and Networking Conference*, pp. 2456–2461, 2014.

[10] R. Haight and J. Fried, Deploying wildland fire suppression resources with a scenario-based standard response model, *INFOR: Information Systems and Operational Research*, vol. 45(1), pp. 31–39, 2007.

[11] J. Hall, The Total Cost of Fire in the United States, National Fire Protection Association, Quincy, Massachusetts, 2014.

[12] B. HomChaudhuri, Genetic Algorithm Based Simulation-Optimization for Fighting Wildfires, M.S. Thesis, Department of Mechanical and Materials Engineering, University of Cincinnati, Cincinnati, Ohio, 2010.

[13] X. Hu and L. Ntaimo, Integrated simulation and optimization for wildfire containment, *ACM Transactions on Modeling and Computer Simulation*, vol. 19(4), article no. 19, 2009.

[14] X. Hu, Y. Sun and L. Ntaimo, DEVS-FIRE: Design and application of formal discrete event wildfire spread and suppression models, *Simulation*, vol. 88(3), pp. 259–279, 2012.

[15] Z. Huang, W. van der Aalst, X. Lu and H. Duan, Reinforcement learning based resource allocation in business process management, *Data and Knowledge Engineering*, vol. 70(1), pp. 127–145, 2011.

[16] C. Isbell, C. Shelton, M. Kearns, S. Singh and P. Stone, A social reinforcement learning agent, *Proceedings of the Fifth International Conference on Autonomous Agents*, pp. 377–384, 2001.

[17] J. Keeley, Fire intensity, fire severity and burn severity: A brief review and suggested usage, *International Journal of Wildland Fire*, vol. 18, pp. 116–126, 2009.

[18] KFH Research, Saudi Petrochemical: "Trade with Caution," Kuala, Lumpur, Malaysia, 2013.

[19] J. Kober, J. Bagnell and J. Peters, Reinforcement learning in robotics: A survey, *International Journal of Robotics Research*, vol. 32(11), pp. 1238–1274, 2013.

[20] Y. Lee, J. Fried, H. Albers and R. Haight, Deploying initial attack resources for wildfire suppression: Spatial coordination, budget constraints and capacity constraints, *Canadian Journal of Forest Research*, vol. 43(1), pp. 56–65, 2013.

[21] D. Martell, A review of operational research studies in forest fire management, *Canadian Journal of Forest Research*, vol. 12(2), pp. 119–140, 1982.

[22] J. Marti, Multisystem simulation: Analysis of critical infrastructures for disaster response, in *Networks of Networks: The Last Frontier of Complexity*, G. D'Agostino and A. Scala (Eds.), Springer, Cham, Switzerland, pp. 255–277, 2014.

[23] J. Marti, J. Hollman, C. Ventura and J. Jatskevich, Dynamic recovery of critical infrastructures: Real-time temporal coordination, *International Journal of Critical Infrastructures*, vol. 4(1-2), pp. 17–31, 2008.

[24] E. Mihailidou, K. Antoniadis and M. Assael, The 319 major industrial accidents since 1917, *International Review of Chemical Engineering*, vol. 4(6), pp. 529–540, 2012.

[25] M. Morais, Comparing Spatially Explicit Models of Fire Spread Through Chaparral Fuels: A New Algorithm Based Upon the Rothermel Fire Spread Equation, M.A. Thesis, Department of Geography, University of California at Santa Barbara, Santa Barbara, California, 2001.

[26] National Fire Protection Association, NFPA 1710: Standard for the Organization and Deployment of Fire Suppression Operations, Emergency Medical Operations and Special Operations to the Public by Career Fire Departments, Quincy, Massachusetts 2010.

[27] L. Ntaimo, X. Hu and Y. Sun, DEVS-FIRE: Towards an integrated simulation environment for surface wildfire spread and containment, *Simulation*, vol. 84(4), pp. 137–155, 2008.

[28] A. Ollero, J. Martinez-De Dios and B. Arrue, Integrated systems for early forest-fire detection, *Proceedings of the Fourteenth Conference on Fire and Forest Meteorology*, vol. 2, pp. 1977–1988, 1998.

[29] N. Petrovic, D. Alderson and J. Carlson, Dynamic resource allocation in disaster response: Trade-offs in wildfire suppression, *PLOS ONE*, vol. 7(4), 2012.

[30] A. Sadeghi-Naini and A. Asgary, Modeling the number of firefighters responding to an incident using artificial neural networks, *International Journal of Emergency Services*, vol. 2(2), pp. 104–118, 2013.

[31] R. Sutton and A. Barto, *Reinforcement Learning: An Introduction*, MIT Press, Cambridge, Massachusetts, 1998.

[32] C. Tymstra, M. Flannigan, O. Armitage and K. Logan, Impact of climate change on area burned in Alberta's boreal forest, *International Journal of Wildland Fire*, vol. 16, pp. 153–160, 2007.

[33] W. Zhang and T. Dietterich, A reinforcement learning approach to job-shop scheduling, *Proceedings of the Fourteenth International Joint Conference on Artificial Intelligence*, vol. 2, pp. 1114–1120, 1995.

Chapter 17

SITUATIONAL AWARENESS USING DISTRIBUTED DATA FUSION WITH EVIDENCE DISCOUNTING

Antonio Di Pietro, Stefano Panzieri and Andrea Gasparri

Abstract   Data fusion provides a means for combining pieces of information from various sources and sensors. This chapter presents a data fusion methodology for interdependent critical infrastructures that leverages a distributed algorithm that allows the sharing of the possible causes of faults or threats affecting the infrastructures, thereby enhancing situational awareness. Depending on the degree of coupling, the algorithm modulates the information content provided by each infrastructure using a data fusion technique called evidence discounting. The methodology is applied to a case study involving a group of dependent critical infrastructures. Simulation results demonstrate that the methodology is resilient to temporary faults in the critical infrastructure communications layer.

Keywords: Distributed data fusion, cautious conjunctive rule, evidence discounting

1.   Introduction

Combining pieces of information through data fusion techniques can enhance the security of critical infrastructure systems by providing improved situational awareness that supports decision making. Usually, critical infrastructure systems combine the information coming from their sensors individually, without sharing information regarding their operating states with other infrastructures. This is mainly due to the fact that the delivery of sensitive information to external entities poses security issues (see, e.g., [6, 21]). However, in real-time environments, there are numerous scenarios in which allowing full information exchange could be beneficial.

Foglietta et al. [9] have applied an algorithm based on the work of Gasparri et al. [11] to share information among a set of critical infrastructures in order to produce common knowledge and decrease the possibility of producing cascading

© IFIP International Federation for Information Processing 2015

M. Rice, S. Shenoi (Eds.): Critical Infrastructure Protection IX, IFIP AICT 466, pp. 281–296, 2015.

DOI: 10.1007/978-3-319-26567-4_17

effects. In their approach, the infrastructures – implemented as "agents" – constitute a connected network and combine their local information about their operating states using a distributed algorithm. However, the approach requires the network to have a spanning tree topology.

Ducourthial et al. [8] have proposed a distributed algorithm that implements data fusion in unknown topologies. The algorithm computes the confidence of each node by combining all the data received from its neighbors using a "discounted cautious operator" and without relying on a central node for data collection. The algorithm converges for any initial configuration and for any unknown network topology. However, the algorithm requires the network topology to become stable (i.e., nodes and links are fixed and agents do not perform any dynamic observations) in order to reach convergence.

Considerable research has focused on applying data fusion techniques to enhance the security of critical infrastructures. Genge et al. [12] have employed cyber-physical data fusion based on the Dempster-Shafer theory [3, 17] to combine knowledge from the cyber and physical dimensions of critical infrastructures in order to implement an anomaly detection system. The system was validated in a scenario involving distributed denial-of-service attacks on an information network whose disturbances propagated to a simulated power grid. However, the centralized nature of this approach (i.e., all the data must be collected by a single node that performs data aggregation) limits its robustness to single node failures.

Oliva et al. [13] have presented a distributed consensus algorithm based on fuzzy numbers and subsequently applied it to a case study related to crisis management. The algorithm provides consensus on the overall criticality of a situation based on the information provided by human operators regarding the state of critical infrastructures. However, the algorithm is complex and requires the generation of appropriate fuzzy membership functions to model operator opinions. Sousa et al. [20] have proposed a critical infrastructure protection methodology based on distributed algorithms and mechanisms implemented between a set of devices that provide secure gossip-based information diffusion among infrastructures. Although the methodology ensures that the data traffic satisfies security policies for mitigating cyber attacks, it lacks flexibility when dealing with physical threats or uncertain threats.

This chapter presents a data fusion methodology for interdependent critical infrastructures based on the algorithm of Ducourthial et al. [8] to exchange information between critical infrastructures and, thus, increase situational awareness. Simulation results show that each infrastructure converges without relying on a static network topology and despite the presence of link failures (e.g., due to natural disasters or cyber attacks). With respect to distributed consensus, the methodology enables each infrastructure to converge and, thus, capture the particular behavior of an infrastructure that, due to its specific dependencies and/or internal failures, may exhibit a particular state. Moreover, the modeling of failures and threats using the Dempster-Shafer formalism takes into account the imprecision and uncertainty in detecting events without the need to specify membership functions as required by fuzzy-based approaches. The cautious operator [5] and an evidence discounting function are used to aggregate information provided by the connected infrastructures. This operator ensures network convergence when the network topology and direct confidences are stable [7, 8]. The evidence discounting concept was introduced by Shafer [17] to account for the reliability of source information. Cherfaoui et al. [2] have applied evidence discounting to a network of agents based on the distance and age of received messages before combining them with local knowledge. The proposed methodology uses evidence discounting to decrease the information content provided by a supporting infrastructure that is loosely coupled.

2. Overview of the Methodology

The theoretical framework of Rinaldi et al. [16] defines several dimensions of an infrastructure interdependency: (i) type of interdependency; (ii) infrastructure environment; (iii) coupling characteristics; (iv) type of failure; (v) infrastructure characteristics; and (vi) state of operation. As will be discussed later, the proposed methodology addresses three dimensions: (i) coupling characteristics (e.g., tight or loose according to Perrow [15]); (ii) type of failure (e.g., cascading or common cause or escalating failures); and (iii) state of operation (e.g., normal or stressed).

In order to effectively model and simulate the dynamic behavior of infrastructures, several researchers have engaged the network-based paradigm [14], representing infrastructures as network nodes and physical connections between the infrastructures as links (edges). The nodes and edges in an infrastructure topology deliver/consume services and/or resources to/from other nodes. However, in the proposed methodology, while infrastructures are represented as nodes, the edges correspond to communications channels that allow the exchange of information about the possible cause(s) of faults. The resulting information sharing framework provides higher information content at each infrastructure layer regarding the possible evolution of the state of operation of each infrastructure. This information can be used by decision makers to take immediate countermeasures and, thereby, decrease the possibility of cascading effects.

The proposed methodology involves three steps:

- **Event Detection:** Each infrastructure produces local information (e.g., by using sensors) called "direct confidence" regarding the credibility of possible normal and stressed operating states.

- **Knowledge Aggregation:** The infrastructures aggregate their local information according to the gossip communications paradigm [1] to produce more informative data called "distributed confidence" regarding the credibility of possible normal and stressed operating states.

- **Convergence:** At a certain time, the information has been distributed to such an extent that the distributed confidence of each infrastructure does not vary (i.e., the agents representing each infrastructure reach convergence).

The Dempster-Shafer formalism [3, 17] is used to deal with the imprecision and uncertainty in detecting events. As explained later, each infrastructure i, when fusing its information with the information received from an infrastructure j, discounts the incoming information according to the degree of coupling between infrastructure i and infrastructure j. In other words, information coming from a loosely coupled infrastructure is considered to be less relevant than information coming from a tightly coupled infrastructure; this expresses the fact that the state of operation of the inputs from the supplying infrastructure would have small or large effects on the receiving infrastructure.

Fusing information from two infrastructures requires knowledge of the degree of coupling of the infrastructures. One approach is to use statistical analysis of historical data about the number of disruptions initiated by one infrastructure that caused cascading failures in a second infrastructure; this provides evidence whether the two infrastructures are tightly or loosely coupled. van Eeten et al. [23] have analyzed public media articles about infrastructure disruptions that occurred in The Netherlands from 2010 to 2014. Their analysis revealed that, depending on the infrastructures where the cascading-initiating failures occurred, certain infrastructures were more frequently affected by cascading failures than other infrastructures. For example, when considering health as the affected sector, 50% of the cascading-initiating failures occurred in the energy sector, 13% in the telecommunications and water sectors, and 24% were the result of internal failures.

With regard to agent (infrastructure) interaction in this work, simulation results demonstrate that the proposed methodology is robust to communications link failures occurring in disaster scenarios. Moreover, a strategy is proposed to update the confidence of each node when a specific communications link is unavailable due to: (i) physical destruction of network infrastructure components; (ii) disruptions in supporting infrastructures; and (iii) disruptions due to congestion [22].

3.   Data Fusion

The theory of evidence is a formalism that can be used to model imprecision and uncertainty. The theory, introduced by Dempster [3] and Shafer [17] (also known as the Dempster-Shafer theory), embraces the intuitive idea of associating a number between zero and one to model the degree of confidence of a proposition with partial (e.g., uncertain or imprecise) evidence. Let $\Omega = \{\omega_1, ..., \omega_n\}$ be the set of possible values of a variable ω where the elements ω_i are assumed to be mutually exclusive. Let $\Gamma(\Omega) \triangleq 2^\Omega = \{\gamma_1, ..., \gamma_{|\Gamma|}\}$ be the associated power set. In this framework, the set Ω, which is referred to as the "frame of discernment," quantifies the confidence of propositions of the form: "the true value of ω is in γ" with $\gamma \in 2^\Omega$.

DEFINITION 1 (BASIC BELIEF ASSIGNMENT) *A function* $m : 2^\Omega \to [0,1]$ *is called a basic belief assignment (BBA)* m *if* $\sum_{\gamma_a \in 2^\Omega} m(\gamma_a) = 1$ *with* $m(\emptyset) = 0$.

DEFINITION 2 (COMMONALITY FUNCTION) *A BBA* m *can be equivalently represented by its associated commonality* $q : 2^\Omega \to [0,1]$ *defined as:*

$$q(\gamma_a) = \sum_{\gamma_b \supseteq \gamma_a} m(\gamma_b), \quad \gamma_a \in 2^\Omega \tag{1}$$

Thus, for $\gamma_a \in 2^\Omega$, $m(\gamma_a)$ is the portion of confidence that supports exactly γ_a (i.e., the fact that the true value of ω is in γ_a) but, due to the lack of further information, does not support any strict subset of γ_a.

The main limitation of the Dempster-Shafer theory is the Dempster combination rule [17], which produces counterintuitive results when strong conflict exists among the sources that are combined [24]. The transferable belief model of Smets [18] also relies on the concept of BBA, but it removes the assumption $m(\emptyset) = 0$. The removal of this assumption applies when the frame of reference is not exhaustive, so it is reasonable to believe that another event, not modeled in the considered frame, will occur. This allows for a refined conjunctive rule that is more robust than the Dempster combination rule in the presence of conflicting evidence [4]. However, this rule and the Dempster combination rule rely on the distinctness assumption with regard to the sources. This limitation can be avoided using an interaction rule called the cautious rule of combination [5], which is associative, commutative and idempotent. The use of the rule is also appropriate when all the sources are considered to be reliable and the assumption of independence is not required.

DEFINITION 3 (WEIGHT FUNCTION) *Let* m *be a generic BBA. Then, the relative weight function* $w : 2^\Omega \setminus \Omega \to \mathbb{R}^+$ *is defined as:*

$$w(\gamma_a) = \prod_{\gamma_b \supseteq \gamma_a} q(\gamma_b)^{(-1)^{|\gamma_b| - |\gamma_a| + 1}}, \quad \forall \gamma_a \in 2^\Omega \setminus \Omega \tag{2}$$

DEFINITION 4 (CAUTIOUS RULE OF COMBINATION $(\oslash)$) *Let* m_1 *and* m_2 *be two generic BBAs with weight functions* w_1 *and* w_2, *respectively. Then, their aggregation using the cautious rule of combination is defined by the following weight function:*

$$w_{1 \oslash 2}(\gamma_a) = min(w_1(\gamma_a), w_2(\gamma_a)), \quad \forall \gamma_a \in 2^\Omega \setminus \Omega \tag{3}$$

The data aggregation algorithm works with the weight function $w(\cdot)$, which is obtained using the commonality function $q(\cdot)$ derived from the initial set of BBAs. Table 1 shows the function $w_{1 \oslash 2}(\cdot)$ obtained by applying the cautious combination rule to the weight functions w_1 and w_2. From now on, $w_{ij}(\cdot)$ will denote the weight function obtained by applying the cautious combination rule to two generic weight functions $w_i(\cdot)$ and $w_j(\cdot)$.

Table 1.   Application of the cautious combination rule.

BBA	∅	a	b	Ω
$w_1(\cdot)$	1.0	0.5	0.3	
$w_2(\cdot)$	0.8	0.7	0.2	
$w_{1 \oslash 2}(\cdot)$	0.8	0.5	0.2	

DEFINITION 5 (DISCOUNTING FUNCTION) *Let m be a generic BBA. Then, the relative discounting function $m^{\alpha}(\gamma_a)$ is defined as follows:*

$$m^{\alpha}(\gamma_a) = \begin{cases} \alpha \, m(\gamma_a) & \text{for } \gamma_a \subset \Omega \\ 1 - \alpha + \alpha \, m(\gamma_a) & \text{for } \gamma_a = \Omega \end{cases}$$

where $\alpha \in [0, 1]$ is called the discounting factor.

Table 2.   BBA $m(\cdot)$ and its relative discounting function $m^{\alpha}(\cdot)$ ($\alpha = 0.2$).

BBA	∅	a	b	Ω
$m(\cdot)$	–	0.30	0.40	0.30
$w(\cdot)$	1.40	0.50	0.40	
$m^{0.2}(\cdot)$	–	0.06	0.08	0.86
$w^{0.2}(\cdot)$	1.00	0.93	0.91	

Table 2 shows an example of BBA $m(\cdot)$ and its relative discounting function $m^{\alpha}(\cdot)$ obtained for $\alpha = 0.2$. The table also presents the weight functions associated with the two BBAs.

4.   Data Fusion Methodology

The goal is to create a model that represents the interdependencies and the communications channels between critical infrastructures as a graph structure. The model embeds the notion of degree of coupling based on the general model of Rinaldi et al. [16] and the specific assumptions described earlier.

4.1   Motivation

In order to motivate the choice of the model, consider $n = 5$ dependent critical infrastructures that can be affected by failures or threats. Each infrastructure is able to produce one BBA expressed as a weight function $w(\cdot)$ from the physical and cyber events detected by the aggregation agents. The frame of discernment is $\Omega = \{a, b, c\}$ where a denotes a possible physical failure, b a possible cyber intrusion or attack and c a normal functioning level.

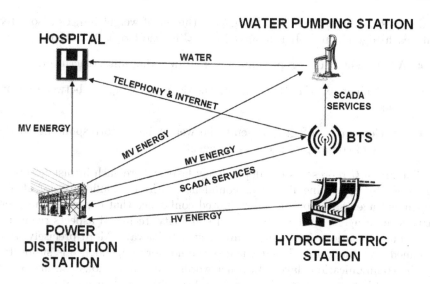

Figure 1. Resources exchanged by the infrastructures.

Assume that the set of systems is geographically distributed and generically corresponds to the infrastructures of a city district. The scenario, derived from [10], incorporates a hydroelectric power station that feeds a power distribution station through a transmission network (not modeled for simplicity). A base transceiver station (BTS) provides telecommunications services required by the SCADA systems of the power distribution station and water pumping station. The base transceiver system receives electricity from the power distribution station. The water pumping station receives electricity from the power distribution station to operate automation devices and water pumps. Failures occurring in the considered infrastructures may produce disruptions at a hospital that receives water from the water pumping station and electricity from the power distribution station. In addition, the hospital may suffer a disruption during a malfunction of the base transceiver system, which provides mobile communications.

Figure 1 shows the dependency layer of the scenario. Assume that the infrastructures can exchange information regarding possible failures or threats. Communications employ virtual private network links between the infrastructures that exhibit non-negligible dependencies.

The model introduced in the following section is able to capture the various couplings between the infrastructures and implement information sharing to enhance situational awareness in the infrastructures.

4.2 Weighted Digraphs

Formally, the model is represented as a weighted digraph $\mathcal{G} = (\mathcal{V}, \mathcal{E}(t), \mathcal{Q})$ where $\mathcal{V} = \{v_1, ..., v_n\}$ with $n > 1$ is the vertex set, $\mathcal{E}(t) = \{e_{ij}\}$ is the edge set and $\mathcal{Q} = \{q_{ij}\}$ with $q_{ij} \in \mathcal{P} = \{l, m, h\}$ is the set of weight indices associated with each edge e_{ij} in $\mathcal{G}$. It is assumed that $\mathcal{G}$ has no loops. Note that:

- An element v_i of $\mathcal{V}$ represents an agent denoting infrastructure i.

- An element e_{ij} of $\mathcal{E}(t)$ represents the degree of coupling between agents v_i and v_j.

- An element q_{ij} of $\mathcal{Q}$ represents the weight index corresponding to the degree of coupling of agent v_j on agent v_i.

The graph $\mathcal{G}$ represents the dependency layer, where each infrastructure or agent v_j, by combining its direct confidence with the confidences of all the dependent agents v_i, obtains a distributed confidence that expresses the operative level of agent v_j. For the sake of simplicity, technical aspects regarding how communications are realized are abstracted away. More precisely, it is assumed that the graph $\mathcal{G}$ that encodes the network dependence is supported by the communications layer. In other words, communications can always be established between a pair of nodes v_i and v_j with coupling w_{ij} if and only if a non-negligible dependence $e_{ij} \in \mathcal{E}(t)$ exists.

Four assumptions are made regarding the network of agents: (i) graph $\mathcal{G}$ has at least a rooted spanning tree; (ii) every node $v \in \mathcal{V}$ produces a local BBA expressed as a weight function $w(\cdot)$ called the direct confidence; (iii) node communications are asynchronous (i.e., at any time t_k, only a pair of agents (v_i, v_j) interacts); and (iv) each agent can store the current direct confidence, the direct confidences of its ancestors and the distributed confidence that is computed via node aggregation.

4.3   Agent Interactions

In the proposed framework, agent actions are modeled using a gossip algorithm [1], which is defined in terms of the triplet $\{\mathcal{S}, \mathcal{R}, \mathfrak{e}\}$ where:

- $\mathcal{S} = \{s_1, ..., s_n\}$ is the set containing the local states $s_i \in \mathbb{R}^q$ of each agent v_i in the network such that $s_i(t) = (w_i(t, \gamma_1), .., w_i(t, \gamma_q))$ at time t with $q = |2^\Omega \setminus \Omega|$.

- $\mathcal{R}$ is the interaction rule based on the cautious operator $\oslash$ and the discounting function $r(\cdot)$ where any two agents $v_i, v_j \in \mathcal{V}$ with $e_{ij} \in \mathcal{E}(t)$ yield $\mathcal{R} : \mathbb{R}^q \times \mathbb{R}^q \to \mathbb{R}^q$ such that:

$$s_j(t) = (w_j(t, \gamma_1) \oslash r(w_i(t, \gamma_1)), ..., w_j(t, \gamma_q) \oslash r(w_i(t, \gamma_q))) \qquad (4)$$

$$r(w_i(t, \gamma_a)) = \begin{cases} r_l(w_i(t, \gamma_a)) = min(1, w_i(t, \gamma_a) + 0.4) & \text{if } q_{ij} = l \\ r_m(w_i(t, \gamma_a)) = min(1, w_i(t, \gamma_a) + 0.25) & \text{if } q_{ij} = m \\ r_h(w_i(t, \gamma_a)) = w_i, (t, \gamma_a) & \text{if } q_{ij} = h \end{cases}$$

Table 3. BBA $m_i^f(0)$ applied to node v_i in case of link failure of e_{ij}.

BBA	$\emptyset$	a	b	c	ab	ac	bc	Ω
$m_i^f(0)$	–	0.10	0.10	–	0.40	–	–	0.40

- $\mathfrak{e}$ is the edge selection process that specifies the edges e_{ij} selected at time t.

When updating the generic agent v_j with an incoming agent v_i, a discounting function $r(\cdot)$ is applied to the weight function $w_i(\cdot)$ according to the degree of coupling of v_j on v_i. Note that the choice of the discounting function is generally application-dependent. The function given above is an effective choice for the case study. When the degree of coupling is high ($q_{ij} = h$), the discounting function leaves $w_i(\cdot)$ unchanged. However, when the coupling is medium or low ($q_{ij} = m$ or $q_{ij} = l$, respectively), the discounting function applies a decreasing constant factor to $w_i(\cdot)$. This way, the refined $r(w_i(\cdot))$ approaches the neutral element $w_\perp$ (unit vector consisting only of one values) with respect to the cautious operator to handle low couplings. In order to render the algorithm robust to communications link failures, when the edge selection process $\mathfrak{e}$ extracts one or more links e_{ij} that are unavailable at a certain time t, the algorithm associates the BBA $m_i^f(\cdot)$ to nodes v_i that cannot communicate with node v_j that performs the update. The BBA $m_i^f(\cdot)$ reported in Table 3 implements the worst-case policy that increases the credibility of failures a and b when no information is available about the state of operation of agent v_i.

The proposed methodology is formalized as Algorithm 1, which extends the approach proposed by Ducourthial et al. [8].

4.4   Graph Construction

Based on the model and the example scenario, a graph $\mathcal{G}$ with $n = 5$ agents was constructed where each agent modeled a specific infrastructure and each link modeled the dependency existing between the corresponding infrastructures. The assignment of weights considered the incident data collected by van Eeten et al. [23] and the application of the method based on the occurrence of historical cascading faults described earlier. For each infrastructure i, let $R_j = \frac{N_j}{N_i}$ be the number of historical faults N_j initiated in infrastructure j that produced a fault in infrastructure i calculated over the total number of cascading failures N_i affecting infrastructure i. For each dependency between infrastructures i and j, four cases exist: (i) $q_{ij} = h$ when $R_j \geq 80\%$; (ii) $q_{ij} = m$ when $80\% > R_j \geq 20\%$; (iii) $q_{ij} = l$ when $20\% > R_j \geq 5\%$; and (iv) a negligible dependency (not modeled as an edge) when $R_j < 5\%$. Because there was no mention of cascading failures occurring among the different infrastructures of the energy sector, it was decided to associate a high dependency on

---

Algorithm 1 : Gossip algorithm.

1: **procedure** GOSSIPALGORITHM($s_j(0) \ \forall \ j \in 1,...,N$)

2: **while** stop_condition **do**

3:    **for** each edge $e_{ij} \in \mathcal{E}(t)$ according to e **do**

       Update the state of agent j according to R:

4:      **if** $q_{ij} = l$ **then**

5:        $s_j(t+1) = s_j(t) \oslash r_l(s_i(t))$

6:      **else**

7:        **if** $q_{ij} = m$ **then**

8:          $s_j(t+1) = s_j(t) \oslash r_m(s_i(t))$

9:        **else**

10:          $s_j(t+1) = s_j(t) \oslash r_h(s_i(t))$

11:        **end if**

12:      **end if**

13:    **end for**

14:      $t = t + 1$

15: **end while**

16:    Return $s_j(t_{stop}) \ \forall \ i \in 1,...,N$

17: **end procedure**

---

the power distribution station of the hydroelectric station and to consider it as an autonomous system.

Figure 2 shows the dependency layer graph $\mathcal{G}$ for the example scenario where each edge is labeled with the service provided and the relative degree of coupling. Note that the l, m and h denote low, medium and high degrees of coupling, respectively. The resulting system can be modeled as a multi-agent platform for distributed data aggregation, where each agent produces a BBA expressing the possible critical event(s) and interacts with other agents via a communications channel.

5. Simulation Results

This section presents the simulation results obtained for two situations in the example scenario: (i) the network topology $\mathcal{G}$ is stable (i.e., the set of agents $\mathcal{V}$ and the set of edges $\mathcal{E}$ are both static); and (ii) the network topology $\mathcal{G}$ is dynamic (i.e., the set of agents $\mathcal{V}$ is static and the set of edges $\mathcal{E}$ is dynamic (time-varying)). For each of the two situations, two cases were considered: (i) the direct confidence produced by each agent is static; and (ii) the direct confidence produced by each agent is dynamic (i.e., time-varying). In the situation where the network topology is dynamic, it is assumed that, at each time step, the graph $\mathcal{G}$ is connected and corresponds to a rooted spanning tree. For all four cases, the pignistic transformation [19] was used to transform the convergent normalized BBA $m(\cdot)$ to a probability measure $P_m = Bet(m)$ as follows:

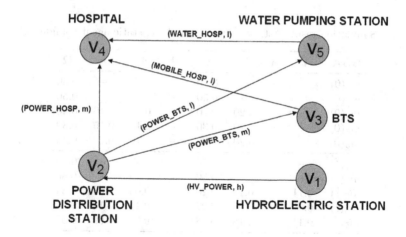

Figure 2. Dependency layer graph $\mathcal{G}$ for the example scenario.

$$P_m(\gamma_a) = \sum_{\emptyset \neq \gamma_b \subseteq \Omega} m(\gamma_b) \frac{|\gamma_a \cap \gamma_b|}{|\gamma_b|}, \qquad \gamma_a \in 2^\Omega \tag{5}$$

This measure is useful to decision makers because it quantifies the probability of occurrence of the operational states of an infrastructure.

5.1   Static Network Topology

This section presents the simulation results obtained for the two cases of static and dynamic direct confidence of agents given a static network topology.

Static (Time-Invariant) Confidence.   This case considers a stable network topology $\mathcal{G}$ where the set of agents $\mathcal{V}$ and the set of edges $\mathcal{E}$ are both static and the direct confidence of the agents is time-invariant. Table 4 shows the simulation results in terms of the convergent BBAs obtained at time $\bar{t} = 5$ and based on a specific set of BBAs for the system of five agents at time $t = 0$. The results show that agent v_4, which monitors the hospital, starts with a probability of normal functioning $P_{m_4}(t = 0) = 0.55$ and reaches a lower probability of normal functioning $P_{m_4}(t = 5) = 0.38$. This can be explained by the fact that the water pumping station and the power distribution grid maintain stable normal functioning levels over time.

Dynamic (Time-Varying) Confidence.   This case considers a stable network topology $\mathcal{G}$ where the set of agents $\mathcal{V}$ and the set of edges $\mathcal{E}$ are both static and the direct confidence of the agents varies over time. Table 5 shows the simulation results in terms of the convergent BBAs obtained at time $\bar{t} = 43$ and based on a specific set of BBAs for the system of five agents through dynamic observations of agents v_2 and v_3 at time $t = 40$. The results show that agent v_4, starts with a probability of normal functioning $P_{m_4}(t = 0) = 0.55$ and reaches

Table 4.　Simulation results (static network topology; static agent confidence).

BBA	∅	a	b	c	ab	ac	bc	Ω
$m_1(0)$	–	–	–	0.70	–	–	–	0.30
$m_2(0)$	–	–	–	0.50	–	–	–	0.50
$m_3(0)$	–	–	0.20	0.20	–	0.10	0.10	0.40
$m_4(0)$	–	–	0.10	0.30	–	0.15	0.15	0.30
$m_5(0)$	–	–	0.20	0.20	–	0.10	0.10	0.40
$\overline{m}_1(\bar{t})$	–	–	–	0.70	–	–	–	0.30
$\overline{m}_2(\bar{t})$	–	–	–	0.50	–	–	–	0.50
$\overline{m}_3(\bar{t})$	0.11	–	0.17	0.20	–	0.09	0.09	0.34
$\overline{m}_4(\bar{t})$	0.09	–	0.09	0.27	–	0.14	0.14	0.27
$\overline{m}_5(\bar{t})$	0.11	–	0.18	0.18	–	0.09	0.09	0.35

Table 5.　Simulation results (static network topology; dynamic agent confidence).

BBA	∅	a	b	c	ab	ac	bc	Ω
$m_1(0)$	–	–	–	0.70	–	–	–	0.30
$m_2(0)$	–	–	–	0.50	–	–	–	0.50
$m_3(0)$	–	–	0.20	0.20	–	0.10	0.10	0.40
$m_4(0)$	–	–	0.10	0.30	–	0.15	0.15	0.30
$m_5(0)$	–	–	0.20	0.20	–	0.10	0.10	0.40
$m_2(40)$	–	0.05	0.30	0.10	0.25	0.05	–	0.25
$m_3(40)$	–	–	0.30	0.20	–	0.20	0.10	0.20
$\overline{m}_1(\bar{t})$	–	–	–	0.70	–	–	–	0.30
$\overline{m}_2(\bar{t})$	–	0.05	0.30	0.10	0.25	0.05	–	0.25
$\overline{m}_3(\bar{t})$	0.12	0.05	0.30	0.13	0.05	0.14	0.07	0.14
$\overline{m}_4(\bar{t})$	0.16	0.03	0.13	0.20	0.07	0.10	0.10	0.20
$\overline{m}_5(\bar{t})$	0.12	0.01	0.19	0.16	0.04	0.08	0.08	0.32

a lower probability of normal functioning $P_{m_4}(t = 43) = 0.29$. This can be explained by the fact that the normal functioning of the power distribution grid has decreased credibility.

Additionally, it was discovered that, if the direct confidences change at time t' with $t' > \bar{t}$ where $\bar{t}$ is the convergence time before the dynamic observations occur, then the edge selection policy does not influence the convergent BBAs. On the other hand, if the direct confidences change at time $t' < \bar{t}$, then the edge selection policy causes the network to reach a different equilibrium point for the convergent BBAs.

Table 6. Simulation results (dynamic network topology; static agent confidence).

BBA	∅	a	b	c	ab	ac	bc	Ω
$m_1(0)$	–	–	–	0.70	–	–	–	0.30
$m_2(0)$	–	–	–	0.50	–	–	–	0.50
$m_3(0)$	–	–	0.20	0.20	–	0.10	0.10	0.40
$m_4(0)$	–	–	0.10	0.30	–	0.15	0.15	0.30
$m_5(0)$	–	–	0.20	0.20	–	0.10	0.10	0.40
$\overline{m}_1(\overline{t})$	–	–	–	0.70	–	–	–	0.30
$\overline{m}_2(\overline{t})$	0.02	–	0.02	0.48	–	–	–	0.48
$\overline{m}_3(\overline{t})$	0.17	0.02	0.19	0.15	0.09	0.06	0.06	0.26
$\overline{m}_4(\overline{t})$	0.16	0.03	0.13	0.20	0.07	0.10	0.10	0.21
$\overline{m}_5(\overline{t})$	0.13	0.01	0.19	0.16	0.03	0.08	0.08	0.32

5.2 Dynamic Network Topology

This section presents the simulation results obtained for the two cases of static and dynamic direct confidence of agents given a dynamic network topology.

Static (Time-Invariant) Confidence. This case considers a dynamic network topology $\mathcal{G}$ where the set of agents $\mathcal{V}$ is static, the set of edges $\mathcal{E}$ varies over time and the direct confidence of the agents is time-invariant. In the dynamic topology, it is assumed that, at each time step, the set of edges $\mathcal{E}(t)$ may or may not contain some of the edges, e_{23}, e_{24}, e_{25}, e_{34} and e_{54}, so that the graph $\mathcal{G}$ is always connected and exhibits at least a rooted spanning tree. For each link, the probability of failure is assumed to be $P_f = 0.5$.

Table 6 shows the simulation results in terms of the convergent BBAs obtained at time $\overline{t} = 31$. The results show that agent v_4 starts with a probability of normal functioning $P_{m_4}(t = 0) = 0.55$ and reaches a lower probability of normal functioning $P_{m_4}(t = 31) = 0.29$. This can be explained by the occurrence of several link failures that are managed by considering $m_i^f(\cdot)$ as a BBA for a node v_i that cannot communicate with node v_j.

Dynamic (Time-Varying) Confidence. This case considers a dynamic network topology $\mathcal{G}$ where the set of agents $\mathcal{V}$ is static, the set of edges $\mathcal{E}$ varies over time and the direct confidence of the agents varies over time. In the dynamic topology, it is assumed that, at each time step, the set of edges $\mathcal{E}(t)$ may or may not contain some of the edges, e_{23}, e_{24}, e_{25}, e_{34} and e_{54}, so that the graph $\mathcal{G}$ is always connected and exhibits at least a rooted spanning tree. Table 7 shows the simulation results in terms of the convergent BBAs obtained at time $\overline{t} = 50$ and based on a specific set of BBAs for the system of five agents through dynamic observations of agents v_2 and v_3 at time $t = 40$. The

Table 7.   Simulation results (dynamic network topology; dynamic agent confidence).

BBA	∅	a	b	c	ab	ac	bc	Ω
$m_1(0)$	–	–	–	0.70	–	–	–	0.30
$m_2(0)$	–	–	–	0.50	–	–	–	0.50
$m_3(0)$	–	–	0.20	0.20	–	0.10	0.10	0.40
$m_4(0)$	–	–	0.10	0.30	–	0.15	0.15	0.30
$m_5(0)$	–	–	0.20	0.20	–	0.10	0.10	0.40
$m_2(5)$	–	–	0.20	0.20	–	0.10	0.10	0.40
$m_3(5)$	–	–	0.10	0.30	–	0.15	0.15	0.30
$\overline{m}_1(\overline{t})$	–	–	–	0.70	–	–	–	0.30
$\overline{m}_2(\overline{t})$	–	0.05	0.30	0.10	0.25	0.05	–	0.25
$\overline{m}_3(\overline{t})$	0.31	0.04	0.24	0.11	0.04	0.11	0.05	0.11
$\overline{m}_4(\overline{t})$	0.16	0.03	0.13	0.21	0.07	0.10	0.10	0.20
$\overline{m}_5(\overline{t})$	0.12	0.01	0.19	0.16	0.04	0.08	0.08	0.32

simultaneous changes of links and direct confidences of the agents over time causes the network to reach a different equilibrium point.

6.   Conclusions

The data fusion methodology described in this chapter enables interdependent critical infrastructures to exchange information about possible threats and failures in order to increase situational awareness. The effectiveness of the methodology was demonstrated using a realistic scenario of critical infrastructures with different degrees of coupling that produce early warnings of possible physical and cyber events. Simulation results reveal that the methodology is robust to communications link failures and converges after the last dynamic observations of the infrastructures. Future work will focus on mathematical proofs of convergence for the static and dynamic network configurations.

References

[1] S. Boyd, A. Ghosh, B. Prabhakar and D. Shah, Randomized gossip algorithms, *IEEE Transactions on Information Theory*, vol. 52(6), pp. 2508–2530, 2006.

[2] V. Cherfaoui, T. Denoeux and Z. Cherfi, Distributed data fusion: Application to confidence management in vehicular networks, *Proceedings of the Eleventh International Conference on Information Fusion*, 2008.

[3] A. Dempster, A generalization of Bayesian inference, *Journal of the Royal Statistical Society, Series B (Methodological)*, vol. 30(2), pp. 205–247, 1968.

[4] A. Dempster, Upper and lower probabilities induced by a multivalued mapping, in *Classic Works of the Dempster-Shafer Theory of Belief Functions*, R. Yager and L. Liu (Eds.), Springer, Berlin-Heidelberg, Germany, pp. 57–72, 2008.

[5] T. Denoeux, Conjunctive and disjunctive combination of belief functions induced by nondistinct bodies of evidence, *Artificial Intelligence*, vol. 172(2–3), pp. 234–264, 2008.

[6] S. De Porcellinis, G. Oliva, S. Panzieri and R. Setola, A holistic-reductionistic approach for modeling interdependencies, in *Critical Infrastructure Protection III*, C. Palmer and S. Shenoi (Eds.), Springer, Heidelberg, Germany, pp. 215–227, 2009.

[7] B. Ducourthial and S. Tixeuil, Self-stabilization with path algebra, *Theoretical Computer Science*, vol. 293(1), pp. 219–236, 2003.

[8] B. Ducourthial, V. Cherfaoui and T. Denoeux, Self-stabilizing distributed data fusion, in *Stabilization, Safety and Security of Distributed Systems*, A. Richa and C. Scheideler (Eds.), Springer, Berlin, Germany, pp. 148–162, 2012.

[9] C. Foglietta, A. Gasparri and S. Panzieri, A networked evidence theory framework for critical infrastructure modeling, in *Critical Infrastructure Protection VI*, J. Butts and S. Shenoi (Eds.), Springer, Heidelberg, Germany, pp. 205–215, 2012.

[10] V. Formicola, A. Di Pietro, A. Alsubaie, S. D' Antonio and J. Marti, Assessing the impact of cyber attacks on wireless sensor nodes that monitor interdependent physical systems, in *Critical Infrastructure Protection VIII*, J. Butts and S. Shenoi (Eds.), Springer, Heidelberg, Germany, pp. 213–229, 2014.

[11] A. Gasparri, F. Fiorini, M. Di Rocco and S. Panzieri, A networked transferable belief model approach for distributed data aggregation, *IEEE Transactions on Systems, Man and Cybernetics, Part B: Cybernetics*, vol. 42(2), pp. 391–405, 2012.

[12] B. Genge, C. Siaterlis and G. Karopoulos, Data fusion based anomaly detection in networked critical infrastructures, *Proceedings of the Forty-Third IEEE/IFIP International Conference on Dependable Systems and Networks; Workshop on Reliability and Security Data Analysis*, 2013.

[13] G. Oliva, S. Panzieri and R. Setola, Distributed consensus under ambiguous information, *International Journal of Systems of Systems Engineering*, vol. 4(1), pp. 55–78, 2013.

[14] M. Ouyang, Review on modeling and simulation of interdependent critical infrastructure systems, *Reliability Engineering and System Safety*, vol. 121, pp. 43–60, 2014.

[15] C. Perrow, *Normal Accidents: Living with High-Risk Technologies*, Basic Books, New York, 1984.

[16] S. Rinaldi, J. Peerenboom and T. Kelly, Identifying, understanding and analyzing critical infrastructure interdependencies, *IEEE Control Systems*, vol. 21(6), pp. 11–25, 2001.

[17] G. Shafer, *A Mathematical Theory of Evidence*, Princeton University Press, Princeton, New Jersey, 1976.

[18] P. Smets, The combination of evidence in the transferable belief model, *IEEE Transactions on Pattern Analysis and Machine Intelligence*, vol. 12(5), pp. 447–458, 1990.

[19] P. Smets and R. Kennes, The transferable belief model, *Artificial Intelligence*, vol. 66(2), pp. 191–234, 1994.

[20] P. Sousa, A. Bessani, W. Dantas, F. Souto, M. Correia and N. Neves, Intrusion-tolerant self-healing devices for critical infrastructure protection, *Proceedings of the Thirty-Ninth IEEE/IFIP International Conference on Dependable Systems and Networks*, pp. 217–222, 2009.

[21] D. Sutton, J. Harrison, S. Bologna and V. Rosato, The contribution of Neisas to EP3R, in *Critical Information Infrastructure Security*, S. Bologna, B. Hammerli, D. Gritzalis and S. Wolthusen (Eds.), Springer-Verlag, Berlin Heidelberg, Germany, pp. 175–186, 2013.

[22] A. Townsend and M. Moss, Telecommunications Infrastructure in Disasters: Preparing Cities for Crisis Communications, Center for Catastrophe Preparedness and Response and Robert F. Wagner Graduate School of Public Service, New York University, New York (`www.nyu.edu/ccpr/pubs/NYU-DisasterCommunications1-Final.pdf`), 2005.

[23] M. van Eeten, A. Nieuwenhuijs, E. Luiijf, M. Klaver and E. Cruz, The state and the threat of cascading failure across critical infrastructures: The implications of empirical evidence from media incident reports, *Public Administration*, vol. 89(2), pp. 381–400, 2011.

[24] L. Zadeh, On the Validity of Dempster's Rule of Combination of Evidence, Memorandum UCB/ERL-M, Electronics Research Laboratory, University of California, Berkeley, Berkeley, California, 1979.

VI

RISK AND IMPACT ASSESSMENT

Chapter 18

USING CENTRALITY MEASURES IN DEPENDENCY RISK GRAPHS FOR EFFICIENT RISK MITIGATION

George Stergiopoulos, Marianthi Theocharidou, Panayiotis Kotzaniko-laou and Dimitris Gritzalis

Abstract   One way to model cascading critical infrastructure failures is through dependency risk graphs. These graphs help assess the expected risk of critical infrastructure dependency chains. This research extends an existing dependency risk analysis methodology towards risk management. The relationship between dependency risk paths and graph centrality measures is explored in order to identify nodes that significantly impact the overall dependency risk. Experimental results using random graphs to simulate common critical infrastructure dependency characteristics are presented. Based on the experimental findings, an algorithm is proposed for efficient risk mitigation. The algorithm can be used to define priorities in selecting nodes for the application of mitigation controls.

Keywords: Dependency risk graphs, graph centrality, cascading failures, mitigation

1.   Introduction

Critical infrastructure dependencies contribute to the evolution of cascading effects in the case of infrastructure failures. Previous research [5–7, 12, 13] has articulated a methodology for assessing the cumulative risk of dependency risk paths (i.e., paths of critical infrastructure nodes that are (inter)connected as a result of one or more dependencies). The methodology takes as input the risk assessment results from critical infrastructure operators and, based on the first-order dependencies between the critical infrastructure nodes, assesses the implied risk values of all the n-order dependency risk chains. Next, by sorting the estimated dependency risk chains based on the cumulative dependency risk of each chain, the most important dependency chains are identified.

Although several methods focus on the identification and assessment of the most critical chains of dependencies, they tend to underestimate the importance

© IFIP International Federation for Information Processing 2015
M. Rice, S. Shenoi (Eds.): Critical Infrastructure Protection IX, IFIP AICT 466, pp. 299–314, 2015.
DOI: 10.1007/978-3-319-26567-4_18

of nodes that do not belong to the most critical risk paths (i.e., dependency risk paths with cumulative dependency risk levels above a risk threshold). Moreover, even when nodes belonging to critical risk paths are examined, there are certain nodes whose effects are not measured properly (e.g., nodes that participate in multiple dependency risk paths but have low-risk first-order connections). Decreasing the probability of failure of these nodes may have a greater overall benefit because they affect multiple dependency paths.

This chapter presents an enhanced methodology that uses graph centrality measures to define node priorities when applying risk mitigation controls. Experiments are conducted to determine the significance of each measure in risk mitigation. The experimental results are used to specify an algorithm for achieving an efficient risk mitigation strategy.

2. Graph Centrality Analysis

Graph centrality measures are used to estimate the relative importance or role of a node in a graph. Multiple centrality measures exist, each measuring a different characteristic:

- **Degree Centrality:** This measures the number of edges attached to each node. Given a node u, the degree centrality is defined as:

$$C_d(u) = deg(u)$$

where $deg(u)$ is the total number of outbound and inbound edges.

- **Closeness Centrality:** This quantifies the intuitive notions of "central" or "peripheral" in a two-dimensional region; it is based on geodesic distances. Closeness centrality is defined as:

$$C_c(u) = \sum_{\forall v \in V(G)} \delta(u, v)$$

where $\delta(u, v)$ is the average shortest path between the examined node u and any other node in the graph.

- **Betweenness Centrality:** This measures the number of paths in which a node participates. Betweenness centrality is defined as:

$$C_b(u) = \sum_{u \neq i \neq j \in V} \delta_{ij}(u)$$

where

$$\delta_{ij}(u) = \frac{\sigma_{ij}(u)}{\sigma_{ij}}$$

Here, $\sigma_{ij}(u)$ denotes the number of geodesic distances from i to j in which node u is present and σ_{ij} is the number of geodesic distances from i to j.

- **Bonacich (Eigenvector) Centrality:** Bonacich centrality [2] attempts to measure the influence of a node in a network. It is defined as:

$$c_i(\alpha, \beta) = \sum_j (\alpha - \beta c_i) R_{i,j}$$

  where α is a scaling factor, β reflects the extent to which centrality is weighted, R is the node adjacency matrix, I is the identity matrix and l is a matrix of ones. Note that an adjacency matrix is an $N \times N$ matrix whose elements have a value of one if an edge exists between nodes; and zero otherwise.

- **Eccentricity Centrality:** This measure is similar to closeness centrality. Essentially, it is the greatest distance from among all the shortest paths between u and any other vertex (in terms of geodesic distances).

3.   Related Work

Centrality analysis has primarily been used in graph-based critical infrastructure protection approaches involving vulnerability analyses in power networks. For example, Verma et al. [16] have simulated node removal strategies that trigger cascading failures in the high-voltage European power grid. They compare: (i) random node removal; (ii) node removal based on centrality (betweenness, degree and closeness); and (iii) node removal based on node significance, a context-based measure that considers power flow through a node to its neighbors. They conclude that betweenness, closeness and node degree centrality measures underestimate power grid vulnerability. This is because removing a node with the highest significance causes much more damage than removing a node with the highest centrality or a random node.

A heuristic methodology [1] uses five centrality measures: degree centrality, betweenness centrality, eccentricity centrality, centroid centrality and radiality. The methodology ranks nodes in five lists, one list for each centrality measure. If a node is present in at least two lists, it is considered to be an important node that must be examined. The methodology has been used to evaluate the effects of targeted attacks on the Swiss power grid.

The electrical centrality measure [4] assesses the structure of a network as a function of its electrical topology instead of its physical topology. Unlike the situation with conventional measures of network structure, power networks appear to have a scale-free structure when measured electrically; specifically, power networks have a number of highly-connected "hub" buses that should be examined thoroughly. A similar approach by Wang et al. [18] concludes that, when the electrical parameters are incorporated in centrality definitions, the distributions of degree centrality and eigenvector centrality become very different from those based only on the topological structure. In the case of electrical degree centrality and electrical eigenvector centrality, a large amount of centrality can reside in a small number of nodes; this helps locate groups of important nodes that cannot be identified otherwise. Cadini et al. [3] have extended the topological concepts of centrality measures to account for the reliability of network connections.

Zio and Piccinelli [19] have highlighted the importance of considering the actual service capacities of nodes as well as other parameters such as the probabilities of node failures and the fact that the flows between network nodes are not restricted to direct, shortest paths as typically assumed. For these reasons, Zio and Piccinelli extend the topological concept of betweenness centrality to account for random flow propagation across a network. Based on network performance characteristics and the random flow betweenness centrality measure, they have identified weaknesses in the network structure of an electrical power transmission system.

Nguyen et al. [9] have studied the optimization problem of detecting critical nodes in interdependent power networks. They introduce novel centrality measures that more accurately assess the importance of each node in interdependent networks; this is achieved by considering intra-centrality (centrality of nodes in each network) and inter-centrality (centrality due to the interconnections between two networks).

In all the approaches discussed above, centrality measures are used topologically and in combination with other parameters to provide a measure of the reliability or failure rate of a node. Many of the approaches demonstrate that a pure topological analysis of power networks is inadequate. On the other hand, the approach presented in this chapter uses centrality measures as an analysis tool for graphs that express the risk dependencies of interconnected critical infrastructures. The edges between the nodes in these graphs do not define physical or topological connections between nodes as in the case of the approaches discussed above. Parameters that indicate the significance of a node are inherently incorporated in the graphs as each risk graph considers the probability of a node failure, the probability of a cascading failure to another node and the impact of the failure. Centrality measures help identify the potentially significant nodes that have larger contributions to the overall graph risk. Thus, the application of mitigation controls to these nodes yields greater overall benefits.

4.   Centrality Measures for Dependency Graphs

This research extends the dependency risk methodology of Kotzanikolaou et al. [5, 6] for analyzing multi-order cascading failures. A dependency is defined as "the one-directional reliance of an asset, system, network or collection thereof – within or across sectors – on an input, interaction or other requirement from other sources in order to function properly" [14]. The methodology of Kotzanikolaou et al. [5, 6] quantifies this concept by identifying direct relations (first-order dependencies) between pairs of critical infrastructures as assessed by critical infrastructure operators and extends them to n-order relations. Each dependency from a node CI_i to a node CI_j is assigned an impact value $I_{i,j}$ and likelihood value $L_{i,j}$ of a disruption being realized. The product of the impact and likelihood values yields the dependency risk $R_{i,j}$ to infrastructure CI_j due to infrastructure CI_i. Dependencies are visualized in a graph $G = (N, E)$ where N is the set of nodes (or infrastructures or components) and E is the set of edges (or dependencies). The graph is directional and the destination critical infrastructure receives a risk from the source critical infrastructure due to its dependency. The numerical value of each edge is the level of the cascade resulting risk for the receiving infrastructure due to the dependency based on a predefined risk scale $\{1, .., 9\}$.

The methodology of Kotzanikolaou et al. [6] extends the direct risk relations in order to estimate the risk of n-order dependency chains. Let $\mathbb{CI} = (CI_1, \ldots, CI_m)$ be a set of critical infrastructures. An algorithm in [6] examines each critical infrastructure as a potential root of a cascading effect. Let CI_{Y_0} denote a critical infrastructure that is the root of a dependency chain $CI_{Y_0} \to CI_{Y_1} \to \ldots \to CI_{Y_n}$ of length n. The algorithm computes the cumulative dependency risk of the n-order dependency chain as:

$$DR_{Y_0,\ldots,Y_n} = \sum_{i=1}^{n} R_{Y_0,\ldots,Y_i} \equiv \sum_{i=1}^{n} (\prod_{j=1}^{i} L_{Y_{j-1},Y_j}) \cdot I_{Y_{i-1},Y_i} \qquad (1)$$

Informally, Equation (1) computes the dependency risk contributed by each affected node in the chain due to a failure realized at the source node. The computation of the risk is based on a risk matrix that combines the likelihood and the incoming impact values of each vertex in the chain. Interested readers are referred to [5] for additional details of the methodology.

4.1   Centrality Measures for Dependency Graphs

This section analyzes the effects of centrality measures in order to construct an algorithm for selecting the most appropriate nodes to apply risk mitigation controls. As mentioned above, the methodology uses risk graphs whose edges denote directed risk relations between nodes, not topological connections or service exchanges between nodes. Several centrality measures in a dependency risk graph formulation are considered in order to identify the nodes that have significant effects on the evolution of the cumulative risk in a dependency chain. Intuitively, nodes with high centrality measures would have high effects on the overall dependency risk. Thus, they are good candidates for implementing risk mitigation controls in a cost-effective mitigation strategy.

Degree Centrality.   A node with high degree centrality is a node with many dependencies. Since the edges in a risk graph are directional, the degree centrality is examined for two cases: (i) inbound degree centrality (i.e., number of edges ending at a node); and (ii) outbound degree centrality (i.e., number of edges starting from a node). Nodes with high inbound degree centrality are called cascade resulting nodes while nodes with high outbound degree centrality are called cascade initiating nodes [8].

Nodes with high outbound degree centrality appear to be the most appropriate nodes to examine when prioritizing mitigation controls. Indeed, if proper mitigation controls are applied to these nodes, then multiple cumulative dependency risk chains are simultaneously reduced. This could result in a cost-effective mitigation strategy that applies controls to high risk edges or high risk paths. Obviously, it is not certain that applying one or more security controls at a node with high outbound degree centrality would positively impact many (or all) outgoing dependencies chains involving the node. However, a mitigation strategy would definitely benefit if it were to initially examine such security controls.

Nodes with high inbound degree centrality in a risk graph are natural "sinkholes" of incoming dependency risk. These nodes are probably subject to multiple independent sources of risk, but reducing the impact of a disruption on these nodes may affect multiple paths. This research has not experimented with such nodes; however, future work will examine mitigation strategies that focus on sinkholes instead of nodes with high outbound degree centrality.

Closeness Centrality. A node with high closeness centrality has short average distances from most nodes in a graph. In the case of a dependency risk graph, nodes with high closeness tend to be part of many dependency chains; sometimes these nodes may even initiate dependency chains. Since cascading effects tend to affect relatively short chains (empirical evidence indicates that cascades rarely propagate deeply [15]), nodes with high closeness centrality would have larger effects on the overall risk of dependency chains than nodes with low closeness centrality. To formalize this idea, consider Equation (1) that computes the cumulative risk of a dependency chain: the closer a node is to the initiator of a cascading event, the greater the effect it has on the cumulative dependency risk. This is because the likelihood of its outgoing dependency affects all the partial risk values of the subsequent dependencies (edges).

A more effective way to exploit closeness centrality in mitigation decisions is to compute the closeness of every node with respect to the subset of the most important initiator nodes. Regardless of the underlying methodology, risk assessors would have *a priori* knowledge or intuition about the most important nodes in cascading failure scenarios. For example, empirical results show that energy nodes and information and communications nodes are the most common cascade initiators [15].

In addition, nodes with high outbound degree centrality are likely to participate in multiple dependency risk chains. Thus, it is possible to first identify the subset of the most important nodes for cascading failures and then compute the closeness of all other nodes relative to this subset of nodes as a secondary criterion for mitigation prioritization.

Eccentricity Centrality. Similar to closeness centrality, eccentricity centrality measures the centrality of a node in a graph that has a small maximum distance from the node to every other reachable node. Note that the small maximum distance corresponds to the greatest distance from among all the shortest-paths between the node and every other node (geodesic distances).

If the eccentricity of a critical infrastructure node is high, then all the other critical infrastructure nodes are proximal to it.

Betweenness Centrality. In a dependency risk graph, a node with high betweenness centrality lies on a high proportion of dependency risk paths. This means that, although such nodes may not be initiating nodes of cascading failures (high outbound centrality) or may not belong to a path with high cumulative dependency risk, they tend to contribute to multiple risk paths and, thus, play an important role in the overall risk calculation. Applying mitigation measures at these nodes (in the form of security controls) is likely to decrease the dependency risk of multiple chains simultaneously.

Upon comparing closeness centrality with betweenness centrality, it appears that closeness should precede betweenness as a mitigation criterion. Although nodes that are between multiple paths will eventually affect multiple chains, it is possible that a node that lies in multiple paths but tends to be at the end of a dependency chain will not (in reality) affect the cumulative dependency risk chain (recall that nodes with high-order dependencies are rarely affected).

Bonacich (Eigenvector) Centrality. A node with high Bonacich [2] (eigenvector) centrality has a high influence on other nodes. In a risk dependency graph, nodes with high eigenvector centrality where $\beta > 0$ are of interest because these nodes are connected to other nodes that also have high connectivity. This is an interesting measure for critical infrastructure risk graphs because such nodes not only can cause cascading failures to more nodes, but they can cause multiple cascading chains of high risk. In contrast, a less connected node shares fewer dependencies with other nodes and is, therefore, affected only by specific nodes in the graph. This means that applying mitigation measures to such a node may not significantly affect the overall risk. However, if mitigation controls are applied to a node with the highest eigenvector centrality (when $\beta > 0$), then the most powerful (or critical) node is modified and this, in turn, affects several other important nodes.

4.2   Centrality Measures for Risk Mitigation

This section examines how the centrality measures described above can be combined to assist in selecting the most appropriate nodes for applying mitigation controls. For example, a critical infrastructure node with high eccentricity and closeness measures might affect a large number of paths with relatively low cumulative dependency risk values. If existing risk assessment methods are applied, potentially serious cascading effects involving these nodes may go unnoticed.

Based on the analysis of the centrality measures on dependency risk graphs discussed in Section 2.4, the following generic method is proposed to assess the selection of candidate nodes for applying risk mitigation controls:

- Use the method of Kotzanikolaou et al. [5] (see Equation (1)) to assess the cumulative dependency risk of all existing dependency paths in a dependency risk graph.

- Compute all the centrality measures for each node.

- Identify alternative mitigation strategies by selecting a subset of nodes for applying risk mitigation controls based on (some) centrality measures.

- Apply the strategy to the selected subset of nodes (i.e., reduce the weights of all the outbound edges for each node in the selected set). Generate a new risk graph (reduced risk graph) by applying mitigation controls to the selected nodes.

- Evaluate the results of the strategy by comparing the new graph with the initial graph. The comparison can be based on the risk of the most critical path, the maximum risk of all paths or the number of paths that have risk values above a specified risk threshold.

The next section uses the generic method to evaluate the effects of various centrality measures on the selection of candidate nodes for risk mitigation. The experimental results are leveraged to develop the most efficient strategy for applying controls to mitigate the overall risk.

5.   Experimental Results

An automatic dependency risk graph generator was developed in Java and the Neo4J graph database model was used for graph construction and analysis. Graph databases provide index-free adjacency and more effective models than relational databases, especially in situations where the relationships between elements are the driving force for data model design [11, 17]. Neo4J builds on the property graph model; nodes may have various labels and each label can serve as an informational entity. The nodes are connected via directed, typed relationships. Nodes and relationships hold arbitrary properties (key-value pairs) that make the Neo4J library ideal for building and testing dependency risk graphs and calculating centrality values. After creating a dependency risk graph, the automated dependency risk graph generator computes the cumulative dependency risk of all paths of length five and the centrality values of each node.

The first step was to study possible relationships between the most critical paths of a risk graph (calculated according to the method of Kotzanikolaou et al. [6]) and the subset of nodes with the highest centrality measures. The experiments were designed to understand how often nodes appear simultaneously in the critical paths (i.e., paths with the highest cumulative dependency risk values) and how often nodes in the paths are members of the set of nodes with the highest centrality measures. The graphs constructed in the experiments were randomized with certain restrictions [8, 15] in order to resemble critical infrastructure dependencies based on real data:

Table 1. Participation rates of nodes with high centrality measurements.

Type of Statistical Experiment	Average
Nodes in 1% of top paths AND 10% of highest centrality values	16.3%
Nodes in 5% of top paths AND 10% of highest centrality values	16.2%
Nodes in 10% of top paths AND 10% of highest centrality values	16.0%
Paths in 1% of top paths AND at least one node in the top 10% of nodes with the highest centrality values	49.0%

- Occasional tight coupling (i.e., occasional high dependencies between critical infrastructures). Some node relationships in a risk graph have high dependencies (randomization applies random risk values with relatively high lower and upper bounds).

- Interactive complexity (i.e., a measure of the degree to which it is not possible to foresee all the ways in which things can go wrong). Real-world critical infrastructure dependencies have high interactive complexity. To achieve this, the experiments constructed random graphs of 50 nodes with high complexity; the critical paths up to fourth-order dependencies had 230,300 to 2,118,760 possible chains.

- One to seven connections (dependencies) per critical infrastructure node.

- Critical paths of three to four hops.

- 62% of critical infrastructure nodes act as initiators.

- Initiators tend to have higher numbers of interconnections.

- 100 random repetitions.

Experiments were conducted on 5,000 random graphs with the aforementioned restrictions. The results demonstrated that the sum of nodes comprising the top 1% of critical paths also appeared in the top 10% of nodes with the highest centrality measures (average of 16%). However, the number of critical paths with at least one high centrality node was extremely high: an average of 49% of the top 1% of the most critical paths always included a high centrality node based on at least one of the measures. This percentage remained the same even for the top 10% of most critical paths, which leads to the conclusion that the top 10% of paths essentially pass through the same nodes as the top 1% of paths. These results appear to hold for all the centrality measures.

The same experiments were conducted using the top 10% of most critical paths against the top 10% of nodes the with the highest centrality values. The participation percentage appeared to remain stable (16,850 out of a total of 141,093 nodes in the top 10% critical paths). Table 1 presents the participation percentages obtained for each experiment. The results show that, with a percentage of 49%, the top 1% of highest ranked critical paths are indeed affected by nodes with very high centrality. Analysis of larger sample sets (more than 50% of critical paths) revealed that almost all the high centrality nodes were part of some critical path.

5.1   Risk Mitigation Based on Centrality

The experimental results demonstrate that, even if nodes with high centrality are only a small fraction of the nodes in the most critical risk paths, they affect the top 1% of the most critical risk paths about half the time. Thus, it is essential to take them into consideration when deciding where to implement risk mitigation controls in a high criticality path. In practice, the controls could involve the repair prioritization of nodes (i.e., where to send a repair crew first) or increasing redundancy at a node to reduce the likelihood or consequences of a failure.

In the experiments, the implementation of mitigation controls at a node i was emulated by reducing the likelihood $L_{i,j}$ that a failure of node i would cascade to another node j with a risk dependency on node i. Specifically, the implementation of mitigation controls at a node i was emulated by reducing the $L_{i,j}$ by 20% for all nodes j that depend on node i. The reduction in cascading likelihood was selected because the focus was on cascade initiating nodes. In the case of sinkholes, the reduction in impact would be more appropriate because these are usually cascade resulting nodes. To measure the results of risk mitigation on each selected subset of nodes, the dependency risk values were computed in the same graph before and after the implementation of risk mitigation, and the corresponding risk reduction in each case was computed.

The effects on two metrics were examined: (i) risk reduction achieved in the most critical path; and (ii) risk reduction in the sum of the risks of the top 20 paths with the highest cumulative dependency risks. Mitigation controls were implemented for 6% of the nodes in the entire risk graph (three out of 50 critical infrastructure nodes in the experiments).

Effect on the Most Critical Path.   Figure 1 shows that the highest risk reduction in the most critical path was achieved when implementing mitigation controls at the top three nodes (6%) with the highest aggregate values of all the centrality metrics. The average risk reduction achieved was 8.1% (over 100 experiments and 100 most critical paths). The highest risk reduction achieved in all the experiments was 31.5%.

The second highest risk reduction was achieved using a combination of the top three nodes (6%) using the eccentricity and closeness centrality measures (highest risk reduction achieved: 27.2%; average: 9.1%). The next highest risk reduction was achieved using betweenness (highest risk reduction: 26.0%; average: 8.1%) and, lastly, using the eigenvector centrality (highest risk reduction: 17.3%; average: 7.4%).

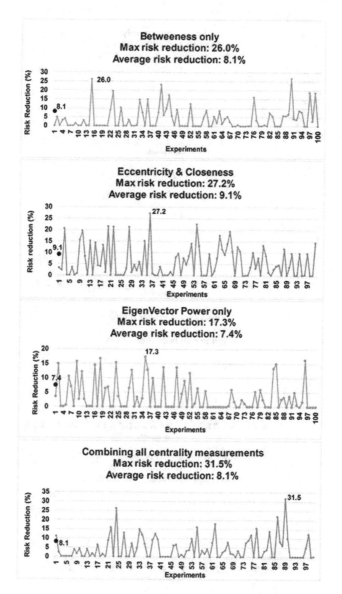

Figure 1. Risk reduction in the most critical path.

Effect on the Top 20 Risk Paths. Figure 2 shows that the highest risk reduction in the sum of risk values derived from the top 20 critical paths is, once again, achieved by implementing mitigation controls at the top three (6%) nodes with the highest centrality for different combinations of centrality metrics. However, the risk reduction achieved has the lowest average reduction of 4.4% despite the fact that the highest maximum reduction is 30.3%.

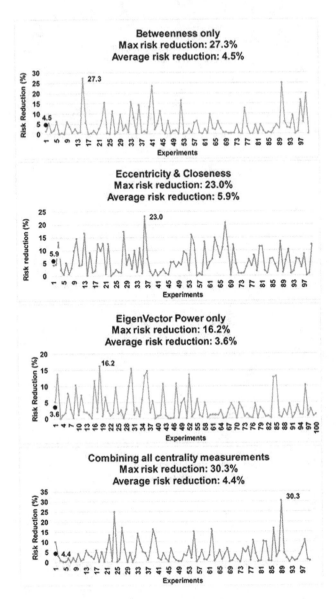

Figure 2. Average risk reduction in the 20 highest critical paths.

Despite aggregating all the centrality measurements, the second highest risk reduction was achieved using a combination of the top 6% of nodes using betweenness centrality only (highest risk reduction achieved: 27.3%; average: 4.5%), followed by the combined use of the eccentricity and closeness centralities (highest reduction: 23.0%; average: 5.9%); and finally using the eigenvector centrality (highest risk reduction: 16.2%; average: 3.6%).

5.2   Efficient Risk Mitigation Algorithm

Algorithm 1 was designed based on the experimental results presented above. In the algorithm, U_1 denotes the subset of the top $X\%$ of nodes with the highest centrality values from among all the centrality sets; U_2 denotes the subset of the top $X\%$ of nodes with the highest eccentricity and closeness centralities; U_3 denotes the subset of the top $X\%$ of nodes with the highest degree and betweenness centralities; and U_4 denotes the subset of the top $X\%$ of nodes with the highest eigenvector centrality. The parameters r_1, r_2, r_3 and r_4 correspond to the average risk reductions for U_1, U_2, U_3 and U_4, respectively, which were measured in the experiments as 8.5%, 9.0%, 4.5% and 3.6%, respectively. S is the subset of nodes belonging to the top 20 critical paths with the highest cumulative dependency risks.

6.   Conclusions

The dependency risk methodology described in this chapter extends the approach of Kotzanikolaou et al. [5, 6] by incorporating graph centrality measures as additional criteria for evaluating alternative risk mitigation strategies. The goal was to identify the nodes that greatly affect the critical risk paths and, thus, are more efficient candidates for the application of risk mitigation controls. The experimental results confirm that the most critical paths in dependency risk graphs tend to involve nodes with high centrality measures. However, multiple centrality measures can be applied and these measures contribute to the overall risk mitigation in differing degrees. Experimental evaluations were performed for each centrality measure and for combinations of measures in order to determine the most appropriate combinations of measures. The results demonstrate that aggregating all the centrality measure sets to identify nodes with high overall centrality values is the best mitigation strategy, a result that matches intuition. Nevertheless, aggregation may not always be a viable choice because a dependency graph may have no nodes that exist in all the high centrality sets or there may be contextual reasons that inhibit the application of controls at these nodes.

For this reason, the methodology was extended to rank different combinations of centrality measures based on the experimental results. The results show that, if the method for calculating dependency risk chains is combined with centrality measures, an average risk mitigation of 8.1% is achieved for the most critical path by only implementing mitigation controls at three out of 50 nodes. The experimental analysis was used to design an algorithm for identifying the optimum set of nodes that achieve greater than average risk mitigation for the overall network of nodes instead of a single node. The algorithm, thus, enables "important" nodes to be targeted for mitigation even if the nodes do not belong to the most critical paths in a risk graph.

Future work will focus on enhancing the methodology by incorporating additional parameters, such as the cost of applying controls and other limitations that may arise during mitigation. These could be contextual, such as sector-

---

Algorithm 1 : Mitigation algorithm.

---

procedure MITIGATION(U_1, U_2, U_3, U_4, S)
    Create subset U_1
    Create subset S   ▷ S has nodes from the top 20 paths
    if $S \cap U_1$ not empty **then**
        Implement controls at the nodes in $S \cap U_1$
        if nodes in $S \cap U_1$ have less nodes than U_1 **then**
            Implement the remaining controls at the nodes in U_1
        end if
    else
        Implement controls at the nodes in U_1
    end if
    if risk reduction $< r_1$ **then**
        CONTINUE
    else
        FINISH
    end if
    Create subset U_2
    if $S \cap U_2$ not empty **then**
        Implement controls at the nodes in $S \cap U_2$
        if nodes in $S \cap U_2$ have less nodes than U_2 **then**
            Implement the remaining controls at the nodes in U_2
        end if
    else
        Implement controls at the nodes in U_2
    end if
    if risk reduction $< r_2$ **then**
        CONTINUE
    else
        FINISH
    end if
    Create subset U_3;
    if $S \cap U_3$ not empty **then**
        Implement controls at the nodes in $S \cap U_3$
        if nodes in $S \cap U_3$ have less nodes than U_3 **then**
            Implement the remaining controls at the nodes in U_3
        end if
    else
        Implement controls at the nodes in U_3
    end if
    if risk reduction $< r_3$ **then**
        CONTINUE
    else
        FINISH
    end if
    Create subset U_4;
    if $S \cap U_4$ not empty **then**
        Implement controls at the nodes in $S \cap U_4$
        if nodes in $S \cap U_4$ have less nodes than U_4 **then**
            Implement the remaining controls at the nodes in U_4
        end if
    else
        Implement controls at the nodes in U_4
    end if
    if risk reduction $< r_4$ **then**
        Implement controls at the nodes with the highest results for all four strategies
    end if
end procedure

---

based characteristics of nodes or constraints imposed by legislation, policy and critical infrastructure operations. Additionally, mitigation strategies for nodes with high inbound degree centrality (sinkholes) will be explored in combination with impact reduction. Finally, since the risk graphs used in this work were based only on normal operating conditions [10], it is necessary to investigate modified risk graphs that depict other modes of operation (e.g., stressed, crisis and recovery modes).

Acknowledgement

This research was partially supported by the European Union's Seventh Framework Programme for Research, Technological Development and Demonstration under Grant no. 312450.

References

[1] E. Bilis, W. Kroger and C. Nan, Performance of electric power systems under physical malicious attacks, *IEEE Systems Journal*, vol. 7(4), pp. 854–865, 2013.

[2] P. Bonacich, Power and centrality: A family of measures, *American Journal of Sociology*, vol. 92(5), pp. 1170–1182, 1987.

[3] F. Cadini, E. Zio and C. Petrescu, Using centrality measures to rank the importance of the components of a complex network infrastructure, in *Critical Information Infrastructure Security*, R. Setola and S. Geretshuber (Eds.), Springer-Verlag, Berlin Heidelberg, Germany, pp. 155–167, 2009.

[4] P. Hines and S. Blumsack, A centrality measure for electrical networks, *Proceedings of the Forty-First Annual Hawaii International Conference on System Sciences*, 2008.

[5] P. Kotzanikolaou, M. Theoharidou and D. Gritzalis, Assessing n-order dependencies between critical infrastructures, *International Journal of Critical Infrastructures*, vol. 9(1/2), pp. 93–110, 2013.

[6] P. Kotzanikolaou, M. Theoharidou and D. Gritzalis, Cascading effects of common-cause failures in critical infrastructures, in *Critical Infrastructure Protection VII*, J. Butts and S. Shenoi (Eds.), Springer, Heidelberg, Germany, pp. 171–182, 2013.

[7] P. Kotzanikolaou, M. Theoharidou and D. Gritzalis, Interdependencies between critical infrastructures: Analyzing the risk of cascading effects, in *Critical Information Infrastructure Security*, S. Bologna, B. Hammerli, D. Gritzalis and S. Wolthusen (Eds.), Springer-Verlag, Berlin Heidelberg, Germany, pp. 104–115, 2013.

[8] E. Luiijf, A. Nieuwenhuijs, M. Klaver, M. van Eeten and E. Cruz, Empirical findings on critical infrastructure dependencies in Europe, in *Critical Information Infrastructure Security*, R. Setola and S. Geretshuber (Eds.), Springer-Verlag, Berlin Heidelberg, Germany, pp. 302–310, 2009.

[9] D. Nguyen, Y. Shen and M. Thai, Detecting critical nodes in interdependent power networks for vulnerability assessment, *IEEE Transactions on Smart Grid*, vol. 4(1), pp. 151–159, 2013.

[10] A. Nieuwenhuijs, E. Luiijf and M. Klaver, Modeling dependencies in critical infrastructures, in *Critical Infrastructure Protection II*, M. Papa and S. Shenoi (Eds.), Springer, Boston, Massachusetts, pp. 205–213, 2008.

[11] B. Shao, H. Wang and Y. Xiao, Managing and mining large graphs: Systems and implementations, *Proceedings of the ACM SIGMOD International Conference on Management of Data*, pp. 589–592, 2012.

[12] M. Theoharidou, P. Kotzanikolaou and D. Gritzalis, A multi-layer criticality assessment methodology based on interdependencies, *Computers and Security*, vol. 29(6), pp. 643–658, 2010.

[13] M. Theoharidou, P. Kotzanikolaou and D. Gritzalis, Risk assessment methodology for interdependent critical infrastructures, *International Journal of Risk Assessment and Management*, vol. 15(2/3), pp. 128–148, 2011.

[14] U.S. Department of Homeland Security, National Infrastructure Protection Plan (NIPP) 2013: Partnering for Critical Infrastructure Security and Resilience, Washington, DC, 2013.

[15] M. van Eeten, A. Nieuwenhuijs, E. Luiijf, M. Klaver and E. Cruz, The state and the threat of cascading failure across critical infrastructures: The implications of empirical evidence from media incident reports, *Public Administration*, vol. 89(2), pp. 381–400, 2011.

[16] T. Verma, W. Ellens and R. Kooij, Context-independent centrality measures underestimate the vulnerability of power grids, *International Journal of Critical Infrastructures*, vol. 11(1), pp. 62–81, 2015.

[17] C. Vicknair, M. Macias, Z. Zhao, X. Nan, Y. Chen and D. Wilkins, A comparison of a graph database and a relational database: A data provenance perspective, *Proceedings of the Forty-Eight Annual Southeast Regional Conference*, pp. 42:1–42:6, 2010.

[18] Z. Wang, A. Scaglione and R. Thomas, Electrical centrality measures for electric power grid vulnerability analysis, *Proceedings of the Forty-Ninth IEEE Conference on Decision and Control*, pp. 5792–5797, 2010.

[19] E. Zio and R. Piccinelli, Randomized flow model and centrality measure for electrical power transmission network analysis, *Reliability Engineering and System Safety*, vol. 95(4), pp. 379–385, 2010.

Chapter 19

ASSESSING CYBER RISK USING THE CISIApro SIMULATOR

Chiara Foglietta, Cosimo Palazzo, Riccardo Santini and Stefano Panzieri

Abstract   Dependencies and interdependencies between critical infrastructures are difficult to identify and model because their effects appear infrequently with unpredictable consequences. The addition of cyber attacks in this context makes the analysis even more complex. Integrating the consequences of cyber attacks and interdependencies requires detailed knowledge about both concepts at a common level of abstraction.

CISIApro is a critical infrastructure simulator that was created to evaluate the consequences of faults and failures in interdependent infrastructures. This chapter demonstrates the use of CISIApro to evaluate the effects of cyber attacks on physical equipment and infrastructure services. A complex environment involving three interconnected infrastructures is considered: a medium voltage power grid managed by a control center over a SCADA network that is interconnected with a general-purpose telecommunications network. The functionality of the simulator is showcased by subjecting the interconnected infrastructures to an ARP spoofing attack and worm infection. The simulation demonstrates the utility of CISIApro in supporting decision making by electric grid operators, in particular, helping choose between alternative fault isolation and system restoration procedures.

Keywords: Critical infrastructure, simulation, cyber attacks, risk

1.   Introduction

Critical infrastructures are vital to modern society. Airports, rail transport, network communications, electric grids, oil refineries and water systems are examples of critical infrastructure assets. Industrial operations adhere to the so-called $N-1$ standard, which refers to the ability to operate without the loss of service after the failure of one key component. Industrial plants also have the ability to operate despite the loss of two key components ($N-2$ standard). However, the $N-2$ standard is inadequate for critical infrastructures because

© IFIP International Federation for Information Processing 2015
M. Rice, S. Shenoi (Eds.): Critical Infrastructure Protection IX, IFIP AICT 466, pp. 315–331, 2015.
DOI: 10.1007/978-3-319-26567-4_19

major service outages, coordinated cyber attacks and faults often initiate in other interconnected infrastructures and propagate to the infrastructure of interest. Conditions within the infrastructure of interest as well as the existing infrastructure interdependencies must be considered and evaluated in order to restore services as soon as possible.

For more than fifteen years, researchers have grappled with the problems of modeling interdependencies and predicting the effects of infrastructure failures. The 2003 North American blackout was the first example of cascading effects after a power outage. The blackout, which was due to a software bug in an electric grid control room, impacted water supply, transportation, communications systems and several industries [1]. Another example is Hurricane Katrina, which interrupted oil production, transportation, refining, ocean shipping and exports as well as electric utilities [10].

Critical infrastructures adhere to the $N-1$ standard and they are protected from failures that initiate in their own sectors. In the event of a failure in the power grid, operators can reconfigure the grid to isolate the fault and restore power to customers (some users might still not have power, but the blackout is not complete). The reconfiguration procedure can be automated or executed manually and it depends on the specific topology (the sequence of opening and closing circuit breakers is related to the topology) as well as on other infrastructures, especially the telecommunications network, which is used to send commands to circuit breakers. This procedure is called fault isolation and system restoration (FISR) or power load shedding.

If a cyber event or a failure occurs in the telecommunications network, the procedure for restoring power may fail without any alerts being sent to power grid operators. In this situation, a routine failure can evolve to become a large-scale blackout that lasts for an extended period of time. One of the most famous cyber attacks on a SCADA network was perpetrated by Stuxnet [9]. This chapter focuses on the modeling and assessment of the impacts of cyber events on interconnected critical infrastructures.

The vast reach of telecommunications networks leads to poorly understood situations that can have uncontrolled effects on physical equipment in critical infrastructure assets. However, the problem of detecting cyber anomalies is outside the scope of this research because the approach presented here is independent of anomaly detection techniques. Indeed, the assumption here is that intrusion detection systems and malware protection software are in place to collect data about potential anomalies.

This chapter demonstrates the application of CISIApro to evaluate the effects of cyber attacks on physical equipment and infrastructure services. A complex environment involving three interconnected infrastructures is considered: a medium voltage power grid managed by a control center over a SCADA network that is interconnected with a general-purpose telecommunications network. The functionality of the simulator is illustrated by subjecting the interconnected infrastructures to an ARP spoofing attack to compromise a secure communications channel, which is then used to launch a worm infection. The simulation demonstrates the utility of CISIApro in supporting decision making by electric operators, specifically helping choose between alternative fault isolation and system restoration procedures.

2.   Related Work

This section conducts a brief analysis of techniques and tools for modeling and simulating interdependent critical infrastructures, with a focus on evaluating the consequences of cyber attacks.

2.1   Infrastructure Modeling and Simulation

Satumitra and Duenas-Osorio [15] have published an exhaustive survey of the principal methods for critical infrastructure modeling and simulation. Their survey reveals that most of the approaches for dealing with infrastructure interdependencies, cascading system failures and risk mitigation are complementary rather than competing. The modeling approaches include techniques based on game theory, graph theory, risk-based models, Petri nets and Bayesian networks. However, many of the interdependency models are primarily conceptual in nature or are limited to simple or high-level scenarios.

Rahman et al. [13] have developed the Infrastructure Interdependency Simulator (I2Sim) based on the well-known cell-channel model. In this model, infrastructures and their interconnections are represented using cells and channels. A cell is an entity that performs a function. For example, a hospital is a cell that uses input tokens such as electricity, water and medicines, and produces output tokens such as the number of patients served. A channel is a means through which tokens flow from one cell to another. The interdependencies between infrastructures are non-linear relationships that are summarized in the form of human-readable tables. I2Sim helps decision makers optimize resources and prioritize system restoration actions after critical events. I2Sim is the core element of DR-NEP (Disaster Response Network Enabled Platform), an advanced disaster management tool that is based on a web services infrastructure and incorporates domain simulators. The modeling technique has been validated by several case studies, including one involving the Vancouver 2010 Winter Olympics. However, the case studies mainly focus on natural disasters and do not consider the impacts of cyber attacks.

A survey of the research literature reveals that the majority of simulators employ the agent-based paradigm, in which a population of autonomous interacting agents coordinate their decisions to reach a higher-level global objective. Each infrastructure is modeled as an agent. Interdependencies are modeled as edges between agents. This enables agents to exchange information: each agent receives inputs from other agents and sends its outputs to other agents (see Nieuwenhuijs et al. [12] for further details). The CISIApro (Critical Infrastructure Simulation by Interdependent Agents) simulator [3] used in this research employs the agent-based paradigm, where each agent has a high-level description of the internal dynamics of an infrastructure. The main goal of CISIApro is to study the propagation of faults/attacks and the resulting degradation in performance [6]. Of course, a disadvantage of the approach is the difficulty in acquiring detailed information about the internal dynamics of infrastructures in order to create the agents.

Another recent trend is the use of co-simulation frameworks, where several domain-specific simulators are connected using a well-defined and generic interface (API) for simulation interoperability [16]. The main goal of a co-simulation framework is to reuse existing models in a common context to simulate complex scenarios. The Mosaik ecosystem [16] has been applied to analyze a smart grid scenario in which telecommunications network and power grid simulators are integrated. This work integrated various simulators for the electrical side, including models of electric vehicles in Python, photovoltaic cells in MATLAB/Simulink, residential loads as CSV time series data and two power distribution grids in Python. Mosaik is still at an early stage of development, but it can cope with different temporal resolutions (e.g., continuous, every minute or every fifteen minutes).

2.2   Cyber Attack Impact Assessment

Motivated by Stuxnet, researchers have focused on understanding how cyber attacks can affect physical critical infrastructure assets by leveraging SCADA telecommunications networks. This problem is complex because it requires deep knowledge from different domains – telecommunications and the specific physical infrastructure. Smart grids and power grids, in general, are perfect environments for evaluating the effects of cyber threats. Power grids have detailed analytic models at almost every level of abstraction and they also have well-documented control algorithms.

Lemay et al. [11] have used an industrial control system sandbox for the cyber portion of a cyber-physical system and optimal power flow algorithms for an electrical simulator to replicate the physical portion of an electrical power grid. The ability to model the physical damage caused by cyber attacks enables defenders to accurately evaluate the risk using metrics such as the delivered power and generation costs.

Sgouras et al. [17] have analyzed the impact of denial-of-service and distributed denial-of-service attacks on a smart meter infrastructure. They demonstrated that an attack on a single meter causes a temporary isolation or malfunction, but does not impact the power grid. However, the partial nonavailability of the demand-response mechanisms in a large number of smart meters due to a distributed denial-of-service attack could impact load shedding when the grid reaches an unsafe zone close to its maximum capacity. For these reasons, an attacker would prefer to conduct a distributed denial-of-service attack during a peak-use period in order to achieve greater impact.

Dondossola et al. [7] have assessed the impact of malware using a cyber-physical risk index that incorporates a probabilistic interpretation of vulnerability existence, threat occurrence and intrusion success. The basic idea underlying the cyber assessment methodology is to adopt a frequency interpretation of probability; specifically, the probabilities comprising the risk index are translated to their corresponding frequencies.

Another approach is to fuse information from the cyber and physical domains. To accomplish this, Santini et al. [14] have developed a data fusion framework using evidence theory. The data fusion framework was used to identify the cause of a cyber-physical attack (i.e., a denial-of-service attack that caused a breaker in a smart grid to malfunction).

Critical infrastructure operators are especially interested in the quality of the the services provided to their customers. Therefore, it is vital to understand the effects of cyber attacks on physical systems and their services. The CISIApro simulator used in this research is specifically designed to help determine the consequences of cyber attacks on physical equipment and the services they provide.

3. CISIApro Simulator

This section describes the main features of the CISIApro simulator, including its reliance on the mixed holistic reductionist (MHR) approach.

3.1 Mixed Holistic Reductionist Approach

The mixed holistic reductionist approach [5] was created to exploit the advantages of holistic and reductionist methods. In holistic modeling, infrastructures are seen as singular entities with defined boundaries and functional properties. On the other hand, reductionist modeling emphasizes the need to fully understand the roles and behaviors of individual components to comprehend the infrastructure as a whole. Different types of analyses require one or both points of view and their boundaries are lost when complex case studies are considered. In the mixed holistic reductionist approach, the relationships between infrastructures can be viewed at different levels via a top-down or bottom-up approach. Critical infrastructures have specific requirements in terms of the quality of the services delivered to customers. This requires the addition of another layer – the service layer – that describes the functional relationships between components and the infrastructure at different levels of granularity. In the mixed holistic reductionist approach, services provided to customers and to other interconnected infrastructures are explicitly considered as a middle layer between the holistic and reductionist layers.

3.2 Simulator Description

CISIA is an agent-based simulator in which all agents have the same structure (Figure 1). An agent receives resources and failures from other agents. A resource is a good, service or data produced and/or consumed by an agent that is represented in CISIA as an entity. The ability to produce resources is summarized by the concept of an operative level, which depends on the availability of received resources, propagation of faults and functionality of the entity itself.

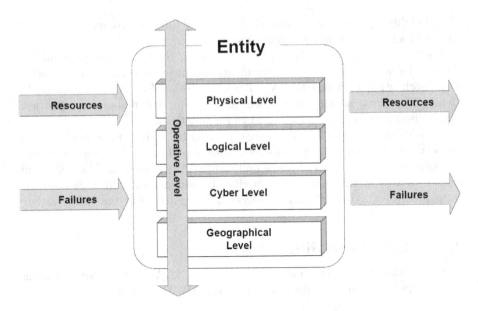

Figure 1.   CISIA entity diagram.

An entity also receives failures via its upstream interconnections and spreads the failures to downstream entities. The failures propagate different types of faults in different ways. The output of an agent depends on the actual value of the operative level. The classes of interdependencies considered are physical, logical, geographical and cyber. Interested readers are referred to [6] for a detailed description of the CISIA simulator.

Risk is defined as the product of the impact, threat and vulnerability:

$$Risk = Impact \times Threat \times Vulnerability \qquad (1)$$

Risk is usually computed as a numeric value from the impact severity, the likelihood of occurrence of the threat and the vulnerability measure. In CISIA applications, the likelihood of occurrence is replaced with the trust of the information. For each entity, a user can also add a vulnerability variable; however, in the case study discussed in this work, it is assumed that the vulnerability depends only on the distance from the source and on the persistence of the attack. The operative level of each agent is associated with a risk level. The risk, which is defined as the amount of harm due to a specific event (e.g., failure), is evaluated as:

$$Risk = 1 - Operative\ Level \qquad (2)$$

where 1 represents the maximum value of the operative level. A high operative level corresponds to a low risk.

In 2014, the CISIApro simulator was developed to overcome certain implementation problems associated with CISIA. The main problem was the possibil-

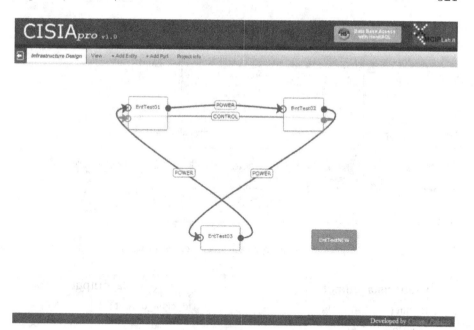

Figure 2. CISIA graphical user interface.

ity of an infinite loop when resources are instantly exchanged between entities. CISIA's main cycle buffers all the information exchanged between entities at each time step. If the exchanges form a cycle, then the simulation time step never ends, which results in an infinite loop. The CISIApro simulator ensures that the information flow is well defined using a maximum execution threshold for a time step; this eliminates infinite loops.

Another disadvantage of CISIA was the extended period of time required to set up and debug the system. In CISIApro, a graphical user interface is provided to create and connect entities and to add the exchanged resources in an efficient manner (Figure 2).

After creating the entities and their interconnections (i.e., interdependencies) and adding the exchanged resources, it is necessary to implement the behavior of each entity. Each entity is composed of four modules that are executed: (i) RECEIVED, which evaluates the received resources and faults; (ii) DYNAMIC COMPUTED, which implements dynamic evolution; (iii) INSTANT COMPUTED, which implements instantaneous evolution; and (iv) SENT, which evaluates the resources that are sent to the downstream entities.

CISIApro uses a database to capture all the information needed to represent multiple critical infrastructures and their interconnections. Figure 3 shows the database structure. Each entity is an instance of an entity type whose status is expressed using variables. Each entity has ports for exchanging resources and creating the mixed holistic reductionist model layers. Each layer embodies various interdependencies.

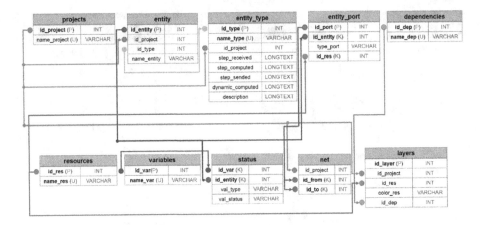

Figure 3. CISIApro database representation.

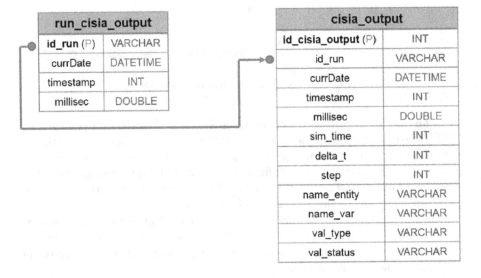

Figure 4. CISIApro output database representation.

The CISIApro output is stored in a separate database (Figure 4). This database stores timestamped data for use by operators.

Adjacency matrices that represent interdependencies existing between entities are generated during the design phase. During the simulation, the matrices are represented as queue data structures to speed up computations.

The ability of CISIApro to support operator decision making has been validated by two European Union projects, FACIES [8] and CockpitCI [4]. Figure 5 shows the information flow from input acquisition to operator display. The physical system data is gathered from the SCADA control center and the cyber threat data is obtained from cyber detection systems such as intrusion

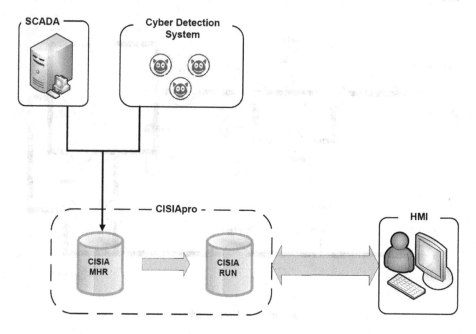

Figure 5. Information flow.

detection systems and anti-virus software. All the information is translated and saved into the CISIApro database (CISIA MHR) and the output is placed in the CISIA RUN database. The CISIApro execution results are displayed to operators via human-machine interfaces (HMIs).

4. Case Study

The case study considers three interconnected infrastructures: a medium voltage power grid controlled by a SCADA network and connected to a general-purpose telecommunications network. Interested readers are referred to [2] for details about the interconnected infrastructures.

Figure 6 shows a portion of the medium voltage power grid. It consists of two lines fed by two substations that transform current from the high voltage grid. During normal conditions, the two lines are usually disconnected by two circuit breakers that are normally open (Breakers #7 and #8 in Figure 6). Also, Breakers #3 and #5 are open in order to maintain a radial topology.

All the circuit breakers, except for the two located at the substations (not numbered in Figure 6), are controlled from the SCADA control center via a telecommunications network. This proprietary network, which belongs to the power grid owner, uses a protocol compatible with TCP/IP. A remote terminal unit (RTU) is directly connected to each circuit breaker, except for the two breakers located at the substations. The SCADA control center in Figure 7

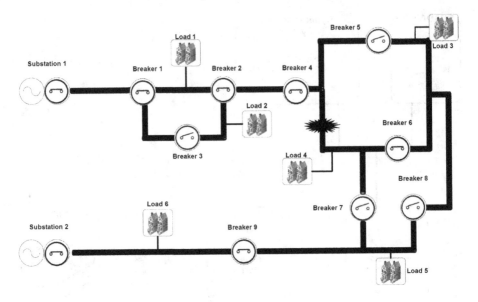

Figure 6.   Power grid.

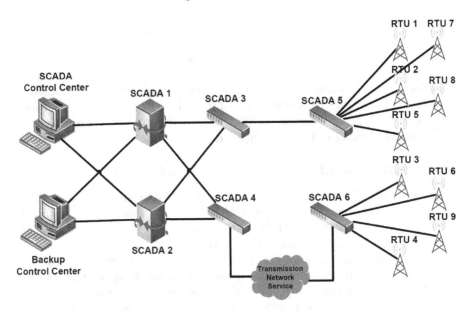

Figure 7.   SCADA control center.

sends commands to the remote terminal units to open or close the associated circuit breakers.

Figure 8 shows the general-purpose telecommunications network (i.e., Internet) that is connected to the SCADA system. The network essentially has a

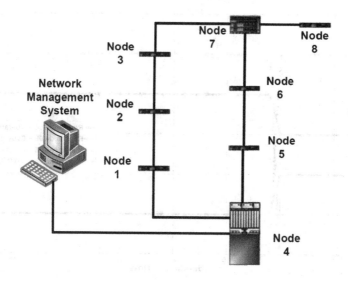

Figure 8. Telecommunications network.

ring topology. In the event of a link failure, network packets are transmitted back to the sending node in order to change the routing protocol.

In the case of a permanent failure in the power grid, the operator executes a fault isolation and system restoration procedure to open or close circuit breakers. This procedure determines where the fault occurred and how to restore power to customers after the damage is repaired. If a cyber fault occurs in the telecommunications network, then the fault isolation and system restoration procedure fails with unpredictable consequences.

The attack scenario considered in this work involves a cyber attacker who attempts to modify the behavior of the power grid using a computer worm to infect the remote terminal units, as in the case of Stuxnet [9]. The attack begins with an ARP spoofing attack that exploits ARP vulnerabilities. The goal is to map the attacker's MAC address to the IP address of a trusted node in the network so that traffic directed at the trusted node is sent to the attacker. The attacker is assumed to be connected to the telecommunications network and uses the connectivity to send the worm to the remote terminal units and their associated circuit breakers.

5.   Simulation Results

The simulation, which lasted 40 seconds, is divided into two parts. The first part, lasting from 1 to 10 seconds, involves the attacker performing a man-in-the-middle attack on Node #6 in the telecommunications network (Figure 8). The second part, lasting from 11 to 40 seconds, involves an infection being spread from Node #6 to the remote terminal units and their associated circuit breakers via the SCADA network (Figure 7).

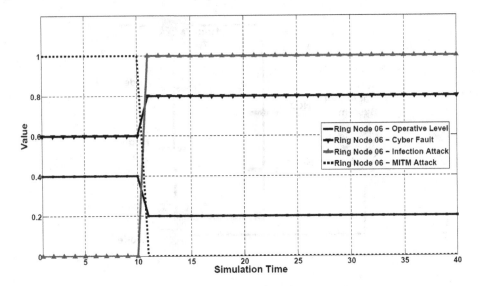

Figure 9.   Telecommunications Node #6 simulation results.

The man-in-the-middle attack has a static aspect – no changes occur during the first 10 seconds of the simulation for the involved entities. The spreading of the cyber attack depends on the distance from the infected node: the greater the number of hops needed to reach a node, the lower is the effect of the cyber attack and the lower is the risk of the node malfunctioning. Figure 9 shows the simulation results for Telecommunications Node #6 (Figure 8) whose operative level was 0.4 during the man-in-the-middle attack. The operative level of the downstream SCADA node (Node #6 in Figure 7) was 0.85 as shown in Figure 10. The operative levels of the remote terminal units connected to SCADA Node #6 (in particular, RTUs #3, #4, #6 and #9 on Figure 7) were also 0.92 as shown in Figure 12.

Figure 9 shows that, after the infection is detected at 11 seconds, the telecommunications node (Node #6 in Figure 8) is greatly affected and with high confidence. Note that the SCADA network has two paths for sending information to the remote terminal units; the bottom path in Figure 7 is via the telecommunications network. The CISIApro simulation did not consider the real path over the telecommunications network, but instead, it considered the global evaluation of the service level of the network, which is referred to as the telecommunications network service (TNS) and whose operative level is shown in Figure 11.

As seen in Figure 10, the downstream node of the SCADA network (SCADA Node #6 in Figure 7) is affected by the infection after 12 seconds. Nodes that are further away from the source of the infection are affected after nodes closer to the source node. Therefore, SCADA Node #6 needs more time to become completely unavailable with respect to Telecommunications Node #6. The

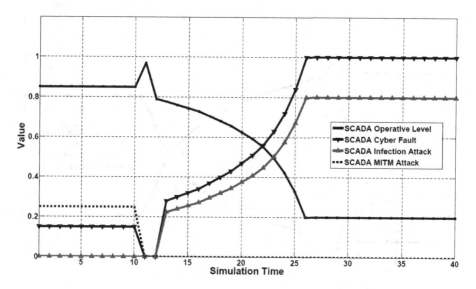

Figure 10. SCADA Node #6 simulation results.

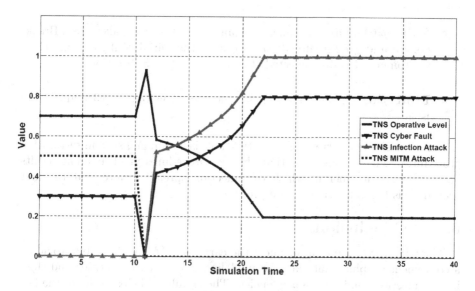

Figure 11. Telecommunications network service simulation results.

remote terminal units (RTUs #3, #4, #6 and #9) that are linked to SCADA Node #6 exhibit similar trends, with delays of one time step (Figure 12).

The CISIApro simulator is designed to enhance operator decision making. The reconfiguration of a power grid is a task that requires the consideration of the interconnected infrastructures. Assume that the fault in the power grid shown in Figure 6 is the result of an explosion. Then, two alternative fault isolation and system restoration (FISR) procedures may be considered:

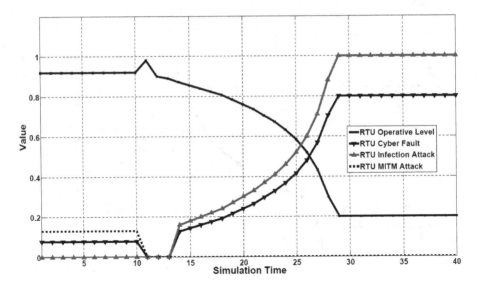

Figure 12.   Simulation results for RTUs #3, #4, #6 and #9.

- **FISR #01:** Open Breakers #4 and #6. Close Breaker #8. Breakers #5 and #7 are already open due to the initial configuration. Only Customer #4 is disconnected. Load #3 is fed by Substation #2.

- **FISR #02:** Open Breakers #4 and #6. Customers #3 and #4 are isolated.

Figure 13 shows the trends for the two fault isolation and system restoration procedures. The graphs show that the two procedures yield different results because of the manner in which the infection spreads. Note that the first procedure is less risky than the second procedure.

6.   Conclusions

The CISIApro simulator advances the earlier CISIA simulator by providing a convenient graphical interface for modeling infrastructure entities and their interconnections and interdependencies. The simulator helps evaluate the impacts of cyber attacks on interdependent infrastructures; the attacks include ARP spoofing, SYN flooding and worm infections. CISIApro has been validated using complex case studies involving approximately 70 entities that exchange around twelve distinct resources. The case study described in this chapter involves three interconnected infrastructures: a medium voltage power grid managed by a control center over a SCADA network that is interconnected with a general-purpose telecommunications network. The real-time simulation involving an ARP spoofing attack and worm infection demonstrates the utility of the CISIApro for supporting decision making by electric grid operators, in partic-

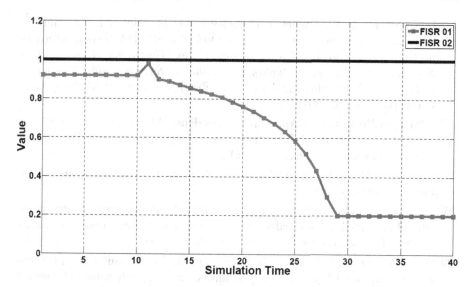

Figure 13. Simulation trends for different FISR procedures.

ular, helping choose between alternative fault isolation and system restoration procedures to reduce the attack impact and enhance system recovery.

Future research will evaluate the impacts of cyber attacks on other critical infrastructures such as water distribution networks and gas pipelines; the goal is to enhance the CISIApro library of cyber attacks and the understanding of their outcomes. Additionally, research will focus on the detailed modeling and simulation of telecommunications networks to better understand attack propagation and to devise approaches for measuring and reducing the impacts of failures within the telecommunications infrastructure as well as failures that propagate from other interdependent infrastructures.

Acknowledgement

This research was partially supported by the DG Home Affairs under the Prevention, Preparedness and Consequence Management of Terrorism and Other Security Related Risks CIPS Grant Action 2013 (HOME/2013/CIPS/AG 2013) (URANIUM – Unified Risk Assessment Negotiation via Interoperability Using Multi-Sensor Data (uranium.theorematica.it)).

References

[1] G. Andersson, P. Donalek, R. Farmer, N. Hatziargyriou, I. Kamwa, P. Kundur, N. Martins, J. Paserba, P. Pourbeik, J. Sanchez-Gasca, R. Schulz, A. Stankovic, C. Taylor and V. Vittal, Causes of the 2003 major grid blackouts in North America and Europe and recommended means to improve system dynamic performance, *IEEE Transactions on Power Systems*, vol. 20(4), pp. 1922–1928, 2005.

[2] E. Ciancamerla, C. Foglietta, D. Lefevre, M. Minichino, L. Lev and Y. Shneck, Discrete event simulation of QoS of a SCADA system interconnecting a power grid and a telco network, in *What Kind of Information Society? Governance, Virtuality, Surveillance, Sustainability, Resilience*, J. Berleur, M. Hercheui and L. Hilty (Eds.), Springer, Heidelberg, Germany, pp. 350–362, 2010.

[3] CISIApro Project, CISIApro: Interdependency Modeling and Simulation Made Easy for Critical Infrastructures, University of Roma Tre, Rome, Italy (cisiapro.dia.uniroma3.it).

[4] CockpitCI Project, CockpitCI, Selex Systems Integration, Rome, Italy (www.cockpitci.eu).

[5] S. De Porcellinis, S. Panzieri and R. Setola, Modeling critical infrastructure via a mixed holistic reductionistic approach, *International Journal of Critical Infrastructures*, vol. 5(1/2), pp. 86–99, 2009.

[6] S. De Porcellinis, S. Panzieri, R. Setola and G. Ulivi, Simulation of heterogeneous and interdependent critical infrastructures, *International Journal of Critical Infrastructures*, vol. 4(1/2), pp. 110–128, 2008.

[7] G. Dondossola, F. Garrone and J. Szanto, Cyber risk assessment of power control systems – A metrics weighed by attack experiments, *Proceedings of the IEEE Power and Energy Society General Meeting*, 2011.

[8] FACIES Project, FACIES: Online Identification of Failures and Attacks on Interdependent Critical Infrastructures, University of Roma Tre, Rome, Italy (facies.dia.uniroma3.it).

[9] N. Falliere, L. O'Murchu and E. Chien, W32.Stuxnet Dossier, Version 1.4, Symantec, Mountain View, California, 2011.

[10] A. Kwasinski, P. Chapman, P. Krein and W. Weaver, Hurricane Katrina Damage Assessment of Power Infrastructure for Distribution, Telecommunications and Back-Up, CEME-TR-06-05, UILU-ENG-2006-2511, Grainger Center for Electric Machinery and Electromechanics, Department of Electrical and Computer Engineering, University of Illinois at Urbana-Champaign, Urbana, Illinois, 2006.

[11] A. Lemay, J. Fernandez and S. Knight, Modeling physical impact of cyber attacks, *Proceedings of the Workshop on Modeling and Simulation of Cyber-Physical Energy Systems*, 2014.

[12] A. Nieuwenhuijs, E. Luiijf and M. Klaver, Modeling dependencies in critical infrastructures, in *Critical Infrastructure Protection*, E. Goetz and S. Shenoi (Eds.), Boston, Massachusetts, pp. 205–213, 2008.

[13] H. Rahman, M. Armstrong, D. Mao and J. Marti, I2Sim: A matrix-partition based framework for critical infrastructure interdependencies simulation, *Proceedings of the Electric Power Conference*, 2008.

[14] R. Santini, C. Foglietta and S. Panzieri, Evidence theory for cyber-physical systems, in *Critical Infrastructure Protection VIII*, J. Butts and S. Shenoi (Eds.), Springer, Heidelberg, Germany, pp. 95–109, 2014.

[15] G. Satumìtra and L. Duenas-Osorio, Synthesis of modeling and simulation methods in critical infrastructure interdependencies research, in *Sustainable and Resilient Critical Infrastructure Systems*, K. Gopalakrishnan and S. Peeta (Eds.), Springer-Verlag, Berlin Heidelberg, Germany, pp. 1–51, 2010.

[16] S. Schutte, S. Scherfke and M. Troschel, Mosaik: A framework for modular simulation of active components in smart grids, *Proceedings of the First IEEE International Workshop on Smart Grid Modeling and Simulation*, pp. 55–60, 2011.

[17] K. Sgouras, A. Birda and D. Labridis, Cyber attack impact on critical smart grid infrastructures, *Proceedings of the IEEE Power and Energy Society Innovative Smart Grid Technologies Conference*, 2014.

[18] A. Singh, K. Srivastava and J. Marti, Reduction techniques in modeling critical infrastructures under the infrastructure interdependencies simulator framework, *International Journal of Critical Infrastructures*, vol. 9(3), pp. 173–189, 2013.

Printed in the United States
By Bookmasters